Creating Economic Order

Record-keeping, Standardization, and the Development of Accounting in the Ancient Near East

■

Volume IV
in a series sponsored by the
Institute for the Study of Long-term Economic Trends
and the International Scholars Conference on
Ancient Near Eastern Economies

A Colloquium Held at The British Museum, November 2000

Edited by
Michael Hudson
Cornelia Wunsch

COVER ART: Mycenaean Linear B tablet from Pylos (Jn 829, obverse) listing expected contributions of recycled 'temple' bronze from the 16 major administrative districts of the kingdom of Pylos; see page 290f. for transliteration and discussion.
This photograph is reproduced from the archives of the Program in Aegean Scripts and Prehistory, University of Texas at Austin, with the kind permission of the Department of Classics, University of Cincinnati.

Library of Congress Cataloging-in-Publication Data

Creating economic order: Record-keeping, standardization and the development of accounting in the ancient Near East / edited by Michael Hudson and Cornelia Wunsch

355 p. 23×15 cm

At head of title: The International Scholars Conference of Ancient Near Eastern Economies, vol. 4

Includes bibliographical references.

ISBN 978-3-949546-10-5 hardbound
978-3-949546-09-9 paperback

1. Accounting–Middle East–History. I. Hudson Michael, 1939- II. Wunsch, Cornelia. III. The International Scholars Conference of Ancient Near Eastern Economics.

TYPESETTING AND DESIGN: Cornelia Wunsch
TYPE: 11/13.2 Adobe Garamond with customized diacritics

Table of Contents

ACKNOWLEDGMENTS

On November 10-11, 2000, our fourth colloquium met at the British Museum to present and discuss the papers presented in this volume. The meeting was hosted by Christopher Walker at the Department of Ancient Near East at the British Museum.

Ogden Goelet and Carl Lamberg-Karlovsky submitted papers but were unable to attend the London meeting. Attending and participating in the discussion but not presenting papers were Johannes Renger from Berlin, Cornelia Wunsch from Perth, and Carlo Zaccagnini from Rome. Also attending were the economist Arno Daastol from Oslo, Lamia al-Gailani from London, and Geoffrey Gardiner, a Fellow of Britain's Institute of Chartered Secretaries and Administrators and member of its National Council from 1973 to 1981.

We are grateful to Harvard University, the Robert Schalkenbach Foundation, and anonymous personal contributors for providing the funding for this colloquium.

INTRODUCTION

The Role of Accounting in Civilization's Economic Takeoff

Michael Hudson
University of Missouri (Kansas City)

There has been a natural progression in these colloquia. Our first meeting, on privatization in 1994, found that the most important asset being privatized was rural self-support land. Our 1996-97 colloquia accordingly focused on land ownership and urbanization. Inasmuch as the primary lever making the land alienable was debt default, our third meeting, held in 2000, focused on debt and royal "Clean Slate" proclamations.

We might well have begun our series of colloquia with this fourth volume's topic of accounting, for all the topics we have been discussing stem from it. Accounting formats are our main source for understanding economic practices from the time the first written records appear. It is from them that we are able to reconstruct how the temples and palaces provisioned their labor and administrators and how they organized their trade and public infrastructure investment. Out of their record-keeping evolved pricing, monetary and debt relations, along with leasing arrangements for land and workshops.

Held at the British Museum in November 2000, this meeting addressed the extent to which accounting practices did more than just reflect the economic dynamics of an epoch prior to descriptive narrative. They actively shaped economic life. The papers in this volume trace the aims and functions of accounting practices from early Uruk c. 3300 BC down through the Neo-Babylonian period, as well as Egyptian practice. Also described are the accounting techniques that diffused from Sumer eastward to the Iranian plateau and, to the northwest, up the Euphrates through Syria and across the Mediterranean to Crete and Mycenaean Greece. Weights and measures were standardized among these regions, with the key measure becoming monetary weights as the basic unit of account.

From counting and accountability to accounting

Some discussion has gone into deciding on the most appropriate title for this volume. The term "accounting" focuses on "counting," and hence on the development of numeracy. "Bookkeeping" is less ambitious. On the one hand it reflects the fact that economic accounts were the first "books," out of which writing and literacy developed as well as numeracy. However, bookkeeping is done mainly for one's own use. It provides the source material but does not formally become an accounting statement until this data is supplied to someone. The essence of accounting is *accountability*, which implies ranking and subordination. Accounting systems are part of a broader system of administration, at least within the public institutions where they initially were developed. Being answerable to a higher party, early scribes followed the categories and format determined by Mesopotamia's palaces and temples.

Symbolic tokens existed already in the seventh millennium BC, as described most thoroughly by Denise Schmandt-Besserat. But these calculi were not organized in the context of a time frame. Full-fledged accounting went beyond merely tracking inventories. It scheduled, ordered and tracked the flow of inputs and output during specific time periods. By quantifying these resource flows, accounting became a management tool for forward planning. As such, it was used increasingly to squeeze out an economic surplus.

An accounting system's categories reflect the logic and world-view at work. The process is dialectical, involving how the accountant's mind operates as well as the "objective" conditions at hand. The formats designed by the Sumerians reflected how the large institutions worked administratively. Underlying their accounting records and categories is the perspective of institutions managing their extensive landholdings and herds, their workshops and specialization of labor.

Accounting systems as a means of ordering the administrative sphere

Non-agricultural labor did not possess its own means of support, but worked in an institutional context whose scale of operations required account-keeping for forward planning to provision this work force. Functions that had been free-form and amorphous within the family household had to be given measure and definition.

To coordinate these activities the Sumerians created a cluster of interlocking innovations in a "big bang" as a unified-field approach. An administrative calendar based on uniform 30-day months led to the sexagesimal system of counting and dividing into 60ths, and a matching sexagesimal set of weights and measures to allocate rations to the work force for monthly and daily use. Mutual price equivalencies were assigned for key commodities and the rental rate for land (see Renger 1995). These prices served as coefficients to form a grid of equivalencies in which barley and silver emerged as the basic reference prices or "money-of-account." Setting these two commodities as a joint standard of value enabled disparate transactions to be organized into an integrated system in which an overall balance could be struck to measure the net gain or loss.

The standardization of time, measures and weights, and prices

The administrative logic can be inferred by working backward to peel away the layers of standardization and simplification that were the keys to shaping economic order out of what had been a more amorphous course of economic life.

Designing an accounting system started by standardizing units of time in order to regularize the distribution of rations and other resource flows within the large institutions. An awareness of calendrical regularities is reflected already in the Ice Age to coordinate group festivals and meetings (Marshack 1972, 1999). By neolithic times seasonal and lunar forecasting timed the planting and harvesting cycles. The calendrical keys were the year and its four quarters marked by the solstices and equinoxes, and the new moons occurring twelve or thirteen times annually.

By the Bronze Age a serious problem confronted planners. The lunation cycle had long been used to time public ceremonies and meeting dates, but the 354⅓-day lunar year is composed of months of varying lengths—"hollow" months of 29 days and "full" months of 30 days. This periodicity does not fit symmetrically into the 365¼-day solar year. It was necessary to subordinate the lunar months to a synthetic system.

To allocate their resources on a regular basis, the large Sumerian institutions devised a 360-day administrative year composed of twelve 30-day months.[1] This divided time into uniform periods so as to avoid

[1] The most elaborate study remains Englund (1988). It seems logical to infer that sexagesimal fractions were developed to handle the monthly or other periodic distribution of resources in keeping with the public-sector calendar. Their legacy persists in today's practice of dividing minutes and hours into 60ths, as well as the 360 degree circle, perhaps one of the most deeply-seated modern vestiges of a practice that emerged initially out of Mesopotamian accounting needs.

the problem of lunar months of varying length, which governed the community's festivals and life outside of the temple and palace internal administrative rhythms. The 360-day calendar did not stem from the heavens as previous calendrical observation had done, but was artificial. It became the foundation for civilization's first managerial revolution, the first step in creating a symmetrically ordered world.

The sexagesimal system's fractions would seem to reflect these calendrical divisions, and Sumerian weights and measures followed suit by being divided into sexagesimal denominations convenient for distribution on the basis of the 30-day administrative month as rations to the workforce (Lambert 1960: 22). Grain was measured in volumetric gur units divided into multiples of 60 (initially into 300 sila and later into 180 and at time only 144 sila) to measure out the food and other materials needed for the smooth functioning of the temples and palaces. And a gur-weight of grain was the unit needed to sow a gur-area of land.

In any accounting format the categories for the columns and lines reflect an implicit economic theory. Babylonian accounts translated food rations into labor time for each distinct category of labor—males, females and children. This enabled the large institutions to calculate the rations needed to produce textiles or bricks, build public structures or dig canals during any given period of time. Administrators calculated the lead times involved in planting and harvesting crops, estimated their prospective yields and rental charges, and set prices for the inventories they advanced to merchants. It was through such organizational planning that these institutions produced systematic annual surpluses.

A precondition for their account-keeping was standardization, starting with ration levels. To enable large quantities and their values to be readily calculated, the commodities being measured and weighed were assigned prices set in conveniently round numbers. "By at least the time of the sales contracts of the ED IIIa (Fara) period, c. 2600 BC," points out Robert Englund, "the concept of value equivalency was a secure element in Babylonian accounting." Major commodities such as gold and copper, wool and sesame oil were assigned values in an overall price grid that also could be used to calculate labor time and land rent. Any element in this grid could be used to measure others, so that accounting prices could be set for barley and silver, copper or gold relative to each other and to other key commodities. (To be sure, these coefficients differed from city to city and from period to period.)

There was little thought of letting market forces affect the administered prices of the major products. Although prices for grain that the temples or palaces bought from outside suppliers sometimes shifted drastically in times of grain failure (as when the kingdom of Ur fell into crisis at the end of the third millennium), it would take many centuries, even millennia, for price-setting markets to evolve. When they did so, it was in the wake of collapsing central authority.

Account-keeping and the origins of money

The monetary breakthrough came when a common denominator was selected out of the overall price grid to measure diverse activities. Money was the ultimate abstraction, the most important price coefficient, providing the large institutions with a standard to value the output of their lands and herds, the products of their work force, the handicrafts they consigned to merchants, and to calculate interest on such advances.

The major commodity being distributed was barley to feed the labor force. The most important metal used in production was copper, which was alloyed with arsenic, antimony, and especially with tin, which is why archaeologists refer to this period as the Bronze Age, 3500-1200 BC. It could equally well be called the Silver Age, for it was an age of commercial outreach, in which silver emerged as the "money of the world" as 18th-century economists would call it. (Gold was used in much smaller quantities and usually in less public contexts.)

Silver owed its high status not to its technological role in production, but to the social role it played in the temples and palaces that served as society's administrative organs. Probably because of its rising status as the major form of religious donation, silver became the preferred payment vehicle for merchants to settle balances owed to the temples. And it was the temples that supplied it to the economy down through Greece and Rome, when mints were located in the temple precincts.

The essence of early accounting systems was the need of the large institutions to administer prices. The monetary pivot of Sumerian accounting practice was established by designating the relative value of silver and barley. A shekel of silver was set as equal in value to a gur "bushel" of barley. By the end of the third millennium, about a thousand years after the inception of Uruk accounting, the large institutions were stating the value of their activities in terms of silver. Minas and shekels were plugged into what originated as a barley-based valuation system for distributing rations and charging rent on temple and palace land.

Starting in Early Dynastic documents, price equivalencies were expressed in terms of ratios to the value of copper that the temples imported and refined. Later, dividing the weight units—the mina—into 60 shekels made barley accounts easily rendered in terms of silver or other metals to quantify the crop rents or debts due upon harvest. The rate of interest was set in simple sexagesimal terms rather than reflecting the actual returns generated in trade and agriculture. In this and many other such cases the standardized rate used by the public institutions was adopted by the economy at large.

Silver's role as the key measure of value led it to become the most generally desirable means of payment. In keeping with what Georg F. Knapp called the State Theory of money, the large institutions gave silver value by making it acceptable in payment for proto-taxes and fees, as well as for goods and services purchased from these institutions.

The striking absence of money in Mycenaean Greek records, c. 1400-1200 BC, shows that tribute lists and tax accounts could be kept without making the monetary breakthrough that Mesopotamia account-keeping achieved. Although the Mycenaean period was highly cosmopolitan throughout the Near East and Mediterranean region, Michael Ventris found no evidence of "anything approaching currency. Every commodity is listed separately, and there is never any sign of equivalence between one unit and another." He was not "able to identify payment in silver and gold for services rendered" in the Linear B lists of "women, children, tradesmen, rowers, troops, flocks of sheep and goats, grain, oil, spices, land leases and yields, tribute, ritual offerings, cloth, vessels, furniture, bronze, chariots and helmets."[2] The delivery schedules found in Linear B records were rake-offs from each department under palace control rather than leading toward commercial relations.

From this long-term perspective, the development of account-keeping by Sumer's temples was as important a contribution to civilization as Quesnay's Tableau Economique and subsequent national income accounting has been for modern economic management.

---

2 Ventris 1956: 113, 198; see also 1970: 101, cited in Buchan 1997: 24.

Social origins and consequences of account-keeping

Writing and classifying as byproducts of accounting practice

Although accounting may seem at first glance simply to report economic phenomena, it has major effects on society's economic shape. Its early development consists of what Carl Lamberg-Karlovsky calls the "technology of social control," starting with the monitoring devices of seals, bullae and sealings, and proceeding via writing and the administration of weights, measures and prices to the creation of what today would be called an economic model to organize the activities of Mesopotamia's large institutions and their relations with the rest of society.

Two parallel developments evolved hand in hand for about half a millennium. First, numeracy and quantitative measurement were needed to extend the control over nature to include the rhythms of the large institutions—their seasonal schedule of planting and harvesting, and the monthly rhythm of provisioning their workshops and dependent labor so as to coordinate the large flows involved. Second, written notation was needed to track and quantify these resource flows, and to classify the disbursements and receipts for a myriad of activities.

As Alexander Marshack (1999) has pointed out in an earlier contribution to these colloquia, the first written notations were calendrical in character. Chiefs, priests and rulers were the time-keepers in early epochs. Yet it was not from their calendrical symbol systems that cuneiform writing evolved, but from the three-dimensional clay tokens that served as proto-accounting devices to represent animals, crop units, oil and other basic commodities starting c. 8000 BC.

The fact that most tokens have been found in temples and other public locations gives a hint that accounting and writing first developed within the large institutions. Their predominantly agricultural character led Schmandt-Besserat to infer that they were associated with the oversight of cultivation and herding. This would make writing an expression of bureaucratic control already at an early date, rather than "bills of lading" arising out of individuals pursuing their gain-seeking through trucking and bartering. "Contrary to a common misconception," she warns (1992: 167), "the exchange of goods per se seems to play no role in the development of reckoning technology, presumably because bartering was done face to face and, therefore, did not require any bookkeeping. ... there is no evidence that [prehistoric long-distance trade] involved any formal accounting ... because the product was bartered by nomads in the course of their annual round or because it was presented as a ceremonial gift, in which cases, the transactions were carried out face to face and, like local trade, did not require any recording."

By the middle of the fourth millennium these tokens and the signs impressed on their envelopes became more complex, denoting "finished products typical of urban workshops, such as textiles, garments, vessels, and tools; processed foods, such as oil, bread, cakes, and trussed ducks; and luxury goods, such as perfume, metal, and jewelry." However, she finds no archaeological indication that they were linked to trade consignments. Rather, they represent "local agricultural staples such as grain and animals" and basic products such as garments.

Late in Lagash's Ur-Nanshe dynasty c. 2500 BC cuneiform tablets deal visibly with commerce. Throughout these early centuries of cuneiform, tablets consist primarily of accounting records and writing exercises to train scribes working in the temples and palaces. A large portion of the documents that survive from the early third millennium are thematic lists of words for metals, animals, trees and other plants, and geographic place names. These lexical texts are the earliest writing not linked to numerical documents, and are the first literate records (Bottéro 2000:26).

To be sure, the words on these lexical lists were intended to be attached to numerical accounts. And having been developed as a byproduct of the need to allocate and track resource flows, writing facilitated the creation of categories and ranks, extending control over nature and civic society by enumerating different species within each group or category. The more categories and species that could be named, measured and tracked, the more could be brought under control. The process of abstraction reflected the epoch's economic ranking, starting with the oft-copied Professions List headed by the ruler and proceeding sequentially down through the administrative hierarchy.[3]

[3] The term "hierarchy" (from *heiro*, sacred) reflects the originally religious organization of corporate households into ranks such as "deacons" and other officers. William Scott's 1907 history of British corporations reveals the extent to which the antecedents of modern corporate practices extend at least as far back as Sumer, including their annual meetings replete with audited income-and-expense statements and balance sheets measuring the surplus being accumulated.

And with this writing went authority, not least because of the intensive scribal training it required. Subordinates reported to their superiors, documenting and sealing each transaction.

The organization of these lists mark the inception of literary texts. They reflect an administrative world view, evolving out of accounting practices in the public sphere that in turn reflected how the large institutions were administered. Out of this notation developed the foundation for writing literary documents, also largely public in character at their inception—ceremonial texts for temple dedications, hymns to the temple and city-gods, mythological stories, laws and letters.

Early records stop at the point where the administrative units end. No trade documentation has survived.

The creation of a bureaucracy to squeeze out an economic surplus

Many societies developed forms of information storage and record-keeping that did not involve writing, from Mesopotamia's early tokens and calculi to the knotted *quipu* strings of Incan Peru and the tally sticks used in England to record royal debts as late as the 18th century. Noting that large Incan and Mayan city-states operated without written records, Piotr Steinkeller concludes that complex economies even on the scale of Uruk and other Sumerian cities could have functioned without accounting, but could not have processed this information for forward planning and economic cost rationalization. Calculations based on past yields and productivity were used to estimate quotas and allocate labor. The Ur III bala taxation system, for instance, "called for an extraordinarily high level of data-recording, since the provincial administration had to know exactly how much goods and labor it expended on behalf of the central government and its officialdom in order to be able to calculate the value of its contributions vis-à-vis the figure that had been assessed for the province by the central government."

Ogden Goelet points out that "all effective systems of management require controls such as accounting and inspections to insure that resources are being allocated and consumed according to plan." His paper cites the Old Kingdom Palermo Stone predicting crop yields on the basis of the level of the Nile's annual inundation, the Abusir archive with its ruled papyrus blanks to be filled in to compare scheduled receipts and disbursements to actual deliveries, and the Wilbour Papyrus recording land rents or taxes as "evidence for the existence of a basic sense of planning and control within the Egyptian state or proto-state . . . a system for checking and controlling a rather extended network of institutions from a distant central point."

The earliest periods had the most detailed and sophisticated accounting practices, largely because of their more centralized character. To explain their quantum leap in management techniques it is necessary to reconstruct the social context. Accountants traditionally have been cost cutters, seeking ways to save money and squeeze more output out of labor by working it more intensively. The Sumerians started this tradition by developing a bureaucracy whose task involved making life more tightly managed. Planning from the Uruk period onward aimed at producing an economic surplus, not just at passively reporting what was happening. The public institutions, if not society itself, were obliged to conform to the dictates of their accountants.

Any review of the early impact of accounting must acknowledge Maurice Lambert's pioneering research on Lagash's royal bureaucracy. In an early article (1960:26) he described how the accounting innovations wrought by the city-state's scribes c. 2380-60 BC "mark a boundary between two epochs: that of empires established uniquely by force of arms, which usually perished with the death of their founder; and that of States adding to the power of their warriors with the vigilance of their scribes and managers, backed by the armature of a methodical bureaucracy, efficacious for its automaticism." Reviewing the flowering of bureaucracy that accompanied the elaboration of this account-keeping into forward planning, he subsequently (1963:83) noted that *ad hoc* solutions to administrative problems were refined into an increasingly schematized "*planification* of the entire royal economy." The word refers to France's "indicative planning" from the 1950s onward.

Our own epoch has discovered that when accountants are put in charge, they aim at working labor harder while cutting wage costs. Sumerian accounts show that this phenomenon has been occurring for over four thousand years. Dependent labor received only the barest subsistence minimum. When the nubanda Eniggal standardized accounting practice under Lagash's rulers Enentarzi, Lugalanda and Urukagina, he did what accountants have been doing ever since: He used cost accounting as a management tool to squeeze more out of the temple labor force.

In scheduling and administering the flow of crops and other raw materials, rations and labor, accounts were used for "planning" in the sense of providing a formal structure to the large institutions and, via their central role, to the world around them. Developing into an integrated system of resource allocation in the Early Dynastic and Ur III periods, accounting played an increasingly sophisticated role in central planning by such refinements as dating statistical records, streamlining their formats and widening their comprehensiveness.

The flowering of accounting between 3300 and 2000 BC imposed an order by a regime of standardization. After the Ur III period, however, planning—along with centralized rulership—became looser as control over agriculture and handicraft production was delegated and privatized. Accounting was little concerned with how the economy outside of the palace and temples operated. Michael Jursa finds that by Neo-Babylonian times the degree of bureaucratic control was limited to setting fiscal targets whose round numbers reflect a lack of empirical realism for sophisticated cost-accounting.

Given the changing role of the palace and temples from one period to the next, the colloquium's participants find the term "planning" to be ambiguous. Jursa asks whether the simple act of setting standard tax and rent quotas really constitutes "planning," or whether the term should be reserved for a more detailed cost management. In his words, is the scope of accounting minimalist or maximalist? "Minimalists emphasize the administrations' restricted scope and claim that Mesopotamian institutional accounting fulfilled primarily what the classicist Moses Finley called a 'police function': keeping track of obligations. … The opposing, 'maximalist' position considers the bureaucratic administration primarily a means of enabling prognostication and planning for the future."

Standardized proportions, from planning to fiscal levies

Steinkeller finds that early Sumerian accounts were used for planning purposes at least to calculate what the palace expected from the land and other resources leased or consigned to managers. Marc Van De Mieroop notes that in making these estimates "the accountant viewed the world on the basis of standard rates, which may have been originally based on observation, but became mathematical formulae detached from reality." Throughout the more than two thousand years of Mesopotamian record-keeping surveyed by this colloquium's members, round numbers were used as the basis for forecasting, setting leasing rates and levying taxes. Standardized proportions were calculated in round numbers using "theoretical constants" according to fixed ratios such as 2:1 or 3:1. This practice led early interpreters to view such tablets as school exercises. But they turn out to be quotas used for planning purposes, proscriptive rather than descriptive.

If this sounds like a Procrustean bed, the fit became looser over time. Jursa finds that when Neo-Babylonian temples calculated expected yields by rule of thumb, they did so optimistically and in round numbers. To the large institutions the "plan" simply listed what the managers and "entrepreneurs" owed. As workshops and agricultural estates shifted into private hands, accounting evolved from what he calls a "maximalist" managerial function to more "minimalist" fiscal quotas and oversight. Reflecting the more limited role of the bureaucracy in Neo-Babylonian times, Jursa concludes, "administrative control over institutional property and economic affairs was . . . overall far less direct and strict than for example in the Ur III period." The palace concerned itself simply with how much it would receive in taxes or rents, leaving the underlying organization and productivity of labor to local proprietors. "Accounting as a source of data with which such rules could have been refined in an objective 'rational' way seems to have played a minimal role at best."

Shortfalls and carry-overs

As a result of such standardization, accounting lacked the realism that would have characterized actual records, being idealized and often in the character of wishful thinking when it pertained to economic forecasting. Van De Mieroop points out that using round numbers meant that a disparity was bound to develop between the rents or quotas assigned to the land and its actual yield, as there is even today with crop forecasts. "If there were more credits than debits, there was a surplus (Sumerian diri), which often could be used for whatever purpose the official accounted for wanted." Otherwise, there was a deficit. "The fact that the scribe indicated both the expected harvest and what was really delivered indicates that actual measurements of the income were made." Goelet finds that in Egypt, projected yields were filled out in advance and shortfalls were written in red ink, inaugurating a tradition that survives in our own language as "red-ink entries." Bureaucrats had to show what they had disbursed and why they no longer had the resources that the palace or temples had provided them.

Shortfalls were carried over to the next year, but Jursa reports that whether the Neo-Babylonian leaser or bureaucrat had to pay the balance seems to have been a rather loose affair, as probably was the case in Old Babylonian times and perhaps also in Ur III. Sharecroppers and other cultivators who fell behind were burdened with onerous debt charges, and forfeited their land rights or other assets when they could not pay. Yet palace claims and carry-overs on the powerful often remained mere bookkeeping items. The large "entrepreneurial" leasers of property apparently were able to defer payment without penalty, at least in times when palace control weakened, until rulers cleared the slates with an *andurarum*, that is, a debt-remission act. A double standard was at work. In much the same manner Goelet points out that while shortfalls were noted in Egyptian records, there is no indication that actual indebtedness resulted when the crops failed. The palace recognized that its collectors had taken all they could.

We thus see that already by 2000 BC a long-standing social principle was being established. Debt claims were strongest when they were held by a person or institution of higher status on someone of lower status. Stated the other way around, it was much harder to collect a debt from a wealthy person or someone in the public sector than to enforce a debt against a lower-status person. Anthropologists have noted this for tribal communities, and it is familiar enough in today's world. Wealth and position always bring advantages in avoiding debt payments.

The technical development of bookkeeping and accounting

The growing articulation of the palace economic system created a need for increasing simplification of account-keeping. Each technical innovation was a step toward greater streamlining. Robson describes the development of the tabular formatting as making it easier to summarize accounts, enabling totals and subtotals to be added up without having to search through the text. The earliest tables with column headings and a horizontal axis of calculation appear full-fledged already in the Early Dynastic period (24th century), and were well established by the 19th century BC.

Hallo points out that the final column of data sums up the preceding columns, making it possible to perform the routine of cross-checking the sums vertically and horizontally. This put in place a precondition for double-entry bookkeeping, which almost was incipient. Or at least it would have been if scribes had written out receipts and produced new tablets immediately as they allocated their resources, for the essence of double-entry bookkeeping is automatic simultaneity.

Hallo has found a set of such tablets whose inflows and outflows nearly match, and poses the question of how closely this meets the criterion for double-entry bookkeeping. Van De Mieroop counters that "There could not be double-entry bookkeeping for which a sheep, for example, appeared as a credit and a debit in the same account, for the time lag between the receipt and the issuing of the animal probably often surpassed the time it took clay to dry." The information needed to create a double-entry account was there, but the medium was not conducive to it as writing on clay could not be amended as readily as, say, Egyptian papyrus. "The scribe could only amend figures or correct mistakes soon after he made them, by erasing them with a wet finger and rewriting the entry. Once the tablet had fully dried, that became impossible." The concept of double-entry bookkeeping was merely incipient.

Van De Mieroop finds that "the greatest challenge to the ancient accountants was not the recording of a single transfer, but the combination of a multitude of transfers into a summary." Adding up daily and monthly statistics to compile annual totals required "that the scribe combine information from various records." Organizing them into an overall set of accounts spanning an entire year or a larger aggregation created problems that stretched the technical capacity of cuneiform documentation to the limit. Jursa points out that the Neo-Babylonian solution was to use wax writing boards to track totals and sub-totals.

The essentially "police function" of cross-checking totals by line and column was in place, creating a potential for double-checking from one set of accounts to another. However, the meeting's consensus was that from the modern point of view the methodology of double-entry bookkeeping was lacking. The accounts to which Hallo points are a tantalizing precursor, almost on the verge of a breakthrough, but not quite getting there. The "balanced accounts" were not balanced in a double-entry manner. The basic conceptual dimension of debts and credits, automatically and instantaneously balanced in a parallel set of accounts, was not achieved.

The fact that it did not quite get there raises the question of whether double-entry bookkeeping as such was so critically important, if the Babylonians achieved nearly the same thing. Hallo's evidence shows what was missing: a thorough-going set of accounts tracking assets and debits as well as receipts and dispersals, such as the Venetians made explicit in the 15th century. As Steinkeller summarizes the situation in a recent paper (2003:38f.): "At least from Pre-Sargonic times (2450-2350 BC)—though probably true as far back as the Uruk III period (3100-2900 BC)—the administrative documents produced by a given institution generally formed a single, interconnected chain of records, tracing the passage of individual items through the local economy. Such a chain begins with a delivery tablet (optional), which is then followed by a sequence of receipt tablets; from the Ur III period onwards, individual receipts are commonly linked to one another by balanced accounts." Strictly speaking, the practice is best described as single-entry accounting in two strands of records, which is why Hallo refers to these "balanced accounts" as "implicit or latent" balance-sheet accounting.

Accounting errors often are found, but do not appear to be the result of fraud. Perhaps the oversight system was strong enough to deter cheating. More likely if someone did set out to cheat, the easiest way was to use false weights and measures. The practice was sufficiently prevalent to be denounced from Babylonian wisdom literature down through the Bible. Indeed, one of the reasons why the Sumerians carved their public weights so beautifully in the form of ducks was that attempts to shave or otherwise alter them would visibly mar the design. Artistically shaped weights thus played a role much like milling the edges of coins in later times.

Interregional contrasts

A decade ago Schmandt-Besserat (1992:170) found that writing and accounting did not emerge automatically out of the neolithic or Bronze Age agricultural and handicraft "mode of production," but from the centralized way in which Mesopotamian society was organized into "ranked societies and the state." Counting was compatible with egalitarian societies, she concluded, but accounting implied a hierarchical social structure.

Although accounting and writing were limited to regions with centralized public institutions, Alfredo Mederos and Carl Lamberg-Karlovsky find a much broader geographic area comprising ten regions whose weight systems dovetailed neatly with each other. This compatibility suggests a process of diffusion as each region fit its weight standards into those of its early trading partners in order to facilitate trade.

To be sure, each region had its own distinct weights based on different unit-fractional systems—10s for Egypt, 2s for the Indus civilization, and 12s for Rome. These weight systems appear fully developed by the time they can be picked up on the archaeological record. But some weights must have come first, the two major candidates are Sumer and the Indus Valley, which traded with Sumer via the island entrepôt of Dilmun-Bahrain.

The Indus practice of dividing by 2s is so basic as to probably be universal. The sequential halving of weights until a suitably small set of fractional sub-units was reached was best suited to calculate halves, quarters, eighths and sixteenths. This procedure could have dealt conveniently with exponential doublings of loans and debts, but was not as well-suited to weigh or measure the flow of inputs and output over the 30-day months or deal with Uruk's sexagesimal system generally. The Indus practice of dividing by twos also could not have dealt easily with the major known annual rates of interest—one-fifth in Mesopotamia (the equivalent of 20 percent, that is, 1⁄60 per month), a tenth (10 percent) in Egypt and Greece, and a twelfth (8⅓ percent) in Rome. This suggests that other regions had gone further than the Indus by the time they developed their own fractional weights.

Lamberg-Karlovsky suspects that the initial set of weight standards most likely came from Mesopotamia as a monitoring device developed as part of its technology of social control. He points out that while weights and measures were adopted nearly everywhere, account-keeping was not. Even syllabic writing seems to have been deliberately rejected, most likely because of its association with the large public institutions as part of their system of accountability and control. Evidently such centralized accountability was not desired outside of Mesopotamia, Egypt, Crete and Mycenaean Greece.

Englund describes the origins of the writing and account-keeping that developed in Uruk toward the end of the fourth millennium and spread outward to a rather narrow sphere of regions via trade, catalyzed by the exchange of prestige goods. Finding the sexagesimal system to be an intrusion into Elam's decimalized usage, he shows in a related paper (2001) that Proto-Elamite derived from Uruk practice. Lamberg-Karlovsky (2003:67) notes that Proto-Elamite happens to be the only known instance of "an illiterate culture adopting the technology of writing." It had only limited success, being abandoned "after a century or two on the entirety of the Iranian Plateau. It took the passing of several centuries in Khuzistan, and over a millennium on the Iranian Plateau, before literacy was once again adopted."

Lamberg-Karlovsky finds that in the wake of Mesopotamia's long contact among different cultures during the third millennium, "in almost every instance we are forced to conclude that the illiterate culture *chose* not to adopt the technology of writing." After the Uruk "colony" at Godin Tepe was abandoned and melted back into the indigenous Godin culture, for instance, writing disappeared along with the use of seals, sealings, inscribed tablets and other control devices that had been introduced. Contrary to what "progressive" evolutionary theory might suggest, "the more 'advanced' organization did not, in fact, replace the indigenous tribal and/or village familial organization. In fact, in this instance the tribal and the familial appear to completely reject that which is deemed more 'advanced.'" He concludes (2003:72): "The export of a technology is no guarantee of its success if the social context is not present."

Egypt was one of the areas where accountability was long maintained. Goelet finds that its accounting records were supplied mainly "for review by a higher outside authority, showing at least indirect evidence that there was some level of revenue control by the central administration during the Egyptian Old Kingdom, a 'paper trail' in modern parlance." Likewise in Mycenaean Greece, Palaima finds that economic records reflect the accountability of local administrators to the central authority.

What emerges from interregional comparisons is that the complex system of accounting practices, weights and measures, and even early writing was not a natural and inevitable mode of organizing handicraft production, trade and exchange. It was a choice to develop in one of a number of possible directions—a choice that became a foundation for much of the subsequent continuum of Western civilization.

As noted above, the mere fact of planning did not necessarily mean that it was enlightened. There are many ways to plan. But although some colloquium members criticize the early reliance on fixed proportions, these served as an early form of coefficient analysis along lines of today's input/output tables. If they were prone to deviate from reality, so does much planning today.

Although the Mesopotamian expansion led to a diffusion of weights, measures and money, as well as many other commercial formalities, not all societies chose to follow the path to which accounting led as a means of economic control. As Palaima notes in the discussion that concludes this volume, it was a mark of subject peoples to aim at "efficiency" in squeezing out an economic surplus, at least under conditions where this was turned over to public institutions which were turned into intermediaries to transfer resources from conquered populations to the most dominant military power as military empires were created. But today, efficiency principles, standardization and the use of accounting procedures to cut costs shapes the entire world. Accountants have become the planners of this world, for corporate business and finance if not on behalf of government bodies.

Why early accounting is important for understanding economic origins

Sumerian, Babylonian, Egyptian and Mycenaean account-keeping may seem anomalous to economic historians who start their narrative in medieval Italy more than four thousand years after accounts first appear in the historical record. Bureaucracy today is associated with inefficiency, not innovation. But when we look back to the epoch when civilization's most basic economic practices were being introduced, they first appear in the public institutions set corporately apart from the family-based households on the land.

The accounting practices developed in Mesopotamia five to six thousand years ago have survived to shape our modern world as part of its genetic DNA molecule, so to speak. Yet historians have neglected the early context of these practices, in particular the catalytic role of the large public institutions. Once having been put in place, the specialization of labor and related economic structures that formed the precondition for market exchange no longer required central planning or even cost accounting. The detailed accounts found in Bronze Age economies survived in late Egypt and in Persia, but no equivalent records are found in classical Greece or Rome. Economies were becoming decentralized and economic control passed into private hands, above all in what had been the western periphery of the earlier Near Eastern core. This is where most historians have chosen to pick up the thread of Western civilization, but they do so in the "second act" as it were.

Accounting and the establishment of formalized economic relationships and markets

The history of accounting practices extends the approach that our group has been developing since its inception in focusing on Near Eastern societies that passed beyond "anthropological" to formalized economic relationships. Neither the modern market-oriented economic view nor that of its anthropologically oriented "primitivist" critics is appropriate to describe the standardization and administered prices that were preconditions for organizing resource flows in the large public institutions.

The essence of accounting was to measure and quantify economic activity. As the large institutions organized their production and standardized weights and measures, society at large adopted their written notation and accounting practices. Also spreading from the public to the "private" sector were contractual formalities for charging interest and rent, along with monetary silver to provide a common denominator for exchange, to settle debts, and to provide a uniform general standard to track the accumulation and drawdown of resources.

Writing at first was an *aide memoire*, an adjunct to account keeping, but soon took on a life of its own. The objective of written records was not merely to help the writer remember, but to enable outside parties to check on how resources were administered. Account-writing evolved into a means of operating on data, using it as the first step in calculating and planning. One hardly can track resource flows by memory or solve algebraic problems in one's head. It is necessary to write down figures in order to add them up, multiply and divide them. It was this combination with mathematical operations that gave writing its early power.

The early evolution of account-keeping and its proto-market exchange has major implications for the social sciences, above all economics. For one thing, an understanding of the economic origins of civilization requires some widely held preconceptions to be abandoned. Anthropologists almost unanimously find that societies since the neolithic have had to plan their economic life. Assyriologists find that the origins of modern economic practices can be traced back to centralized planning. Yet modern ideology holds public planning to be inherently inefficient at all times and places? Free-market economists have created a timeless and unhistorical mythology of individuals spontaneously creating free-form price-setting markets, money and interest.

This is not the picture that emerges from a review of civilization's first few thousand years of documentation.

Accounting concepts, weights and measures, money and prices, and the charging of stipulated rates of interest and land rent were part of the "technology of social control" that constituted civilization's quantum leap from personalized reciprocity to bulk resource acquisition, production and distribution. Public institutions developed these new modes of control to coordinate their resource flows and long-distance trade.

In contrast to the individualistic model used by free-enterprise ideologues to deduce the origins of economic practices, the findings of this colloquium are in line with Karl Polanyi's "redistributive" system of administered price equivalencies. Mesopotamia's experience and that of its trading sphere provides the missing link between reciprocity (gift exchange) and the modern price-setting markets that most historians have traced back only as far as classical Greece and Rome. Rather than assuming that such markets emerged naturally at the hands of individuals acting by themselves, these papers focus on the basic building blocks that took many centuries and even millennia to evolve in place in Sumer, Babylonia and their neighbors.

The initial objective was to provide stable value equivalencies, not to open the way for price flexibility responding to shifts in supply and demand. Such fluctuation was perceived as disorder, especially for transactions in barley and other crops at the interface with the family-based economy on the land.

The lesson of Near Eastern economic history in the fourth, third and second millennia BC is that free-market models that portray government planning and allocation as inherently destabilizing and self-defeating are products of modern ideology rather than historically grounded. The origins of most economic practices find their roots in Mesopotamia's public institutions.

BIBLIOGRAPHY

Bottéro, Jean (2000), "Religion and Reasoning in Mesopotamia," in Jean Bottéro, Clarisse Herrenschmidt and Jean-Pierre Vernant (eds.), *Ancestor of the West* (Chicago: University of Chicago Press): 3-66 .

Buchan, James (1997), *Frozen Desire: An Inquiry into the Meaning of Money* (London: Picador/Macmillan).

Damerow Peter, and Robert K. Englund (1987), "Die Zahlzeichensysteme der Archaischen Texts aus Uruk," in M. Green and Hans Nissen, *Zeichenliste der Archaischen Texte aus Uruk* (ATU 2): 165-66.

Englund, Robert K. (1988), "Administrative Timekeeping in Ancient Mesopotamia," *JESHO* 31: 121-85.

— (2001), "The State of Decipherment of Proto-Elamite," in S. Houston (ed.), *First Writing* (Cambridge), available at http://cdli.ucla.edu/education.html.

Hudson, Michael (2000), "How Interest Rates Were Set, 2500 BC–1000 AD: *Máš, tokos* and *fœnus* as Metaphors for Interest Accruals," *JESHO* 43: 132-61.

Knapp, Georg Friedrich (1924), *The State Theory of Money*. London [first published in German, Leipzig 1905].

Lamberg-Karlovsky, Carl C. (2003), "To Write or Not to Write," in Timothy Potts, Michael Roaf and Diana Stein (eds.), *Culture through Objects: Ancient Near Eastern Studies in Honour of P.R.S. Moorey*" (Oxford: Griffith Institute): 59-75.

Lambert, Maurice (1960), "La naissance de la bureaucratie," *Revue historique* 224: 1-26

— (1961), "La premier triomphe de la bureaucratie," *Revue historique* 225: 21-46.

— (1963), "L'Usage de l'argent-metal a Lagash au temps de la IIIe Dynastie d'Ur," *RA* 57: 79-92.

Marshack, Alexander (1972), *The Roots of Civilization*. New York: McGraw Hill.

— (1988), "North American Indian Calendar Sticks: The Evidence for a Widely Distributed Tradition," in A.F. Aveni (ed.), *World Archaeoastronomy* (Cambridge): 308-24.

Polanyi, Karl (1957), *Primitive, Archaic, and Modern Economies: Essays of Karl Polanyi*, ed. George Dalton (New York: Doubleday Academic Books).

— (1977), *The Livelihood of Man* (New York).

Renger, Johannes (1995), "Subsistenzproduktion und redistributive Palastwirtschaft: Wo bleibt die Nische für das Geld? Grenzen und Möglichkeiten für die Verwendung von Geld im alten Mesopotamien," in W. Schelkle and M. Nitsch (eds.), *Rätsel Geld. Annäherungen aus ökonomischer, soziologischer und historischer Sicht* (Marburg: Metropolis-Verlag): 271-324.

Schmandt-Besserat, Denise (1977), *An Archaic Recording System and the Origin of Writing* (Malibu).

— (1992), *Before Writing, Vol. 1: From Counting to Cuneiform* (Austin, Texas: University of Texas Press).

Steinkeller, Piotr (2003), "Archival Practices at Babylonia in the Third Millennium," in Maria Brosius (ed.), *Ancient Archives and Archival Traditions: Concepts of Record-Keeping in the Ancient World* (Oxford: Oxford University Press): 37-58.

Ventris, Michael (1970), *The Decipherment of Linear B* (Cambridge).

Ventris, Michael and John Chadwick (1956), *Documents in Mycenaean Greek* (Cambridge: Cambridge University Press).

1.

Proto-Cuneiform Account-Books and Journals

Robert K. Englund
University of California, Los Angeles

Historians of ancient Babylonia are confronted with a myriad of hurdles in their work. First and foremost is the fact that they deal with a long-dead civilization, so that in the absence of informants they must interpret the material remains from Near Eastern excavations as best they can, often with very limited tools.

More daunting is the task for those who want to make sense of the social system that produced the documents from the Late Uruk period. Associates of the Berlin research project *Archaische Texte aus Uruk*,[1] to whom I owe most of my understanding of the earliest written records in Mesopotamia, are often forced to oversimplify archaeological and epigraphic data from Uruk and the other late fourth millennium BC settlements of the Near East, and in a sense to falsify into apparent meaningfulness what remains a disturbingly unclear picture. We may apply to our data the models developed in the social, above all ethnographic sciences, yet we should remember that with the onset of urbanization in the mid-fourth millennium we are dealing with an historical,

---

1 The working constellation of this long-term research project was described by its founder and director Hans Nissen in R. Englund and H. Nissen (2001):9-10. Primary contributors to the decipherment of the archaic (now generally called "proto-cuneiform") texts include, beyond the original editors Falkenstein and Nissen, the following (in the order of their work on the archaic texts and on Late Uruk cylinder seal function and iconography): R.M. Boehmer, M.W. Green, K.-H. Deller, J. Friberg, R.K. Englund, P. Damerow, J.-P. Grégoire, A. Cavigneaux, R. Matthews. The publication of the Uruk exemplars of the archaic corpora will continue with a second volume on the texts of the Vorderasiatisches Museum (ATU 6, forthcoming) and two volumes on those in the collection of the Iraq Museum, for understandable reasons currently on hold (ATU 8-9). A revised Late Uruk sign list will be reserved for the pages of the *Cuneiform Digital Library Initiative* (http://cdli.ucla.edu/).

developed society in Babylonia; there is a danger of ascribing to this historically distinct period the same ahistorical nature that characterizes most general histories of Mesopotamia.[2]

Control of the movement of goods and services is a critical element in the economic dimension of social power.[3] As is clear from a review of the emergence of proto-cuneiform in the latter half of the fourth millennium BC, it was an ever-present component of urbanization in the ancient Near East. M. Hudson has offered in the introduction to this volume a concise description of most of the salient elements of early accounting in Babylonia, elements that most Assyriologists have considered in working on their specific periods of specialization, and to a lesser degree in terms of general developments in Mesopotamia. Among these is the development of writing itself; a system of calendrical metrology; and systems of quantification and bookkeeping that led to the formation of equivalence values based on the commodity silver.

Considering the importance of precious metals in most early civilizations, it might seem surprising to learn that we have no clear evidence in the archaic texts of the use of weights, nor any evidence that silver was in any way used in early households in a manner comparable to later, third millennium usage. We indeed are hard pressed to cite evidence for the utilization of equivalence values in the Late Uruk period, with the possible exception of ration days.

An attempt is made in the following pages to give a general impression of the little we know about the accounting methods in the archaic period, with occasionally formalistic information culled from early texts, starting with a review of the development of writing; discussing in short fashion the importance of archaic numerical and metrological systems as elements of social control; illuminating the use of writing with some examples drawn from grain administration archives; touching on the matter of labor management; and closing with a tentative discussion of the implications the labor accounts have for our understanding of archaic ideology of class.

---

[2] This is a criticism of most integrative treatments of early Mesopotamia. For a recent example see R. Bernbeck's 1999 review of M. Van De Mieroop's *The Ancient Mesopotamian City*, in which he describes the author's proclivity of distilling into a homogeneous Babylonian community what must have been a developing social construct through time and space.

[3] See the discussion by M. Mann (1986).

Account-keeping and the emergence of writing

More so than other writing systems, cuneiform has been described as a script based on a long history of preliterate accounting devices. Most who have studied the matter have considered early writing to be a collateral development from the exploitation of an increasingly complex method of fixing quantitative data.

Urbanization in southern Babylonia during the Middle and Late Uruk periods resulted in the growth of the settlement of southern Mesopotamian Uruk into an expanse of 200 hectares, with a population estimated to have approached 40,000 or more. Very large numbers of this population evidently were available for the construction and maintenance of the massive public district known as Eanna, with its monumental architecture surely the clearest testimony to the extraordinary new surplus economy supporting Uruk.

Hand in hand with these urban developments are found in the archaeological record a series of accounting devices known popularly as "tokens" since the publications of Schmandt-Besserat. While the Texas

	Period	Writing Phase	Historical Developments
3400		Clay bullae and numerical tablets	Beginning of large-scale settlement of Babylonia
3300	Late Uruk	Archaic texts from Uruk: Writing Phase Uruk IV,	
3200		Writing Phase Uruk III	First urban centers
3100			Age of early civilization
3000	Jemdet Nasr		
2900	Early Dynastic I		
2800		Archaic texts from Ur	
2700	Early Dynastic II		Formation of large irrigation networks
2600		Texts from Fara	
2500	Early Dynastic III		Rival city-states
2400		Old Sumerian texts	

Figure 1: An overview of the chronology and historical developments of the earliest literate periods in Babylonia.

archaeologist has been faulted for over-interpreting both the systematization and the iconic differentiation of these small clay objects,[4] there can be little doubt that at least a subset consisting of many of her simple geometrical artifacts represents the precursors of writing in Mesopotamia, and therefore that cuneiform began with numerical signs.

This assertion is based on two phenomena. First, the simple tokens were gathered in discrete assemblages and encased in clay balls in the periods immediately before the emergence of proto-cuneiform ca. 3300 BC, and these balls were then sealed with impressions from cylinder seals—the hallmark of 3000 years of Babylonian administrative history. Second, the plastic tokens were themselves impressed on the outer surfaces of some balls, leaving marks which, both physically and also in their context, conform exactly to the impressed numerical signs of the early so-called numerical tablets and the curvilinear tradition of Babylonian accounts down to the Ur III period at the end of the third millennium. We have little doubt that a statistical analysis of the overbearing numbers of tokens still encased within clay envelopes would lead even further, to the establishment of the preliterate use of numerical sign systems with the same abstraction of unit bundling as has been shown for proto-cuneiform numerical notations. We should anticipate that we will find the two most important numerical systems in these tokens, one used to count discrete objects and one used to quantify capacity measures.

It is of historical interest that the so-called Uruk expansion continued down through the use of bullae and sealed numerical tablets. Further, as R. Dittmann demonstrated at the Tübingen conference on the Jemdet Nasr period, this contact continued into the earliest phase of "ideographic" inscriptions of the Late Uruk period, those that I have called the numero-ideographic tablets.[5] These texts from the Susa level

---

[4] Her publications have been conveniently consolidated into a two-volume work *Before Writing* (Austin 1992), itself reprinted in an abbreviated version, *How Writing Came About* (Austin 1996). Specialist reviewers from the fields of Near Eastern archaeology and Assyriology have not been kind to the scholarship represented by this work, while it has received a generally positive press from non-specialists, and as is evident from its wide publicity, from science editors of leading media organizations.

[5] R. Dittmann (1986): 332-66; R. Englund (1998): 51-56.

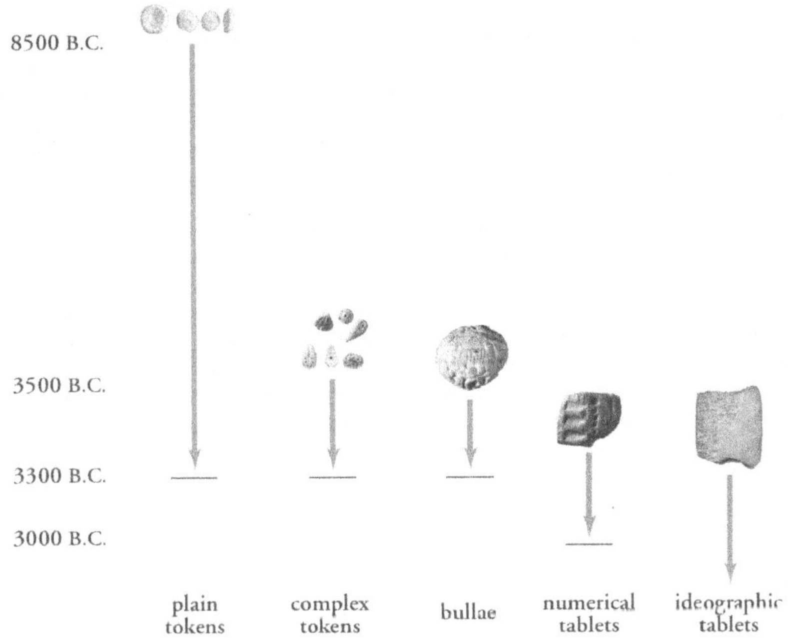

Figure 2: Schmandt-Besserat's writing history

17Ax "contact"[6] correspond nicely with texts found in the area of the Red Temple at Uruk, characterized by their inclusion of seal impressions, numerical notations and one or at most two apparent ideograms representing the basic agricultural commodities: butter oil, textiles and small cattle.

[6] See P. Damerow and R. Englund (1989): 15 n. 37. This artificial stratigraphic construct of Dyson, Le Brun and Dittmann has not been proven by excavations of Susa, nor evidently can the epigraphic finds from the area of the Red Temple in Uruk serve to strengthen the argument for a linear development, from numerical through numero-ideographic to ideographic tablets, in either center of early writing (cf. R. Englund, *ATU* 5, pp. 13-16). Renewed excavations of Susa are required, although recent discoveries of very early tablets from Iraqi sites might point archaeologists to native Mesopotamian sources for a sound Late Uruk stratigraphy so painfully absent in the Uruk data. See the following footnote.

At this point there is an abrupt conclusion of interregional Uruk influence, with a continuation of development of writing in Uruk alone.[7] The archives from Uruk consist above all of administrative documents, accompanied by a group of texts generally known as lexical lists, although there is good reason to assert that we have among these lists the earliest known example of literature.[8] It should be remembered that the numbers generally cited in this connection, 85% administrative and 15% lexical texts, represent averages; less than one percent of the earliest, the Uruk IV tablets, are of the lexical genre, while close to 20% of the following Uruk III tablets belong to this type of document. Whereas Uruk IV documents known to us derive without apparent exception from Uruk, those of the Uruk III (also called Jemdet Nasr) period come from a number of Babylonian sites, including Jemdet Nasr, Kish, Uqair, Larsa, from transtigridian Tell Asmar, and as post-Kuwait excavations streaming through London have shown, from Umma and from Adab.[9] We should include here too the c. 1500 tablets and fragments of the so-called proto-Elamite phase in the Susiana and regions to the east.

The categories of administrative documents

We can divide proto-cuneiform administrative documentation into the two major bookkeeping types known from later periods in Babylonia, namely into primary and secondary documents. The easiest way to recognize the former type, consisting of receipts, bills and simple transfers, etc., is by the physical size and the spatial format of the tablets. As a rule these are quite small, perhaps up to c. 8×8 cm, and might be divided into at most several cases. At present we can only anticipate that these sorts of simple documents contain no more than the most basic elements of a transaction or inventory record, as a rule including desig-

---

7 It appears from some recently excavated but as yet unpublished tablets from Iraq that a revision of this monogenesis theory is immanent. Although these artifacts are moving through the antiquities markets and are therefore unprovenienced, there is reason to identify the ancient cities of Umma (Jokha and/or al-Aqirib) and possibly Adab as their sites of origin, and thus as further centers of Uruk IV proto-cuneiform. Based on paleographic analysis, both MS 2963 and MS 4485 of the Oslo Schøyen Collection appear to predate Uruk III.

8 R. Englund and H. Nissen (1993): 25-9.

9 See above, n. 7.

nations of quantified objects and of one or more actors involved in a relationship of some sort with those objects, often together with an indication of the administrative positions of these actors, as well as their geographical affiliations. In less frequent cases these simple texts would appear to include predicate information in the form of transaction qualifications, for instance, the signs BA or GI, which qualify, evidently for purposes of accounting clarity, the nature of the movement or storage of goods, including parcels of agricultural land.

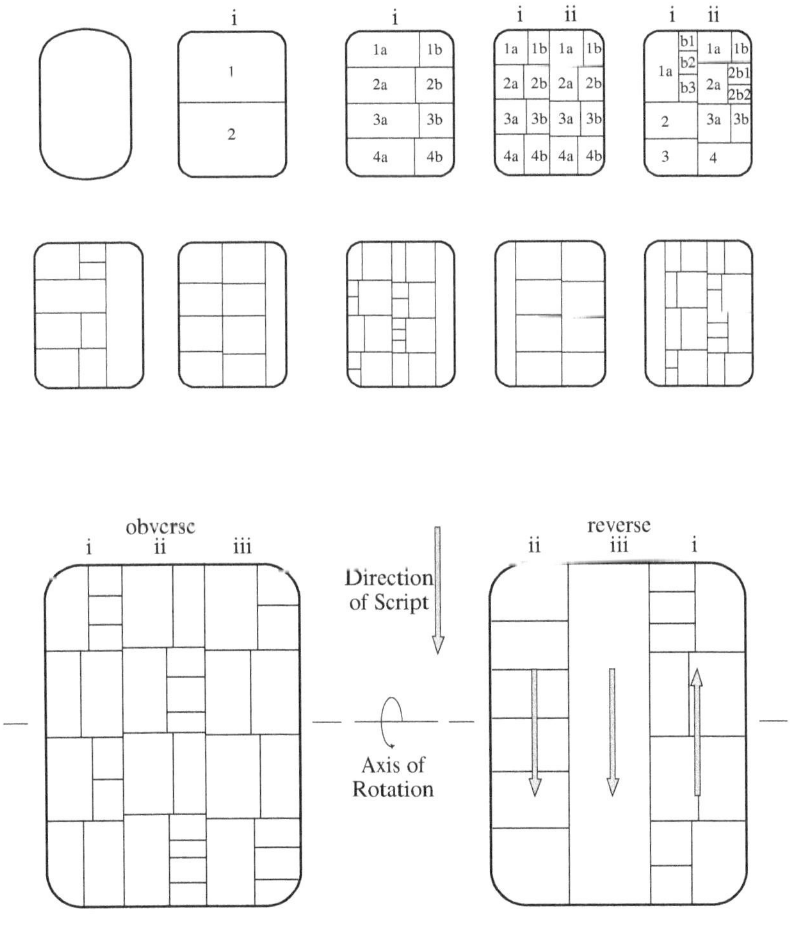

Figure 3: Formats of the proto-cuneiform texts.
The two upper rows represent primary, the lower row a secondary document.

The more interesting but rarer secondary documents can be twice or three times as large. They contain relatively large numbers of entries, and their surfaces often are divided into a complex format. As has been stated in numerous publications, this tablet format may be presumed to fulfill the syntactical functions of the more developed language representation found in later texts, particularly those of the Fara period and thereafter.

While we should be circumspect in our judgment of the syntactical force of the archaic ideographic record, there can be little doubt that the highly formalized system of numerical notations, with its roots in the token assemblages found in clay envelopes in Persia, Babylonia and Syria, followed a wholly conventionalized internal syntax, and represented concrete facts in the archaic record that have played an imposing role in our partial decipherment of proto-cuneiform and of proto-Elamite.

Numerical and metrological systems

P. Damerow of the Max Planck Institute for the History of Science in Berlin, and J. Friberg of the Chalmers University of Technology in Göteborg must be credited with having early on discovered the importance of the numerical signs in the archaic record and making progress in this decipherment. It should be obvious that accounts deal with numbers and measures; however, the treatment by Assyriologists of numerical notations in cuneiform texts has been one of the worst blemishes in a field otherwise marked by close attention to detail. Friberg was so vexed by the copies and interpretations of the important Jemdet Nasr texts by S. Langdon[10] that, in preparation of his groundbreaking re-edition of a number of these, together with archaic texts from other European collections,[11] he made and exploited Xerox copies of the physical tablets in Oxford to aid in his work.

Langdon's *Pictographic Inscriptions from Jemdet Nasr* must be the worst example of cuneiform text editions on record. But a tradition of cavalierly dispensing with numerical notations in editions of administrative documents continues today in transliteration publications of primary sources with decimally interpreted sexagesimal notations, despite the appeals of the associates of the Cuneiform Digital Library Initiative[12] to adhere to a system of transliteration that reflects in a strict fashion the physical realities of the cuneiform inscriptions. This should be a basic convention in text-analytical treatments of Babylonian literature.

---

10 *OECT* 7 (Oxford 1928).

11 Friberg (1978-1979).

12 http://cdli.ucla.edu/cdli_methods.html.

In considering proto-cuneiform accounts, the first signs that command one's attention must be the numerical signs. These were deeply impressed in the clay surface with the butt ends of two round styli of different diameters. As a rule, impressions of the larger stylus represent larger numbers or measures, those of the smaller styli numbers and measures from the lower scale of the numerical systems they represented. In most cases these numerical notations come first, followed by some designation of the objects they qualify, then by representations of persons or offices. Although within discrete notations the signs were, with some few exceptions, entirely unambiguous and therefore might have been inscribed in free order,[13] numerical notations conformed to a rigid syntactical sequence, from signs representing the largest to those representing the smallest order of quantity or measure.

The rigidity of these notational sequences can be explained partly by the fact that many of the signs were ambiguous across system borders. Dependent on the object quantified by numerical notations, the sign N_{14} (a simple small circular impression) can represent ten clay pots of butter oil, a measure of grain corresponding to about 150 liters of barley, or a field of about 6 hectares. The real power of a clear understanding of the array of archaic numerical systems was first exploited by Friberg, who in 1978-1979 published in preprint form an analysis of the Uruk III period texts from Jemdet Nasr and other sites, in part made accessible to him by the Ashmolean Museum.[14] Friberg's correction of an age-old misinterpretation of the structure of the archaic capacity system led to the partial decipherment of large numbers of accounts. Based in part on his work, Damerow and I were in the 1980s and 1990s able to abstract the systems in figure 4 from a data set including the large numbers of texts from the German Uruk excavations.[15]

---

[13] The few exceptions involve the second use of signs representing irregularly high quantities. For instance, the text W 19726,a has been cited in the literature (*ATU* 2, 140; *Spektrum der Wissenschaft*, March 1988, 47; *Archaic Bookkeeping*, 32-5) as an example of the ambiguous use of the sign N_{46} to represent both 60 and 10,800 of the basic units N_4 of emmer wheat (N_4 corresponds to N_1 in the basic grain capacity system, see fig. 4). This practice corresponds closely to the attachment of Sumerian gal, "large," to the sign šar$_2$ to signify the sexagesimal step above what would have otherwise been the largest commonly known number (šar$_2$, "3600"; thus šar$_2$ gal represents 216,000 in the sexagesimal system, 3600 bur$_3$ in the surface metrology system).

[14] See n11.

[15] An English update of the German publication that derived from that early effort (Damerow and Englund 1987) will appear in our edition of the Erlenmeyer collection in *MSVO* 3 (in preparation).

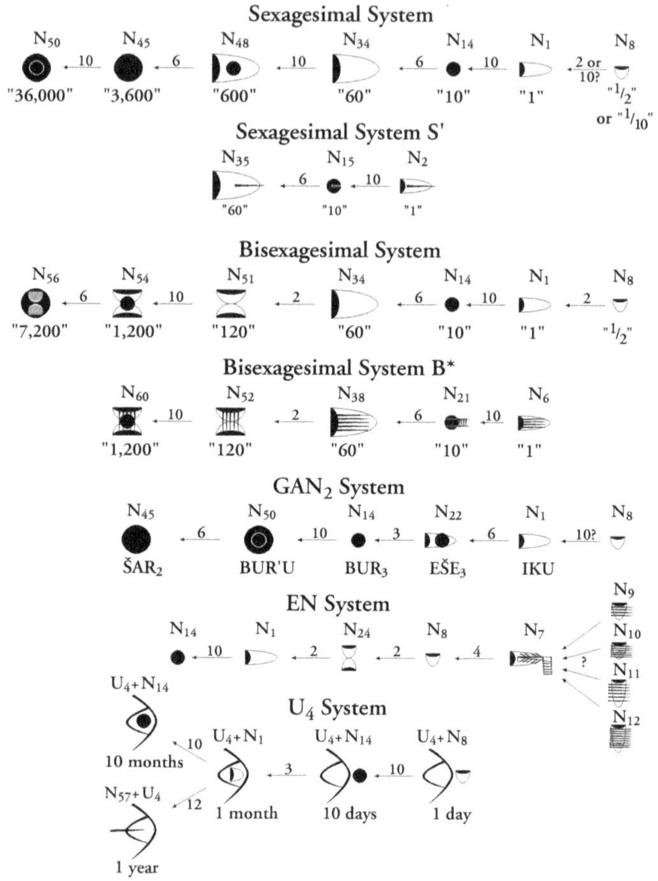

Figure 4a: Proto-cuneiform numerical sign systems.
Several systems of numerical signs served to qualify discrete objects (Fig. 4a), while others qualified measures of grains, (semi-)liquids and time (Fig. 4a and 4b).

The standardization of time in grain administration archives

These numerical representations afforded those working on the problem sufficient evidence to make a number of advances in the decipherment of proto-cuneiform, including the observation that already in the archaic period household administrators had imposed on the natural cycle of time an artificial year consisting of 12 months, each month of

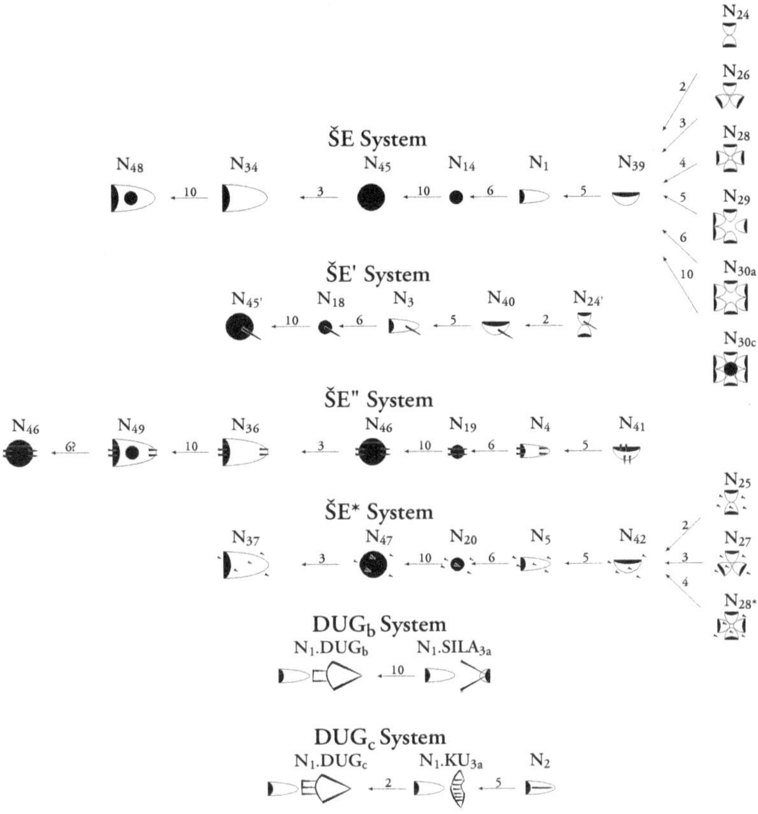

Figure 4b: Proto-cuneiform numerical sign systems

30 days.[16] This realization and the subsequent discovery of the widespread use of time calculations in apparent rationing texts led to a fruitful exchange between Friberg and myself that identified a number of different grain measure sizes employed in this rationing system, and to the plausible interpretation first advanced by Friberg that texts such as *MSVO* 1, 89 and 90,[17] recording the daily disbursement of an amount of grain corresponding to the measure N_{24} (c. 2½ liters) or N_{39} (ca. 5 liters) over a span of three years, might document a system of long-term temple offerings. It is hard to understand why an account should reckon through several years the daily disbursement of a small amount of grain if this were not meant as regular alimentation for a cult figure or for a person dedicated to serve the donor in the cult.

---

[16] R. Englund (1988): 121-85. [17] R. Englund (1988): 138.

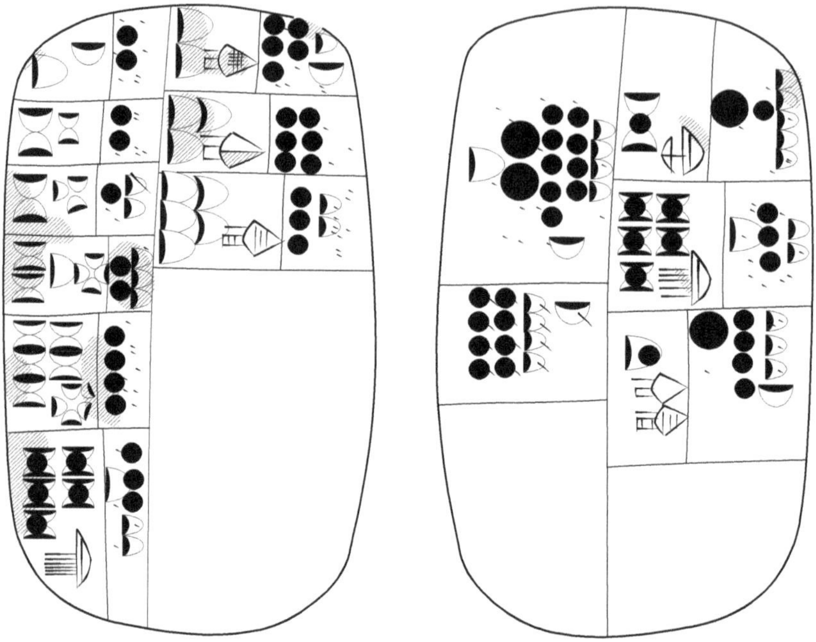

Figure 5: The administrative exercise tablet MSVO 4, 66.
This text formed the basis for Friberg's identification of the structure of the archaic metrological system used to count grain measures, in particular the relationship of 1:6 between the two signs N_{14} and N_1, earlier believed to be 1:10.

The strengths and limitations of numerical analyses of archaic texts can be demonstrated using a group of documents from the Uruk III period recording the dispensation of agricultural products, above all dry and liquid grain products.

The key to understanding the important grain texts is in fact an artificial account, one of a number of school exercises known from the archaic period. Examples from later periods have received little attention. The text *MSVO* 4, 66 (figure 5), possibly from Larsa, is something of a Rosetta stone in the decipherment of proto-cuneiform. In terms of both text format and sign meaning, this text resolved nearly all questions concerning a complex accounting mechanism. The individual entries of the text consist of notations that represent on the one hand discrete numbers of grain products—if dry products in the bisexagesimal; if liquid products in the sexagesimal system—and on the other hand notations that represent measures of grain equivalent to the amount necessary to produce the individually recorded products.

The calculations implicit in the text MSVO 4, 66 (see fig. 4 for sign designations):

obv. i 1	$60\times \frac{1}{5} N_1$		$= 12\times N_5$	$= 2\times N_{20}$			
2	$120\times \frac{1}{10} N_1$		$= 12\times N_5$	$= 2\times N_{20}$			
3	$120\times \frac{1}{15} N_1$		$= 8\times N_5$	$= 1\times N_{20}$	$2\times N_5$		
4	$300\times \frac{1}{20} N_1$		$= 15\times N_5$	$= 2\times N_{20}$	$3\times N_5$		
5	$600\times \frac{1}{25} N_1$		$= 24\times N_5$	$= 4\times N_{20}$			
rev. i 1	1200			$1\times N_{47}$	$1\times N_{20}$	$5\times N_5$	
obv. i 6	$6000\times \frac{1}{30} N_1$	$(GAR+6N_{57})$	$= 200\times N_5 = 1\times N_{37}$		$3\times N_{20}$	$2\times N_5$	
ii 1	$120\times \sim\frac{1}{4} N_1$	(DUG_a+U_{2a})	$\times\ 30\times N_5 =$		$5\times N_{20}$	$1\times N_5$	$1\times N_{42}$
2	$180\times \frac{1}{5} N_1$	$(DUG+AŠ_a)$	$= 36\times N_5 =$		$6\times N_{20}$		
3	$300\times \frac{1}{15} N_1$	$(KAŠ_a)$	$= 20\times N_5 =$		$3\times N_{20}$	$2\times N_5$	
rev. i 3	600			$1\times N_{47}$	$4\times N_{20}$	$3\times N_5$	$1\times N_{42}$
			$1\times N_{47}$		$1\times N_{20}$	$5\times N_5$	
			$1\times N_{37}$		$3\times N_{20}$	$2\times N_5$	
			$1\times N_{47}$		$4\times N_{20}$	$3\times N_5$	$1\times N_{42}$
Grand total of flour used:		$1\times N_{37}$	$2\times N_{47}$		$9\times N_{20}$	$4\times N_5$	$1\times N_{42}$

Grand total of malt used:

$1N_{47}\ 4N_{20}\ 3N_5\ 1N_{42a}$ (rev. i 3) $\times \frac{3}{5} \approx 8\times N_{18}\ 4\times N_3\ 1\times N_{40}$

Once the information from *MSVO* 4, 66, could be marshaled, numbers of other complex accounts from the Uruk III period became clear to us, at least in their bookkeeping form. For instance, the Jemdet Nasr text *MSVO* 1, 93 (figure 6 with reconstructions), shares much of its form and content with *MSVO* 4, 66.[18] The obverse face of the tablet records in successive cases numbers of grain products together with notations that represent the amount of grain required for their production. As seems obvious based both on sign identifications and on production technology implicit in the types of cereals used, the first column lists dry goods—probably rough-ground flour and types of breads—while the first half of the second column lists liquid goods, certainly a type of beer represented by pictograms of ceramic vessels.[19]

[18] R. Englund (2001): 1-35.

[19] See H. Nissen, P. Damerow and R. Englund (1993), in particular 43-46.

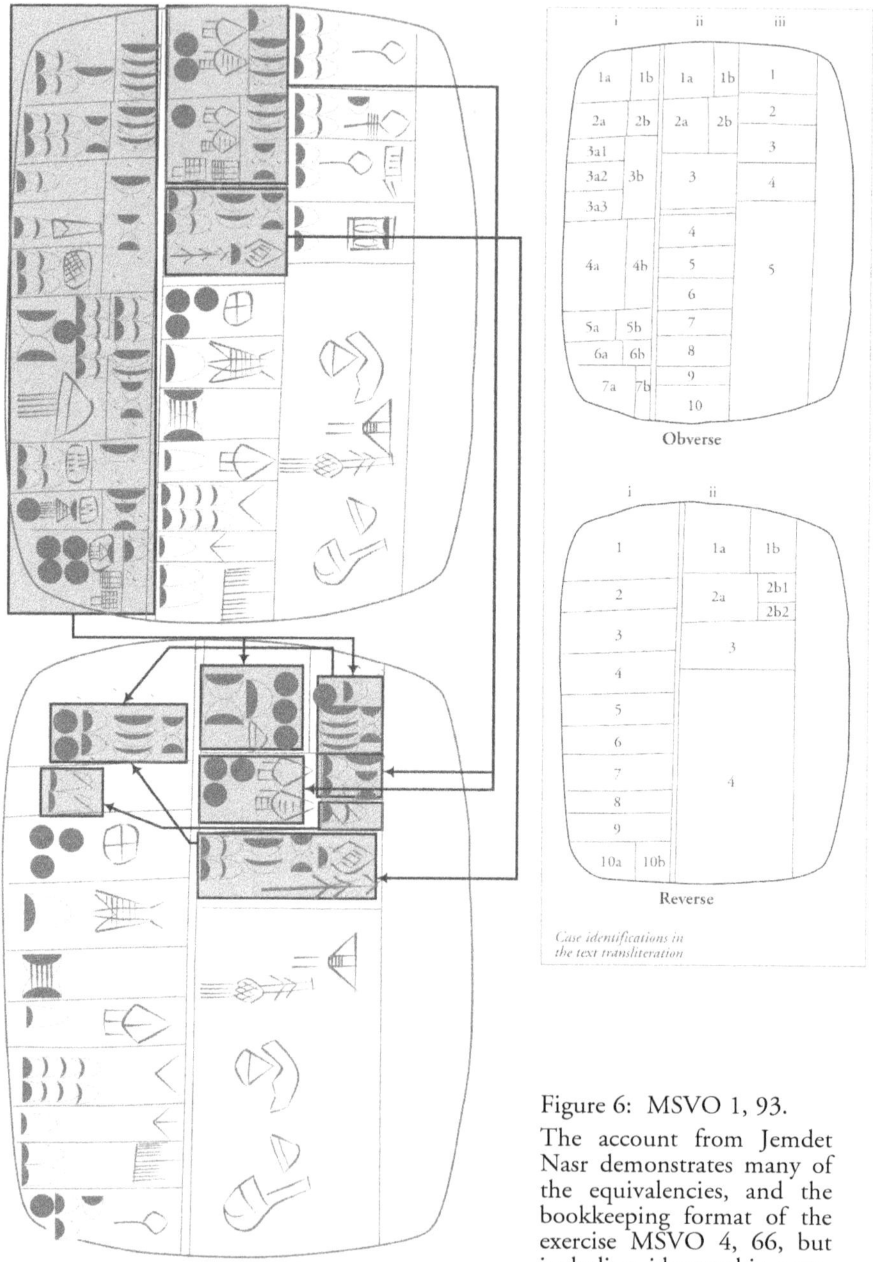

Figure 6: MSVO 1, 93.
The account from Jemdet Nasr demonstrates many of the equivalencies, and the bookkeeping format of the exercise MSVO 4, 66, but including ideographic notations representing agents, actions and time spans connected with the account.

Following a double dividing-line, and therefore an accounting format device employed to indicate information derived from different primary sources, the scribe registers varying numbers of animals, animal products (butter oil, textiles, processed fish), and strings of dried fruit. Both sections are qualified, finally, with a set of ideograms representing the type of transaction recorded ("ration", GU_7), the originating place or office of the account (NI+RU, possibly representing the small settlement Jemdet Nasr itself), and the period of time covered in the account.[20]

The ration system

The basic format of those entries recording dry goods is straightforward. In the first of two sub-cases of each entry, discrete objects were counted using what we have, due to its continuation past the bundling phases of the more common sexagesimal system into units representing 120, 1200, and, probably, 7200 units (see figure 4), designated the bisexagesimal system.[21] The second sub-case records a notation corresponding to the amount of grain requisite for the production of the units recorded. The system used in this case corresponds in its numerical structure to the common grain capacity sign system, but is qualified by the addition of an arbitrary number of impressed dots that seem to graphically represent the ground barley used in the grain products.

Grain equivalencies

As is usually the case with proto-cuneiform accounts, eventual subtotals and totals are inscribed on the reverse face. Here too, the categories of goods are treated differently, with a full tally of products in a first sub-case of the right column. The second sub-case was used here to tally all grain products with grain equivalencies. These equivalencies evidently represent the final value of these goods and thus alone included in the grand total of the left column.

---

20 Englund (2001): 18-21.

21 No compelling explanation has been advanced for the numerical structure of the sexagesimal or the bisexagesimal system. It should nonetheless be noted that the only factors that make sense in compounding an original primitive counting system with a first limit at either ten ("Euphratic," the unknown first users of the sexagesimal system) or twenty (probable original Sumerian vigesimal counting system) to limits of both 60 and 120 are those of the artificial calendrical system of strictly 30-day months (see n16). A mix of discrete rations or meals and monthly accounts would result in counting units of 60 or 120 based on the daily rations involved.

This formation and use of grain product equivalencies as exemplified by the texts *MSVO* 1, 93 and *MSVO* 4, 66, must be considered an important step in the direction of general value equivalencies best attested in the Ur III period for silver, but then still generally applicable for other commodities such as grain or fish, including finally also labor time. It is not possible to determine whether, as would seem intuitively likely, these equivalencies simply describe the amount of grain expended in producing different types of bread, beer, and other cereal products. But even if this is the case and the accounts presume no value equivalencies for products that might, for instance, require in their processing more labor or different ingredients than would be represented by a one-to-one relationship between the capacity of the finished product and the amount of barley corresponding to the product's grain capacity, still the *seeds* of value equivalencies among disparate goods may have been sown in these accounting procedures. The concept of value equivalency was a secure element in Babylonian accounting by at least the time of the sales contracts of the ED IIIa (Fara) period, c. 2600 BC.[22]

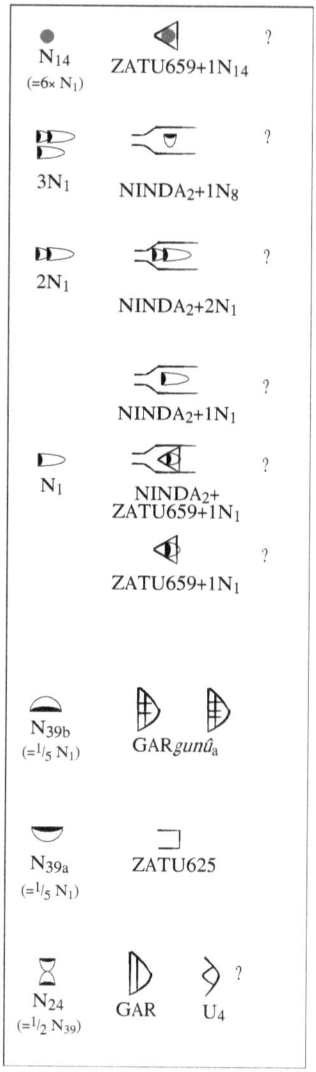

[22] We do not clearly understand the function of those early "kudurrus" in I. Gelb, P. Steinkeller and R. Whiting (1991): 27-43, and see Steinkeller (1987): 11-27, in particular the mechanism through which prices might have been calculated and expressed in the accounts (*OIP* 104, nos. 1-11, in any case, are in all likelihood to be dated to no earlier than the period of the archaic texts from Ur, either ED I or II; see *ATU* 5, 12, n. 7). The sign that in the third millennium represented "value equivalence," "exchange amount," was sa$_{10}$. Its pictographic correspondence in the proto-cuneiform corpus, possibly representing some sort of grain scoop and containing the sign for "barley," is with 60 attestations not uncommon in these texts, yet in no instance is it found in a context suggestive of equivalency values, including the ED I/II texts.

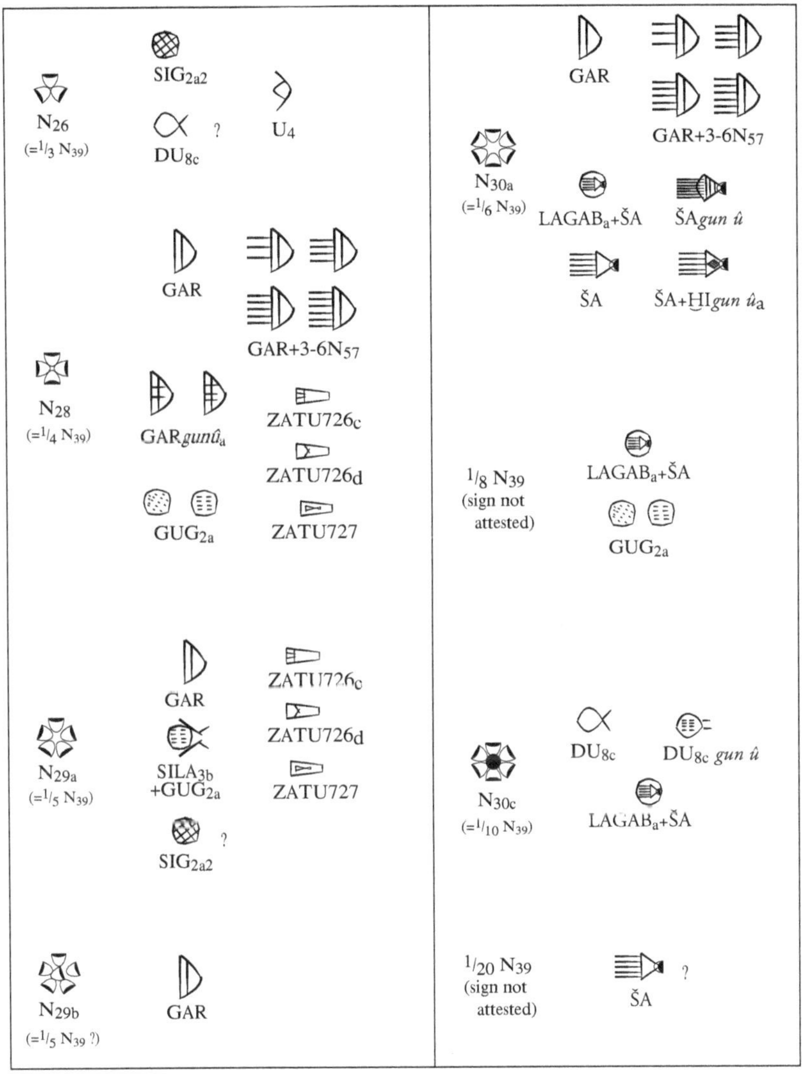

Figure 7: Equivalencies in grain accounts.
The table lists, in order from largest to smallest attested values, the grain equivalences of products found in the proto-cuneiform record together with their respective ideographic correspondences (ideographic correspondence of the same numerical signs is not included).

While there are no evident notations in the archaic texts which exhibit the level of labor time and production norm complexity of the Ur III period, still at least two components of archaic accounts are instructive about the accounting procedures at the dawn of literacy. In the first place there appears to have been a close connection between the graphic system employed to record calendrical units and that used to quantify measures of grain. In both cases the unit month played a central role. Only those calendrical notations representing one or more months employed the standard forms of the sexagesimal system, with the sexagesimal unit representing the discrete unit "one." Notations for days and years alike employed derivative numerical signs (N_8 and N_{57}, respectively). At the same time the capacity system centers on this same unit sign N_1, yet with diverging relationships between this and other signs in the system.

In particular the signs representing lower values in the system are arranged in a sequence that successively divides the basic unit into fifths, and further on down to the sign N_{30a}, which represents a measure of grain 1/30 the size of the basic unit. It cannot be a coincidence that this sign so regularly corresponds in the archaic accounts to the ideogram GAR. This latter sign is the pictographic representation of the beveled-rim bowl, a clay vessel with a capacity equal to a standardized daily ration in Mesopotamia. It therefore seems reasonable to assume that the numerical sign N_1 represents one month-ration for one laborer in the archaic period.

In the second place we find in the archaic accounts good evidence for the quantification of household-dependent labor entirely compatible with later tradition. The Jemdet Nasr accounts *MSVO* 1, 212-214, belong together in a relationship of secondary and primary documents and represent an accounting transfer without any gaps.[23]

---

[23] Note that the treatment of this complex in Nissen, Damerow and Englund (1993):72-75, and in particular figure 62, suffered a certain "graphic overload"; text *MSVO* 1, 213 (62b) rev. i 1-2 was entered into text *MSVO* 1, 212 (62a) obv. i 8-9, 213 obv. ii 2-4 into 212 rev. i 3-5, 213 rev. ii 7-8 into 212 rev. 1-2. The primary entry column of text 212 reverse was evidently reserved for the dependent laborers qualified with the sign N_2 and thus, according to our interpretation, probably "dead slaves" that would disappear from subsequent accounts. The large account *MSVO* 1, 212, incidentally, also presents a good example of what is referred to as a complex tablet rotation, whereby the tablet is flipped on its vertical axis to continue low-level individual entries, but then on its horizontal axis to inscribe subtotals and totals. Comparable accounts with complex rotations and/or evidence of primary document entries are not common in the archaic corpus, but are well enough attested to justify the claim that account consolidation was a regularly used technique by the time of the Uruk III period ca. 3100-3000 BC (see for instance the accounts *MSVO* 3, nos. 11 and 6; Nissen, Damerow and Englund [1993]:43-46).

It should be noted that the ideographic qualifications of those persons recorded by name in the individual entries of *MSVO* 1, 212-214—namely, with the sign combinations SAL+KUR and SAG+MA, and with ERIN_2 —are designations of dependent laborers, probably slaves taken as plunder in violent actions against Babylonian neighbors. The 27 individuals so qualified do not constitute a large number of slaves, but other accounts are suggestive of larger groups, for instance W 9827 with a minimum of 211 such individuals.[24]

Accounting for labor

The method of bookkeeping employed by archaic scribes to record groups of laborers is not particularly complex. We have approximately a dozen recognizable accounts of this sort with numbers qualified by sign combinations that represent "laborer" and including sign combinations evidently representing personal names. These persons are also qualified according to gender and age. For instance, the text W 23999,1[25] in figure 8 distinguishes subgroups of 5 female and 3 male humans, these subgroups in each case further divided according to age, whereby presumable infants are qualified with sign combinations that might be translated as "womb-suckling." It is noteworthy that precisely the same

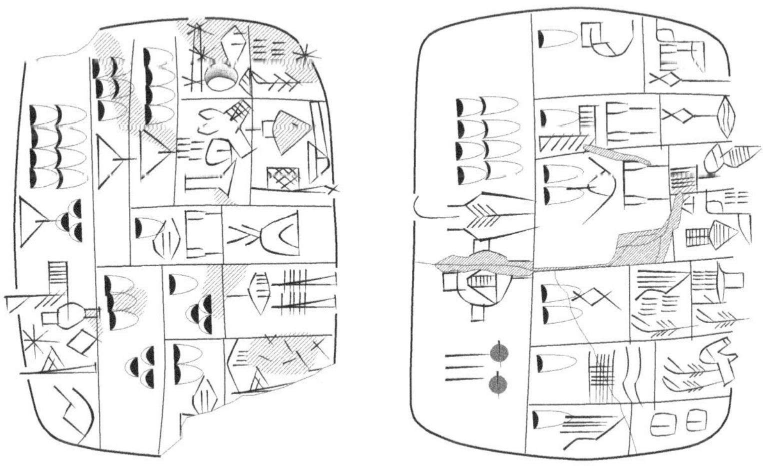

Figure 8: Accounts of domestic "herds" of slaves. Formal accounting practices suggest that these two Uruk III period accounts from Uruk record the make-up of two eight-member "herds" of human laborers.

[24] R. Englund, *ATU* 5, pl. 118. [25] A. Cavigneaux (1991):74.

accounting format is employed in the records of animals. Here too, pigs are separated according to age, and in the case of small and large cattle, animals are divided according to sex. The gender qualifications for the young of these animals are represented by SAL and KUR, the same signs that generally describe men and women. Furthermore, as A. Vaiman has shown,[26] Uruk accounts record young animals and young "slaves" with the same derived numerical sign N_8 (see figure 9), which generally qualifies a half (in some limited applications one-tenth) of some unit counted in the sexagesimal and bisexagesimal systems. This may derive from an apportioning of rations to children of productive age of approximately half that of adults, as was administrative labor practice in later periods.

Labor and slavery

We cannot be certain that the taxonomic differentiation in archaic Babylonia between higher-status humans on the one hand, and lower-status humans and animals on the other, is a meaningful one. Still it might be of interest to compare Babylonian with archaic Persian data. The sadly neglected field of proto-Elamite studies has demonstrated the use of the same numero-metrological systems as those known in archaic Babylonia, with the addition of a purely decimal system. As far as we can tell, the sexagesimal system qualifies discrete goods in the same field of application as that of Babylonia, except that some objects were qualified specifically with the decimal system. This decimal system, employing signs borrowed from the bisexagesimal system, qualifies what apparently are domestic animals, but also what we believe are lower-status humans. It appears that high-status humans—foremen and high officials—were, as all humans in Babylonia, qualified sexagesimally. If as we suspect these unusual numerical systems were introduced into Persia during the period of the Uruk expansion, then we can speculate that the inclusion of high-status humans in the Babylonian sexagesimal system represents a vestige of a two-tiered taxonomy of living beings practiced in Babylonia, including domestic laborers with domestic animals. The concept of *homo sapiens sapiens*, seen relatively in different populations even today, must well have been a much more fluid concept in prehistoric times.

---

[26] In German translation from the Russian original: Vaiman (1991): 121–33.

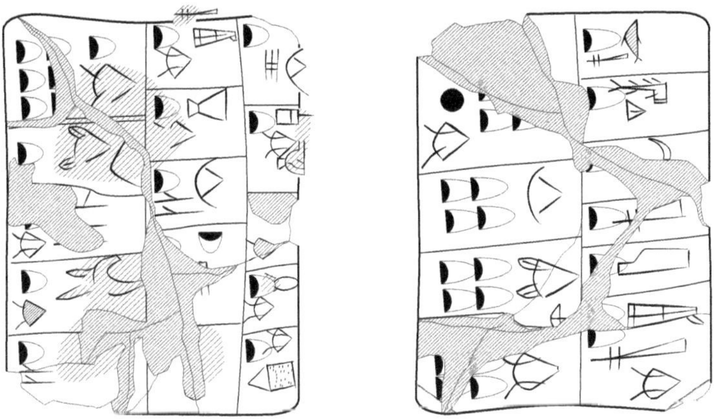

W 9656,ex

Figure 9a: Numerical qualification of young animals.
The Uruk IV period texts record numbers of cattle (Fig. 9a, top) and humans (Fig 9b, bottom), in both cases including the numerical sign N_8 designating young animals.

Figure 9b: Numerical qualification of humans

W 9655,t

Can we call the proposed taxonomy of the Late Uruk "slave" = "animal" an ideological perspective? It may be that we are looking at the enslavement and exploitation of foreign populations, reflecting a deep element of the earliest native Babylonian population.

But it may also reflect a developing class consciousness. G. Algaze has stated in a recent paper that the identification of humans with domestic animals is even a *necessary stage* in the formation of early states.[27] Certainly when we speak of "work force," "farm hands" or "factory hands" we abstract laborers little less than Babylonian scribes who recorded pigs and laborers in similar fashion, both serving the community of man. Our archaic accountants may have forgotten how close they were to membership in the same fraternity.

---

27 Algaze (2001), esp. 211-13 (comments pp. 215-28 and 415-18). The author states that this primitive categorization represents "a new paradigm of the nature of social relationships in human societies."

BIBLIOGRAPHY

Algaze, Guillermo. (2001), "Initial Social Complexity in Southwestern Asia: The Mesopotamian Advantage," *Current Anthropology* 42: 199-233.

Bernbeck, Reinhard (1999), Review of M. van der Mieroop, *The Ancient Mesopotamian City*, *BASOR* 315:78-80.

Cavigneaux, Antoine (1991), "Die Texte der 33. Kampagne," *BaM* 22:74.

Damerow, Peter and Robert Englund (1987), "Die Zahlzeichensysteme der Archaischen Texte aus Uruk," in M. Green and H. Nissen, eds., *Zeichenliste der Archaischen Texte aus Uruk* (ATU 2): 117-66.

— (1989), *The Proto-Elamite Texts from Tepe Yahya* (American School of Prehistoric Research Bulletin 39; Cambridge, Mass.: Harvard University Press).

Dittmann, Reinhard (1986), "Seals, Sealings and Tablets," in U. Finkbeiner and W. Röllig, eds., *Ǧamdat Naṣr: Period or Regional Style?* (Beihefte zum Tübinger Atlas des Vorderen Orients, Reihe B 62; Wiesbaden: L. Reichert): 332-66.

Englund, Robert, (1988), "Administrative Timekeeping in Ancient Mesopotamia," *JESHO* 31: 121-85.

— (1998), "Texts from the Late Uruk Period," in J. Bauer, R.K. Englund, and M. Krebernik (eds.), *Mesopotamien: Späturuk-Zeit und Frühdynastische Zeit* (OBO 160/1): 51-56.

— (2001), "Grain Accounting Practices in Archaic Mesopotamia," in J. Høyrup and P. Damerow (eds.), *Changing Views on Ancient Near Eastern Mathematics* (BBVO 19): 1-35.

Englund, Robert and Hans Nissen (1993), *Die lexikalischen Listen der archaischen Texte aus Uruk* (ATU 3).

— (2001), *Archaische Verwaltungstexte aus Uruk: Die Heidelberger Sammlung* (ATU 7).

Friberg, Jöran (1978-79), *The Early Roots of Babylonian Mathematics: II. Metrological Relations in a Group of Semi-Pictographic Tablets of the Jemdet Nasr Type, Probably from Uruk-Warka* (= Research Report, 1979-15; University of Göteborg. Department of Mathematics, Chalmers).

Gelb, Ignace J., Piotr Steinkeller and Robert Whiting (1991), *Earliest Land Tenure Systems in the Near East* (OIP 104).

Mann, Michael (1986), *The Sources of Social Power*, vol. 1 (Cambridge: Cambridge University Press).

Nissen, Hans, Peter Damerow and Robert Englund (1993), *Archaic Bookkeeping* (Chicago: University of Chicago Press).

Steinkeller, Piotr (1987), "Grundeigentum in Babylonien von Uruk IV bis zur frühdynastischen Periode II," *Jahrbuch für Wirtschaftsgeschichte* 1987: 11-27.

Vaiman, Aisak (1991), "Die Bezeichnungen von Sklaven und Sklavinnen in der protosumerischen Schrift," *BaM* 20: 121-33.

2.

Accounting in Early Mesopotamia: Some Remarks

Marc Van De Mieroop
Columbia University, New York

Scholarship on Ancient Mesopotamia presents a contradictory situation: The abundance of bureaucratic accounts is oftentimes and appropriately stressed, but there is no long-term history of accounting, no tracing of how these records originated and developed over time. The basis of such a work would be the investigation of what is found in individual periods, a classification of records—and such a task is daunting. Confronted with perhaps 100,000 Ur III accounts, how will someone establish a typology of them? Fortunately, serious strides forward have been made in recent years,[1] but there is no diachronic history of text types or the like available. In this paper I will make some comments about accounting techniques as attested in Mesopotamian records from the third and early second millennia. This is not intended to be a survey of what we have, but merely a set of remarks to point out some questions and suggest some avenues for further research.

The format of accounts

A surprising aspect of early Mesopotamian accounting is how much variation there was in the format of records, even if the majority of documents can be easily classified. This was true even in settings where institutional accountants seem to have been exceedingly well-organized.

---

[1] The books of Bauer, Englund and Krebernik (1998) and Sallaberger and Westenholz (1999) provide excellent surveys of the materials of the traditionally delineated early time-periods up to 2000 BC. Their formats vary, however, and the ancient records are not always the focus of the discussions.

The relatively small twentieth-century BC Isin craft archive provides a good example (Van De Mieroop 1987). The large majority of the 900+ texts falls into two groups: receipts of materials by the workshop, and issues of finished products by it.

The first group contained the information of what the workshop official received from the outside (šu ba-an-ti), the second what he issued (ba-zi). These documents were thus written from the point of view of the institution, which is not surprising, but both transactions sometimes were recorded as well from the other perspective, that of the outsider. Sometimes the first was presented as a delivery to the workshop (mu-DU; *e.g.*, BIN 9 505), the second as a receipt from it (šu ba-an-ti; *e.g.*, BIN 9 111). There is no indication at all that these records from the outsider's point of view were written by a scribe other than the institutional one, or that they belonged to another archive. These documents provide the same information—but in a different format. We know from the same archive that delivery records were routinely made in two copies, one to be kept by the outsider, the other by the institution. The Isin archive contains mostly the second copies, which were explicitly identified as such by the Sumerian term, gaba-ri, "copy."

Is it possible that these were actually not duplicates, but records of the same transaction from a different point of view? Could it be that the institution's scribe usually kept the correct record, but sometimes made a mistake and unintentionally gave it away while he[2] kept the original? Even in this relatively small and coherent archive we cannot assume that every text with the verb šu ba-an-ti, "he received," indicates that the workshop was the recipient.

When we are confronted, then, by the thousands of records from Ur III Umma or Puzriš-Dagan, a typology based on the formulary of the texts cannot be used without strict caution about the context of the record. Sigrist has pointed out, for example, that in Puzriš-Dagan the Sumerian term mu-DU followed by a personal name (PN) can mean both delivery from the person or delivery to that person (1992:57). Terminology by itself is thus not a guide for the interpretation of a record.

---

[2] Women scribes were active in early Mesopotamia, especially in organizations that primarily served women (see, for example, Lion 2001). As I will not discuss those organizations here, I will use the masculine form when referring to scribes for simplicity's sake.

The most crucial question is to determine whose record we have, that is what individual or institution kept it in an archive. That can be difficult when we have different bureaus or offices interacting with one another. Usually we are unable to rely on archaeology for such information as most of the large corpora of texts were looted and sold to museums and collectors rather than excavated with a secure provenience.

The personal names of the officials provide the best clue for the identification of offices and a good prosopography is a necessity for any archival analysis. At Puzriš-Dagan, for example, there were three bureaus that administered the movements of animals: one for registering deliveries to the cattle yard, another for transfers within Puzriš-Dagan, and a third for distribution to the outside. All of them produced receipts in which they indicated the transaction with the term ì-dab$_5$ "he received." Since the term was used by the various bureaus, the modern interpreter needs to be cautious to determine what movement is really recorded. An entry in a modern catalogue that refers to a "delivery of an animal, PN received," could indicate many different transactions.

Summaries

The greatest challenge to the ancient accountants was not the recording of a single transfer, but the combination of a multitude of transfers into a summary. When information piles up and is not synthesized, it becomes useless: a good bureaucrat needs to be able to compress data. The summary account requires that the scribe combine information from various records, and more important, that he excludes what is redundant or overly specific. He also has to organize the results in a systematic whole. In the end he must account for every unit for which he is responsible.

In their work Mesopotamian accountants used different materials than scribes in most other cultures. As Edward Chiera poignantly stated in his survey of Mesopotamian culture in 1938: "They Wrote on Clay." Writing on clay placed great restrictions on the scribes. Unlike with paper or papyrus, with clay they could not build up a single account over time, cumulatively. There could not be ledgers in which entries were added for days in a row. There could not be double-entry bookkeeping for which a sheep, for example, appeared as a credit and a debit in the same account, for the time lag between the receipt and the issuing of the animal probably often surpassed the time it took clay to dry. The scribe could only amend figures or correct mistakes soon after he made them by erasing them with a wet finger and rewriting the entry. Once the tablet had fully dried, that became impossible.

The Mesopotamian scribes thus were presented with the challenge to produce a summary at a single moment, either with the individual records laid out in front of them, or (most likely when large numbers of records were involved) on the basis of preparatory accounts that summarized smaller groups of texts.

We see development over time, with the procedures becoming more refined. The mid third-millennium archives from Šuruppak show a stage where summaries were basically the compilation of single documents with the totaling of amounts at the end. The summary lists of grain rations (*Sammeltafeln* in the terminology of Pomponio and Visicato 1994) sometimes just strung together a set of basic accounts, adding or dropping no information. Only at the end was the total amount of grain calculated (for example, texts 14 to 18 in Pomponio and Visicato 1994). The scribes could just as well have read the basic tablets one by one to get the same result and we can wonder why summaries of this type were produced at all. Also interesting is the fact that different compilations were produced. Some gathered information for a specific time period, others for the subordinates of a specific overseer, and so on (Pomponio and Visicato 1994:21-2). There seems to have been a proliferation of overlapping records whose exact purpose eludes us.

With the growth of the central organizations and the expansion of their activities, the work of scribes became more complex. In the Ur III period (twenty-first century BC), we see a culmination of their activities and of the complexity of their task. A good example of this allows us to study the scribe's difficulties in detail. The text is UET 3 1498, a twelve-column tablet dated to the fifteenth year of King Ibbi-Suen (IS) of Ur (*c.* 2014 BC), 25 by 24 centimeters large and deposited in the British Museum. It is a well-known year summary, whose composition I have studied in detail before (Van De Mieroop 1999/ 2000). It is a fabulous source for the study of accounting techniques, because we have available to us some 400 day accounts that were used in its composition. The day accounts dutifully record who delivered what on what day, and which workshop official was in charge. For instance, "9 minas of silver to make 9 bowls of 1 mina each, from Ur-gu'edena, Ahuwaqar received, month 6, day 1, year IS 15" (UET 3 500). One hundred and twelve tablets that record the delivery of silver have survived until today, and on the basis of the totals in the summary text we can estimate that the scribe worked with some 210 in total when he drew up that account. In the summary account the details about the purpose of the silver were omitted by the scribe to abbreviate the information.

The same was true for the gold deliveries, of which we actually have 185 individual records at present, but I estimate that the total number used easily could have amounted to about 325 tablets. Confronted with an abundance of information, the scribe extracted only the amounts. It is clear that these precious metals, often used in the workshop, were kept elsewhere and were delivered by specially designated men only when needed. Thus the amounts recorded in the day records were very small.

For materials that were less valuable, deliveries were made much less often and in larger amounts. Ivory, for instance, appears only in a handful of records. The delivery records indicate why the material was brought in, for the fashioning of statuettes, for example, and the summary account repeats that information. The scribe did add amounts together, however. Five separate deliveries were intended for the making of bird statuettes and in the summary account all these were added together. Various bundles of wood were delivered, which in the summary account were carefully organized in descending order of length. In these cases the scribe did omit information, but not much. He did however combine the information of several day accounts, adding up amounts delivered, or objects to be made from the material.

More startling is another task he had to fulfill: to add information not explicitly available in the day accounts. The workshop at Ur had eight sections: the ateliers of the sculptors, the goldsmiths, the stonecutters, the carpenters, the blacksmiths, the leatherworkers, the felters, and the reedworkers. These studios often worked with specific materials, and deliveries of copper, for instance, were always intended for the blacksmiths. But other products were used in more than one section, including gold and silver used by both goldsmiths and blacksmiths, or ivory used by both sculptors and carpenters. The day accounts do not indicate for what section of the workshop the products were intended, although the year account does distinguish between deliveries to the different sections. Thus summaries of gold, silver and ivory appear twice each.

There is even one text that combines the deliveries of ivory to two sections of the workshop, and somehow the scribe of the year account was able to separate the information in it. UET 3 768, dated V/15, reads:

41 ma-na 10 gín zú-am-si	41 minas 10 shekels of ivory
ba-sur šà-ba	were broken up
1 gu-za umbin sal$_4$-la	and applied to
ba-an-gar	a chair with thin legs.
½ ma-na 8 gín zú-am-si	½ mina and 8 shekels ivory
ba-sur šà-ba	were broken up
1 dar-Me-luḫ-ḫa-tur	and applied to a statuette
	of a francolin
1 mar zà-ḫi-li-tur	and a small spoon.
ba-an-gar	
ki *Ìl-su-ra-bí*-ta	Ahuwaqar received it
A-ḫu-wa-qar šu ba-ti	from Ilsurabi

This corresponds to two separate entries in UET 3 1498, col. V: lines 28-32 there records the first part of UET 3 768:

41 ma-na 10 gín zú-am-/si / ba-sur šà-ba / 1 gu-za umbin sal$_4$-la / ba-an-gar / ki *Ìl-su-ra-bí*-ta.

It is included among the deliveries to the carpenters, and the entire day account was entered in the summary. The second section of the day account found its way into a set of deliveries made to the sculptors. UET 3 1498, col. I: lines 2-15 includes these entries:

21 ma-na 9½ gín zú-am-si / ba-sur šà-ba / 8 dar Me-luḫ-ḫa^{ki}-tur / 5 mar zà-ḫi-li / ba-an-gar / ki *Ìl-su-ra-bí*-ta.

The single delivery of ivory was thus put together with others to make up a grand total of 8 bird statuettes and 5 spoons. How could the scribe, more than six months after the delivery was made, remember what amount of ivory went where? The combination of the ivory and the chair must have told him that the carpenters' shop was involved, but he must have read the document carefully to observe that, and must have had the foresight to keep the record available for two entries in his final text. A part of his duties thus involved the identification of the section of the workshop that received the material, a piece of information that was not stated in the daily records he used.

The scribe who had to write out the year summary needed to undertake several steps. He first had to sort the day accounts by section of the workshop—information that was not explicitly indicated in these texts. About 400 of these records are preserved today, but he must have worked with many more. From these he needed to abstract the necessary data to be entered in the year account. The amounts of primary materials were added together, making a distinction between levels of quality and size. They were listed in a specific order. For example, bundles of wood were distinguished by type of wood, girth of the bundle, and length of the logs in descending order:

a bundle, 66 centimeters in girth, of 50 centimeters-long mes-wood
a bundle, 83 centimeters in girth, of 43 centimeters-long mes-wood
a bundle, [ ] centimeters in girth, of 40 centimeters-long mes-wood
a bundle, [ ] centimeters in girth, of 35 centimeters-long mes-wood
a bundle, [ ] centimeters in girth, of 28 centimeters-long mes-wood
(UET 3 1498, col. VI: lines 23-7)

In summarizing the deliveries of gold the scribe distinguished between different qualities of the metal, the purer red gold and the regular quality, which were often recorded on the same day account. The small amounts had to be added together to compute the total value of a specific material that had been delivered to the workshop.

There are relatively few summary accounts from the Ur III period whose source documents can be identified, although the ongoing cataloguing of these numerous tablets will make this easier in the future. A totally different type of record for which the summary account and source records were brought together derived from a labor supervisor in Umma, Lu-Šara (Englund 2003). During the year 2036 (Šu-Suen 2), he supervised 6,518 2/60 man-days of labor in such tasks as agriculture, shipping, and canal works. The scribe used source accounts that are still preserved, registering limited numbers of work days and the tasks in which the men were engaged. These usually added the amounts for a certain category together and the scribe merely copied out the sealed tablet he had received, omitting some information such as the date. Sometimes several source accounts dealt with the same type of work and the same supervisor, and the scribe merged the information of two tablets together. In such cases, he acknowledged that he had used two tablets. For example, one source tablet (UTI 3 1630) records that 135 worker days were spent on irrigation work in the Šara-gugal field. Another one, now lost, must have accounted for 42 more days, since the total in the summary was 177 days and that record acknowledges the use of two sealed tablets from the overseer Agugu (Englund 2003:9).

At other times, this simple work of addition was not undertaken. Under the lead of Akalla, a barge was punted three times from Apisal to Nippur and back to deliver oil and cheese to the royal estate. These trips required 45, 50, and 60 worker days respectively. For some reason the accountant did not bother to add up those three numbers. Thus the level of synthesis in these records was relatively restricted.

The calculations undertaken by the scribe could become complex if he used numerous source accounts. He must have used tallies and partial summaries of specific products before he drew up the final account. It is unclear, however, whether he wrote the final accounts fully out on a wax board or the like before writing his tablet. On many cuneiform tablets, including some summary accounts (Englund 2003: top of obverse column III), scratch-pad calculations appear, which indicate that the scribe did not have all information at hand when he started to write.

Without a full draft version of the final tablet, the scribe must have had considerable skill to estimate the tablet size he needed to write out the entire record. Usually the large multi-column accounts have some extra space, but not very much. The work must have been time consuming and required a great deal of attention to detail. Mistakes were easily made, and modern editors of cuneiform accounts are often eager to point those out. We should admire the computational skills of these accountants, however. The scribes of the Ur III bureaucracy produced accounts for all assets of the state, ranging from a single lamb to the entire grain harvest of a province. The complexity of their work should not be underestimated, and we should not deny them the respect they deserve.

The account from Ur's craft workshop for the year 2014 BC, discussed above, provides only half the information that was important to the central administration. None of the materials issued were ultimately to remain in the workshop, but were used to produce goods that had numerous destinations. There must have been records of the various issues by the workshop, but in the Ur archive these rarely survived. Ahuwaqar, the official who received all materials, is attested only twice as issuing finished products (Loding 1974:151 n. 28). An example is

UET 3 862 in which he issued reed gakkul-containers to the temple of Ninsun. The record was sealed by the official recipient, Humanzi, nu-banda of the temple.

Such accounts cannot have been rare in the workshop's archive when complete, but the tablets must have been stored elsewhere and have not been found by modern excavators. Receipts are the most common records in most Ur III archives. As Steinkeller has pointed out, records of disbursements are more important for organizations than those of acquisitions. For any bureaucrat it was important to be able to prove that an asset had been legitimately disbursed, and a sealed receipt would show why it was no longer available. The difference can be more easily accounted for than what has been removed (Steinkeller 2003:37f.). The general early Mesopotamian practice was that the party that issued something was given a receipt, often sealed by the recipient (Potts 1997:245). The archive of the issuer thus contained a set of such receipts.

Whereas the Ur account listed only receipts by the workshop, the one from Umma had two parts: the men assigned to the supervisor Lu-Šara (a total of thirty-three named individually) were listed first, and then the labor they provided was accounted. The first section also was based on source accounts, as is clear from the find of a record for a single man (Englund 2003: text no 2): one Undaga, who was to work half-time only, was assigned to Lu-Šara by the foreman Lu-dingira. The scribe of the Umma account had thus probably thirty-three records for such individuals at hand when he drew up his summary.

Balanced accounts

The combination of both sets of data—income to an institution or individual and expenditures—was found in the most refined work of the Ur III accountants, the so-called balanced accounts. Every office produced such records, as all accountants had to ascertain the balance of their area of responsibility: labor, animals, craft goods, or whatever. Balanced accounts typically are made up of three sections. The first, usually relatively short, records what was at hand, the second what had been deducted, and the third calculated the positive or negative balance.

Here again it is very important to determine whose account we are reading in order to establish the use of the record. The large majority of Ur III balanced accounts derive from Umma and are part of the state's archives. They are designed to present matters from the point of view of the state which provided assets to the office or individual whose account was produced. The first section listed what was provided by the state, and was to be repaid. This was the debit side of the account. The second section listed the goods or services provided to the state. This was the credit side. It represented the obligations which the office or individual had fulfilled.

The end of the account calculated the balance. If there were more credits than debits, there was a surplus (Sumerian diri), which often could be used for whatever purpose the official accounted for wanted. If not all debits had been provided for, there was a deficit (Sumerian lá-ì) that was passed on to the next year. For example, a long distance merchant received funds from the state at the beginning of the year. With these, he imported goods. At the end of the year the value of his acquisitions had to equal what he had received. If he had not spent enough, the state's silver balance left over would be passed on to the next year as a debit. Although the silver was an asset to the merchant, it was represented as something for which he still owed the state.

It is likely that some organizations and individuals made up balanced accounts of their own to determine what assets they had left, as an inventory. All these records had to summarize the information of a set of source accounts. For example, a balanced account of the labor provided by 37 female workers in the year 2034 BC indicates the different activities in which they were involved (Englund 1991). Milling work took up 5,986 labor-days. The time dedicated to this task was calculated on the basis of the amounts of their finished products, that is, flour of various qualities.

The source tablets for the balanced account provided the total amounts of the different types of flour milled. The time needed to produce these was calculated on the basis of standardized performance expectations. The accountant knew, for example, that 860 liters of fine flour had been produced during the year. As it was expected that one woman milled 20 liters of that type of flour in one day, it was easy to calculate that 43 labor days had been involved.

The women also provided agricultural labor, which needed to be incorporated into their service record. That labor was recorded on other tablets, sealed by officials who were explicitly named in the balanced account (*e.g.*, Englund 1991:265, col II: line 15). The source tablets were summaries of work provided in different locations, and must have been made up on the basis of other, more specific accounts that focused on one activity, for example. It might be possible to reconstruct a hierarchy of tablets, ranging from a day's note regarding the production of some flour to a year's balance, but the profusion of tablets from the Ur III period and the absence of a scholarly prosopography makes this work still very difficult. Moreover, many of the source tablets may have been discarded in antiquity, even if there is evidence that they were kept in labeled bags for a while.

Estimates

A scribe had to do more than just write down information. Not only did he measure and calculate, he also had to be able to evaluate the quality of products. If he could not do so himself, he needed the advice of people who could provide that information. As an example of where these skills were needed, we can follow an ear of grain from the field to the bakery. Along the way several scribes had to account for it. Even before the crops were full-grown, estimates were produced about the size of the harvest. In the Ur III period these were recorded on the so-called Round Tablets (Pettinato 1969), which gave the size of the field, the productivity level of the areas within it, and sometimes an amount of rent to be paid by the plow teamleader (Maekawa 1984: 84).

Recently it has been argued that many of the records of early Mesopotamia were estimates to plan ahead rather than actual accounts (Selz 1999). That seems somewhat of an overstatement, since numerous accounts recorded past activities and actual facts and figures. But estimates were indeed important. An owner of property which someone else worked, for example, had to determine what to expect as income before productivity requirements were imposed. Likewise, before a project such as digging an irrigation canal was started, one had to calculate how many people to assign to the task. These problems were solved using standard rates, some of which survived in the Old Babylonian mathematical school literature (Robson 1999: 139-40). A male laborer was supposed to excavate a certain volume of earth every day, and it was easy to divide the total of earth to be moved by that figure to determine the number of man-days required. There was no consideration of the actual conditions of the work. The ground could be stone hard or soft, which must have affected how much earth a man could dig up. The accountant viewed the world on the basis of standard rates, which may have been originally based on observation, but became mathematical formulae detached from reality. We can only wonder what pain this inflicted on the working population. Were the quotas they needed to provide so low that they could easily manage or so high that they needed to break their backs to attain them?

If large tracts of land were to be harvested, it was important that the correct number of people were sent to do the work. That probably did not require too much forethought. Experience gave guidance, but the information had to be communicated to the central labor office.

Once the harvest was completed, it had to be measured. Initially the grain heaps were used as a basis, as a skilled farmer can estimate their volume by inserting a stick into them (Civil 1994:96). Later, more accurate measures were needed, probably often based on the size of the granaries. This detailed information had to be passed on to a central office, which in the end could calculate the harvest of an entire province. Some of the texts available account for enormous amounts of grain. For example, Thureau-Dangin 1903: no. 407 gives totals of more than 37, 35, and 27 millions of liters for three years in the province of Lagaš:

> 74,426 iku (= 267.72 sq. km.) of field, its grain is 124,035 royal gur (= 37,210,500 liters)
> from which 129,000 gur 5 sìla (= 38,700,005 liters) were deli[vered]
> [excess of 4,965 gur 5 sìla (= 1,489,505 liters)]
> [Year: (Šulgi year 28?)]
> [... iku of field, its grain is ...]
> from which 118,200 gur (= 35,460,000 liters) were delivered
> deficit of 7,502 [+] gur (= 2,250,600 + liters)
> Year: the royal daughter married the king of A[nshan] (Šulgi year 30)
> 76,698 iku (= 275.89 sq. km.) of field, its grain is 91,830 gur (= 27,549,000 liters)
> from which 42,462 gur 100 sìla (= 12,738,700 liters) were delivered
> deficit of 42,207 gur 200 sìla (= 12,662,300 liters)
> Year: Simurrum was destroyed for the third time (Šulgi year 32)
> [Fields?] divided among five šabra-officials.

The fact that the scribe indicated both the expected harvest and what was really delivered indicates that actual measurements of the income were made in this case. In the record above, the third year's entry is amazing as the estimate was almost twice the size of what was actually delivered. This must have been a terrible harvest year, as the estimate even expected less income per square kilometer than it did for the first entry.

Grain that was transported had to be registered when loaded onto a boat and probably checked again when it arrived at its destination. The fact that boats had standard sizes of capacity—or at least were accounted for as such—presumably helped one calculate what was shipped, but someone still had to certify that the cargo was intact. When it reached its destination the grain had to be stored until it was issued to the millers. These produced varied qualities of flour depending on the fineness. A single miller could grind 10 liters of the basic type, dabin in Sumerian, in a single day; of a coarser type called eša, 20 liters could be produced in one day.

The scribe worked with standardized expectations: a woman was given 10 liters of barley, and was allotted a day in order to produce dabin. Yet, there was an acknowledgment that different circumstances could lead to different results. In a balanced account studied by Englund (1991) the quota of a flour called zì-sig$_{15}$ is only 6⅔ liters a day rather than the usual 10. As Englund points out, this may have been a mistake, but

> may support the interpretation that Ur III bookkeepers enjoyed some measure of flexibility in the regulation of labor output, whereby numerous factors such as the categories of employed laborers or the season during which the work was performed played a role only implicitly recorded in the running account. (1991:272)

Quality control

One of the amazing characteristics of Mesopotamian accounts is the systematic presence of evaluations of the quality of the work produced. For instance, in textile production four to five levels of wool quality were indicated. There was also a large terminology to distinguish the final products by type and color, all of which could appear in various qualities. The time spent in weaving was indicative here, yet the scribe or someone else had to determine a standard by which acceptable work had been done. Similarly, many different brews of beer appear in the accounts, which were distinguished by the amount of cereals used and the additives. Someone had to ascertain that the correct quality was attained. When goods were involved an equivalency in silver was often established. For instance, gold was available in values from 7 times to 21 times its weight in silver. Someone had to take the responsibility to appraise the gold and other goods, in order to enable the scribe to keep track of the assets for which he was responsible.

The power of classification connects administrative accounts to the other textual genre that is found throughout Mesopotamian history from the beginnings of writing: lexical material. Like the account texts, compilations such as urra-*ḫubullu*, a seemingly endless lists of objects, goods, animals, etc., make very careful distinctions according to quality, color, size, breed, and so on. The large variety of animals found in the Ur III Puzriš-Dagan texts, for example, is paralleled in the lexical lists. It is unlikely that the Ur III account texts provided the original entries for lists such as urra-*ḫubullu*, since these lists postdate the Ur III period, but the two types of sources show the same concern for classification.

Taxonomies represent a way in which the world is viewed and how knowledge is ordered. The lexical material shows how systematic the Mesopotamians were. The Old Babylonian version of urra-*ḫubullu*, for example, is divided into tablets of 500 to 700 lines each. Each one of them deals with a different subject. Tablet I lists trees and wooden objects, tablet II reed and reed objects, vessels and clay, hides and leather objects, and metals and metal objects, and so on (Veldhuis 1997:47). Each tablet is carefully organized. In the wood list, for example, boats are listed together, as are axes or siege engines (Veldhuis 1997:85). In this way every phenomenon is classified.

The purpose of these lists was not simple classification of the existing reality. There was no *Listenwissenschaft*, in the sense that von Soden suggested many years ago (von Soden 1936:425), the ordering of the world through lists. Lexical lists could easily expand on the existing world by extending patterns into areas where they did not exist or were irrelevant. They shared these patterns with other genres, such as omen texts which also include options beyond the realm of the possible (Bottéro 1991:134-35). For example, the same sequence of colors was systematically applied to a wide variety of entities, including animals and fruits: white, black, red, spotted and yellow. These were assigned to cats as well as to unripe dates, where their occurrence is highly unlikely (Veldhuis 1999:114).

Veldhuis has shown that the myriad variations in the lists derive from a concern with writing rather than with reality. Because the Sumerian language renders words of the same category with similar signs—for instance, all wooden objects are preceded with the giš-sign—the categorizations in the lexical lists group together Sumerian words whose written forms are similar. Expansion of the lists based on the visual patterns of word compounds was thus easy, and combinations of signs could lead to the recording of *realia* that did not exist or were highly obscure. Instead of a *Listenwissenschaft*, there was a science of writing in Mesopotamia (Veldhuis 1997: 137-46).

The Old Babylonian student thus learned words that had no value in practical life, and one can say that part of his training had no concrete benefits for his later profession. On the other hand it seems unlikely that this habit would not have affected his view of the world, and that it would not have urged him to see reality with a classificatory concern in mind. A sheep was not just a sheep, but was fattened or not, had a heavy fleece or a light one, was black or white, and so on. These may not have been unimportant distinctions, but the wealth of details provided may have exceeded purely utilitarian goals.

Conclusions

Accounts thus provide insights on different aspects of early Mesopotamian culture. They were utilitarian in that they established responsibility for an asset. The work of a scribe made a disbursement legitimate, as it documented that a transfer from one administrative entity to another had been genuine. The disbursing unit was relieved of the responsibility for the asset, the recipient had taken it over (Van De Mieroop 1997).

The scribes also evaluated and ascertained the quality of the things they entered into the accounts—numerous qualifications of everything that was produced or grown. Flour, cloth, beer, sheep, and much else were available in many varieties, which needed to be recorded because their values depended on them. These values were established through a set of equivalencies that were fully standardized. The whole process shows a passion for classification that also is visible in other Mesopotamian writing.

We need not imagine that an army of accountants was present all over the early Mesopotamian states. The scribes were highly efficient, and a small number of them could undertake the tasks assigned. Their rarity gave them a very select status. They worked in a non-literate society where the majority of people did not understand the details of what was written on the clay. But people must have realized how important documents were, how they protected them against accusations of theft or careless loss. The scribe had thus certain esoteric powers, a control over people's lives that was expressed in ways most of them could not grasp.

In return, the scribe bore an enormous responsibility: the accounts had to add up properly, the debits and credits had to represent reality so that the unit for which the scribe worked wasn't short-changed. At a time when it is hard to ascertain who won the majority of 6 million votes in Florida in the technologically most advanced nation, we should have great admiration for those scribes who 40 centuries ago could determine the exact whereabouts of each one of 38 million liters of barley.

BIBLIOGRAPHY

Bauer, Josef, Robert K. Englund and Manfred Krebernik (1998), *Mesopotamien. Späturuk-Zeit und Frühdynastische Zeit* (OBO 160/1).

Bottéro, Jean (1992), *Mesopotamia. Writing, Reasoning, and the Gods* (Chicago: The University of Chicago Press)

Chiera, Edward (1938), *They Wrote on Clay. The Babylonian Tablets Speak Today* (Chicago: The University of Chicago Press).

Civil, Miguel (1994), *The Farmer's Instructions. A Sumerian Agricultural Manual* (AuOr, Supplementum 5).

Englund, Robert K (1991), "Hard work—Where will it get you? Labor Management in Ur III Mesopotamia," *JNES* 50:255-80.

— (2003) "The Year: 'Nissen returns joyous from a distant island'," *Cuneiform Digital Library Journal* 2003:1 (http://cdli.ucla.edu/pubs/cdlj/2003/001.html).

Lion, Brigitte (2001), "Dame Inanna-ama-mu, scribe à Sippar," *RA* 95:7-32.

Loding, Darlene (1974), *A Craft Archive from Ur* (Ann Arbor: University Microfilms).

Maekawa, Kazuya (1984), "Cereal Cultivation in the Ur III Period," (BSA 1): 73-96.

Pettinato, Giovanni (1969), *Texte zur Verwaltung der Landwirtschaft in der Ur-III Zeit* (Analecta Orientalia 45; Rome: Pontificium Institutum Biblicum).

Potts, Dan T. (1997), *Mesopotamian Civilization. The Material Foundations* (Ithaca: Cornell University Press).

Robson, Eleanor (1999), *Mesopotamian Mathematics, 2100-1600 BC. Technical Constants in Bureaucracy and Education* (Oxford: Clarendon Press).

Sallaberger, Walther and Aage Westenholz (1999). *Mesopotamien. Akkade-Zeit und Ur III-Zeit* (OBO 160/3).

Selz, Gebhard J. (1999) "Vom 'vergangenen Geschehen' zur 'Zukunftsbewältigung'. Überlegungen zur Rolle der Schrift in Ökonomie und Geschichte," in B. Böck, E. Cancik-Kirschbaum and Th. Richter (eds.), *Munuscula Mesopotamica. Festschrift für Johannes Renger* (AOAT 267):465-512.

Sigrist, Marcel (1992), *Drehem* (Bethesda, Md.: CDL Press).

Steinkeller, Piotr (2003), "Archival Practices at Babylonia in the Third Millennium," in Maria Brosius (ed.), *Ancient Archives and Archival Traditions* (Oxford: Oxford University Press):37-58.

Thureau-Dangin, François (1903), *Receuil des tablettes Chaldéennes* (Paris: Ernest Leroux).

Van De Mieroop, Marc (1987), *Crafts in the Early Isin Period* (Orientalia Lovaniensia Analecta 24; Leuven: Departement Oriëntalistiek).

— (1997), "Why Did They Write on Clay?," *Klio* 79:7-18.

— (1999/2000), "An Accountant's Nightmare: The Drafting of a Year's Summary," *AfO* 46-47:111-29.

Veldhuis, Niek (1997), *Elementary Education at Nippur. The Lists of Trees and Wooden Objects* (Groningen: Unpublished Ph.D. dissertation).

— (1999), "Continuity and Change in the Mesopotamian Lexical Tradition," in B. Roest and H. Vanstiphout (eds.), *Aspects of Genre and Type in Pre-Modern Literary Cultures* (Groningen: Styx): 101-18.

von Soden, Wolfram (1936), "Leistung und Grenze sumerischer und babylonischer Wissenschaft," *Die Welt als Geschichte. Zeitschrift für universalgeschichtliche Forschung* 2:411-64, 509-57.

3.

The Function of Written Documentation in the Administrative Praxis of Early Babylonia*

Piotr Steinkeller
Harvard University

Developing some of the ideas I recently have offered elsewhere,[1] this article examines the role and place of written documentation in the Ur III administrative praxis in order to address a number of broader and more fundamental issues. Why did Babylonian administrators prepare written records in the first place? Were such records indispensable for the operation of the economic system? Did writing have an impact on the development of Babylonian institutions and, if so, to what degree and in which areas? To put it differently, could Babylonian society and its economy as we know it have developed without the use of written documentation?

These questions, especially the last one, are by no means trivial. We know of many successful ancient states with complex political and economic systems that never developed writing. For example, the exceedingly centralized Inca state operated without the benefit of writing, fulfilling all its accounting needs with the *quipu* recording system. On the other hand Mayan city-states did employed a hieroglyphic writing system, but only, it appears, to keep historical and chronographic records.

---

* I wish to offer my thanks to P.-A. Beaulieu, G. Magid, G. Marchesi, and B. Studevent-Hickman for reading and critiquing the preliminary version of this paper. Their input is warmly appreciated. It goes without saying that the responsibility for the final product rests with me alone. The drawings in fig. 1 are reproduced by courtesy of Time-Life Books Inc.

[1] Steinkeller 2003.

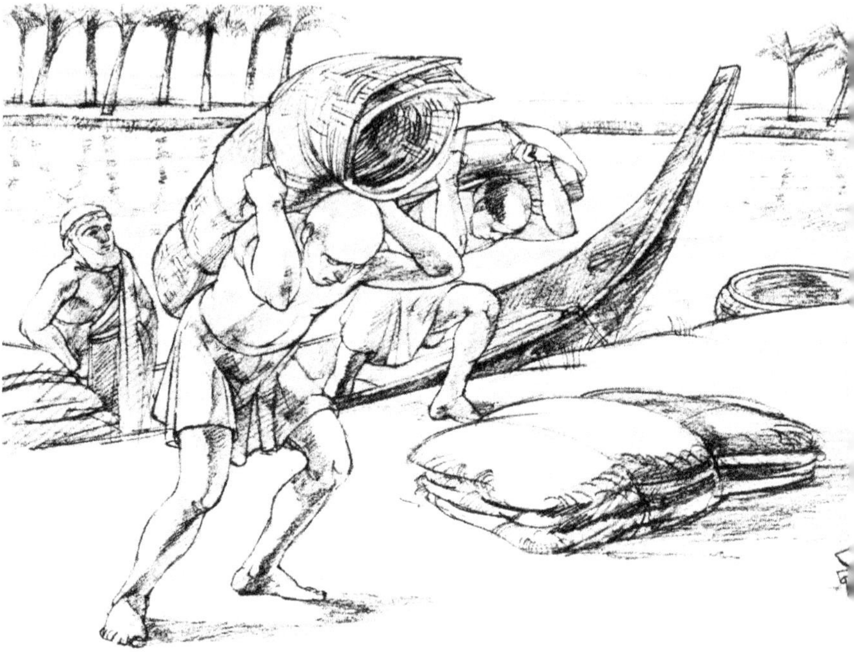

Fig. 1.

What's Wrong With These Pictures? (reproduced after Robert Claiborne and the Editors of Time-Life Books, *The Emergence of Man: The Birth of Writing* [New York: Time-Life Books, 1974]: 83).

Although the use of writing for accounting purposes was historically a rare phenomenon, the archeological and ethnographic data permit a safe generalization: Virtually every illiterate society, modern and ancient, possessed the capacity to store copious and complex information through the use of an array of para-writing devices such as calculi, counting sticks, cords, etc. Apart from being stored, such information also could be transferred routinely over distance, by recourse to pictographic letters, talking drums, and smoke signals, to mention only the best known examples.[2]

I begin with the question of the nature of third-millennium administrative records. The article I just referred to was primarily concerned with the following two issues: the interdependence of records, *i.e.*, the way they formed a complete system and related to one another; and the place of written documentation in the accounting process. For reasons of clarity and simplicity I left out the question of what these documents actually "say" and how they relate to the facts they are purportedly concerned with.

In my view the two most important characteristic features of cuneiform administrative documents are the following. First, such records were usually if not always written *post factum*, meaning that the document is not contemporaneous with but subsequent to the economic fact in question. Contrary to what commonly is imagined by non-specialists and scholars alike (see fig. 1), it was prepared only later (very often much later) and in a different location and setting than those of the original transaction. The second—and even more important—feature of such records is that they describe a special type of reality.

Even in the simplest and most straightforward types of transactions, such as the disbursements and the receipts of commodities, the facts as stated in documents are not what happened in real life. Consider, for example, the receipt tablets of the functionary Arad (see Texts 1-5 below), the chief official in charge of grain processing, storage, and distribution at Umma.[3]

---

[2] Gelb 1963:24-51. For pictographic letters as a means of conveying complex information, see, in particular, the example discussed *ibid.* 30f. and fig. 9.

[3] Arad held the title of ka-guru$_7$, "granary superintendent." In all probability he was the brother of Ur-Lisi, at onetime the governor of Umma: Árad šeš Ur-^{d}Li$_9$-si$_4$-ka (ASJ 19 [1997]:226-27 no. 72 ix 7)

Text 1 (Sigrist Yale 366:1-9)

0.4.2 še lugal	260 liters of barley
é-kikkin-ta	(removed) from the mill;
7.2.1 še gur	2,230 liters of barley
A-šag$_4$-^{giš}ma-nu-ta	(removed) from (the hamlet of) Ašag-manu[4];
ki Árad-ta	from Arad
Lugal-ḫé-gál	Lugal-ḫegal
šu ba-ti	received.
Date	Šulgi 44/xii.

Sealed with the seal of: Lugal-ḫé-gál / mu$_6$-sùb ^{d}Šára / dumu Ur-nìgin-gar, "Lugal-ḫegal, shepherd of (the god) Šara, son of Ur-nigingar."

Text 2 (Sigrist Yale 576:1-11)

0.1.0 še lugal	60 liters of barley
é-kikkin da bàd-ta	(removed) from the mill at the city-wall (of Umma);
1.1.2 še sumun gur	380 liters of old barley
igi É-maḫ-šè-ta	(removed) from (the hamlet) in front of Emaḫ[5];
šag$_4$-gal anše-kúnga	the fodder of mules;
ki Árad-ta	from Arad
Lú-^{d}Nin-šubur	Lu-Ninšubur
šu ba-ti	received.
Date	Šulgi 48/iii.

Sealed with the seal of: Lú-^{d}Nin-šubur / SAḪAR / árad ^{d}Šára, "Lu-Ninšubur, the equerry, servant of Šara."

---

4 Documented also as É-duru$_5$-<a-šag$_4$->^{giš}ma-nu, "Hamlet of <Ašag>manu (Sigrist Yale 298:3). A rural hamlet, which housed a grain silo (guru$_7$) (YOS 4 41:8-9; Sigrist Yale 1023:2-4, 1828:8-9) and a threshing floor (ki-sur$_{12}$) (Istanbul 772:6, 972:2; etc.).

5 Documented also as É-duru$_5$-é-maḫ (MVN 21 412 rev. v 4). A hamlet associated with Emah, a rural temple-estate of Šara. It housed a grain silo (Istanbul 104:3, 2299:7; etc.) and a threshing floor (Istanbul 1641:11, 2361:2; etc.).

Text 3 (Sigrist Yale 584: 1-9)

0.3.3 še lugal	210 liters of barley
Ḫa-ḫa-ša	(for) Ḫaḫaša;
0.3.3 še Nimgir-di-dè	210 liters of barley (for) Nimgir-dide
sá-dug$_4$ ^{d}Nanše	(as) the regular offering of Nanše;
ki-sur$_{12}$ gu-la A-šag$_4$-lá-maḫ-ta	from the big threshing floor of (the hamlet of) Ašag-lamaḫ[6];
ki Árad-ta	from Arad
kišib Ḫa-ḫa-ša	received by Ḫaḫaša.
Date	Šulgi 48/xi.

Sealed with the seal of: Ḫa-ḫa-ša / dumu Lugal-[...], "Ḫaḫaša, son of Lugal-[...]."

Text 4 (Sigrist Yale 857: 1-6)

1.2.0 še ur$_5$-ra maš nu-tuku gur	420 liters of barley, a loan without interest,
ki-sur$_{12}$ Gáb-temen-na-ta	(removed) from the threshing floor of (the hamlet of) Gabtemena[7];
ki Árad-ta	from Arad
kišib Na-ba-šag$_5$ šidim	received by Nabašag, the mason.
Date	Amar-Suen 5/xi.

Sealed with the seal of: Na-ba-šag$_5$ / dumu Lugal-nesag-e, "Nabašag, son of Lugal-nesage."

[6] Documented also as É-duru$_5$-a-šag$_4$-lá-maḫ (Sigrist Yale 635: 5). A rural hamlet, which housed, apart from several threshing floors, a grain silo (Istanbul 9: 3; Sigrist Yale 1290: 7; etc.).

[7] Documented also as Du$_6$-gáb-temen-na, "Hill of Gabtemena" (Nikolski 2 140: 8; MVN 20 156: 5-6; etc.). A rural hamlet, which housed a grain silo and a threshing floor (Sigrist 1617: 3-6; Istanbul 2038: 2; etc.).

Text 5 (Sigrist Yale 859: 1-7)

7.2.3 še gur	2,250 liters of barley,
sá-dug$_4$ ^{d}En-ki	(as) the regular offering of Enki,
Gú-eden-na-ta	(removed) from (the hamlet of) Gu'edena[8];
ki Árad-ta	from Arad
kišib Ur-nìgin-gar	received by Ur-nigingar.
Date	Amar-Suen 5/i.

Sealed with the seal of: Ur-nìgin-gar / gúda ^{d}En-ki, "Ur-nigingar, the gúda priest of Enki."

In such documents, dozens (if not hundreds) of which survive,[9] Arad is identified as the issuer of grain, flour, and other cereal products: "from Arad Party so-and-so received." While many of those disbursements took place in Umma itself, where several mills and extensive storing facilities are known to have existed, the majority of them were made from the grain silos in the countryside. Certainly Arad was not physically present at all those diverse locations to make expenditures. The same probably was true of the "recipients" named in the documents; very likely, they too were not there in person to receive the items in question. What apparently happened is the following:

(1) first, an authorization of the expenditure would be given by Arad or his office (possibly in the form of a letter-order) to the "recipient";
(2) then, a representative/subordinate of the "recipient" would collect the item in question from the unnamed official in charge of the grain-storing facility in location X;
(3) finally, the "recipient" (or his representative) would show up in Arad's office at Umma; at that time a receipt document would be prepared, duly sealed with the seal of the "recipient," and deposited among Arad's records.

[8] Documented also as É-duru$_5$-gú-eden-na (Sigrist Princeton 400: 2). A rural hamlet, which housed a grain silo (Nikolski 2 159: 6-7; Watson Birmingham 2 218: 9; etc.) and a threshing floor (Istanbul 1458: 2, 2855: 2-3; etc.).

[9] Further examples are MVN 3 122, 127, 132, 135, 138, 141, 142, 144, 146, 148, 149, 155, 157, 158, 163, 164, 167, 168, 169, 171, 175, 176, 180, 181, 182, 186, 191, 192, 193, 194, 195, 216, 249; MVN 13 176, 177, 179, 180, 181, 182, 183, 184, 202, 205; etc.

This reconstruction finds confirmation in the fact that many a document records multiple withdrawals made in different locations, as in Text 1, where two separate expenditures of barley were made "from the mill (of Umma)" and "from (the storing facility of the hamlet of) Ašagmanu" respectively.

Similar operational principles may be detected behind other types of receipt tablets:

Text 6 (Sigrist Yale 424: 1-7)

3.0.0 gur lugal	900 liters of barley,
šag$_4$-gal gud niga	(as) the fodder of grain-fed oxen,
Uš-gíd-da-ta	from (the hamlet of) Ušgida[10];
ki énsi-ta	from the governor,
A-ab-ba šu ba-ti	A'abba received.
Date	Šulgi 45 (or Amar-Suen 2)/xii.

Sealed with the seal of: Íd-pa-è / dub-sar / dumu Lú-^{d}Šára sag-du$_5$, "Idpa'e, the scribe, son of Lu-Šara, the field-recorder."

Text 7 (Sigrist Yale 361: 1-6)

1 gud-giš	1 plow-ox
ki A-tu-ta	from Atu
Lú-dùg-ga engar	Lu-duga, the head of a plowing team,
ì-dab$_5$	took.
kišib Uš-mu	Received by Ušmu.
Date	Šulgi 44.

Sealed with the seal of: Uš-mu / dub-sar / dumu Lugal-šag$_5$-ga, "Ušmu, the scribe, son of Lugal-šaga."

The literal sense of Text 6 is that A'abba received from the governor 900 liters of barley in Ušgida. But this is not what actually happened. The phrase "received from the governor" rather signifies that the governor (specifically, his office) authorized the transaction. As the events can plausibly be reconstructed:

---

[10] Documented also as É-duru$_5$-uš-gíd-da (Istanbul 3669: 3). A rural hamlet, which housed a grain silo (Istanbul 800: 5, 1815: 3; etc.) and a threshing floor (Istanbul 994: 4, 2888: 7; etc.).

(1) the governor's office at Umma authorized the expenditure;
(2) A'abba (or his representative) withdrew the grain from the silo at Ušgida;
(3) information (apparently in an unwritten form) about the withdrawal was conveyed to Umma; and
(4) finally, the governor's office prepared a receipt tablet, which was sealed by Idpa'e, who was either a member of the governor's office or A'abba's superior.

Text 7 concerns the activities of Ušmu, a one-time head of Umma's cattle and sheep office.[11] In this instance a plowing ox was apparently physically withdrawn by Lu-duga, the head of a plowing team, from a certain Atu. But the document clearly was written in a bureau setting after the receipt had taken place. The significance of the phrase "sealed (receipt) of Ušmu" is that Ušmu authorized the transaction; more specifically, he gave his *imprimatur* to Lu-duga's withdrawal. It is doubtful, though, that he rolled his seal himself; more likely, it was one of his subordinates.

As yet another illustration of the disparity between the physical event and its administrative version may serve the Puzriš-Dagan delivery tablets, which are characterized by the use of the term mu-DU, "delivery" or "delivered."[12] Written (or at least dated) daily, these documents invariably record multiple deliveries of livestock from various sources. Given the fact that no delivery tablets recording individual deliveries are known, it follows that such records were produced at the end of a business day/period, and not when the animals were physically brought into the corals of Puzriš-Dagan. What is more, it is clear that many of the recorded deliveries did not take place at Puzriš-Dagan at all. Rather, the animals in question were brought to one of Puzriš-Dagan's local branches, especially those at Ur and Uruk.

All these facts show beyond any doubt that usually, if not as a matter of course, the document offers an administrative version of the events, not an objective description of what actually happened. More often than not, there is no one-to-one correspondence between the event as it really occurred and as it is described in the tablet. One could say, therefore, that the administrative records operate within a kind of

---

[11] See Stępień 1996:187-90, 202, 206-08; Sharlach (in press).

[12] See Maeda 1989:69-107; Sigrist 1992:54-56.

"accounting reality" or even "accounting fiction," in that the events and their temporal sequence are re-interpreted and regrouped to suit best the purposes of the administrative procedure.

Not uncommonly, this abstraction from reality reaches a very high level, such as in the Umma records of labor extracted from the various types of dependent workers.[13] Being modeled after the receipts of movables and commodities, the documents of this type are formulated as the receipts of man-days, and are invariably sealed. Their pattern is as follows:

> x workers for y days;
> description and location of the work assignment;
> under the supervision (ugula) of PN_1;
> the seal (kišib) of PN_2;
> date.

As I analyzed this pattern elsewhere:

> In this laconic formulation, PN_1 is the foreman of the work-gang (usually numbering ten men). The sealing official is to be identified as the receiving party, since the phrase kišib PN_2 is identical with the formula PN_2 ì-dab$_5$/šu ba-ti 'PN_1 received,' the latter formulation being used in unsealed receipts. As for the item that was received in this transaction, it was the conscripted workers or, more correctly, the man-days they spent working on the assignment in question. Accordingly, in purely accounting terms the sense of this record is as follows: 'PN_2 received from PN_1 x man-days to perform such-and-such a work-assignment.' What happened in reality, however, was the following sequence of events: (a) PN_2 commissioned PN_1 to do job x at location y; (b) PN_1 brought his workers to y and completed job x as requested; (c) PN_2 prepared for PN_1 a sealed receipt tablet (kišib) for the expended man-days.[14]

Thus, although the document has the form of a receipt, there was no real "recipient," nor was there a real "disbursing party." It is also likely that the "recipient" (PN_2) never showed up at the site of the project in question. The document was prepared much later in an office setting. As that part of the operation may be reconstructed, some time after the project had been completed, the "disbursing party" (PN_1) came to PN_2's office and offered the evidence of the project's performance. PN_1 (or, more likely, one of his subordinates) then prepared a respective receipt, sealed it with his official seal, and handed it over to PN_2.

---

[13] Steinkeller 2003:44-48.

[14] Steinkeller 2003:45f.

While in the records of this type the numbers of workers employed are given accurately (since it was significant to know how many members of a given gang were actually used), this information became irrelevant once the data on the performance of multiple gangs were compiled. At that stage only the total numbers of man-days expended mattered, and so figures were routinely reduced to a single worker. In this way, instead of listing, for example, five workers each contributing 10 days of labor, it was sufficient (and much more economical) to have a record of one worker with a 50 man-day contribution.

Since written records were prepared *post factum* and in locations different from those where the facts in question had actually occurred, the following question unavoidably arises: How was the relevant information gathered and stored until it was converted into a written form? Clay drafts are one candidate here, but this possibility can immediately be discounted, since no examples of such drafts have survived. Even more important, clay tablets would be a highly inefficient medium outside of the office setting, since it is difficult—if not impossible—to conceive of a scribe carrying with him supplies of wet clay on his errands.

A much more likely possibility is that wooden boards, called li-um in Sumerian, were used for that purpose. Although the widespread use of writing boards is well documented during the first millennium, both in Babylonia and Assyria,[15] as well as in Egypt throughout most of her history,[16] there is, however, very little evidence of the use of such devices in third-millennium Mesopotamia.[17] This rarity of the men-

[15] See MacGinnis 2002:217-36; Baker 2003:252f.; Postgate 2003b:133-36.

[16] For the Egyptian writing boards see Vernus 1984:703-09; Reisner 1911: 113-14; Brovarski 1987:27-52; Manuelian 1996:566-68. I owe these references to Dr. Peter Der Manuelian. A picture of the 19th dynasty writing board in the collection of the Kunsthistorisches Museum, Vienna, is available on the WEB: <http://www.khm.at/staticE/page1525.html>. The board measures 18.5 × 14.8 cm in size and is coated with a thin layer of white plaster. For the place of such boards in administrative praxis, particularly informative are the reliefs and frescos depicting the measuring of grain at the conclusion of harvest. For the examples, dating from the Old through the New Kingdom, see Ifrah 1981:138 fig. 3.14, 153 fig. 3.38; Erman 1894:432; Shaw 2000:224. Customarily included in such scenes are scribes, some of whom make calculations on their fingers, while others record the results on writing boards. The information so gathered would later be converted into proper archival records, written on papyrus.

[17] This situation notwithstanding, it may be taken for granted that such boards were used as a matter of course in land-surveying. In fact, there exist two examples of li-um (both cited courtesy of G. Marchesi) which appear to

tions of li-um probably indicates that wooden boards, while certainly known and used earlier, did not become a standard administrative device until late in the second millennium.[18]

If it was not wooden boards, then the only possibility left is that, essentially, information was preserved through the reliance on human memory and the use of various para-writing accounting and recording devices, such as the clay or stone calculi and counting sticks. Although there is no direct evidence to support such a supposition, it would seem certain that the records such as the daily records of receipts from Puzriš-Dagan I discussed earlier were prepared based on the information collected in this manner, either through the recourse to calculi or perhaps even some early form of the counting board or abacus.[19]

---

concern that particular application: ŠUKU dù-dù-a li-um-ta dib-ba šag$_4$ é-dub-ba-ka, "(records of) the subsistence land under cultivation that had been transferred from the wooden tablet(s) (and subsequently stored?) in the archive" (MVN 11 93:34-36); 60+10×3(bùr) 4(iku) gána a-šag$_4$ Ambar-Lagaš^{ki} li-um-ta mú-a im-ma-an-tur NI-da mu-ni-gíd, "the field Ambar-Lagaš has 'grown' (in the records) by 90 bur (and) 4 iku of land since the (preparation of the) wooden tablet. It has now been reduced (in the records). NI-da had measured (it) out (originally)" (MVN 11 91 rev. 1-4).

The other Ur III attestations of li-um known to me are the following ones: deliveries of animals … li-um-ma nu-ub-gi-in, "were not verified in the wooden tablet(s)" (Szlechter TJA IOS 15:1-11); 1 ^{gi}pisan li-um-ma dagal-bi 2 kùš gíd-bi 3 kùš (Istanbul 2870:6); (zú-lum) li-um-ma nu-ba-gar (UET 3 1097 colophon); 60 li-um GAG (RTC 221 v 10); […] li-um-ma (in a broken context) (MVN 13 241:5; courtesy of G. Marchesi); ur-sag-gá-àm á mu-gur li-um za-gìn šu im-mi-du$_8$ é-a giš-ḫur-bi im-gá-gá … ur-sag-gá-àm á mu-gur$_8$ li-um za-gìn šu bí-du$_8$-a ^{d}Nin-dub-kam é-a giš-ḫur-ba im-mi-sì-sì-ge (Gudea Cylinder A v 2-4, vi 3-5); Mar-ḫa-ši^{ki} li-um-ma gur-ru-dè ("Curse of Akkade" line 20). See also ^{gi}pisan im-sar-ra im-li-um in the Old Babylonian text YOS 5 61:2. Another term describing writing boards is possibly ^{giš}da, "wooden board," as in the following Ur III example: 30 lá 1 ^{gi}pisan im-sar-ra ^{giš}da-a ésir su-ba, "29 baskets caulked with bitumen (for) tablets (and?) writing? boards" (Istanbul 797:1f.).

[18] An additional problem in this connection is presented by the rarity of the references to wax (gaba-làl = *iškuru*, làl-àr = *lallāru*) in third-millennium sources. Only a couple of such attestations survive, involving either *iškuru* or gaba-làl and dating to Ur III times. See CAD I/J, 251b; [x] gín eš-ku-ru-um (Snell Ledgers no. 9 iii 23); 2 ma-na eš-ku-ru šag$_5$ dam-še-lu-um dam-šè (Sigrist Yale 1613:2-3). This evidence appears to indicate that wax was not available in large quantities during the third millennium, which, in turn, would speak against the widespread use of writing boards. Or should one speculate that a different malleable substance was employed for that purpose?

If I am correct that the overwhelming majority of administrative documents were written *post factum* (and the extant evidence leaves no doubt that that was the case), it becomes apparent—and this point is of even greater significance—that the operation of the whole system at least on the level of individual / primary economic units did not depend on the presence of written records. More often than not—and probably even as a general rule—within individual components of the system information was gathered, processed, stored, and consulted without the recourse to writing. Because of this, whenever written documentation was part of the administrative procedure, it invariably represented an additional and purely optional feature. Written records were prepared only in special circumstances, and those circumstances were created by outside factors, and not by the internal needs of the economic unit in question.

Similar conclusions about the place of writing within the administrative praxis of ancient Mesopotamia have been reached by the archaeologist Gian Giacomo Fissore.[20] Writing nearly a decade ago, he too believed that under normal conditions written documentation was not necessary for the operation of a given administrative system, and that it co-existed together with various traditional para-writing recording and accounting practices.[21] Unfortunately Fissore's zeal to foster the importance of the latter led him to mistaken views about the function of the written records themselves, and of how they relate to para-writing devices such as clay-stoppers and other types of sealings. It therefore is necessary to review these views in some detail.

In the main, Fissore's article is a passionate tirade against the "mistaken viewpoint … of wanting to see the written text as an autonomous form of administrative expression."[22] Rather, Fissore believes

---

[19] A possible example of such a counting device is ^{giš}níg-ŠID, Akk. *nikkassu*, *uttuk(k)u*, *māḫiṣātu*, see Civil 2000: 115-16. For the ancient examples of the abacus, as well as for the counting devices employing strings and knots, see Ifrah 1981: 121-59.

[20] Fissore in Ferioli *et al.* (eds.) 1994: 339-54. With a response by Th.G. Palaima, pp. 355-58, and discussion, pp. 359-61.

[21] Similar conclusions were reached by Th.G. Palaima, based on the evidence of the Old Babylonian Mari texts ARMT 10 12 and ARMT 13 22: "Both examples show us that writing enters the routine administrative process in anomalous situations, but is not used in regular circumstances: *i.e.*, that written records are not an integral part of the normal transactional processes," in Ferioli *et al.* 1994: 358).

[22] Ferioli *et al.* 1994: 343.

that writing played only "a supplementary, often redundant, role compared to the unwritten records devised and developed earlier."[23] In his opinion written documents represented but an appendage to clay sealings: "writing is not an absolute parallel of the clay sealing system, but a partial and, perhaps, mainly casual complement to it, entrusted in all likelihood to the actual presence and availability of scribes, a presence which was then neither generalized nor compulsory in a rigid bureaucratic structure."[24] From the historical perspective, written documents are merely adaptations of prehistoric clay bullae "without the slightest modification and without any improvement other than intrinsic in the analytical potential of the written language."[25] The only differences between the two is that the former offer more information.[26]

Fissore certainly deserves credit for recognizing the importance of non-writing devices and stressing their co-existence with written documentation. But his understanding of the purpose of writing records is fundamentally wrong, bordering on a caricature.[27] As I have shown

---

[23] *Ibid.* 342. [24] *Ibid.* 343. [25] *Ibid.* 343.

[26] "Compared to the clay sealing, a written document essentially offers more information about the people involved in the administrative act" (*ibid.* 342).

[27] In all fairness to Fissore, his conclusions depend in large part on the unfortunate article by Enrica Fiandra (1981), which offers a completely wrong explanation of the function of cuneiform receipt tablets. In particular, Fiandra thinks that the term kišib PN, "sealed receipt tablet of PN/ sealed by PN," which appears on the envelopes of Ur III receipt documents, and replaces the phrase PN šu ba-ti, "PN received," in the tablets, refers to the sealing which was applied to the door of the warehouse after the goods were withdrawn. She bases this view on the mistaken assumption that the PN invoked in the envelope and the one named in the tablet were two different individuals: the recipient of the goods in question, who sealed the doors of the warehouse subsequent to the goods' removal, and the official responsible for the drawing of the document respectively. Hence this (and many similar) misrepresentations of the facts: "The periodic checking of the names and amounts on the document and the clay stopper bearing the impression of the seal mentioned in the text, was thus facilitated. So it was not necessary to open the envelope to check whether the clay stopper with the seal corresponding to the person who withdrew the goods existed. After the audit, the tablet in its original envelope could be stored intact and indefinitely in the archives while the clay stopper could be thrown away" (*ibid.* 34). None of this is true. It is absolutely certain that both the envelope and the tablet identify the same person, who is the sealing party = the recipient of the goods in question. Accordingly, there is no connection whatsoever between the receipt tablets and the sealings that were applied to containers and door locks.

earlier, administrative documents were not part, physically and mentally, of what may be described as "the warehouse context." We have seen that even the simplest receipts of commodities are fully abstracted from the physical occurrences they are concerned with; what they are about is an administrative reality, and not a factual reality. It follows, therefore, that written records were not complementary—and certainly not redundant—to clay sealings as Fissore wants us to believe. Their purpose was distinctly different from that of non-writing devices. Such a conclusion is unavoidable if only on common-sense grounds alone, since it would have been quite uneconomical and impractical simultaneously to use two different accounting systems serving the same purpose.

But what then was the true purpose of written records? For this question the following fact is of absolutely basic importance: From the perspective of a single (primary) economic establishment, such as the Umma labor office or the bureau in charge of Umma's grain stores (to use the examples just discussed) there was no need to prepare written documentation for its own internal purposes, since it operated perfectly well without such records. As I would argue, it was only when an office was required to report to higher authorities that written documentation became necessary.

We need to ask, therefore, why such reporting was required in the first place. This problem was considered recently by Marc Van De Mieroop, who suggested that written documentation was prepared to justify the activities of an administrator, especially his expenditures, to higher authorities.[28] In other words, documents were an instrument of administrative control, which enabled a superior official to audit the performance of his subordinates.

Certainly, considerations of this kind must have been a factor, though in my opinion a secondary one, since for the purposes of simple accountability unwritten forms of reporting would have been quite sufficient. In my view the main reason why written records were compiled was to enable a given office to provide the top management with the summary (or even statistical) information, presented in a form intelligible to an outsider, which would permit global economic prognostication or planning. Clearly, this kind of information could have been gathered and further manipulated only through the use of detailed written documentation.

---

[28] Van De Mieroop 1997.

In suggesting that the main function of cuneiform administrative documents was to provide a database for economic forecasts I am not alone. Very similar views have recently been expressed by Gebhard J. Selz.[29] Selz's position is made clear by the title "Verwaltungsurkunden als Planungsdokumente" he assigns to one of the subsections of his study. And note the following statement: "Selbst wenn in einem Bereich nur Abrechnungen und Bestandskontrollen vorgenommen bzw. überliefert sein sollten, so verfolgen sie innerhalb dieser Wirtschaftsform einen auf die Zukunft gerichteten Zweck: sie sind Unterlagen für eine Planung."[30]

In fact, it has been noted more than once that no economic activity is possible without some form of planning. As the anthropologist Jack Goody puts it:

> By means of a written record of income, an organization can increase its control over the internal allocation funds—for example, in calculating the amount to be spent on investment or set aside for saving as distinct from the sum needed for meeting the running costs and consumption needs. All societies require some forward planning from their members, some allocation of resources over time, some husbandry. But for an elaborate organization, budgeting increases its 'efficiency,' 'its rationality,' and extends its depth of control.[31]

It is not by accident, therefore, that a considerable percentage of the economic records from the third millennium are precisely of the estimate type. For example, most of the Ur III documents dealing with agricultural matters are estimates, beginning with the projections of yields based on the soil quality and past history of the fields in question; through the estimates of seed-grain, animal fodder, and human labor to be expended during the agricultural cycle from the soil preparation through the harvest; and ending with the forecasts of the actual harvest and its subsequent distribution. Babylonian administrators even had specific terms for estimating. One of them is the verb káb … dug_4, meaning primarily "to calibrate, to adjust," but also "to project, to make an estimate." Hence the noun káb-dug_4-ga, "adjustment,

---

[29] Selz 1999.

[30] *Ibid.* 489.

[31] Goody 1986: 104.

estimate."[32] A similar expression is gún ... gar "to impose/project yield, income," with its derivative gún gá-ra, "projected / expected yield."[33]

While these suggestions about the economic records as a planning tool remain somewhat speculative (as they cannot be proved—or disproved—without further extensive study of the role of forecasting in Mesopotamian economies), few would disagree with the proposition that there is a direct connection between the volume of economic documentation produced by a given economic system and the level of centralization and planning within that system. The more centralized an economy is and the greater degree of prognostication it employs, the more written documents it produces. At the same time, the information contained in such records becomes progressively more and more detailed. These facts permit us to formulate a general rule that the presence of written documentation is predicated on the level of centralization and economic planning within the entire system, and not on the degree of internal complexity of its components.

---

[32] See Civil 1994: 153-63; Attinger 1993: 575 ("... par extension, il pourrait signifier 'estimer'"). The sense "to estimate" of káb ... dug_4-ga is clear in the Umma estimates of the productivity of date-palms, which conclude with the phrase zú-lum káb-dug_4-ga, "estimated/projected dates," or $^{giš}kiri_6$ káb-dug_4-ga, "estimated orchards" (for the occurrences, see Civil 1994: 154-55). In this connection, note also 1 pisan im-sar-ra EN im zú-lum káb-dug_4-ga ba-an-gá-ar, "1 basket (for) large?? tablets, the tablets with date estimates were placed in it" (Istanbul 1169: 2-4); pisan-dub-ba zú-lum káb-dug_4-ga $šag_4$ $Umma^{ki}$ ì-gál, "a tablet basket; the date estimates (of the orchards) in Umma are contained in it" (Sigrist Yale 1972: 1-4). Similar usage is found in the estimates of apples, garlic, and agricultural land: ḫašḫur ... káb-dug_4-ga (N. Koslova, SANTAG 6 196: 13-14); sum káb-dug_4-ga (Koslova, SANTAG 6 321 rev. iii 2, 340 iv 9); 9(bùr) 2(eše) 4(iku) gána 9-ta a-$šag_4$ Urgu ... gána káb-dug_4-ga (Sigrist Yale 1093: 1-18).

[33] Vegetables $gún^{un}$ gá-ra $^{giš}kiri_6$ 1(iku) gána-kam, "estimated produce of 1 iku of orchard land" (Boson Tavolette 364: 1-8); 10×4+9(bùr) gána še $gún^{un}$ gá-ra še-bi 1,080.0.0 gur gána-gud-ta íb-ta-zi mu $gún^{un}$ gá-ra-a íb-tab-ba-šè $šag_4$ im Lú-^{d}Ḫa-ià-ka-ta níg-ŠID-ka lá-a še gur_x(ŠE.GUR)-a zàr-tab-ba A-pi_4-sal_4^{ki}, "49 bùr of land, with an estimated barley yield of 1,080 gur, has been deducted from the institutional holdings, on account of the doubled barley estimate; (deducted) from the tablet of Lu-Haya; the reduced balanced-account of the harvest (work) and grain-stacking in Apišal" (Sigrist Yale 1641 iii-iv 3).

A perfect illustration of this rule is the Ur III economic records, since no appreciation of this documentation is possible without the understanding of the nature of the Ur III economy itself. Of particular importance in this connection is the *bala* taxation system, which imposed on all the provinces of the Ur III state specific quotas of taxes and other types of economic obligations.[34] This system called for an extraordinarily high level of data-recording, since the provincial administration had to know exactly how much goods and labor it expended on behalf of the central government and its officialdom in order to be able to calculate the value of its contributions vis-à-vis the figure that had been assessed for the province by the central government. Needless to say, the *bala* system also called for a great deal of budgeting and planning.

When we juxtapose this picture with that obtaining in the following period, we see that the Old Babylonian economic system was closely similar, though considerably less centralized. The individual components of the Old Babylonian economy, such as the crafts, labor, animal husbandry, and even agriculture, were organized and operated in very much the same way as in Ur III times. It also seems certain that all those components retained the earlier level of internal complexity. Thus, there is no reason to think that, for example, the Old Babylonian agricultural system was any less complex—as regards both its technological and managerial aspects—than its Ur III counterpart. The only difference was that, in Old Babylonian times, the central government no longer was directly engaged in agricultural production, nor were there any serious attempts, at that highest command level, at global planning and forecasting. The king and his government left all the agriculture-related decisions to local officials, who ran the royal estates very much like private entrepreneurs. As a result, a great deal less documentation pertaining to agriculture was generated by the administration.

The last point has important implications for the evaluation of the Old Babylonian textual corpus as a whole. The fact that the surviving body of economic documents from that period is comparatively small is almost certainly not an accident of discovery. Rather, this fact is directly related to the relative insignificance of central economic planning in Old Babylonian times.

---

[34] Sharlach 2004.

I turn now to the question of the impact of written administrative records and of writing more generally on the development of Mesopotamian institutions. Of particular interest is the problem of how the invention of writing in the late Uruk period related to the momentous economic and social developments known to have taken place about the same time. If my earlier conclusions about the nature of economic records and their place in administrative praxis are correct, then it becomes fairly clear that the presence of a writing-based recording system had not been a condition *sine-qua-non* for those developments to have occurred. In other words, it is fair to assume that much of those changes would have taken place irrespective of whether or not cuneiform writing had been invented.[35] This, however, does not diminish writing's importance—on the contrary. I would argue that what the written records did enable was the possibility of engaging in forward economic planning. This, in turn, led to the development of much more complex and efficient forms of economic organization and management. While the precise impact of writing on the Uruk institutions is difficult to judge, it is fair to conclude that much of the organizational fabric that one finds in southern Babylonia during the second half of the third millennium would not have been possible without the presence of written records. This is particularly true of the Ur III economic organization, which almost totally depended on this form of record-keeping and reporting.

The contribution of written records to the rise and flourishing of the Mesopotamian civilization was thus of the first order. However, at the same time we should give full recognition to the role of other, non-written forms of recording and accounting in the administrative procedure. That recognition is slow in coming, I suspect as a result of our literary conditioning, which too often is responsible for an absolutist attitude toward writing. The tendency has been to presuppose writing to be the only possible way in which information may be stored and transferred from one location to another.

---

[35] Compare Postgate, who, having considered the question of the impact of writing on trade in Uruk and historical times, concludes as follows: "... although in historical times traders used writing in ways which helped them finance their collaborative ventures and respond to market conditions, written documents were not indispensable to the movement or the exchange of goods as such" (2003: 16f.).

This limitation of the literary mind to appreciate the possibilities of non-written forms of recording is nicely illustrated by a story involving two Lutheran lay missionaries who settled in Australia in the second half of the 19th century:

> Mr. Ernst Jacob, who was out on the run looking after the sheep, sent word to "Father" Vogelsang, who was in charge of the store, that he would like him to send some tobacco. A native boy was sent with the parcel together with a letter in which it was mentioned how many plugs of tobacco were forwarded. The boy, knowing what the package contained, could not resist the temptation, and took a few plugs and hid them in order to pick them up on his return trip. The boy was questioned about the missing tobacco by Mr. Jacob, and immediately admitted his guilt. The boy was at a loss to understand how the letter, which was closed up, had managed to see him taking the tobacco.[36]

This amusing anecdote was cited by Piotr Michalowski in his study of early writing and literacy as an illustration of the otherness of writing for those who are not familiar with it.[37] Surely, Michalowski makes a splendid point, but there is a problem with the anecdote itself: it almost certainly is apocryphal. One may be fairly confident that this story goes back (possibly via various intermediate retellings) to the account told in a book by John Wilkins, which was first published in 1641.[38] The latter story reads as follows:

> How strange a thing this Art of Writing did seem at its first Invention, we may guess by the late discovered Americans, who were amazed to see Men converse with Books, and could scarce make themselves to believe that a Paper could speak.
>
> ...
>
> There is a pretty Relation to this Purpose, concerning an Indian Slave; who being sent by his Master with a Basket of Figs and a Letter, did by the Way eat up a great Part of his Carriage, conveying the Remainder unto the Person to whom he was directed; who when he

[36] Ferguson 1987:223-37. The original source of the story is E.H. Proeve, *Three Missionary Pioneers* (Tanuda, Australia: Auricht's Printing Office, 1946), which I have not been able to locate.

[37] Michalowski 1994:49-50.

[38] Wilkins 1707:3-4, cited after Eco *et al.* 1992:40f.

> had read the Letter, and not finding the Quantity of Figs answerable to what was spoken of, he accuses the Slave of eating them, telling him what the Letter said against him. But the Indian (notwithstanding this Proof) did confidently abjure the Fact, cursing the Paper, as being a false and lying Witness.
>
> After this, being sent again with the like Carriage, and a Letter expressing the just Number of Figs, that were to be delivered, he did again, according to his former Practice, devour a great Part of them by the Way; but before he meddled with any, (to prevent all following Accusations) he first took the Letter, and hid that under a great Stone, assuring himself, that if it did not see him eating the Figs, it could never tell of him; but being now more strongly accused than before, he confesses his Fault, admiring the Divinity of the Paper, and for the future does promise his best Fidelity in every Employment.

There is little reason to think that Wilkins's tale is any truer than the former one. Even if they originated independently of one another, both stories are obvious fabrications, meant to extol the power of writing and, by extension, the superiority of Western culture. What betrays it is their patent literary bias, since the notion that the ability to convey information is unique to writing could have been spawned only by a literate mind. As assured by the examples of pictographic letters I referred to at the beginning of this article,[39] the Australian Aborigine and the Indian slave these stories make fun of would undoubtedly have known better.

[39] See above p. 68 and n. 2.

Bibliography

Abbreviations used for text editions are those of the *Assyrian Dictionary of the Oriental Institute of the University of Chicago* and the *Sumerian Dictionary of the University of Pennsylvania Museum* with the following additions: Istanbul (see Yildiz *et al.*); Sigrist Yale (see Sigrist 2000); SANTAG: Arbeiten und Untersuchungen zur Keilschriftkunde (Wiesbaden).

Attinger, Pascal (1993), *Eléments de linguistique sumérienne* (OBO Sonderband).

Baker, Heather D. (2003), "Neo-Babylonian Record-Keeping Practices," in Brosius 2003: 241-63.

Brosius, Maria, ed. (2003), *Ancient Archives and Archival Traditions: Concepts of Record-keeping in the Ancient World* (Oxford: Oxford University Press).

Brovarski, Edward (1987), "Two Old Kingdom Writing Boards from Giza," *Les Annales du Service des Antiquités de l'Égypte* 71: 27-52.

Civil, Miguel (1994), *The Farmer's Instructions: A Sumerian Agricultural Manual* (AuOr, Supplementa 5).

— (2000), "From the Epistolary of the Edubba," in A.R. George and I.L. Finkel (eds.), *Wisdom, Gods and Literature: Studies in Assyriology in Honour of W. G. Lambert* (Winona Lake: Eisenbrauns): 105-18.

Eco, Umberto, with R. Rorty, J. Culler, and Ch. Brooke-Rose (1992), *Interpretation and Overinterpretation* (S. Collini, ed.; Cambridge: Cambridge University Press).

Gelb, Ignace J. (1963), *A Study of Writing*, rev. edition (Chicago: University of Chicago Press).

Erman, Adolf (1894), *Life in Ancient Egypt* (London: Macmillan and Co.).

Ferguson, Charles A. (1987), "Literacy in a Hunting-gathering Society: The Case of the Diyari," *Journal of Anthropological Research* 43: 223-37.

Ferioli, Piera *et al.* (eds., 1994), *Archives before Writing* (Torino: Scriptorium).

Fiandra, Enrica (1981), "The Connection between Clay Sealings and Tablets in Administration," in H. Härtel (ed.), *South Asian Archaeology 1979* (Berlin: Dietrich Reimer): 29-43.

Fissore, Gian Giacomo (1994), "Conceptual Development and Organizational Techniques in the Documents and Archives of the Earliest Near Eastern Civilizations," in Ferioli *et al.* 1994: 339-54.

Ifrah, Georges (1981), *Histoire universelle des chiffres: L'intelligence des hommes raconté par les nombres et le calcul* (Paris: Editions Robert Laffont). English edition (2000): *The Universial History of Numbers. From Prehistory to the Invention of the Computer* (New York: John Wiley & Sons).

Goody, Jack (1986), *The Logic of Writing and the Organization of Society* (Cambridge: Cambridge University Press).

MacGinnis, John D. (2002), "The Use of Boards in the Neo-Babylonian Temple," *Iraq* 64: 217-36.

Maeda, Kazuya (1989), "Bringing (mu-túm) Livestock and the Puzrish-Dagan Organization in the Ur III Dynasty," *Acta Sumerologica (Japan)* 11: 69-107.

Manuelian, Peter Der (1996), "Presenting the Scroll: Papyrus Documents in the Tomb Scenes of the Old Kingdom," in P. D. Manuelian (ed.), *Studies in Honor of William Kelly Simpson* (Boston: Museum of Fine Arts): 561-88.

Michalowski, Piotr (1994), "Writing and Literacy in Early States: A Mesopotamianist Perspective," in D. Keller-Cohen (ed.), *Literacy: Interdisciplinary Conversations* (Cresskill, N.J.: Hampton Press): 49-70.

Postgate, J. Nicholas (2003a), "Learning the Lessons of the Future: Trade in Prehistory through a Historian's Lens," *BiOr* 60: 5-25.

— (2003b) "Documents in Government under the Middle Assyrian Kingdom," in Brosius 2003: 124-38.

Reisner, George (1911), "A Scribe's Tablet Found by the Hearst Expedition at Giza," *Zeitschrift für ägyptische Sprache und Altertumskunde* 48: 113-14.

Selz, Gebhard J. (1999), "Vom 'vergangenen Geschehen' zur 'Zukunftsbewältigung': Überlegungen zur Rolle der Schrift in Ökonomie und Geschichte," in B. Böck, C. Cancik-Kirschbaum and Th. Richter (eds.), *Munuscula Mesopotamica: Festschrift für Johannes Renger* (AOAT 267): 465-512.

Sharlach, Tonia M. (2004), *Provincial Taxation and the Ur III State* (Cuneiform Monographs 26; Leiden: Brill–STYX).

Shaw, Ian, ed. (2000), *The Oxford History of Ancient Egypt* (Oxford: Oxford University Press).

Sigrist, Marcel (1992), *Drehem* (Bethesda: CDL Press).

— (2000), *Texts from the Yale Babylonian Collections, Parts 1 and 2: Sumerian Archival Texts 2 and 3* (Bethesda: CDL Press).

Steinkeller, Piotr (2003), "Archival Practices at Babylonia in the Third Millennium," in Brosius 2003: 37-58.

Stępień, Marian (1996), *Animal Husbandry in the Ancient Near East: A Prosopographic Study of Third-Millennium Umma* (Bethesda: CDL Press).

Van De Mieroop, Marc (1997), "Why Did They Write on Clay?," *Klio* 79: 7-18.

Vernus, Pasqual (1984), "Schreibtafel," in *Lexikon der Ägyptologie* V/5 (Wiesbaden: Harrassowitz): 703-09.

Wilkins, John (1707), *Mercury; Or, the Secret and Swift Messenger*, 3rd ed. (London: Nicholson).

Yildiz, Fatma *et al.* (1988-2001), *Die Umma-Texte aus den Archäologischen Museen zu Istanbul*, vol. 1 = MVN 14 (Rome, 1988); vol. 2 = MVN 16 (Rome, 1994); vol. 3 (Bethesda, 1993); vol. 4 (Bethesda, 1997); vol. 5 (Bethesda, 2000); vol. 6 (Bethesda, 2001).

4.

Bookkeeping in the 21st Century BCE

William W. Hallo
Yale University

Welche Vorteile gewährt die doppelte Buchhaltung dem Kaufmanne! Es ist eine der schönsten Erfindungen des menschlichen Geistes, und ein jeder guter Haushalter sollte sie in seiner Wirtschaft einführen.
J.W. von Goethe, *Wilhelm Meisters Lehrjahre* I/1/10; cf. Ijiri 1993:266.

I. Bookkeeping in the Renaissance

The Italian Renaissance of the Quattrocento and the Cinquecento (15th and 16th centuries CE) is justly famed for reviving the knowledge of classical antiquity in arts and sciences, though it is now increasingly if grudgingly acknowledged that the present era is enjoying its own, more modest, risorgimento thanks to the ongoing recovery of the pre-classical antiquity of the ancient Near East.[1] But Renaissance Italy also figures in most histories of economics as the fountainhead of modern financial techniques, including banking and double-entry bookkeeping. It will be my purpose here to see whether theses claims stand up to newer insights.

To begin with some definitions, double-entry bookkeeping is typically defined as any method whereby each transaction is entered twice in a record, once as a debit and once as a credit; debit (German *Soll*) is defined as "the recording of an asset, or a decrease in liability or net worth value"; credit (*Haben*) is defined as "the recording of a liability or net worth value or a decrease in the value of an asset"; assets are defined as the sum of liabilities and net worth.[2]

In practice, however, what is meant is that a transaction is entered four times; a simple sale, for example, would appear as a credit and debit in the books of the seller and as a debit and credit in the books of the purchaser.

---

[1] Cf. in brief Hallo 1996:324-33. [2] Johnson 1962:240f.

The two earliest preserved modern examples of the genre date to 1340; they represent the books of the Commune of Genoa, one kept by two treasury officials of the city called "stewards" (*massari*), and one, a duplicate of the foregoing ledger, maintained by two officials called *maestri razionali*, whose duty it was to watch and check the work of the *massari*. They probably borrowed their technique from prior practices of the "banks" (*banchi*), but the earliest preserved bank ledger dates to 1408, also from Genoa. Debits and credits were entered in paragraph form, debits on the left-hand page and credits on the right-hand page.[3]

The next innovation took place at Florence, where the "lateral accounts" of Venice (and Genoa) were introduced into the already fully developed Florentine system of double-entry bookkeeping complete with debits, credits and balances, but hitherto listed in simple successive entries, one below the other. Florence had forged to the fore as a commercial power as early as the 13th century when (in 1252) it began to mint the "gold florin" (*fiorino d'oro*) and succeeded in having that accepted across Europe as *the* gold standard.[4] (To this day the English call their standard 2-shilling piece a "florin," and until recently at least it was interchangeable in coin machines with the Dutch guilder, abbreviated fl. for florin.) By the end of the 14th century (1382), the "memorandum book" (*vacchetta*) of a certain Paliani of Pisa already placed debits and credits on facing pages. Also at Pisa, the Datine Compagnia ledgers from 1383-1408 employed the new method. The individual entries were cross-indexed with the ledgers from which they had been derived, and at the end a balance was calculated and carried forward to the next ledger.

The final refinement takes us back to Venice where, by the early fifteenth century, the ledger and memorandum books where replaced by the journal (1430), which combined the virtues of both. "Debits" (identified by *per*) and "credits" (identified by *a*) are combined in one paragraph each, with money values carried to the right margin and cross-references to the ledgers to the left margin. By 1494, the new rules of double-entry bookkeeping were summed up by Fra Luca Paciolo in his *Summa de Arithmetica, Geometria, Proportioni et Proportionalita* (Everything about arithemtic, geometry, proportion, and proportionality) in a section called *De Computis et Scripturis* (Of reckonings and writings), which became one of the earliest books printed with moveable type. There have been many refinements in double-entry bookkeeping

---

[3] Peragallo 1938:4f.

[4] Peragallo 1938:18.

since then, but no fundamental departures from the Florentine and Venetian models. Let us then see whether, in their essentials, they were anticipated in antiquity.

II. Bookkeeping in the 21st century BCE

Mark Twain is credited with the observation that he was finished with letting his friends into his personal library because, as he said, "though they were mostly poor mathematicians, they were all excellent bookkeepers." The scribes of ancient Mesopotamia, by contrast, were good at both: mathematics *and* bookkeeping.[5] And they learned both in the scribal schools, best attested for the 18th century BCE but whose foundation undoubtedly goes much further back. Karen Nemet-Nejat has conveniently assembled more than two hundred (actually 227) mathematical texts of all periods which reflect daily life in Mesopotamia.[6] By way of illustration, let me cite just one—or part of one: an Old Babylonian text which was hidden among the archival documents from Ur but which represents an interesting exercise in dividing an inheritance, UET V: 121: 1-8.[7] First a transliteration:

> 26 ma-na 15⅔ gín 15 [še kù]-babbar
> dumu *Ṭa-bi-ia* šeš-gal šeš-tur-meš
> igi-5-gál ḫa-la-kam ḫé-íb-diri
> šeš-gal e 7⅔ ma-na 8⅔ gín 15 še
> šeš-2-kam 6 ma-na 15 gín
> šeš 3 kam 5 ma-na
> šeš-4-kam 4 ma-na
> šeš-5-kam 3 ma-na 12 gín

---

5 Lambert (1985: 92 n. 17) even claims the Sumerian professional name sag-su_{18} for the meaning "book-keeper," though CAD Š/2 (1992): 145 translates the term by "land registrar, recorder." For the wider significance of Lambert's text, see Hallo 2001:245f.

6 Nemet-Nejat 1993.

7 Eleanor Robson (2000: 104) maintains that "Mathematical problems from the same [OB] period ... do not reflect contemporary practice but rather use inheritance and loan scenarios to set up pseudo-realistic word problems on topics like artihmetic progressions and division by irregular numbers." For the importance attached to divisions of inheritance, at least from the legal and moral points of view, see most recently Hallo 2002. For inheritance problems in Babylonian mathematics in general, see Muroi 1988; for UET 5: 121 in particular, see now Friberg 2000: 138-40, 149, 151.

My translation converts all entries into še (grains), of which 180 make a gín (shekel) and 60 × 180 or 11,400 make a ma-na (pound):

283,635 grains of silver,
the sons of Ṭabia, the big brother and the little brothers,
let (each one) have ⅕ more by way of an inheritance share:

the big brother (gets):	84,375	grains
the second brother:	67,500	grains
the third brother:	54,000	grains
the fourth brother:	43,200	grains
the fifth brother:	34,560	grains
(Total:	283,635	grains)

The exercise involves an arithmetic progression, as the following calculations show:

⅕ of 84,375 = 16,875;	84,375–16,875 = 67,500
⅕ of 67,500 = 13,500;	67,500–13,500 = 54,000
⅕ of 54,000 = 10,800;	54,000–10,800 = 43,200
⅕ of 43,200 = 8,640;	43,200– 8,640 = 34,560

The Neo-Sumerians of the 21st century have no school texts to compare with the numerous examples from the 18th century. But they more than make up for this lack of exercise texts with a wealth of actual archival texts. And these furnish abundant evidence of their mathematical skill as applied to bookkeeping procedures.[8] This evidence will be considered here under three headings: debits and credits, balance sheets, and letters of credit. It will also be useful to review the role of money and the question of formats.

III. Debits and credits

If double-entry bookkeeping is defined as entering each transaction twice in ONE record (cf. above, I), then the Neo-Sumerian accounts of the 21st century BCE cannot lay claim to the technique, and "the primacy of medieval Italy in the development of the double-entry account is thus apparently assured."[9] But if it is defined more broadly as entering each transaction twice at a time, albeit in two different records, then there is ample evidence for the practice in the detailed documentation from Drehem, ancient Puzrish-Dagan, the great cattle-yards constructed

[8] Cf. Hallo 1979:4-13, Grégoire 1970 No. 135, and Van De Mieroop 1999-2000 for some particularily telling examples.

[9] Snell 1982:53.

by King Shulgi of Ur (c. 2093-2046 BCE) in the 38th year of his reign (c. 2056 BCE) to service the religious capital of his realm at nearby Nippur as well as the political capital at more distant Ur. A comprehensive survey of its operations has been provided by Marcel Sigrist,[10] but I will confine my attention here to what has long been understood as its "basic organization."[11]

As Jones and Snyder recognized, there are numerous examples of pairs of texts dated on one and the same day of which one records the receipt or "delivery" (mu-túm) of certain animals from certain sources, and the other records the "disbursement" (zi-ga or, from Shulgi 47 on, ba-zi) of the same animals from the same sources.[12] They took these entries literally as meaning that the animals in question were routed to their ultimate destinations on the day they were received. Alternatively, one can regard these as bookkeeping operations only, in which a receipt (debit) was matched by a corresponding entry described as a disbursement (credit). If so, we would have here at least an implicit form of double-entry bookkeeping.

To illustrate, I will juxtapose two Drehem texts dated Shulgi 47/V/1:

Debit (mu-túm) (CST 174)	Credit (ba-zi) (PDT 1:415)
1 lamb [Urmesh] the cupbearer	1 lamb for Enlil, delivery of Urmesh the cupbearer
1 goat Zikur-ili	
1 lamb Zabar-dab	1 lamb for Nusku, delivery of Zabar-dab
1 lamb Irmu	
2 fatted goats Lu-GUL-zida	1 fatted goat for Enlil, 1 fatted goat for Ninlil, delivery of Lu-IZKIM-zida
1 lamb Ṣillush-Dagan	
2 lambs Shesh-dada the priest	1 lamb for Enlil, 1 lamb for Ninlil, delivery of Shesh-dada 1 lamb for Hursag-galamma, delivery of Ṣillush-Dagan
1 lamb Kur-girnishe	1 lamb for Nanna, delivery of Kur-girnishe,

[10] Sigrist 1992; cf. also Sigrist 1999. [11] Jones and Snyder 1961:212-38.

[12] *Ibid.* 215-17. They operated with a reign of 49 years for Shulgi, rather than 48, so their "Shulgi 48" is the equivalent of what is today regarded as Shulgi 47.

	Zabar-dab being deputy
	1 lamb for the é-uzga,[13]
delivery	delivery of Irmu,
	Aa-kalla being deputy.
Nasha took in charge.	Withdrawn from Nasha.

As can be seen from this juxtaposition, each of the entries in the mu-túm text (except for the second one) corresponds precisely to one in the ba-zi text—though not always in the identical order. Numerous other examples of such pairs of Drehem texts could be added to the handful offered by Jones and Snyder. I have collected them over the years and will note them here without the slightest pretense at being exhaustive.

mu-túm	zi-ga/ba-zi	date
OIP 115:201 (A 5546)[14]	NBC 2272	Shulgi 46/IV/18
OIP 115:188 (A 4164)	TRU 267	Shulgi 46/VIII/5
An.Or. 7:150[15]	LB 142*[16]	Shulgi 47/VI/20
OIP 115:265 (A 4434)	NBC 6536	Shulgi 47/XI/2
NBC 6655	TrDr 14	Amar-Suen 2/V/2

Exceptionally, the mu-túm text may be a bulla, as in the case of PDT 389, which bears comparison with CST 155, both dated Shulgi 46/XII/28.

Halfway through the reign of Amar-Suen, the accounting usage changed. Starting with the king's fifth year, deliveries were now first transferred from one official to another, who "took them in charge" (ì-dab), before they were disbursed to their final destination (whether in reality or in bookkeeping). In the first instance they were no longer identified by the name of the person who had delivered them. Thus it is less certain that reference is to the same day's deliveries. Still it may be suspected in cases like the following, both dated Amar-Suen 5/II/23:

---

[13] On this structure(?), see most recently Sigrist 1992:158-62.

[14] I transliterated this and hundreds of other Drehem texts from the Oriental Institute collection nearly fifty years ago; the Shulgi texts are cited here from the publication by Hilgert 1998, the Amar-Suen texts from Hilgert 2003.

[15] Although the day of the date is damaged, and could be restored as any number from 20 to 29, it can confidently be read as 20 on the basis of the parallels with LB 142*.

[16] LB 142 was published by me as TLB 3:113; hence the notation must refer to another text.

mu-túm (CST 304)	ì-dab (PDT 109)
1 ox 1 cow 1 *a-lum* sheep	
2 fat-tailed sheep	
2 fat-tailed ewes	
Gulkunum the Amorite	
4 gazelles, selected[17]	
Igiannakezu	
1 lamb from Namu	
3 fatted sheep, 1 fatted female lamb	5 fatted sheep, 1 fatted female lamb
1 *a-lum* sheep for breeding	1 *a-lum* sheep
Naram-Ea	
2 fatted sheep 1 lamb	
Nur-Dagan	
2 fat-tailed sheep, 1 lamb	4 fat-tailed sheep
... ib-ḫa-in	
1 goat Ur-Ninsun	
1 goat Lugal-azida	
delivery	
Abba-shaga took in charge	from Abba-shaga Nalul took in charge

At the same time, there emerged a tendency to lump all of one day's transfers together for a given day. This further complicates their identification with a specific delivery, but it does not necessarily rule it out, as in the following cases:

mu-túm	i-dab	date
1 lamb Nig-Mama	2 lambs	Amar-Suen 5/V/5
1 lamb Puzur-Eshtar		
delivery		
Abba-shaga took in charge	from Abba-shaga Intae'a took in charge	
(PDT 141)	(CST 315)	
1 lamb Puzur-Irra	1 lamb	Amar-Suen 5/VII/14
the temple steward (šabra)	from Abba-shaga	
delivery	Intae'a	
Abba-shaga took in charge	took in charge	
(PDT 144)	(CST 324)	

[17] For this approximate meaning of šu-gíd see Sigrist 1992:40-42.

Similarly, 13 of the 14 lambs delivered in Amar-Sin 5/VIII/25 to Abba-shagga by 12 different parties (MVN 4:116)[18] are quite likely summed up as transferred by Abba-shaga to Intaeʾa on the same day (PDT 64). Of the 82 lambs and 3 goats delivered to Abba-shaga by as many different named individuals in Amar-Sin 5/X/9 (TCL 2:5504), 77 lambs and 3 goats made it into the transfer to Intaeʾa whicḥ was recorded on the same day (PDT 128). It is harder to reconcile the deliveries (CTC 11) and transfers (PDT 93) for Amar-Sin 5/X/18.

Disbursement to final destinations also continued to be recorded, but now more often separately instead of, as before, listing all together for a given day. So for example, we can read Jean, SA LVIII 35:15[19] as "1 gazelle buck (amar-mašda), Puzur-Eshtar" in light of PDT 143: "1 gazelle buck for the é-uz-ga, delivery of Puzur-Eshtar" since both texts are dated Amar-Suen 5/VI/12 and involve Abba-shaga. In Amar-Sin 5/VII/11, we can probably equate the one lamb delivered by the governor of Nippur to Abba-shaga (OIP 121:92=A 3297) with the one lamb for Ninurta received by Abba-shaga from the governor of Nippur (OIP 121:238=A 4763).

IV. Balance sheets and balanced accounts

All these examples could be multiplied *ad libitum*, but the point is clear: under a looser definition, these accounts qualify as examples of double-entry bookkeeping in the sense that for each debit recorded in one text, there is a corresponding credit entered at the same time in another text. The next question virtually imposes itself: are there cases which combine both entries in one ledger? The answer, given long ago by Jones and Snyder, is yes. They follow their chapter on "The basic organization at Drehem" with one on "balanced accounts" which begins: "Balanced accounts, the Sumerian form of double-entry bookkeeping, list the receipts and expenditures for a day, a month, or a longer period." An example from their own catalogue will illustrate the genre, based on a single day (SET 102).

196 sheep, balance forward from the balanced account of the fourth day
139 sheep from the property of Ili-ili
25 adult goats via Allamu
1 sheep 2 lambs ...-ta via Nigingar-kidu

[18] The text was previously published by Deimel in Or. 26 (1927):187, but with many errors. The new copy also has a problem: the total on the left edge says "20 sheep" though the text enumerates 23.

[19] For the preceding lines of this text see Michalowski 1975:717.

(total on hand) 363 out of which:
10 adult goats receipt of Shu-ili man of Babati
2 adult goats receipt of Beli-bani
via Allamu
1 sheep Lu-ushgina
1 adult goat receipt of Lu-gina
28 sheep: first time
17 sheep: second time
17 sheep: third time
via Babati
1 sheep slaughtered out of 12 via Ir-Shara
16 kids out of 26 via Ur-kununna
10 sheep via Urgar
1 sheep via Ishme-ilum

Shu-ili took in charge 90
10 kids for breeding Abi-ṭab took in charge via Adallal
10 sheep slaughtered receipt of the dog-herders
(total:) 126 disbursed
237 sheep on hand
balanced account of Urgar
Amar-Sin 7/III/18

The credit side of this ledger lists 363 small cattle (sheep and goats) including a balance of 196 brought forward from the previous accounting 14 days earlier; the debit amounts to 126—although the individual entries add up to only 124[20]—and the positive balance of 237 will presumably be brought forward to the next balanced account.

Here follows an example of a balanced account of one month (SET 101):

5 lambs for extispicy[21], 19 assorted goats and kids,
balance of II/5
6 lambs for extispicy, 2 lambs delivery via Duga
2 lambs for extispicy, 2 sheep 7 lambs "on the books,"[22]
2 lambs 1 kid for breeding remaining outside (the books)[23] from Aallamu
9 assorted kids and lambs from Shu-ili

---

20 The numbers in the interior of lines 17, 18 and 22 clearly do not figure in the calculations.

21 For this possible meaning of kin-gi$_4$-a see Sigrist 1992: 123.

22 For this sense of šà-kišib-ba (šà-dub-ba) see Sigrist 1992: 93, 113.

23 For this sense of bar-ta-gál-la, see *ibid.* 93. PSDB 95 translates "additional, extra, extra available."

Their tablets were not sealed[24]
(total:) 55
(capital on hand) out of which:
1 lamb for offering in the palace on the 14th day
1 lamb for Inanna of Uruk on the 15th day
3 lambs 1 kid for offering in the palace on the 21st day
1 kid for Irra-ZU on the 22nd day
(2 lines lost)
1 kid …
1 lamb for extispicy
1 lamb for Lu-shalim
1 kid selection …
1 lamb receipt of Dada the cupbearer
1 sheep receipt of Adda the cupbearer
1 lamb receipt of Daian-ili the amar-ga
2 kids seal of Ur-alla the door-keeper
1 sheep receipt of Lugal-unuga
3 lambs for extispicy receipt of Zazi
1 kid Urshu the cook
disbursed …
(total:) 32 having been disbursed
his (balance) brought forward: 23 assorted kids and lambs
balanced account of Lu-Shalim
Amar-Sin 7/II/30

Here it is clear that a positive balance at the end of the month is called lá-ni, though the positive balance brought forward from the preceding month is called *si-ì-tum*. It is this discrepancy which has led Robert Englund to a complete reevaluation of the terminology of the balanced accounts.[25]

According to him, *si-ì-tum* is a negative balance, and lá-ni a deficit. But the examples of successive balanced accounts (see below) show clearly that the lá-ni of one year (or half-year) became the *si-ì-tum* of the next. Not surprisingly, other interpreters have returned to the more traditional understanding of the terminology.[26]

---

[24] For this sense of kišib(!) nu-kišib see Sigrist 1992:97; but perhaps we should read kišib-bi nu-um(!)-túm, "their sealed tablets were not delivered."
[25] Englund 1991.
[26] Note especially Lafont 1992.

V. Money before coinage

The existence of double-entry bookkeeping, in the broader if not the stricter sense of the term, can thus be argued where accounting procedures concerning cattle are involved. One could equally suggest its existence on the evidence of balanced accounts involving the "great organizations" of the Ur III kingdom. One can cite, *e.g.*, labor performed for the state at Umma[27] or deliveries to the temple of Shara there.[28] The next question is logically: are the accounts always in kind (cattle, votive offerings, labor etc.) or can they be in money/silver? The answer is not in doubt. In fact, the balanced account is most typically employed for the so-called merchant's balanced accounts in which all entries are routinely expressed in or converted into money terms.

The question of what constitutes money before the invention of coinage in the first millennium BCE—traditionally by Croesus of Lydia in the sixth century[29]—is a much debated issue. Commonly, silver served the function, typically cast into spirals that could conveniently be carried on the person like bracelets or armbands. Silver served in all the classical functions of money: as a unit of account, a medium of exchange, or a standard (store?) of value. But on occasion, these functions could be served as well by other commodities, the so-called "exchangeable goods," most notably barley, as was recognized tellingly in the proverbial wisdom of Sumer.[30]

The merchant's balanced accounts have been the subject of numerous studies over the years, most systematically by Daniel Snell.[31] Thus it is unnecessary to go over the ground again. Instead I will illustrate the genre by a precis of two of Snell's texts which happen to represent successive accounts by the same merchant, Ur-Dumuzida. The first is Snell's Sequence no. 26, published in copy (pls. xvf. = No. 9) only; it belongs to the Morgan Library Collection at Yale and will be cited here by its accession number as MLC 2602. The second is his Sequence no. 28, published in copy (pls. xviif. = No. 10), transliteration (pp. 19f.) and translation (pp. 20-22); it belongs to the Nies Babylonian

---

27 Englund 1991.

28 Lafont 1992.

29 See most recently NY Times August 14, 2000, Science Section. Kagan 1982 dated the origin of coinage already to seventh-century Lydia.

30 Hallo 1996: 18-25, with earlier literature. Cf *ib.* 73f.

31 Snell 1982.

Collection at Yale and will be cited here by its accession number as NBC 11448.[32]

The merchants of Umma seem to have typically balanced their accounts twice a year. They are thus dated, if at all, to the beginning, middle or end of the year. This is true of 12 of the accounts that include a month name;[33] only three are dated to other months.[34] MLC 2602 is dated Amar-Suen 6/XI and possibly covers the preceding eleven months. NBC 11448 is dated Amar-Suen 7/VII and covers the intervening months. Both texts convert all entries into their money (= silver) equivalents. MLC 2602 carries forward a positive balance of 52 shekels and 150 grains from the preceding year (Amar-Suen 6), and then adds capital on hand in the form of wool, dates and other "exchangeable commodities" to the value, apparently, of 365 shekels and 110 grains to make for a total capital on hand of 418 sh. 80 gr. Against this credit are posted a total of 338 sh. 163 gr. of debits or purchases, leaving a positive balance of 79 sh. 97 gr. to be carried forward.[35] And indeed this figure recurs as the first entry in NBC 11448.

Snell himself objected that the merchants' balanced accounts did not, strictly speaking, meet the crucial criterion of double-entry bookkeeping since "only rarely do the same products occur as both capital and expenditure and never in the same amounts."[36] But in the first place we would not expect to see entries occur in both capital and expenditure sections since they are fundamentally different, whether we treat them respectively, as he tends to, as sales and purchases, or, as I prefer, as exports and imports.[37] In the second place, once converted to money equivalents, the entries *do* appear in both sections, albeit not individually but in the respective totals. This is not so different from usage in the Italian system, where individual entries in the debit and credit sections could differ as long as the totals coincided. But admittedly it falls short of the systematic "matching" of receipts and expenditures, which is the essence of double-entry bookkeeping.

---

[32] *Ibid.* 15-17 for a tabular summary of the 44 examples of the genre known to Snell.

[33] Snell's Sequence nos. 7, 8, 12, 18, 25, 26, 27, 28, 30, 31, 32, 39.

[34] Sequence nos. 24 (II), 29 (IX), 34 (X).

[35] The figures in col. vi line 31 are slightly damaged but can be restored with confidence.

[36] Snell 1982: 53; cf. above, n. 9.

[37] Snell 1982: 55-75; Hallo 1996: 73 and n. 240.

VI. The question of format

Thus the Ur III bookkeeping system was a highly sophisticated one. But it remained stubbornly linear, or one-dimensional. That is, all entries were made in linear succession, with little or no effort to dispose the entries on the surface of the clay tablet in any manner designed for greater ease of visualizing the relationship among the entries. Modern transliterations often make good on this shortcoming by presenting the contents of the accounts in tabular, or two-dimensional format. (Eleanor Robson favors the term "tabular."[38]) A word is in order on this format.[39]

As long ago as 1957, I coined the term "two-dimensional" to characterize the underlying character of the Neo-Sumerian account texts, especially from Drehem, and I gave Thorkild Jacobsen credit for applying the technique, though not the term, to the elucidation of the Old Babylonian Grammatical Texts (OBGT) in MSL IV. I employed the technique myself in subsequent publications, encouraged Baruch Levine to use it on "the descriptive tabernacle texts of the Pentateuch," and collaborated with him on a joint presentation of two elaborate Old Babylonian accounts of "offerings to the temple gates at Ur."[40] In 1974, Jacobsen first used the term, but only to emphasize that the OBGT had *avoided* the technique in presenting their paradigms. He did, however, note that it was used in contemporary archival texts, citing TCL 11:236 by way of a random example.[41] I had made the same point a decade earlier, citing TLB 1:52-55.[42]

The examples cited by Levine and myself were equally random, and can be multiplied almost at will not only for Old Babylonian times,[43] but also for Middle Babylonian[44] and Late Babylonian times.[45] The move

38 Cf. also Robbins 1996. I have used the term myself on occasion; cf. Hallo 1960:101 *ad* text 22; 1992:54 *ad* text 7 and 55 *ad* text 9.

39 Hallo *apud* Sigrist 1999:146f.

40 All references in Levine and Hallo, 1967:20 n. 16.

41 Jacobsen 1974:44 and 61, n. 2.

42 Hallo 1964:61, n. 29.

43 *E.g.*, JCS 2:80f.; VS 13:86.

44 Gurney 1983 Nos. 66-68, 79. I had already called attention to such MB tables in 1964:62 and n. 47. For MB bookkeeping techniques in general, see Petschow 1973.

45 YOS 1:46-51. For other *ḫitpu* texts see Robbins 1996; for the concept of *ḫitpu* see Hallo 1999. For NB bookkeeping techniques in general, see Sack 1979; van Driel and Nemet-Nejat 1994.

from one-dimensional to two-dimensional format may be compared, *mutatis mutandis*, with the evolution of modern bookkeeping from the paragraph format to the "lateral" format.[46] Its principal evidentiary value is in showing that the interpretation of the bookkeeping techniques of the 21st century BCE is not simply a modern construct but implicit or latent in the texts themselves, though not realized in patent form until two or three centuries later.[47] Indeed it is not too much to expect that, as the most archaic account texts, those from Uruk, begin to yield their secrets to modern decipherment, the rudiments of modern bookkeeping techniques may yet be traced back by another millennium.

VII. Letters of credit and the question of banking

As long ago as 1958 I pointed out that, "if money did not turn the wheels of economic activity under the Third Dynasty of Ur, something else must have, and the letters show the motivation for at least some of the innumerable transactions which are attested for the period. The letters, better described as letter-orders, are in effect drafts or orders to pay (in kind), drawn on the great storage centers of Drehem, Umma etc., in favor of the bearer."[48] The point was reiterated in 1969,[49] and the term "letter-order" has become standard not only for the Neo-Sumerian genre but also for its counterparts in Old Babylonian,[50] Neo-Babylonian,[51] and even Elamite.[52] In connection with the last, Richard Zettler noted that "The letters [from the Persepolis treasury] generally request the treasurer to transact payments for services rendered by various kinds of workmen, artisans, and officials. It is always the addresser who has sealed the tablet."[53]

---

[46] Peragallo 1938:24-27

[47] For a recent example of the transcription of a massive cuneiform account from its linear format to a two-dimensional format, see Hallo *apud* Sigrist 1999:148.

[48] Hallo 1958:98.

[49] Hallo 1969:172. For the latest survey of the genre see Lafont 1990.

[50] CAD I/J (1960):245c referring to YOS 5:164, followed by Stol BSA 5 (1990):198 n. 2; Greengus 1986:63 referring to Greengus 1979 No. 24.

[51] McEwan 1981:131; 1982:59-63 (no. 47-51); Beaulieu 1989:7-11; MacGinnis 1995.

[52] Vallat 1994:264-71.

[53] Zettler 1979:263, n. 12.

In spite of all this unanimity on the part of Assyriologists regarding the concept and modern designation of the letter-order, the notion of its functional equivalence to a modern bank check or draft has found little favor with the historians of banking, notably Raymond Bogaert. He "questioned the notion that Drehem (and other entrepôts) served as a bank, preferring to regard it as a 'caisse de l'État'. Perhaps (as I said in 1969) this is a matter of definition, *i.e.*, is banking a question of technique or of the private vs. the public sector of the economy?"[54] It is in fact a question, if the classical (Greek) model is followed, of interest charged on the debits and credits. Without such interest, one can more properly speak of a simple warehousing function for deposits and withdrawals.

Fortunately the debate can move marginally closer to resolution with the help of new evidence. In 1972, David Owen published "a unique Ur III letter-order" in which the letter-order is enclosed in an envelope inscribed with the corresponding šu-ba-ti receipt. According to Owen, this envelope must have replaced the original envelope after the order had been filled.[55] If he is right, one should expect to find other examples of letter-orders and their corresponding receipts whether in the form of envelopes or of simple tablets.[56] Given the fact that, in the present case at least, neither is dated, such a search would need to rely on other criteria. In effect, we see that in the present case, the two texts coincide precisely in respect to the payee and the amount to be paid; in respect to the "bank," the letter-order simply names the temple of Shara (in Umma) while the receipt specifies Ilum-bani, the temple-administrator (šabra) of the temple of Shara.

Letter-orders thus represent the ancient equivalent of modern letters of credit or bills of exchange. They satisfy one of the criteria of a banking operation, though not as yet the other, that of imposing or granting interest. They also provide a further example of double-entry bookkeeping, since the letter-order represents a credit and the receipt a debit in the identical amount. I rest my case.[57]

---

[54] Bogaert 1966:67, n. 142, cited by Hallo 1969:172, n. 3.

[55] Owen 1971-72; cf. now COS 3 (2002) 296:3.132.

[56] Christopher Walker informs me that the British Museum has "hundreds" of unopened Ur III letter-orders.

[57] My thanks to Stanley Dalnekoff (New Haven) for helpful comments on this paper.

BIBLIOGRAPHY

Beaulieu, Paul-Alain (1989), *The Reign of Nabonidus King of Babylon 556-539 B.C.* (YNER 10).

Bogaert, Raymond (1966), *Les origines antiques de la banque de dépôt* (Leiden: Sijthoff).

Englund, Robert K. (1991), "Hard Work—Where Will It Get You? Labor Management in Ur III Mesopotamia," *JNES* 50: 255-80.

Friberg, Joran (2000), "Mathematics at Ur in the Old Babylonian Period," *RA* 94: 97-188.

Greengus, Samuel (1979), *Old Babylonian Tablets from Ishchali and Vicinity* (PIHANS 44).

— (1986) *Studies in Ishchali Documents* (BiMes 19).

Grégoire, Jean-Pierre (1970), *Archives Administratives Sumériennes* (Paris: Geuthner).

Gurney, Oliver R. (1983), *Middle Babylonian Legal and Economic Texts from Ur* (London: British School of Archaeology in Iraq).

Hallo, William W. (1953), *The Ensi's of the Ur III Dynasty* (M.A. Thesis: University of Chicago).

— (1958), "Contributions to Neo-Sumerian," *HUCA* 29: 69-107 + xxvii plates.

— (1960), "A Sumerian Amphictyony," *JCS* 14: 88-114.

— (1964), "The Road to Emar," *JCS* 18: 57-88.

— (1969), "The Neo-Sumerian Letter-Orders," *BiOr* 26: 171-75.

— (1979), "*Obiter Dicta ad SET*," in *Studies Jones* 1-14.

— (1992), "A Guided Tour through Babylonian History: Cuneiform Inscriptions in the Cincinnati Art Museum" (with David B. Weisberg), *JANES* 21: 49-90.

— (1996), *Origins: The Ancient Near Eastern Background of Some Modern Western Institutions.* (Studies in the History and Culture of the Ancient Near East 6; Leiden: Brill).

— (1999), "A Ugaritic Cognate for Akkadian *ḫitpu*?," in *Studies Levine* 43-50.

— (2001), "Seals and Seal Impressions," in RAI 45/2: 239-54.

— (2002), "A Model Court Case Concerning Inheritance," *Studies Jacobsen* 141-54.

Hilgert, Markus (1998), *Drehem Administrative Documents from the Reign of Šulgi* (OIP 115).

— (2003), *Drehem Administrative Documents from the Reign of Amar-Suena* (OIP 121).

Hymes, Dell, ed. (1974), *Studies in the History of Linguistics: Traditions and Paradigms* (Indiana Studies in the History and Theory of Linguistics; Bloomington: Indiana University Press).

Ijiri, Yuri (1993), "The Beauty of Double-Entry Bookkeeping," *Economic Notes* 2:265-85.

Jacobsen, Thorkild (1974), "Very Ancient Linguistics," in Hymes 1974:41-62.

Johnson, Arnold W. (1962), "Bookkeeping," in *The Encyclopedia Americana* 4:238-44.

Jones, Tom B. and John W. Snyder (1961), *Sumerian Economic Texts from the Third Ur Dynasty* (Minneapolis: University of Minnesota Press).

Kagan, Donald (1982), "The Date of the Earliest Coins," *AJA* 86:342-60.

Lafont, Bertrand (1990), "Nouvelles lettres du temps des rois d'Ur," *RA* 84:165-69.

— (1992), "Quelques nouvelles tablettes dans les collections américaines," *RA* 86:97-111.

Lambert, W.G. (1985), "The History of the *muš-huš* in Ancient Mesopotamia," in *Les Cahiers du Centre d'Étude du Proche-Orient Ancien, Université de Genève* 2:87-94.

Levine, Baruch A. and William W. Hallo (1967), "Offerings to the Temple Gates at Ur," *HUCA* 38:17-58 and figs. 1-4.

MacGinnis, John (1995), *Letter Orders from Sippar* (Poznań: Bonami).

McEwan, G.J.P. (1981), "Arsacid Temple Records," *Iraq* 43:131-43.

— (1982), *Late Babylonian Tablets in the Royal Ontario Museum* (Royal Ontario Museum Cuneiform Texts 2).

Michalowski, Peter (1975), "The Bride of Simanum," *JAOS* 95:716-19.

Muroi, Kazuo (1988), "Inheritance Problems of Babylonian Mathematics," *Historia Scientiarum* 34:11-19.

Nemet-Nejat, Karen Rhea (1993), *Cuneiform Mathematical Texts as a Reflection of Everyday Life in Mesopotamia* (AOS 75).

Owen, David I. (1971-72), "A Unique Ur III Letter-Order in the University of North Carolina," *JCS* 14:133f.

Peragallo, Edward (1938), *Origin and Evolution of Double Entry Bookkeeping* (New York: American Institute Publishing Co.).

Petschow, Herbert (1973), "Zur mittelbabylonischen ‚Buchhaltungstechnik' und zur Tempelwirtschaft der NIN.DINGIR-Priesterinnen," in *Studies Böhl* 299-307.

Picchioni, S.A. (1975), "Miscellanea Neo-Sumerica, II," *OrAn* 14:153-68.

Robbins, Ellen (1996), "Tabular Sacrifice Records and the Cultic Calendar of Neo-Babylonian Uruk," *JCS* 48:61-87.

Robson, Eleanor (2000), "The Uses of Mathematics in Ancient Iraq, 6000-600 BC" in H. Selin (ed.), *Mathematics Across Cultures: The History of Non-Western Mathematics* (Dordrecht: Kluwer).

Sack, Ronald H. (1979), "Notes on Bookkeeping in Eanna," in *Studies Jones* 111-18.

Sigrist, Marcel (1992), *Drehem* (Bethesda, Md.: CDL Press).

— (1999), "Livraisons et dépenses royales durant la Troisième Dynastie d'Ur," in *Studies Levine* 111-49 (Postscript by W.W. Hallo).

Snell, Daniel C. (1982), *Ledgers and Prices* (YNER 8).

Vallat, François (1994), "Deux tablettes élamites de l'Université de Fribourg," *JNES* 53:263-74.

Van De Mieroop, Marc (1999-2000), "An Accountant's Nightmare: The Drafting of a Year's Summary," *AfO* 46-47:111-29.

Van Driel, G., and K.R. Nemet-Nejat (1994), "Bookkeeping Practices for an Institutional Herd at Eanna," *JCS* 46:47-58.

Zettler, Richard L. (1979), "On the Chronological Range of Neo-Babylonian and Achaemenid Seals," *JNES* 38:257-70.

ABBREVIATIONS

COS 3 = William W. Hallo and K.L. Younger, Jr. (eds.), *The Context of Scripture. Vol. III: Archival Documents from the Biblical World* (Leiden etc.: Brill, 2002).

RAI 45/2 = W.W. Hallo and I.J. Winter (eds.), *Seals and Seal Impressions: Proceedings of the XLVe Rencontre Assyriologique Internationale. Part II: Yale University* (Bethesda, Md.: CDL Press, 2001).

Studies Böhl = M.A. Beek *et al.* (eds.), *Symbolae Biblicae et Mesopotamicae Francisco Mario Theodoro de Liagre Böhl Dedicatae* (Leiden: Brill).

Studies Jacobsen = T. Abusch (ed.), *Riches Hidden in Secret Places: Ancient Near Eastern Studies in Memory of Thorkild Jacobsen* (Winona Lake, Ind.: Eisenbrauns, 2002).

Studies Jones = M.A. Powell, Jr., and R.H. Sack (eds.), *Studies in Honor of Tom B. Jones* (AOAT 203, 1979).

Studies Levine = R.Chazan *et al.* (eds.), *Ki Baruch Hu: Ancient Near Eastern, Biblical, and Judaic Studies in Honor of Baruch A. Levine* (Winona Lake, Ind.: Eisenbrauns, 1999).

SET = Tom B. Jones and John W. Snyder, *Sumerian Economic Texts from the Third Ur Dynasty* (Minneapolis: University of Minnesota Press, 1961).

5.

Accounting for Change: The Development of Tabular Book-keeping in Early Mesopotamia*

Eleanor Robson

All Souls College, Oxford

Introduction

Tables are ubiquitous in the modern world: almost any dataset, it appears, is subject to tabulation, from huge and complex databases published for academic analysis to bus timetables on lampposts. We are so familiar with the idea of handling information in this way that we hardly notice or question the presence of tables in the ancient historical record: in concentrating on their content we miss their very table-ness. But this is not simply a blindspot within our own field: the history of table-making in general is only just beginning to attract attention from historians in other areas, perhaps because of its very cross-disciplinary nature. A recent collaborative work on the history of tables within mathematics and related disciplines puts it thus:

* Many kind colleagues aided my hunt for tabular accounts: Jo Renger, Piotr Steinkeller, Marc Van De Mieroop, and Niek Veldhuis (who pointed me to the Ur III example). Christopher Walker indefatigably tracked down relevant unpublished tablets in the British Museum for me, and Jane Siegel gave access to those in the Columbia Rare Book and Manuscript Library. Seth Richardson generously provided transliterations of over twenty late OB tabular accounts from his doctoral thesis. I thank all of them for their help (and blame none of them for the results). But I owe a particular debt of gratitude to two people: Stephanie Dalley, the driving force behind *OECT* 15, who has worked patiently with me on the Ashmolean tabular accounts for over a decade now; and the late and much-missed John Fauvel, who first gave me the idea that the topic was worth exploring.

> Their importance as a central component and generator of scientific advance ... can be underestimated by sheer familiarity. Like other apparently simple technological or conceptual advances (such as writing, numerals, or money) their influence on history is very deep. The history of tables now deserves, and is ready, to be brought forward from the narrow floodlights of particular special studies into the open sunlight.
>
> The issues turn out to be very interesting. From the earliest times there has been a range of different kinds of table, from the representation of mathematical functions to documents summarizing empirical values. What they have in common is an expression of complex information in a two-dimensional form. From the start, issues of design and legibility jostle with issues of abstract information processing. The structure of tables, the transition from one-dimensional to two-dimensional layout in the location of information, has a far greater significance than might naively be expected. (Fauvel in Campbell-Kelly *et al.* 2003: 1-2)

Given the great strides made in studying the history of ancient Near Eastern data storage, from preliterate accounting tokens to the document formatting reforms of the Ur III period, the rise of the table deserves to be discussed and problematised too. I have attempted a general survey of tables within Mesopotamian culture in the volume just cited (Robson 2003); here I explore in more depth the development and spread of tabular formatting within accounting practices of the Old Babylonian period.[1]

The matter has been on my mind for some years now. In the early 1990s, as part of my doctoral work, I was trying to track down the origins of the labouring constants that appear frequently in Old Babylonian school mathematics. This involved delving into a lot of Ur III agricultural accounts (though my search was by no means exhaustive). At the same time I was working with Stephanie Dalley on copying Old Babylonian tablets, mostly from Larsa, in the Ashmolean Museum for *OECT* 15. I noticed, as has everybody before me, that the Ur III documents were all formatted as rather cumbersome lists.

---

[1] The only explicit reference I can find in the specialist literature to the origins of tabularisation is Hallo's observation that "In accounts and other ledger-like texts, the transition from one-dimensional lists to two-dimensional graphs [*i.e.*, tables] began in the Old Babylonian period" (Hallo 1964: 61, n. 29).

For instance, CBS 8162 (Example 1 on p. 110f.; *NATN* 61; Robson 1999:158-59), found at Nippur, is concerned with the work, labour and wages for repairs to walls and ditches in an orchard. Each linear entry gives the lengths, widths, and heights of one section of wall, and where this information is too long to fit the column width the next line is indented. Entries are separated by horizontal lines. Total volumes are given immediately below each group of entries, followed by wage calculations and the name of the workman responsible. Totals of wages in grain and in wool end the account, and there is a summary of its purpose on the left edge of the tablet. The tablet is not dated, but can be assigned to early Ur III Lagash through its association to the well-known figure of Ur-meme (Hallo 1972; Zettler 1984).

On the other hand, many of the Old Babylonian tablets I was copying were clearly tabular, with quantitative and qualitative information organised and stored separately and categorised into columns as well as rows. Like CBS 8162, Ashmolean 1922.290 (Example 2 on p. 112-15; *OECT* 15 18) also records the lengths, widths, and depths of earth works. The volumes of canals dug and not yet dug are calculated and assigned to named workmen or overseers, with subtotals and totals of lengths and volumes given at various points in the document. But unlike CBS 8162, Ash 1922.290 groups each category of information into headed columns, only breaking out of columnar format to give linear descriptive comments to totals and subtotals. The tablet is not dated, but the palaeography and prosopography lead to a likely attribution to the Larsa area around the time of Hammurabi or Samsu-iluna.

Example 1: CBS 8162

obv. I 1½ ninda 5 kùš gíd ½ kùš dag̃al 3 kùš sukud
1½ ninda 3 kùš gíd ½ kùš dag̃al 2 kùš sukud
5 ninda gíd ½ kùš dag̃al 3 kùš sukud
21 ninda 3 kùš gíd ⅔ kùš dag̃al 3 <kùš> sukud
im-du$_8$-a-bi 4⅔ sar ½ gín 22½ še
guruš-bi 1 14⅚ ud-1-šè
še-bi 1 gur 4 barig 5 bán 8⅔ silà gur
á šà-gal 8 [sìla]
lugal-ì-⌜sa$_6$⌝ [um-mi-a]
[……]

obv. II 11½ ninda 1 kùš [gíd……] 3 [……]
im-du$_8$-a-bi […… sar] igi-4-g̃ál 7 [še]
guruš-bi 2 08 ud-[1-šè]
še-bi 3 gur 2 barig 4 silà gur
ur-^{d}⌜bil$_4$-ga⌝-mes um-mi-a
g̃iš-kiri$_6$ gu-la
14 ninda 4 kuš gíd ⅔ kuš [dag̃al] 3 kùš sukud
⌜34 ninda⌝ [……]
[……]

rev. III Missing
rev. IV [……]
im-⌜du$_8$⌝-[a-bi ……]
guruš-bi [……]
še-bi 1 barig 2 bán [……]
6 nindan gíd 1 [kùš dag̃al 3 kùš sukud]
saḫar-bi 1½ sar
guruš-1-e 6 gín-ta
guruš-bi 15 ud-1-šè
síg-bi 4 ma-na
g̃iš-kiri$_6$ bàd še-ga
dug$_4$-ga um-mi-a
šu-nig̃ín á 8 41 guruš ud-1-šè
še-bi 13 gur 4 barig 2 bán ⌜8⌝⅓ silà
šu-nig̃ín 15 guruš ud-[1-šè]
síg-bi 4 ma-na

l.e. im-du-a ak ù pa$_5$ ba-al-la
g̃iš-kiri$_6$ lugal-kù-zu
g̃ìr ur-^{d}iškur
ur-me-me ugula

Translation

obv. I $1\frac{1}{2}$ rods 5 cubits length, $\frac{1}{2}$ cubit width, 3 cubits height
$1\frac{1}{2}$ rods 3 cubits length, $\frac{1}{2}$ cubit width, 2 cubits height
5 rods length, $\frac{1}{2}$ cubit width, 3 cubits height
21 rods 3 cubits length, $\frac{2}{3}$ cubit width, 3 <cubits> height
Its mud wall: $4\frac{2}{3}$ sar $\frac{1}{2}$ shekel $22\frac{1}{2}$ grains
Its workers: $74\frac{5}{6}$ for 1 day
Its grain: $598\frac{2}{3}$ litres
Food wages: 8 [litres]

Lugal-isa [the craftsman]
Rest of column missing

obv. II $11\frac{1}{2}$ rods 1 cubit [length ……]
Its mud wall: [……] a quarter, 7 grains
Its workers: 128 [for 1] day
Its grain: 1024 litres
Ur-Bilgames the craftsman
The large orchard
14 rods 4 cubits length, $\frac{2}{3}$ cubits [width], 3 cubits height
34 rods [……]
[……] *Rest of column missing*

rev. III *Missing*
rev. IV *Top of column missing*
[Its] mud wall: [……]
Its workers: [……]
Its grain: 80(+) litres
6 rods length, 1 [cubit width, 3 cubits height]
Its volume: $1\frac{1}{2}$ sar
Each worker at 6 shekels (volume daily rate)
Its workers: 15 for 1 day
Its wool: 4 minas
Repairing the orchard wall
Duga the craftsman

Total: wages for 521 workers for 1 day
Its grain: $4168\frac{1}{3}$ litres
Total: 15 workers [for 1] day
Its wool: 4 minas

l.e. Making a mud wall and digging a ditch
Lugal-kuzu's orchard
Under the authority of Ur-Iškur
Ur-meme, overseer

Example 2: *Ashmolean 1922.290*

Obverse

⸢UŠ⸣	SAG	GAM
4½ NINDA	1 NINDA	5 KÙŠ
13 NINDA	½ NINDA 5½ KÙŠ	4 KÙŠ
47 NINDA		3½ <KÙŠ>
27½ NINDA 4 KÙŠ		3 KÙŠ
1 UŠ 27½ NINDA 4 KÙŠ		
25 NINDA	½ NINDA 5½ KÙŠ	4 KÙŠ
10 NINDA		3½ KÙŠ
1 UŠ 39 NINDA		3 KÙŠ
2 UŠ 14 NINDA		
9 UŠ 59½ <NINDA> 2 KÙŠ	½ NINDA 5⸢½⸣ <KÙŠ>	3 KÙŠ
3 UŠ 33½ <NINDA>		2½ KÙŠ
13 UŠ 33 NINDA 2 KÙŠ		
½ DANA 2 UŠ 15 <NINDA>		
ša AD.DA-^{d}MAR.TU.MEŠ		
7 UŠ 20 NINDA	½ NINDA 5½ KÙŠ	3 KÙŠ
[40] ⸢NINDA⸣		2½ KÙŠ
[......]		2½ KÙŠ
[......]		

Rest of obverse missing

Translation

Obverse

Length (rods)	Width (rods)	Depth (cubits)
4;30	1	5
12	0;57 30	4
47	<ditto>	3;30
27;50	<ditto>	3
1 27;50		
25	0;57 30	4
10	<ditto>	3;30
1 39	<ditto>	3
2 14		
9 59;40	0;57 30	3
3 33;30	<ditto>	2;30
13 33;10		
17 15		
That the Amorites		
7 20	0;57 30	3
[40]	<ditto>	2;30
[...]		2;30
[...]	[...]	[...]

Rest of obverse missing

SAḪAR *na-as-ḫu*	SAḪAR *la na-as-ḫu-⌜ú⌝*	ŠU.NIGÍN SAḪAR	[.]	[MU.BI.IM]
	22½ SAR	22½ SAR		KA.ÍD.DA
49⅚ SAR		49⅚ SAR		KI.1
0.0.1½^{gána} 7⅔ SAR		0.0.1½^{gána} 7⅔ SAR		KI.2
0.0.½^{gána} 30 SAR		0.0.½^{gána} 30 SAR		KI.3
0.0.2½^{gána} 37½ <SAR>		0.0.2½^{gána} 37½ <SAR>	*ša*	*e-ri-ib-*^{d}SUEN *i-pu-šu*
	0.0.½^{gána} 45⅚ <SAR>	0.0.½^{gána} 45⅚ <SAR>		KI.1
	33½ <SAR>	33½ <SAR>		KI.2
0.0.2½^{gána} 34⅔ <SAR>		0.0.2½^{gána} 34⅔ <SAR>		KI.3
0.0.2½^{gána} 34⅔ <SAR>	0.0.1^{gána} 29⅓ <SAR>	0.0.4^{gána} 14 SAR	*ša*	*i-din-*^{d}*en.líl*^{lí} *i-pu-šu*
0.2.5^{gána} 23½ <SAR>		0.2.5^{gána} 23½ <SAR>	24	KI.1
0.0.4½^{gána} 42⅓ <SAR>		0.0.4½^{gána} 42⅓ <SAR>	2	KI.2
1.0.4^{gána} 15<⅔> SAR		1.0.4^{gána} 15<⅔> SAR	26	*ša ì-lí-i-din-nam i-pu-šu*
1.1.3½^{gána} 37<SAR> 10 GÍN	1^{gána} 29⅓ SAR	1.1.5^{gána} 16½ <SAR>	26	*i-pu-šu*
0.1.4^{gána} 35	0.0.2^{gána} [30] SAR	0.2.0 ½^{gána} 15 SAR		KI.1
0.0.½^{gána} 45⅚ [<SAR>]	[(…)]	0.0.½^{gána} 45⅚ <SAR>		KI.2
[……]	[(…)]	[…]^{gána} 37		KI.3
[……]	[0.0.2^{gána} 30 SAR]	[……]	*ša*	*gi-*X X [*i-pu-šu*]

Volume excavated (sar)	Volume not excavated (sar)	Total volume (sar)	[…]	[Its name]
	22;30	22;30		River mouth
49;50		49;50		First one
2 37;40		2 37;40		Second one
1 20		1 20		Third one
4 47;30		4 47;30	that	Erib-Sîn did
	1 35;50	1 35;50		First one
	33;30	33;30		Second one
4 44;40		4 44;40		Third one
4 44;40	2 09;20	6 54	that	Iddin-Enlil did
28 43;20		28 43;20	24	First one
8 12;20		8 12;20	2	Second one
36 55;40		36 55;40	26	that Ili-iddinam did
46 27;10	2 09;20	48 36;30	26	did
17 15	3 50	21 05		First one
1 35;50		1 35;50		Second one
[…]	[…]	[.] 37		Third one
[…]	[…]	[…]	that	Gi-…… [did]

Beginning of reverse missing

Reverse

[......]	[......]	[......]
[......]	[......]	[......]
[......]	[......]	[......]
[2 07? NINDA]	[4?] KÙŠ	3 KÙŠ
[4 UŠ]	4 KÙŠ	3 KÙŠ
5 38 <NINDA>	4 KÙŠ	3 KÙŠ
8 20 <NINDA>	½ <NINDA> 2 KÙŠ	3 KÙŠ
5 52½ <NINDA>	1 NINDA	2 KÙŠ
1 DANA 2 UŠ 5½ NINDA		
2 DANA 9 UŠ 5½ NINDA		
[*ša*]	*pi-il-kum na-du-ú-ma*	
⸢5 40⸣ <NINDA>	1 NINDA	1½ KÙŠ
⸢*ša*⸣		
9 40	ZAG PA$_5$ *a-bi-i-li-i* EN.NA ^{íd}*ú-ma-nu-ur*	
13 15	ZAG ÍD *ú-ma-nu-ur ša* É.UD.NAGA	
⅓ DANA 2 55 NINDA		
ša	*ik-ka-as-sà-mu-ú-ma*	
3 DANA 2 UŠ ½ NINDA		
ÍD?		

Beginning of reverse missing

Reverse

[......]	[......]	[...]
[......]	[......]	[...]
[......]	[......]	[...]
[2 07?]	[0;20?]	3
4 00	0;20	3
5 38	0;20	3
8 20	0;40	3
5 52;30	1	2
32 05;30		
1 09 05;30		
[of]	the work zone that was abandoned	
5 40	1	1;30
That was dug		
9 40 <rods>		
13 15 <rods>		
22 55 rods		
whose (trees)	were cut down but	
1 32 00;30 rods		
Ka-...... canal		

[……]	[……]	[……] 22 SAR	ZAG […] EN.[NA …]
[0.0.1^{gána}] 28 SAR		0.0.1^{gána} 28 SAR	ZAG […] EN.NA […]
[22] SAR		22 SAR	ZAG *ti*-[…] EN.NA […]
[0.0.1]^{gána} 27 SAR		0.0.1^{gána} 27 SAR	ZAG PA$_5$ […] EN.NA […] ^{giš}KIRI$_6$ ^{d}SUEN-*ú-sé-li*
	0.0.2^{gána} 40 SAR	0.0.2^{gána} 40 SAR	ZAG ^{giš}KIRI$_6$ ^{d}SUEN-*ú-sé-li* EN.NA *mi-iḫ-ṣi-im*
	0.0.3^{gána} 38 <SAR>	0.0.3^{gána} 38 <SAR>	ZAG *mi-iḫ-ṣú-um* EN.NA GÚ *ḫa-šu-úr*^{ki}
0.1.5^{gána} 45 SAR		0.1.5^{gána} 45 SAR	ZAG GÚ *ḫa-šu-úr*^{ki} EN.NA KASKAL LARSA^{ki}
ša i-na up-pu-ši-im SAḪAR ŠÀ ÍD.DA *wa-aṣ-bu*			
0.0.½^{gána}	0.1.0 ½^{gána} 5 SAR	0.1.1^{gána} 5 SAR	ZAG KASKAL LARSA^{ki} EN.NA ^{id}*ú-ma-nu-ur ù* [..]
0.2.5^{gána} 22 SAR	0.2.1^{gána} 5 SAR	1.2.0^{gána} 27 SAR	KI.2 *ša e-tel*-KA-^{d}AMAR.UTU *i-pu-šu*
3.2.5^{gána} 1 SAR 5 GÍN	1.0.3½^{gána} 28½ <SAR>	5.0.2½^{gána} 29 SAR *i-iḫ-ḫi-ru-ú*	
iḫ-ḫi-ru-ú	0.1.0^{gána} 15 SAR	0.1.0^{gána} 15 SAR	ZAG ^{íd}*ú-ma-nu-ur ù* […] EN.NA PA$_5$ *a-bi-i-li-i*
ša É.UD.NAGA ^{d}NIN.GIŠ.ZI.DA ^{d}NIN.GIŠ.ZI.DA EN.NA URU^{ki} *za-wa-ar*			
		la iḫ-ḫi-ir-ru-ú	
		KA	[………]

[……]	[…]	[…] 22	Right: […] Left: […]
[2] 08		2 08	Right: […] Left: […]
[22]		22	Right: […] Left: […]
[2] 07		2 07	Right: […]. Left: [(..)] Sîn-uselli's orchard
	4 00	4 00	Right: Sîn-uselli's orchard. Left: swamp??
	5 38	5 38	Right: swamp.?? Left: the edge of Ḫašur town
15 45		15 45	Right: the edge of Ḫašur town. Left: the Larsa road
to which the volume of the river has been added in the calculated amount?			
50	10 55	11 45	Right: the Larsa road. Left: Umanur river and …
28 42	21 45	50 27	Second one that Etel-pî-Marduk did
1 58 21;05	36 18;30 but	2 34 49 dug	
	10 15	10 15	Right: Umanur river and … Left: the Abi-ili canal
Right: the Abi-ili canal; Left: the Umanur river of Ningišzida's …… temple Right: the Umanur river of Ningišzida's …… temple; Left: Zawar town			
	that was	not dug	
1 32 00;30 rods Ka-…… canal			

To talk about tables clearly and effectively we need a consistent terminology to describe them. I shall define a *formal* table as having both vertical and horizontal rulings to separate categories of information; *informal* tables, on the other hand, separate quantitative and qualitative data by spatial arrangement only, without explicit delimiters. All the tables discussed here are formal; informal tables are found, for instance, in Old Babylonian mathematics (Robson 2003). *Headed* tables have columnar headings, while *unheaded* tables do not. Some tables are preceded by *titles* or introductory *preambles*; others are followed by *summaries* and/or *colophons*. In Old Babylonian tables, any other qualitative or descriptive information is almost invariably contained in the final right-hand column, or interrupts the table as an *explanatory interpolation*, as in Ash 1922.290. Documents like CBS 8162 with no tabular formatting at all we might call *prose-like* or *prosaic*.

Ash 1922.290, both formal and headed, is at the upper limits of Old Babylonian tabular complexity. We could describe it as having two *axes of organisation*: the horizontal axis, along which different types of numerical information are categorised, and the vertical axis, down which the data is attributed to different individuals or areas. All tables are organised along two axes. Calculations, however, are a different matter. Some tables exhibit just one, usually vertical, axis of calculation, or none at all—in which case I refer to them as *tabular lists*. Ash 1922.290, though, has two *axes of calculation* too: horizontally, the volumes dug and not yet dug are totalled, while vertically the lengths of canal and the three categories of volume (dug, not dug, total) are subtotalled and totalled. The logic of tabular calculations always moves from left to right, from top to bottom (Robson 2001). Ash 1922.290 has three *levels of calculation*, shown here with degrees of shading. The first level subtotals are marked with the phrase 'that PN did' in the final column; the second by a descriptive phrase running the whole width of the tablet; the third is the grand total at the end (which does not include the final second-level total of length of canal not yet dug).[2]

[2] For the purposes of this paper my definition of (cuneiform) tables is restricted to those which contain *more than one* column of quantitative information. Documents with one column of numbers and one of description could be considered simply as formal numerical lists, or as rather trivial and uninteresting tables. They very rarely have headings, and by their very structure can have at most one axis of calculation.

When, how, and to what extent did tabular document formatting develop? Why did it happen and what were its effects? These are the questions that I shall deal with here.

The third millennium

The earliest table in the cuneiform record appears fully fledged in the Early Dynastic period, with headings and a horizontal axis of calculation: the well-known table of square areas from Shuruppag (*SF* 82; Nissen *et al.* 1993: fig. 119), in which the first two columns each contain lengths from 9 (UŠ) down to perhaps 1 (ninda) and the third their products in area measure. A roughly contemporary tablet from Adab (*IA*: 70) contains similar data, in prosaic layout, showing that tabulation was not the only choice scribes made in formatting metrological conversions. The Shuruppag table is all the more remarkable, not only for pre-dating any other cuneiform table by some five centuries, but for being the first of just two truly tabular documents in the whole of the cuneiform mathematical tradition—the other being the famous table Plimpton 322, also headed and with a horizontal axis of calculation (Robson 2001; 2003: 29-35).

There is, to my knowledge, just one published tabular account securely datable to the Ur III period. AUAM 73.0400, probably from Puzrish-Dagan (Example 3, *AUCT* 1 56, Robson 2003: 23-24), is an account of sheep and goats. It is dated to Ibbi-Suen year 1 (2028 BC by the Middle Chronology), the penultimate year of known operations at Puzrish-Dagan.

Example 3: AUAM 73.0400

obv. 1	3	3	⌜3⌝	⌜2⌝	1	udu-sila$_4$
	1 33	1 33	1 33	1 [02]	31	udu-a-lum
	6	6	6	4	2	máš-gal
	1 42	1 42	1 42	1 08	[3]4	
5	puzur$_4$	^{d}šul	a-ba	si-⌜sá⌝	[...]	
			(*traces*)	(*traces*)	[...	...]
	ki ⌜sipa⌝-[......]					
rev. 1	iti [......]					
	mu ^{d}⌜i-bí-^{d}suen lugal⌝					

Like later administrative tables, the row labels (types of ovids) are at the end of each row, but the column 'headings' are at the bottom of the obverse below each column total. They appear to be abbreviations, perhaps for personal names. Strikingly, the entries are always in the same proportions 1 lamb : 31 sheep : 3 goats down the rows and 3 : 3 : 3 : 2 : 1 across the columns. On the damaged edge and reverse the column formatting seems to be abandoned in order to give the usual sort of summary information: the names of the official(s) responsible for the record and the date on which it was drawn up.

Ashmolean 1910.759 (Example 4; *TAD* 42; *MKT* 1:82; *AAICAB* 1: pl. 17) is less securely attributable to the Ur III period, but it shares many of the same features.

Example 4: Ashmolean 1910.759

obv.	8	4	sig$_5$
	12	6	uš
	20	10	eš
	20	10	za
	1 00	30	še
	2 00	1 00	
	ša	an	

rev. *blank*

Once again, the row labels are on the right, the column labels at the bottom. Both sets of labels appear to be single-sign abbreviations. The entries are in proportion 2 : 1 across the columns and 2 : 3 : 5 : 5 : 15 down the rows. All are conspicuously round and regular, especially the columnar totals. The numeral 3, written on the left edge, may be the grand total, as Neugebauer (*MKT* 1:82) suggests.

Why such a tiny number of tabular documents in a published corpus not far short of 50 000?[3] The conspicuous roundness of the entries in the tables hints at school exercises (*MKT* 1:82), but the date on AUAM 73.0400 suggests otherwise. The use of abbreviations implies

[3] The CDLI database <http://cdli.ucla.edu> contained some 46 600 Ur III administrative documents as of July 2003.

that this was a tablet format designed for rough jottings, estimates, and calculations, which was not intended to be viewed by superiors or archived for posterity—just as Powell (1976) suggested many years ago for Ur III sexagesimal calculations. This raises the interesting (but untested) possibility that the 'accountant's nightmare' of drawing up annual accounts from daily records (Van De Mieroop 1999-2000) might not have been as labour-intensive as it appears if the scribes were able to collect, summarise, and calculate the quantitative data involved in tabular format before transferring it to the final, non-tabular version.

Old Babylonian tabular accounting

Over the course of the nineteenth century BC, tables gradually became established as an acceptable format for presenting accounts but it was never a popular presentation method in the Old Babylonian period. In all, I have found over 320 examples (Table 1), the earliest and most abundantly attested of which belonged to a single archive from Nippur, c. 1850-36 (Table 2). They are attested elsewhere—or at least published—in increasing numbers for about half a century, until the middle of Rim-Sin's reign, 1837-1784 (Tables 3-5) and then reappear thirty years later in the last years of Hammurabi and the first decade of his successor Samsu-iluna, 1758-25 (Table 6). I have found no tables from the later years of Samsu-iluna or his successors for half a century. The final group dates to the reigns of Ammi-ditana and Ammi-ṣaduqa, 1679-26 (Table 7). The undatable tablets are listed in an Appendix (Table 8).

Is this a true reflection of the waxing and waning of tables in administrative fashion, or an outcome of larger patterns of preservation, with bureaucratic finds clustering towards the ends of regimes (Civil 1992: 38-39)? More modern factors are at work too. I have used a very simple, even simplistic, evidential methodology, seeking examples of tables in the major publications of Old Babylonian cuneiform copies from southern Babylonia. What I have found is limited by what earlier scholars have chosen to copy: recalling Bob Englund's recent observation that 'few Assyriologists like numbers' (Englund 1998: 111), there is a strong likelihood that tabular accounts are underrepresented in publications. Of the 122 OB tabular accounts outside the Nippur archive fully half of them were not in the public domain when I began this study in late 2000 (*OECT* 15; Richardson 2002; Robson forthcoming).

Many of those new tablets fill large gaps in the pattern of attestation (1790s, 1670-20s). That said, I doubt I have collected all published examples. A further weakness in my method is that not every copyist clearly marks vertical rulings; on the reverse of VAT 7874 (*VAS* 18 83), for instance, they gradually disappear under the script. If no vertical rulings show at all on copies of tables, then I have not been able to detect them. This can be no more than a provisional study then, and I look forward to the developmental scheme presented here, which is necessarily an *argumentum ex silentio*, being revised or abandoned as new material comes to light.

Table 1: Tabular accounts from the Old Babylonian period

Publication	Tabular acc.	Dated	Undatable	Provenance	Dates
BBVO 1	2	1	1	Larsa	1637
BiMes 7	1	–	1	Kish	–
BiMes 11	201	201	–	Nippur	1850?-36
CT 45	10	3	7	Sippar	1748-1626
OECT 13	4	1	3	Kish	1796
OECT 15	19	4	15	Larsa	1822, 1758
PBS 8	8	7	1	Nippur	1837-1797, 1752
Richardson 2002	21	16	5	Sippar	1679-30
Robson forthcoming	21	20	1	Larsa area	1792-91, 1758-25
Sanati-Müller 1991-93	4	3	1	Uruk	1821-10
Scheil 1918	1	1	–	Larsa	1744
Sigrist 1985	1	1	–	Larsa area	1837
TCL 10-11	8	4	4	Larsa	1758-53
TLB 1	4	1	3	Larsa area	1784
UET 5	8	3	5	Ur	1837-00
VAS 18	3	1	2	–	1748
YOS 5	3	2	1	Ur or Larsa	1822-13
YOS 12	2	2	–	–	1748-47
YOS 13	1	1	–	–	1629
Total number of tables	322	272	50		

The Nippur sattukkum *tablets*

Some two hundred tabular accounts from Nippur record regular *sattukkum*-offerings of bread, flour, and beer made in Ninurta's temple E-šumeša, over about eighty years of the nineteenth century BC. The whole archive, as recovered, comprises around 420 tablets, excavated in the fifth season of post-War excavations at Nippur and published by Marcel Sigrist (Sigrist 1984 = *BiMes* 11). The tablets were all found in the Parthian period fill near the Inana Temple, but it is unclear whether they had been transported there directly from their original site of use and storage, or from some secondary locus such as a rubbish tip. Most are in very bad condition.

Sigrist classified the tablets in the archive according to the number of columns they contain (Sigrist 1984: 17-33); the two- and six-column tablets, along with most of the smaller categories and the unclassifiable and fragmentary tablets, exhibit simple linear or list-like structures, with vertical rulings used only as column markings and not as classification separators. The 201 five-column tablets, however, are partially tabular.

The obverse sides of the five-column tablets, as exemplified by 5NT 95 (Example 5, p. 122f.; Sigrist 1984:73), list the offerings made to each of the divine statues and other cult objects in the E-šumeša. The first column is always divided into five narrow sub-columns to the left, listing quantities of bread (ninda), shortbread (ninda-ì), eša-flour, utú-flour, and beer (kaš) in that order. The wider sub-column to the right lists the objects of the offerings, always in the same order within a single administrative year. The second column is split vertically into three, with the first two narrow sub-columns holding quantities of unknown commodities (the headings, if there were any, do not survive), and the final column again naming the divine recipients. There is no sign of totalling at the bottom of the columns, as far as I can judge; we could thus describe these tables (partially) headed but with no axes of calculation. They are, in other words, tabular lists.

The reverse sides of the tablets, which record the redistribution of these offerings to human functionaries and dependents of the E-šumeša, are always in list format, with clear spatial separation of the numbers and the names. As on the obverses, the order of entries remains fixed throughout each administrative year. The best preserved is 5NT 90 (Example 6, p. 124f.; Sigrist 1984:84).

Example 5: 5NT 95

obv. I

⸢ninda⸣	ninda-ì	eša	utú	kaš	[...] kaš ^{giš}gu-za
[...]	[...]	2	31		^{d}nin-urta
			5		é-igi-šu-galam-ma
1(bán) 6	1(bán) 1		8		^{d}nuska
4	1(bán)				^{d}suen
⸢2(bán)⸣ 6	1(bán) 2		8		^{d}en-ki
[2(bán)] 6	1(bán) 4	1	4		^{d}innin
⸢2(bán)⸣ 4	1(bán) 2		4		^{d}iškur
⸢5⸣	1(bán)	1		2	^{d}utu
		1			^{d}⸢nin-gur-gi$_4$-lu^{ki}⸣
3	1(bán)	2	2		^{d}nè-irigal
3	1(bán)	1			^{d}nin-tin-ug$_5$-ga
					^{d}da-mu
					^{d}nin-šubur
[......]	[......]	1	3		^{d}ba-ú
[......]	[......]				^{d}nin-sumun
[......]	[......]		4		^{d}nin-in-si-na
[......]	[......]				^{d}nin-kir$_4$-maš-a
[......]	[......]				^{d}šul-pa-èd
[......]	[......]				^{d}šu-zi-an-na
[......]	[......]		4		^{d}nin-nibru^{ki}
[......]	[......]	[..]			^{urud}mi-tum
[......]	[......]	[..]			^{urud}alam-gu-la
[......]	[......]	[..]			^{urud}alam-3-a-bi

obv. II

[...]	[...]	[^{d}nin-ĝiš-zi-da]
1	3	[^{d}nin-si$_4$-an-na]
		^{d}[na-na-a]
		^{d}⸢kal⸣-[kal]
		^{d}mar-[tu]
		^{d}pa-bil-[saĝ]
		^{d}en-á-[nun]
5	1(bán)	ká-gal-[maḫ]
1(bán) 1	1(bán)	^{d}en-nu-[gi$_4$]
sá-		dug$_4$
1 (bán)		^{d}nuska
2	[...]	[*erasures*]
1		[*erasures*]
1		[*erasures*]
2		[*erasures*]

rev. I *missing*

rev. II *missing until:*

iti-še-kin-kud ⸢ud⸣-[4-kam]

mu-^{d}en-líl-[*ba-ni*] lugal é-me-zi-[da] é-ki-áĝ-ĝá-ni ^{d}en-ki-ra

mu-⸢na-an-dù⸣

Translation

obv. I

bread (in silà)	short-bread	*eša*-flour	*utu*-flour	beer	[…] beer for for the throne
[…]	[…]	2	31		Ninurta
			5		E-igi-šu-galama
16	11		8		Nuska
4	10				Suen
⌜26⌝	12		8		Enki
[2]6	14	1	4		Innin
[2]4	12		4		Iškur
⌜5⌝	10	1		2	Uru
		1			Nin-gur-gilu
3	10	2	2		Nergal
3	10	1			Nintinuga
					Damu
					Ninšubur
					Bau
[……]	[……]				Nin-sumun
[…]	[……]			4	Nininsina
[…]	[……]				Nin-kirmaša
[…]	[……]				Šul-pa-ed
[…]	[……]				Šuzi-ana
[…]	[……]			4	Nin-Nibru
[…]	[……]		[..]		*mitum*-weapon
[…]	[……]		[..]		big statue
[…]	[……]		[..]		third statue

obv. II

[…]	[…]	[Ninĝišzida]
1	3	[Ninsiana]
		[Nanaya]
		Kalkal
		Martu
		Pabilsaĝ
		En-anun
5	10	Great gate
11	10	Ennugi
sattukkum-offerings		
10		Nuska
2	[…]	[……]
1		[……]
1		[……]
2		[……]

rev. I *missing*

rev. II *missing until:*

Month xii, day 4.

The year that Enlil-bani the king built E-mezida, his beloved temple, for Enki. (Enlil-bani year i)

Example 6: 5NT 90

rev. I

šà-bi-ta	From it:
2(bán) 3 silà é-sikil	23 litres for the E-sikil
5 silà àr-àr šu-nu-nu	5 litres for the miller of Šununu
kaš-a-gub-ba	<nothing> for the beer attendant
18 silà ugula-é	18 litres for the temple overseer
àr-àr ^{d}nuska	<nothing> for the miller of Nuska
muš-laḫ$_4$	<nothing> for the snake-charmer
10 a-ù-a ^{d}nuska	10 for the ferryman of Nuska
5 silà ^{d}en-líl-za-me-en	5 litres for Enlil-zamen
4 kù-^{d}nanna	4 for Ku-Nanna
10 lú-^{d}nanna	10 for Lu-Nanna
2 silà kap-sar	2 litres for the stone-carver
1 silà ì-du$_8$ kisal-luḫ	1 litre for the door-keeper and courtyard sweeper
6 silà àr-àr ^{d}innin	6 litres for the miller of Inana
4 silà àr-àr ^{d}suen	4 litres for the miller of Sîn
àr-àr ^{d}en-ki	<nothing> for the miller of Enki
2 silà gìr-sì-ga	2 litres for the *gerseqqum*-official
8 silà nin-dingir ^{d}nin-urta	8 litres for the Nindingir-priestess of Ninurta
7 silà išib ^{d}nin-urta	7 litres for the *išippum*-priest of Ninurta
1(bán) nar-gal	10 litres for the chief singer

rev. IV

1(gur) 4(barig) [2 silà é-gal-tuš]	54[2 litres for the palace residentsu̯]
2 silà [a-bal]	2 litres [for the water-drawer]
2 silà sagi-lugal	2 litres for the royal butler
5 silà é-sikil ninda dirig	5 litres for the E-sikil: extra bread
7 silà *na-kam-tum* ka-^{d}innin	7 litres for the storehouse: Pî-Inana
10 zabar-dab ^{d}nin-urta	10 for the *zabardabbum*-official of Ninurta
30 *be-lí-i-di-ni* kisal-luḫ	30 for Beli-iddini the courtyard-sweeper

rev. V

še-ba-àm	Its grain is:
1 30 dumu-sag̃-^{d}nin-urta	1 30 for the heir of Ninurta
2(barig) 15 dumu ^{d}nanna-da-X	135 litres for the son of Nanna-da…
iti apin-a ud-1-kam	Month vii, day 1
mu ^{d}en-líl-*ba-ni* lugal g̃iš-gu-za bará kù-sig$_{17}$ ^{d}nanna-ra mu-na-dím	Enlil-bani year 1 ('The year that Enlil-bani the king had a throne and a golden dais built for Nanna')

Table 2: Chronological distribution of the E-šumeša sattukkum tablets

Dynasty	*Ruler*	*Year of reign*	*Date*	*2-col. (prosaic)*	*6-col. (prosaic)*	*5-col. (tabular)*	*Other & fragments*	*Total*
Larsa	Sumu-el	24	1871	27				27
Larsa	Sumu-el	25	1870	9				9
Isin	Lipit-Enlil	5	1869				1	1
Larsa	Sumu-el	27	1868				1	1
Larsa	Sumu-el	28	1867		1			1
Isin	Erra-imitti	da	1866-61		22			22
Isin	Enlil-bani	1	1860		1		1	2
Isin	Enlil-bani	h	1859-44				3	3
Isin	Enlil-bani	?	1859-44		5			5
Isin	Enlil-bani	?	1859-44		6			6
Isin	Enlil-bani	?	1859-44		2			2
Isin	Enlil-bani	i	1859-44			42		42
Isin	Enlil-bani[4]	d	1859-44			8	1	9
Isin	Enlil-bani	l	1859-44			40		40
Isin	Enlil-bani	c	1859-44			4		4
Isin	Enlil-bani	aa	1859-44			11		11
Isin	Enlil-bani	?	1859-44			5		5
Isin	Enlil-bani	?	1859-44			6		6
Larsa	Sin-iddinam	7	1843			4		4
Larsa	Sin-eribam	1	1842			3		3
Larsa	Sin-eribam	2	1841			2		2
Larsa	Sin-iqišam	1	1840			3		3
Larsa	Sin-iqišam	2	1839			6		6
Larsa	Sin-iqišam	3	1838			47	10	57
Larsa	Sin-iqišam	4	1837				1	1
Larsa	Sin-iqišam	5	1836			20		20
Larsa	Warad-Sin	1	1835				3	3
Larsa	Warad-Sin	4	1832				1	1
Isin	Damiq-ilišu	?			1			1
Isin	Damiq-ilišu	13	1804				1	1
Larsa	Rim-Sin	28	1795				7	7
Larsa	Rin-Sin	?					3	3
	Undated		–	15			87	102
	Total			51	38	201	120	420

[4] This group was dated to Lipit-Enlil 1 (1874) by Sigrist on the basis of the partially preserved year name ⌜x⌝ ᵈen-líl-lá on 5N-T 109 (Sigrist 1984:45). But in that case one would expect the last signs to be lugal-e not lá. A better fit for these remains would be [mu] ⌜lagar⌝ ᵈen-líl-lá <ba-ḫun> of Enlil-bani d.

Looking at the chronological distribution of the tablets across the archive, a clear pattern emerges (Table 2). The earliest datable records in the archive, dating from the 24th year of Sumu-el of Larsa (1871), are twenty-seven simple linear tablets, a style which seems to have been replaced in 1867, the last year of Sumu-el's reign, by an expanded, six-column version of this same format. The six-column tablet continued in use even after the re-conquest of Nippur by Isin under Erra-imitti the following year, but was replaced in favour of the five-column tabular structure at some point during the regime of his successor Enlil-bani.

Because the order of Enlil-bani's year names are not yet established, we cannot pin down the exact date of the change-over, but we can at least make an estimate. Eleven of the sixteen relevant regnal years 1859-44 are attested in the archive. If we assume that all the six-column and fragmentary tablets predate the tabular ones, then the change cannot have happened before 1855 or after 1850.

Nippur was retaken in 1843, Enlil-bani's seventeenth regnal year, by Sin-iddinam of Larsa, then in his seventh year of office. The use of the tabular account documents continued uninterrupted in the E-šumeša for a further six years until the accession of Warad-Sin in 1835. Thereafter a variety of tabular and non-tabular book-keeping methods were used, but the archive peters out with only a dozen or so documents attesting to the last forty years of its existence.

In short, the tabular records fall into a single phase of 15-20 years from 1855 or 1850 to 1838. Changes in political rule, either of individual kings or between the rival states of Isin and Larsa, seem to have had little or no effect on bureaucratic style. Rather, my feeling is that the chronological distribution of these tablets is more a function of the length of scribal careers: the six-column prosaic format and the five-column tabular list which succeeded it both have a life-span consonant with the working life of a senior administrator. Tables are so rare in the cuneiform record we should consider their adoption a matter of individual choice—even if those individuals are anonymous to us—rather than the outcome of large-scale, impersonal forces.

Outside the E-šumeša: Before Rim-Sin

It may simply be the accidents of discovery and publication that explain why just as the E-šumeša archive tails off, accounts in tabular format begin to appear elsewhere in cities under Larsa control (Table 3). All but one of the earliest tablets are unheaded and just one has one, vertical, axis of calculation. In other words, they are essentially tabular lists, just like the five-column accounts of the E-šumeša.

Table 3: Dated tabular accounts before the reign of Rim-Sin[5]

Publication	*Museum no.*	*Proven*	*Cols*	*Hdgs*	*Or*	*Axes*	*Notes*	*Year*	*Date*
PBS 8/1 24	CBS 15216	Nippur	3		P			Siq 4	1837
UET 5 806		Ur	3		P	V1		Siq 4	1837
Sigrist 1985	PSR	Ur	8+	O	–	–	–	Siq 4	1837
PBS 8/1 26	CBS 15169	Nippur	5		L			WS 11	1824

PBS 8/1: 24 ration account? Tabular format abandoned after a few lines; thereafter continues prosaically.

UET 5 806 account of cows and bulls, first column totalled after tabular formatting ends.

Sigrist 1985 summary of shepherd's annual accounts. Year names in all surviving columns; tablet too fragmentary to determine orientation; no entry entirely numerical as all qualified by lá-ì or dirig.

PBS 8/1 26 non-sexagesimal number notation in columns 1-3, column 4 grain measure. Many erasures (calcuations?) on reverse.

---

5 Tables 3-8 use the following abbreviations and conventions:
Columns: lists the number of tabular columns, including the final row label; '+' indicates that more columns may be missing. Occasionally abbreviated to 'Cols.'
Headings: I = introductory preamble; M = with final heading MU.BI.IM, O = with some other final heading; Y = yes, final heading missing or illegible; – = existence of headings undetermined. Occasionally abbreviated to 'Hdgs'.
Orientation: L = landscape, with width longer than height; P = portrait, with height longer than width; R = round; S = square; – = orientation undetermined. Occasionally abbreviated to 'Or'.
Axes (of calculation): V1 = vertical, 1 level; H2 = horizontal, 2 levels, etc.; – = undetermined.
Notes (explanatory interpolations within the body of the table): L = linear, breaking the tabulation; C = within a single cell of the table; – = undetermined.
Year: Siq = Sin-iqišam; WS = Warad-Sin; RS =Rim-Sin; Di = Damiq-ilišu; Ha = Hammurabi; Si = Samsu-iluna; Ad = Ammi-ditana; Aṣ = Ammi-ṣaduqa.
Date: according to the Middle Chronology; – = date undetermined
Comments on individual tablets follow each table.

The early years of Rim-Sin

Just two years after this cluster YBC 4721 (Example 5; *YOS* 5 103) already exhibits a much more sophisticated structure. First, the tablet is shaped to fit the data, so that it has a 'landscape' orientation with the width longer than the height, rather than the more usual 'portrait' format. Many of the tables in this group have the same orientation (as does *PBS* 8/1: 24, the last tablet in the very early group, Table 3, which predates YBC 4721 by just two years).

Second, column headings are used consistently for the first time. The final, qualitative column is labelled MU.BI.IM, literally 'its name'. This will remain the standard heading for the final column throughout the Old Babylonian period.[6] Headings are necessary because the horizontal axis of calculation comes into use: the final column of quantitative data is derived from preceding columns, and (in this case) is used to double-check the values in the first column. Vertical and horizontal additions can be totalled for double-checking for the first time.

Third, explanatory *interpolations* can note information outside the categories of the tabular columns. We could almost say that YBC 4721, dating to 1822 BC, is the world's earliest attested spreadsheet.

Example 7: YBC 4721

obv.

ŠE SAG.NÍG.GA	*a-na* URIM^{ki}	*a-na* X-[...^{ki}]	*a-na* ⌈LARSA$^{?}$⌉^{ki}-*ma*	ŠU.NIGÍN	MU.BI.IM
5 01.0.0	5 01.0.0			5 01.0.0	*li-pí-it*-^{d}SUEN
5 01.0.0		3 ⌈3⌉4.⌈3.4⌉, 5	1 26.1.1, ⌈5⌉	5 01.0.0	*nu-úr*-^{d}*da-gan*
4 56.2.0	3 00.0.0	[1 00.0.0]	56.2.0	4! ⌈56⌉.2.0	*ì-lí*-URU^{ki}
4 37.3.2		[ ]	4 37.3.2	4 37.⌈3.2⌉	^{d}UTU-*ki-ma*-⌈*ap*⌉-[*lu*]

iš-tu 2⌈3.1.4⌉ ERÉN ⌈^{d}UTU-*ki-ma-ap-lu*⌉

rev.

19 36.0.2	8 01.0.0	⌈4⌉ 34.3.4, 5	7 00.1.3, 5	19 36.0.2	

iš-tu ŠE.GUR LÚ.NE.X

ù 2⌈3.1.4 GUR⌉ ERÉN ^{d}UTU- ⌈*ki-ma-ap-lu*⌉

ITI BÁRA.ZAG.GAR UD.7.KAM

MU ^{d}*ri-im*-^{d}SUEN LUGAL

---

[6] MU.BI.IM is also the final column heading of the OB mathematical table Plimpton 322 (Robson 2001).

Translation

obv.

Grain available	For Ur	For …	For *Larsa*	Total	Its name
5 01	5 01			5 01	Lipit-Suen
5 01		3 34;45	1 26;15	5 01	Nur-Dagan
4 56;24	3 00	[1 00]	_ 56;24	4 56;24	Ili-alim
4 37;40		[ ]	4 37;40	4 37;40	Šamaš-kima-aplu

from which 23;20 gur (are for) Šamaš-kima-aplu's labourers.

rev.

19 36;04	8 01	4 34;45	7 00;19	19 36;04	

From which grain for Lu-……
and 23;20 gur for Šamaš-kima-aplu's labourers.

Month I, day 7
Year of Rim-Sin the king (Rim-Sin year 1)

All other known tabular accounts from the early years of Rim-Sin's reign are headed too, have at least one, more often two axes or levels of calculation, and often include linear notes (Table 4). The fully functional table has arrived—not only in the kingdom of Larsa but in Isin and Uruk too.

Table 4: Dated tabular accounts from early in the reign of Rim-Sin

Publication	*Museum no.*	*Provenance*	*Cols*	*Hdgs*	*Or*	*Axes*	*Notes*	*Year*	*Date*
YOS 5 103	YBC 4721	Ur or Larsa	6	M	L	H1 V1	L	RS 1	1822
OECT 15 10	Ash 1922.281	Larsa?	3	M	P	V2	L	RS 1	1822
SaMü 1991: 156	W 20472,88	Uruk	3	O	P	V2	L	Anam a	1821-17
SaMü 1992: 167	W 20472,87	Uruk	3	O	P	H1 V1		Anam a	1821-17
PBS 8/1 34	CBS 15167	Nippur	6+	Y	L	H?		RS 5	1818
SaMü 1992: 168	W 20472, 121	Uruk	6	O	L	H1 V1+	L	Irda-nene d	1816-10
YOS 5 196	YBC 6209	Ur or Larsa	7	O	L	H1 V1	L	RS 10	1813
UET 5 647	U 17216	Ur	3	M	–	V2?	L	RS 16	1807
PBS 8/1 13	CBS 15173	Nippur	8	Y	P	V1	LC	Di 13	1804
UET 5 857	U 7802G	Ur	5	O	–	H1 V^1	L	RS 23	1800
PBS 8/1 36	CBS 15171	Nippur	5	–	P	V^1	L	RS 24	1799
PBS 8/1 33	CBS 15174	Nippur	4	I	P	V2	L	RS 26	1797
OECT 13 87	Ash 1924.1036a	Larsa area?	3	O	P	V1		RS 27	1796

SaMü = Sanati-Müller (1991-93).

OECT 15 10 account of workers and grain, grouped by ethnicity (?): vertical addition with subtotals and totals.

SaMü 1991: 156 account of oil delivered by merchants (final column heading dam-gàr-me-eš), with column for silver value unused. Vertical subtotals according to oil type (ì-giš, ì-šaḫ), when silver equivalent is calculated: 8 sìla per shekel of vegetable oil, 12 sìla per shekel of animal fat. Total silver equivalent at end of document.

SaMü 1992: 167 account of rams and their silver equivalents (calculated); delivered by merchants (column heading blank). Totals of each given.

PBS 8/1 34 account of deliveries. Commodities unspecified, but units change from ma-na to sìla near bottom of obverse. No vertical totalling; horizontal structure not clear.

SaMü 1992: 168 account of four different types of ovid totalled for plucking (final column heading, zú-si-ga-ku$_4$-ra). Totalled horizontally by shepherd, for whom the total hair/wool is also totalled, and yield per ovid calculated, within linear comments. Columnar totals, if there were any, are now missing from the damaged reverse of the tablet.

YOS 5 196 account 6 types of ovids, ŠU.NIGÍN 'total' as last column heading. Interlinear notes give names of shepherds. Column totals at bottom, grand total on reverse in prosaic summary. Wool/hair total given too but not tabulated.

UET 5 647 no horizontal calculations. Appears to be subtotal in line 9 before interlinear note UGULA [+ PN?]. First headings to the two numerical columns apparently identical: unclear.

PBS 8/1 13 tabular offering account, like *sattukkum* archive. Commodities in tiny illegible signs over numerical columns at top of table. Interlinear summary comments assigning lines above to individual temples. Totals for each commodity given in non-tabular form on reverse.

UET 5 857 account of canal repairs. Columns all numerical, with interlinear notes assigning entries to particular locations (including Nirda and Kurhianum (see *OECT* 15 7, Table 6). Calculates volume of canal horizontally from dimensions, with notes in last column as to whether finished or not. Total length given in non-tabular summary on reverse.

PBS 8/1 36 fragmentary account of *sattukkum* offerings. Totals given prosaically on the edge, with interlinear notes assigning lines above to individual temples.

PBS 8/1 33 account of *sattukkum* offerings. Totals of three types of sheep and grand total given at bottom of table. Interlinear comments ascribe days of the month to the entries above.

OECT 13 87 account of *sattukkum* offerings. Totals given outside tabular formatting on reverse.

The later years of Rim-Sin's reign

Towards the end of Rim-Sin's reign we start to find clusters of tablets showing how the minutiae of tabular formatting could vary over a matter of days or months within single archive (Table 5). At the same time, there is striking cross-archive consistency in formatting: the final heading of all these accounts is MU.BI.IM and there is a heavy preponderance of landscape orientations.

Table 5: Dated tabular accounts from the last years of Rim-Sin

Publication	*Museum no.*	*Provenance*	*Cols*	*Hdgs*	*Or*	*Axes*	*Notes*	*Ruler*	*Date*
Ro fc. 1	Col P 292	Larsa	8	M	L			RS 31	1792
Ro fc. 2	Col P 286	Larsa	8	M	L			RS 31	1792
Ro fc. 3	Col P 314	Larsa	5	M	L			RS 31	(1792)
Ro fc. 4	Col P 291	Larsa	5	M	L			RS 31	1792
Ro fc. 5	Col P 324	Larsa	4	M	L	H1 V1		RS 31	(1792)
Ro fc. 6	Col P 287	Larsa	7	M	L	H1 V1	L	RS 31	1792
Ro fc. 7	Col P 288	Larsa	8	M	L		L	RS 31	1792
Ro fc. 8	Col P 289	Larsa	5	M	L		L	RS 31	1792
Ro fc. 9	Col P 293	Larsa	5	M	L		L	RS 31	1792
Ro fc. 10	Col P 290	Larsa	8	M	L		L	RS 31	1792
Ro fc. 11	Col P 294	Larsa	5	M	L		L	RS 31	1792
Ro fc. 13	BM 85260	Larsa area	4	M	P	H1 V2	L	RS 31	1792
Ro fc. 14	BM 85269	Larsa area	4	M	P	H1 V2	L	RS 31	1792
Ro fc. 15	BM 16391	Larsa area	7	M	L	H2 V1		RS 32	1791
Ro fc. 16	BM 85232	Larsa area	7	M	L	H2 V1		RS 32	1791
TLB 1:55	LB 1075	Larsa area	3	M	L	H2	L	RS 39	1784

Ro fc. = Robson (forthcoming).

TLB 1:55 account of beer bread and salt, listed by city. Two groups of entries are subtotalled and the second amount taken away from the first: the earliest subtraction attested in tabular accounts.

The Columbia tablets are all daily allocations of cattle feed to a small group of cowherds over the space of a few months (discussed in detail by Robson forthcoming). The same four men are accounted for in each of the first group, another three in second. The accounts of the first group vary as to whether columns for deficits in three commodities (grain, bran, straw) are given—sometimes they are marked in even when empty. They record no calculations at all, except in the undated tablet Col P 324 associated with them, which totals the number of oxen (GUD) and cows and calves (ÁB.AMAR) allocated to each man. The second group, which covers the same time period, uses linear interpolations to assign each cowherd to a deity: Enlil, Šamaš or Suen. Otherwise the content and formatting is identical to the first group, with columns for deficits sometimes included and left blank, sometimes omitted. The undated tabular account *UET* 5 46 (Table 8; Robson forthcoming) is very similar in content and format, but with different personal and divine names. One tablet, Col P 287, subdivides the cattle into oxen (GUD) and cows and calves (ÁB.AMAR) with totals and a grand total.

The BM tablets, almost exactly contemporaneous with the Columbia group, calculate work allocations (*šerʾānum*) for a dozen or so named workers. The two four-column tables compare the work days owed with the work days done, calculating the totals and differences for each individual, each group assigned to a particular property (NÍG.ŠU PN) or to the royal share (ḪA.LA LUGAL), and a grand total. The two seven-column tablets take identical data but also calculate the volume of earth worked by each worker using the theoretical constant 1½ shekels, rather smaller than those found in Old Babylonian mathematical problems on labouring for earthworks (cf. Robson 1999: 98-109; 157-61). On these tablets the workers are not grouped or subtotalled, but a total for each column is given at the bottom of the table.

A further group of three undated tabular accounts from the Larsa area is probably contemporary with these tablets (*TLB* 1 52-54; Table 8). All account for disbursals of grain, but whereas two are organised by day across the columns (UD.1, UD.2, UD.3, ŠU.NIGÍN, MU.BI.IM) with personal names in the final columns and totals in the final row, the third has days in the row labels and ration types (cultic meal, palace subsistence, ..., donkey fodder) in the column headings—the earliest attested tabular account to be structured chronologically like this (Example 8: LB 1095 = *TLB* 1 54).

Example 8: LB 1095

na-ap-ta-nu-um	ŠUKU É	A [...]	ŠÀ.GAL ANŠE	ŠU.NIGÍN	MU.BI.IM
2 SÌLA	0.0.2, 1 SÌLA	0.0.2	0.0.1	0.0.5, 3 SÌLA	UD.3.KAM
2 SÌLA	0.0.2, 1 SÌLA	0.0.1, 9 SÌLA	0.0.1	0.0.5, 2 SÌLA	UD.4.KAM
8 SÌILA	0.0.2, 1 SÌLA	0.0.1, 6 SÌLA	0.0.1, 5 SÌLA	0.1.0 ŠE	UD.5.KAM
0.0.1	⌜0.0.2, 1 SÌLA⌝	9 SÌLA	0.0.1, 5 SÌLA	0.0.5, 5 SÌLA	UD.6.KAM

The mid-Old Babylonian period

Over the following thirty years further formatting innovations took place, so that tabular accounts post-dating Hammurabi's conquest of Larsa typically resemble Ash 1922.290 (Example 2), with two or three levels of calculation and plenty of interlinear comments (Table 6). Theoretical constants continue to be used. Of particular interest is a group of accounts from Hammurabi's reign estimating the yield of fields (NÍG.GAR, *šukunnûm*) in small settlements in the Larsa area which uses yield rates of between 10 and 40 GUR per BÙR. The undatable accounts *OECT* 15 15. 16. 122. 134 (Table 8) have an identical format and must originate in the same archive (Robson fc.) The accounts in this group almost all use long introductory preambles to describe the contents of the table (Example 9; *OECT* 15 121), as does a slightly later account of fish, also from the Larsa area. One tabular account from Larsa also doubles as a legal document, with witnesses and seals (Robson forthcoming: 27).

Example 9: Introductory preamble to Ash 1923.340

obv. 1 *šu-ku-un-na* A.GÀR *a-a-ni-a-tim ù* A.GÀR DAM *la-ga-nu*
A.ŠÀ É ^{d}NANNA *ù* AGA.ÚS.MEŠ *ša* AB.SÍN *iš-ta-ad-du*
URU *šu-un-na-mu-un-dím*^{ki}
GÚ ÍD *al-bi-an-na* BAL.RI A.A.BI

obv. 1 Estimated yield of the Ayaniatim meadow and DAM laganu$^{?}$ meadow.
Fields belonging to Nanna's temple and to soliders, in which cultivation has been abandoned
Sunnamundim town
On the banks of Albianna river on the opposite bank to the marshes.

Table 6: Dated tabular accounts from the reigns of Hammurabi and Samsu-iluna

Publication	*Museum no.*	*Provenance*	*Cols*	*Hdgs*	*Or*	*Axes*	*Notes*	*Year*	*Date*
OECT 15 7	Ash 1922.277	Larsa	4	I M	P	V3	L	Ha 35	1758
OECT 15 12	Ash 1922.283	Larsa	5	I M	–	H1+	L	Ha 35	1758
OECT 15 121	Ash 1923.340	Larsa	9	I M	L	H2 V1		Ha 35	1758
TCL 10 151	AO 8385	Larsa	4	I O	P	H1 V1	L	Ha 35	1758
Ro fc. 26	BM 85205	Larsa	6	I M	L	H1 V1	L	Ha 35	1758

Ro fc. 27	BM 22738	Larsa	10	O	L	H2		Ha 35	1758
TCL 10 166	AO 6408	Larsa	4	M	P			Ha 38	1754
TCL 10 159	AO 8423	Larsa	6	M	L	H1		Ha 38	1754
TCL 10 171	AO 8425	Larsa	5	M	P	H2 V1	L	Ha 39	1753
PBS 8/2 126	CBS 7185	Nippur	4	M	P	H1		Ha 41	1752
YOS 12 56	YBC 7252	–	7	M	P	H V1	L	Si 2	1748
VAS 18 103	VAT 8400	–	3	M	P	–	L	Si 2	1748
CT 45 32	BM 80169	Sippar	12	M	S	V1	C	Si 2	1748
YOS 12 101	YBC 7075	–	4	M	P	H1 V1	L	Si 3	1747
Scheil 1918	HE 113	Larsa	4	I M	P	H1 V1		Si 6	1744
Ro fc. 28	BM 85211	–	7	O	P	H2 V2	L	Si 7	1743
Ro fc. 29	BM 85238	–	7	O	P	H2 V2	L	(Si 7)	(1743)
Ro fc. 30	BM 13934	–	4	M	L	H1 V2		Si 11	1739

Ro fc. = Robson (forthcoming).

OECT 15 7 inspection of estimated yields (*šukunnu*) of fields in Nirda and Kurḫianu (Robson forthcoming: 17). Running totals of cultivated land (A.ŠÀ AB.SÍN), its grain (ŠE.BI) and unsown land (AB.SÍN ŠE NU) belonging the palace and temple, with grain subtracted (in interlinear comments) for the ENSÍ.

OECT 15 12 fragmentary account of estimated yields of fields in Iazilum and Iakinku (Robson forthcoming: 18). For each cultivated field (A.ŠÀ AB.SÍN) a theoretical yield rate (NÍG.GAR) is used to estimate the yield (ŠE.BI). Uncultivated land is also noted (AB.SÍN NU).

OECT 15 121 account of estimated yields of fields in Šunnamundim (Robson forthcoming: 19). The account is divided horizontally between palace property (NÍG É.GAL) and the property of Nanna's temple (NÍG É.^{d}NANNA). For each cultivated field (A.ŠÀ AB.SÍN) a theoretical yield rate (NÍG.GAR) is used to estimate the yield (ŠE.BI). In each case the column for unsown land (ŠE NU) is blank. Some of the totals at the bottom of the acount are erroneous.

TCL 10 151 account of estimated yields of fields in Ukua (Robson forthcoming: 20). For each field (A.ŠÀ) a theoretical yield rate (NÍG.GAR) is used to estimate the yield (ŠE.[BI]). Uncultivated land is not noted. The heading of the final column listing personnel reads [...] A.GÀR 'meadow'. Final totals are in the summary, outside the tabular format.

Ro fc. 26 account of fields assigned to various people (in column headings) and to towns (row labels and interlinear notes). Areas totalled horizontally and vertically.

Ro fc. 27 account of harvest shortfalls in date harvests at Ili-ištikal over two years (Ha 33 and 34, in fifth and final column heading). For each year the yield of the orchards are calculated at 12 GUR per IKU. (Small) payments and (large) deficits are recorded for each owner and cultivator. The account is witnessed and sealed by the town elders, who promise to pay back the crown the dates it is owed.

TCL 10 166 tabular list of garment allocations to named individuals.

TCL 10 159 account of date orchards in Ea-Šulgi with only one line of data in the table.

TCL 10 171 account of estimated yields of fields in Ea-Šulgi (Robson fc.: 21). For each cultivated field ([A.ŠÀ AB].SÍN) a theoretical yield rate (NÍG.GAR) is used to estimate the yield (ŠE.BI), which is then halved (ŠU.RI.A.BI). Column totals are given at the bottom of the table.

PBS 8/2 126 account of grain assigned to individuals. If the balance (Ì.SÁ) is below 4 GUR the deficit (LÁ.Ì) is recorded; otherwise a surplus (DIRIG) may be shown.

YOS 12 56 Grain account over three years (Ha 42, Si 1, Si 2).

VAS 18 103 fragmentary account of deliveries (MU.TÚM) and deficits (LÁ.Ì) from Ha 38 to Si 1.

CT 45 32 Account of baked bricks over days 6 to 15 (UD.6-UD.15) in column headings, all entries for days 12 onwards blank. On some days the workers are recorded as NA.GADA 'shepherds'. Grand totals for obverse and reverse are recorded separately in non-tabular format, where the daily work rate is explicitly stated to be ÉŠ.GÀR LÚ.1.E 20 SIG_4 AL.ÙR.RA.

YOS 12 101 Account of grain deliveries and deficits.

Scheil 1918 Account of sea fish (KU_6.HI.A A.AB.BA), their price (KÙ.BI) and market rate per shekel of silver (GANBA *a-na* 1 GÍN). The different types of fish are listed in the final column. Some are counted, others sold by capacity measure. The total amount of silver is given in the non-tabular summary at the end.

Ro fc. 28 and 29 two versions of the same account, with the same data in slightly different formats. Lengths, upper widths, widths, depths, and two types of volume (UŠ, SAG AN, SAG, GAM, SAḪAR, SAḪAR.ḪI.A) assigned to various people. The first volume is calculated from data in the first four columns; the derivation of the second is unclear. Subtotals and totals of lengths and the second volumes are given in linear format.

Ro fc. 30 account of grain lost between the threshing floor (SAG.NÍG.GA *ra-ḫi-ṣu*) and delivery at the warehouse (MU.TÚM É.KIŠIB.BA): deficits (LÁ.Ì) are recorded for various days of the month. Subtotalled by temple and totalled at the end of the account.

The late Old Babylonian period

By the reigns of Ammi-ditana and Ammi-ṣaduqa tabular accounts had become much less complex (Table 7). Extant examples tend to have fewer columns and are no longer used for horizontal calculations. Vertical totals are typically given in the final, non-tabular summary but tabular lists, with no calculations at all, now account for a quarter of the known corpus. Introductory titles remain common, and often replace column headings. MU.BI.IM remains the most frequent final column heading, even when its contents are not necessarily personal names. The use of interlinear comments, however, declines. The latest attested OB tabular account is from about three decades before the last known documents of the period.

Table 7: Dated tabular accounts from the reigns of Ammi-ditana and Ammi-ṣaduqa

Publication	*Museum no.*	*Provenance*	*Cols*	*Hdgs*	*Or*	*Axes*	*Notes*	*Year*	*Date*
Ri 2002:3.13	BM 78306	Sippar	3	M	P	V1	–	Ad 5	1679
CT 45 48	BM 78182	Sippar	4	Y D	P	V2	L	Ad 8	1676
Ri 2002:3.01	BM 13168	Sippar	3		P	V	–	Ad 13	1671
Ri 2002:3.02	BM 86439	Sippar	3	M	P			Ad 36	1648
Ri 2002:3.02	BM 79967	Sippar	6	M	L		–	Aṣ 3	1644
Ri 2002:3.02	BM 78720	Sippar	3	O	L	V2	C	Aṣ 4	1643
BBVO 1 106	–	Larsa	3	O	P	V1		Aṣ 10	1637
Ri 2002:3.12	BM 79959	Sippar	3	I	L	–		Aṣ 10	1637
Ri 2002:3.02	BM 16543	Sippar	4	I M	P			Aṣ 13	1634
Ri 2002:3.02	BM 79075	Sippar	3	I	R			Aṣ 13/17	1634
Ri 2002:3.12	BM 79930	Sippar	3	I	L	V2	L	Aṣ 14	1633
Ri 2002:3.12	BM 79951	Sippar	3	I	L	V		Aṣ 14	1633
Ri 2002:5.11	BM 79981	Sippar	3	I	P	V1		Aṣ 14	1633
Ri 2002:3.01	BM 86452	Sippar	4	M	P	–		Aṣ 15	1632
Ri 2002:3.07	BM 79788	Sippar	7	I M	L	V1		Aṣ 16	1631
Ri 2002:3.07	BM 79956	Sippar	7	I M	L	V1		Aṣ 16	1631
Ri 2002:3.01	BM 79010	Sippar	4	I M	P	V1	L	Aṣ 17	1630
Ri 2002:3.12	BM 79485	Sippar	4	I M	P	V2	L	Aṣ 17	1630
YOS 13 182	MLC 721	–	3	M	P			Aṣ 18	1629
CT 45 61	BM 80627	Sippar	3	M D	L	V2	L	Aṣ 21	1626

Ri 2002 = Richardson (2002).

BM 78306 fragmentary account of beer, with column totals in tabular format at the bottom.

BM 78182 fragmentary account of three commodities, subtotalled and totalled. Tabular formatting breaks up two-thirds of the way down the obverse.

BM 13168 fragmentary account of two types of grain.

BM 86439 tabular list of wool and silver; no calculations.

BM 79967 fragmentary tabular list, perhaps of days worked. Most of the column headings are missing; no calculations survive.

BM 78720 account of land, in which the columnar formatting, with headings UŠ, SAG, A.ŠÀ A.GÀR MAR.TU, is adapted to accommodate upper and lower widths (UŠ AN.TA, UŠ KI.TA, SAG AN.TA, SAG KI.TA, written as notes within the table). The average length and width are entered in each column and the area of the field recorded in non-tabular format.

BBVO 1 106 account of silver and men. Silver totalled at the end in non-columnar format.

BM 79959 account of rations, with PNs in final two columns. No calculations survive.

BM 16543 fragmentary tabular list of days worked; no calculations survive.

BM 79075 tabular list of days worked.

BM 79930 account of two types of grain rations, subtotalled by column and totalled at the end of the table.

BM 79951 account of grain, with PNs in two columns. Totals in non-tabular format at the end of the account, somewhat damaged.

BM 79981 account of wages and rations; totals in non-tabular format at the end of the account.

BM 86452 account of grain, silver, and beer. No horizontal calculations; presumably columnar totals at the end of the account, now missing.

BM 79788 tabular list of fabrics produced, with days (UD.4.KAM etc.) in the column headings and PNs in the row labels.

BM 79956 tabular list of work days, with days (UD.4.KAM etc.) in the column headings and PNs in the row labels.

BM 79010 account of silver, oil, and animal fat assigned to individuals, with occasional damaged interlinear comments. Commodity totals at the end of the account in non-tabular format.

BM 79485 account of rations, listed by month (in the column headings) assigned to female PNs. Columnar subtotals and perhaps a total in the damaged non-tabular summary at end of the account.

BM 79485 account of two types of animal, for UD.10.KAM and UD.20.KAM, subtotalled by UGULA.MAR.TU and totalled at the end of the account, in non-tabular format. Dead specimens are noted interlinearly after the subtotals and subtracted from the account; a separate total is given for them in the final summary.

After the Old Babylonian period

The heyday of the cuneiform tabular account was not in fact the 18th century BC, despite the evidence presented so far. That accolade goes to Nippur in the 14th and 13th centuries, where a full third of the six hundred-odd surviving administrative records are in tabular format (*BE* 14-15; *PBS* 2/2; *TMHNF* 5). Showing a remarkable structural similarity with tables from the time of Hammurabi and Samsu-iluna, many of them have introductory preambles, column headings of which the last is MU.BI.IM over the row labels. Calculations, of which there may be several levels, are organised horizontally from left to right and vertically from top to bottom. They are deserving of an in-depth structural study.

For the first millennium the evidence is much scarcer. The few Neo-Assyrian tables tend rather to be tabular lists, with no horizontal axis of calculation and rare columnar or summary totals.[7] A large, headed tabular account from Sultantepe (*STT* 1 47) with fourteen columns and at least three levels of horizontal calculation and two vertical shows that Neo-Assyrian scribes could and did use tabulation very effectively; but it is likely that they mostly used waxed writing boards to do so.

The evidence from Babylonia comes primarily from the Eana temple in Uruk. A dozen tabular lists with two to six columns record animals sacrificed during the reigns of Nebuchadnezzar and Nabonidus in the first half of the 6th century BC (Beaulieu 2003). A headed table from 559 BC records the growth of Eana's flocks over the past decade (van Driel and Nemet-Nejat 1994). There are two levels of horizontal calculation over its 11 columns and a very complex vertical layering of running additions and subtractions, with perhaps three or four levels of calculation. Not surprisingly, there are cumulative numerical errors. Forty-odd four-column tabular lists of *sattukku*-offerings span the reigns of Nabonidus to Cambyses, 551-525 BC (Robbins 1996). All have introductory preambles, in six variants, but only four are headed or partially headed. No doubt there are more tabular accounts from the first millennium, both published and unpublished, which would fill out the picture of tabulation in the cuneiform record. For instance, there are copies of over sixty tabular accounts in CT 55-57 among the tablets from the E-babbar temple in Neo-Babylonian Sippar.

Conclusions

The use of tabular formatting in the cuneiform record was fitful and patchy. After two false starts in the Early Dynastic and Ur III periods, tabulation became recognised as as an efficient way of recording, storing, and sorting data only in the mid-19th century BC:

---

[7] *E.g.*, *CTN* 2 125. 139; *CTN* 3 98. 107. 110. 111; *SAA* 7 116. 132. 137-139. 157; *SAA* 11 80-82. 126. 223.

- It enabled the horizontal separation of different categories of quantitative information associated with named individuals, from around 1850 at the latest (Table 3).
- This led to easy addition of quantitative data, along a vertical axis, by at least 1837 (Table 4).
- At the same time, data could be sorted by criteria such as destination, or date of transaction.
- Headings, attested first in the E-šumeša archive and then regularly after about 1822, obviated the necessity to repeat descriptive information.

When columns of derived data were introduced, again from at least 1822, they enabled calculations to be performed along both horizontal and vertical axes for the purposes of double-checking. At the same time, the columnar format could be ignored where necessary to provide note-like explanatory interpolations. It was at this point, arguably, that tables became truly powerful information processing tools, cognitively distinct from well-organised lists. Their evolution, it appears, took no more than thirty years.

Thereafter further refinements were made and uses found:

- From the 1790s standard calculation constants (for work rates, harvest yields, market rates) were used in tables to *make predictions* as well as to record events that had already happened.
- From the 1750s tabular accounts could function as legal records, with witnesses and seals.
- At the same time, introductory preambles added transparency to complex tables, especially when multiple levels of calculations were made.

These further developments, including horizontally organised calculations, appear on present evidence to have been exclusive to the south. Late OB tabular accounts from the Sippar area show much less complexity and are predominantly vertical in calculational structure. Tantalisingly, the format and structure of Kassite tabular accounts from Nippur suggest a direct line of descent from the mid-OB period.

What drove the development of tabular documents?

My initial hypothesis, before I started to collect the data, was that tables would somehow be linked to, or come out of, the development of the sexagesimal place value system in the 21st century BC. The meagre evidence of the Ur III period points suggestively in that direction, but much more is needed before this untested proposition can be confirmed or refuted.

I also wondered whether tables were related somehow to language change, but I can see no obvious correlation so far. Partly this is because the tables have a high density of numerical notations, logograms, and personal names. The prosaic explanatory interpolations, attested from 1822 onwards, are all in Akkadian; maybe this is relevant.

The use of tables does not seem to be imposed from political centres, as the pattern of use in the E-šumeša archive shows (Table 2). The only other possible motivation I can suggest is individual, or at least bureaucratically internal, innovation driven by a desire for efficiency and accuracy. This of course is a highly speculative proposal, but it is nevertheless clear that tables were *not* the accounting method of choice for most scribes of the Old Babylonian period. Excluding the E-šumeša archive, less than 1 percent of the published tablet copies I searched through showed tabular formatting. Even allowing for under-representation in the dataset, as outlined in the introduction, tabular accounts can never have accounted for more than about 5 percent of OB institutional archives—and had no place at all in family records. Prosaic document formatting continued to be the norm, even for complex multi-commodity, multi-personnel annual accounts.[8]

Much remains to be done on the topic of tabulation—in lexical and scholarly works as well as the administrative record. I hope that this brief sketch will provide a preliminary framework for further and deeper exploration of this fascinating thread in the history of literacy, numeracy, and cognition.

8 *E.g.*, YBC 7478 (*YOS* 5 208), an annual account of two shepherds' flocks from Larsa, RS 11 (1812 BC), or CBS 7197 (*PBS* 8/2 134), from Nippur, an account of fields to be harrowed and sown, Si 21 (1729 BC).

Appendix

Table 8: Undatable tabular accounts from the Old Babylonian period

Publication	*Museum no.*	*Provenance*	*Cols*	*Hdgs*	*Or*	*Axes*	*Notes*	*Date*
BBVO 1 94	–	Larsa	4		P	H1V	L	
BiMes 7: Ki 46	Ist Ki 46	Kish	3+	O	–	–		
CT 45 81	BM 78212	–	4	I D	P	V?		
CT 45 85	BM 78211	–	7	M	L	V1	C	
CT 45 97	BM 80432	–	5	Y	L	H1		
CT 45 100	BM 78303	–	3		P			
CT 45 107	BM 78349	–	3	I M	L	V		–
CT 45 108	BM 78331	–	4		P			
CT 45 116	BM 80211	–	3		P			
OECT 13 28	Ash 1924.534	–	4+	–	–	–	L	–
OECT 13 91	Ash 1924.1046	–	3	O	P			
OECT 13 205	Ash 1931.139	–	4	–	P			
OECT 15 1	Ash 1922.166	–	11+	–	P	H V	L	–
OECT 15 2	Ash 1922.172		4	–	–	H V	L	
OECT 15 3	Ash 1922.173		5	–	P	H V	L	–
OECT 15 5	Ash 1922.180	–	18	–	–	H V	L	–
OECT 15 7	Ash 1922.278	Bad-Tibira	34	V	L	H1 V1	C	
OECT 15 15	Ash 1922.286	Larsa	4	–	P	H1 V	L	–
OECT 15 16	Ash 1922.287	Larsa	5	–	P	H1 V	L	–
OECT 15 18	Ash 1922.290	Larsa	8	Y	P	H V	L	
OECT 15 71	Ash 1922.346	Larsa	3	O	R	–	–	–
OECT 15 122	Ash 1923.341	Larsa	5	–	P	H V	L	–
OECT 15 132	Ash 1923.365	Larsa	3	Y	P	V		M
OECT 15 134	Ash 1923.375	Larsa	5	–	P	H V	L	–
OECT 15 230	Ash 1932.266		3	O	P			
OECT 15 240	Ash 1932.279		10	M	L	H		
OECT 15 262	Ash 1932.389		3	–	P	–		–
PBS 8/1 75	CBS 11313	Nippur	3		S	V1		M
Ri 2002:3.01	BM 96955	Sippar	4	–	P	–		–
Ri 2002:3.05	BM 81021	Sippar	4	M	L	H	C	
Ri 2002:3.07	BM 79965	Sippar	5	I M	P	V1		
Ri 2002:3.12	BM 79765	Sippar	5	–	P	–		–
Ri 2002:7.151	BM 96969	Sippar	4	–	P	–		
Ro fc. 12	Col P 323	Larsa	4	M	L	H1 V1		
SaMü 1993:199		Uruk	4	–	P	H1		
TCL 11 236		Larsa	5	O	L	V2		
TCL 11 244		Larsa	4	M	P			
TCL 11 247		Larsa	3	Y	S	V1		

TCL 11 249		Larsa	4	M	P			M D
TLB 1 52	LB 2055	Larsa	5	M	P	H1 V1		M
TLB 1 53	LB 1024	Larsa	4	–	P	H1 V1		M
TLB 1 54	LB 1095	Larsa	6	M	L	H1		
UET 5 468	–	Ur	4	M	P	H1 V		
UET 5 515	U 8806d	Ur	4	–	S	V1		M D
UET 5 573	U 11519	Ur	7+	Y	–	H V		–
UET 5 846	U 16061n	Ur	5	M	L	H1 V1	L	
UET 5 875	U 7735	Ur	11	M	L		C	
VAS 18 83	VAT 7874	–	3	–	P	V1		
VAS 18 102	VAT 5801	–	4	M	P		L	
YOS 5 102	YBC 4740	Ur or Larsa	4	–	P	H1 V?	L	–

M = month; D = day, Ri 2002 = Richardson (2002); Ro fc. = Robson (forthcoming); SaMü 1993 = Sanati-Müller (1993).

BBVO 1 94 very long grain account, in which the first column is the sum of the second and third. Interlinear comments with subtotals; final column damaged.

CT 45 116 the tablet was ruled into four columns but the entries for the first column consistently spill over into the second.

OECT 15 5 substantial fragment of large summary account of grain yields of different meadows.

OECT 15 7 small tablet with tiny columns; headings almost illegible. Final column gives meadow names.

OECT 15 15. 16. 122. 134 the same format as the estimated yield accounts from Ha 35 and 38 (Table 6), Robson (forthcoming: 22-25).

OECT 15 18 see Example 2.

TLB 1 52-54 see comments on the later years of Rim-Sin, above.

UET 5 515 tabular formatting starts after a line or two in prosaic format.

UET 5 648 tabular formatting stops a third of the way down the reverse of the tablet.

UET 5 846 account of cattle, very similar to the Columbia Plimpton tablets (Table 5).

UET 5 875 month names in column headings, PNs in row labels. Entries consist of day names plus NÍG.ŠU PN; most cells of the table are blank, including all of those for the last 5 months.

Bibliography

For abbreviations of text editions (which are not included in the following list) see the Cuneiform Digital Library Initiative's list of standard abbreviations for Assyriology <http://cdli.ucla.edu/Tools/abbrev.html>.

Beaulieu, Paul-Alain (2003), *The Pantheon of Uruk during the Neo-Babylonian Period* (Cuneiform Monographs 23; Leiden: Brill/STYX).

Campbell-Kelly, M., M. Croarken, R.G. Flood, and E. Robson (2003), *The History of Mathematical Table-Making, from Sumer to Spreadsheets* (Oxford: Oxford University Press).

Civil, Miguel (1992), "Ur III Bureaucracy: Quantitative Aspects," in McG. Gibson and R. D. Biggs (eds.), *The Organization of Power: Aspects of Bureaucracy in the Ancient Near East*, 2nd ed. (Chicago: The Oriental Institute): 35-44.

van Driel, G. and K.R. Nemet-Nejat (1994), "Bookkeeping Practices for an Institutional Herd at Eanna," *JCS* 46: 47-58.

Englund, Robert K. (1998), "Texts from the Late Uruk Period," in J. Bauer, R.K. Englund, and M. Krebernik, *Späturuk-Zeit und Frühdynastische Zeit* (OBO 160/1): 15-233.

Hallo, William W. (1964), "The Road to Emar," *JCS* 18: 57-88.

— (1972), "The House of Ur-Meme," *JNES* 31: 87-96.

Nissen, Hans J., Peter Damerow, and Robert K. Englund (1993), *Archaic Bookkeeping: Writing and Techniques of Economic Administration in the Ancient Near East* (Chicago: University of Chicago Press).

Powell, Marvin A. (1976), "The Antecedents of Old Babylonian Place Notation and the Early History of Babylonian Mathematics," *Historia Mathematica* 3: 417-39.

Richardson, Seth C. (2002), *The Collapse of a Complex State*, Ph.D. thesis, Columbia University.

Robbins, Ellen (1996), "Tabular Sacrifice Records and the Cultic Calendar of Neo-Babylonian Uruk," *JCS* 48: 61-87.

Robson, Eleanor (1999), *Mesopotamian Mathematics: Technical Constants in Bureaucracy and Education* (Oxford Edition of Cuneiform Texts 14; Oxford: Clarendon).

— (2001) "Neither Sherlock Holmes nor Babylon: A Reassessment of Plimpton 322," *Historia Mathematica* 28: 167-206.

— (2003), "Tables and Tabular Formatting in Sumer, Babylonia, and Assyria, 2500-50 BCE," in Campbell-Kelly *et al.* 2003: 18-47.

— (forthcoming), "Old Babylonian Tabular Accounts: A Structural Study."

Sanati-Müller, Shirin (1991-93), "Texte aus dem Sînkāšid-Palast, 4–6: Texte verschiedenen Inhalts I–III," *BaM* 22: 313-30; 23: 119-62; 24: 137-84.

Scheil, Vincent (1918), "Sur le marché aux poissons de Larsa," *RA* 15: 183-94.

Sigrist, R. Marcel (1984), *Les* sattukku *dans l'Ešumeša durant la période d'Isin et Larsa* (BiMes 11).

— (1985), "Mu Malgium basig," *RA* 79: 161-68.

Van De Mieroop, Marc (1999-2000), "An Accountant's Nightmare: The Drafting of a Year's Summary," *AfO* 46-47: 111-29.

Zettler, Richard K. (1984), "The Genealogy of the House of Ur-Me-me: A Second Look," *AfO* 31: 1-14.

6.

Accounting in Neo-Babylonian Institutional Archives: Structure, Usage, Implications*

Michael Jursa
Universität Wien

„Herrlich was Baco sagt (Novum Organum. L I. 45 aphor.), der Mensch, wo er ein bißchen Ordnung sieht, vermutet gleich zuviel.“
(G.C. Lichtenberg, *Sudelbücher*, J 1045)

Ever since the decipherment of cuneiform, many Assyriologists have been impressed by the wealth of Mesopotamian administrative texts and by the scope and efficiency of the bureaucracies that produced these records. It was assumed that at least in some periods accounting procedures in palace and temple administrations covered every aspect of the economic (and social) life of the households in which they originated. In the words of the pioneering historian of Mesopotamian law, Paul Koschaker, the Babylonians were not just bureaucrats but "bureaucratissimi."[1]

---

* Research for the present paper was conducted in the context of a project on *The Economic History of Babylonia in the First Millennium BC* funded by the Fonds für die Förderung der Wissenschaftlichen Forschung (Vienna). I have profited from material collected for this project by H.D. Baker, B. Janković and C. Waerzeggers. Unpublished tablets from the Yale Babylonian Collection and the British Museum are cited with kind permission of Benjamin Foster and Ulla Kasten and of the Trustees of the British Museum respectively. I am indebted to Claudia Römer for information on Ottoman bookkeeping and to Michaela Weszeli for reading the manuscript and suggesting several improvements.

[1] Cited by Edzard in Hudson and Levine 1996: 277.

Only in recent years has research focussed on the limitations of institutional bureaucracy and accounting.[2] It was realised that the administrations by no means exercised bureaucratic control over all aspects of the institutional economy in the same way. Research on diachronic change in this respect has only just begun.[3] Furthermore, the issue of the efficiency (or inefficiency) of bureaucratic administrations needs to be addressed, both by comparison of administrative systems with their precursors and successors and, more important, by judging the potential of an administration in relation to its own aims. These aims cannot be considered to be self-evident.

Simplifying the discussion slightly, one can distinguish two opposed opinions currently held in the field. I shall dub them "minimalist" and "maximalist." Minimalists emphasise the administrations' restricted scope and claim that Mesopotamian institutional accounting fulfilled primarily what the classicist Moses Finley called a "police function:"[4] keeping track of obligations. For them, only such information was recorded in writing upon which there might be need to recur in the future in such a context.[5] The opposing, "maximalist" position considers the bureaucratic administration primarily as a means of enabling prognostication and planning for the future.[6] While minimalists have little faith in the written documentation's potential as a source of information on which decision-making for the future might be based, maximalists see precisely this use as the real raison d'être of the bureaucratic apparatus. This dichotomy mirrors closely a discussion in the field of ancient history, where papyrologists such as Dominic Rathbone[7] have challenged Finley's "minimalist" position. For Rathbone, accounting in the archive from Roman Egypt studied by him was not primarily a tool for monitoring the honesty of the persons involved but a means to furnish administrators with the quantitative

---

[2] Not suprisingly, perhaps, considering the average academic's experiences with his or her university administration, grant-giving institutions or ministry of science. It is after all one of the basic tenets of (so-called) "post-modern" historiography that the questions asked by historians are determined by their experiences in their own contemporary life.

[3] *E.g.*, Postgate 2001; the papers in Brosius 2003.

[4] Finley 1987:33.

[5] See *e.g.*, Van De Mieroop 1997.

[6] See Steinkeller 2003 and his contribution in the present volume for the Ur III period.

[7] Rathbone 1991.

data necessary to optimise the economic efficiency and profitability of their decision-making. The interdisciplinary import of the discussion of Rathbone's thesis is self-evident: it touches upon some of the issues which Assyriology will have to tackle if an understanding of Mesopotamian institutional archives on any but the most superficial levels should be achieved.

Methodologically, it is necessary to distinguish between what an administration could potentially achieve and what it was created to achieve. Of the two questions which need to be asked in this context, the first addresses the potential of the information collected in institutional archives: which kind of planning could it have made possible: rough guesses of likely income, or rational quantitative evaluation of alternatives leading to the choice of the most promising strategy for the future? Secondly, the question of the emphasis placed by individual bureaucratic systems on either control of obligations or planning for the future needs to be evaluated. This has to be discussed independently of the first question. Even if a given archive proves to be a potentially rich source of information useful for economic forecasting, it still must be demonstrated that it was actually used for this purpose.[8]

The purpose of the present study is therefore twofold. It will present a survey of the bookkeeping procedures in Neo-Babylonian institutional archives and discuss what they could have achieved and what they were meant to achieve. The conclusion of the paper will explore the bearing of the results of this survey on some of the issues raised by the ongoing discussions mentioned above, most importantly on the question if these Neo-Babylonian bureaucracies are better explained by reference to the minimalist or the maximalist model or even the rational (in the technical, Weberian sense) bureaucracy posited for Roman Egypt by Rathbone.

---

8 A glance at the history of national budgeting in some early modern European nation states can serve as an illustration of the importance of not approaching even bureaucracies of fairly recent times with too modern expectations. Annual budgeting by European states began in the 16th and 17th centuries. However, in the French system even the yearly final summaries were just rough approximations (not to speak of the estimated budgets established at the beginning of each fiscal year). In Spain in the 17th century, expenditures were still made without consulting the Council of Finance. In England, data on fiscal matters were collected in such a way to make comprehensive budget estimates impossible until the 19th century, Darling 1996: 237f. note 47.

Neo-Babylonian institutional archives

From first millennium Babylonia, three large temple archives have come down to us. The two largest are those of the Ebabbar temple from northern Babylonian Sippar and the Eanna temple from southern Babylonian Uruk, consisting of about 30 000 and 9 000 tablets and fragments respectively which are now housed in Western collections.[9] It is these texts, dating to the 6th and 5th centuries BC, on which this paper is mostly based. Material from other archives will be used only occasionally.

Before bookkeeping procedures attested in these archives can be discussed, however, a number of preliminary issues have to be tackled. Foremost among these is the question of the nature of the archives.

It has been stated repeatedly in the past by van Driel, Bongenaar and myself that the Ebabbar archive is to be considered a dead archive, that is an agglomeration of texts selected from the main working archive and discarded or at least set aside.[10] However, there has been no proper discussion of this issue, in contrast to the Eanna archive, which has to be considered to be a dead archive too.[11] As this matter is important for understanding the structure of the extant documentation, we will begin with a short survey of the main arguments that can be advanced in support of this thesis.

The main characteristics of a dead archive—which, it should be noted, have been defined in the past mostly by reference to material from private archives—are as follows:

---

[9] About 8 500 Ebabbar tablets and 4 600 Eanna tablets are either published or known to me through unpublished transliterations. For general information on these archives see *e.g.*, Pedersén 1999: 193f. and 205ff. The third large archive is that of the main temple of Babylon, Esangila, of which several hundred tablets, mostly from the 4th and 3rd centuries BC, are known to be housed in the British Museum and some other collections. The structure of this archive is still very poorly understood due to the one-sidedness of the documentation (which strongly favours ration lists). See preliminarily Boiy 2000 with further references. A number of 6th and 5th century administrative texts originally from the archives of the Ezida temple at Borsippa have now surfaced within unpublished private archives from this site. These texts will be analysed by C. Waerzeggers in the context of the project mentioned in the note at the beginning of this article.

[10] See MacGinnis 2002: 227+64.

[11] For "dead archives" in general and the Eanna archive in particular see van Driel 1998. On the matter of "dead" private archives see Jursa 1999:8ff. and Bongenaar 2000: 73ff.

a. The temporal distribution is uneven. There are fewer tablets from the last years of the period covered by the archive.
b. Property documents, in particular for real estate, are generally missing: no-one would throw away title deeds of continuing value. The few extant texts of this type from dead archives are copies or date to the beginning of the time covered by the archive.
c. In general, the documents in a dead archive tend to be ephemeral; the younger they are, the shorter their period of usefulness for the archive holders must have been.

There are various ways to classify large groups of administrative cuneiform texts belonging to institutional archives. The following, not mutually exclusive approaches suggest themselves:[12]

1. Formally, one can distinguish records of income, expenditures and stock-taking (so-called "inventories"), subordinating all other distinctions to this threefold division.
2. A variant of this approach would be a typology based on the documents' keywords.
3. One can focus on the records' subject matter, thus distinguishing *e.g.*, a grain file, a metal file, a personnel file, and so forth. Van Driel has presented such a list of 'files' or dossiers from the Eanna archive.[13]
4. Finally, one can try to take the administrative structure of the institution as one's guideline, thus grouping the documents according to the different departments in which they were issued or at least kept for reference purposes. For this approach, a rough typological analysis must be supplemented by prosopographic data.[14] Also the archaeological record, as far as available, has to be considered.

In the present context it seems best to concentrate on the internal structure of the temples and their archives by adapting this final type of approach.

[12] See in general Edzard 1982 [1989]:33ff. on the Ebla archives.

[13] Van Driel 1998:71ff.

[14] Outstanding examples are Steinkeller 1987, 1996 and, on a more abstract level, 2003.

Typology[15]

Typologically, there is a fundamental distinction between witnessed legal documents and unwitnessed administrative texts. Only the latter, by far more numerous, shall be analysed here, as the formulary of the legal texts is not only sufficiently well understood, but also less relevant for our topic.

The vast majority of administrative texts documents the transfer of some commodity or at least the transfer of the responsibility for some commodity from one party to another. Simple inventories, *i.e.*, texts listing commodities without a transaction clause, occur much less frequently. For the temple's bookkeeping, a single transaction is the most basic occurrence it has to deal with. If complete, its documentation provides the following information:

1. amount and type of object transferred
2. type of transaction
3. parties involved. The temple's involvement may simply be implied tacitly.
4. date

An example:

"2 minas, 20 shekels of iron have been given to the smith Arad-[Gula] for a chisel for the doors of [...]. Sixth of Kislīmu, year five of Nabonidus, king of Babylon." (CT 55 214, Ebabbar archive)[16]

Here, I shall refer to such texts as "single transaction receipts" for simplicity's sake, without differentiating between the various text types according to the verb used in the transaction clause and the direction of the transaction. On this level of analysis, there is no distinction between records of income and expenditures.[17]

---

[15] The rough typology presented here is valid for Eanna and Ebabbar tablets. I will hint only occasionally at the differences between the two archives, since they are usually irrelevant as far as the general structure of the texts is concerned. For the early Ebabbar archive see Da Riva 2002: 19ff.

[16] 2 ma.na ⅓ gín an.[bar], *a-na ma-aq-qa-ri*, *šá* ^{giš}ig^{meš} *šá* D[U$^{?}$ x], *a-na* ^{I}ìr-[^{d}*gu-la*], ^{lú}simug sum^{in} (Date).

[17] Structurally, most contracts fall into this category too, since usually only one (type of) commodity (or the obligation for one type of commodity) is transferred.

The tablets recording such single transactions are usually easily recognisable as they tend to have a distinct physical layout: They are small, pillow-shaped and landscape oriented. Quite often, the reverse of the tablet is uninscribed but for the date.

If more than one transaction was to be recorded on a single tablet, the scribe had several possibilities. He could stick to the format of the single transaction tablets, repeating the entire information (except the date, usually) for every single transaction. This was done in particular in those cases in which transactions of different types were treated on one tablet. The physical layout of such tablets is usually landscape oriented. Alternatively, if a certain element was common to all transactions, *e.g.*, if they all concerned silver from a certain source, the scribe could place this information at the beginning of the text. Such a heading is invariably concluded by the date and usually by a horizontal ruling separating it from the rest of the text, which records the information pertaining to individual transactions only. Also here, the landscape format tablets are more frequent than the portrait format ones.

An example:

"[Barley] issued from the storehouse on the fourth of Abu, year seven of Nabonidus, king of Babylon

270 litres, the *malâtu* (a supplementary payment related to a prebend) of Mu[šallim-Marduk], son of Lâbâši, have been given to Ḫašdāya, son of Niqūdu.

540 litres of barley, in addition to the earlier 360 litres, [have been given] as rations to Kurbanni, the guardian of the shrine of Gula."

(CT 57, 55, Ebabbar archive)[18]

Here I shall refer to tablets of this kind as "multiple transaction receipts," again not distinguishing between records of income and expenditures. Such texts can include transactions of quite different types without any apparent internal connection. Another typical example, a portrait format tablet, shall be quoted.

---

[18] [še.bar (*šá*) t]a é níg.ga sum$^{na\text{-}tu_4}$, iti.ne ud.4.kam mu.7.kam ^{Id}ag-i lugal e^{ki} (horizontal ruling), 1 gur 2 (pi) 3 bán *ma-la-tu*$_4$ *šá* ^{I}*mu-*[*šal-lim-*^{d}amar.utu], a-*šú šá* ^{I}*la-ba-ši a-na* ^{I}*ḫaš-d*[*a-a*], a-*šú šá* ^{I}*ni-qu-du* sum^{i}[^{n}], 3 gur še.bar *e-lat* 2 [gur], *maḫ-ru-tu*$_4$ pad.ḫi.a [*a-na*], ^{I}*kur-ban-ni* ^{lú}en.nun [0], *šá* é ^{d}*gu-la* [sum^{in}].

"540 litres (of barley or dates) (have been given to) Anu-iqbi, Nūrēa and Ina-ṣilli-Tašmēt, the hirelings who do service in the New Year's temple.

90 litres (have been given to) Anu-bēlu-uṣur of the *bīt qātē* storehouse as his rations for the month Ṭebētu.

6 *neseppu* jars and one litre of oil (have been given to) Šumu-uṣur, son of Nabû-šar-aḫḫēšu.

Half a mina and 2.5 shekels of silver, (the weight of) a broken *karallu* object (used) for the greeting-of-the-temple ceremony, is at the disposal of Šamaš-iddin, the goldsmith, for repair work.

Two talents, 20 minas of bronze (and) 14 minas of tin (have been issued) for scrapping.

A carcass of a duck has been received by Ištar-rēṣūa.

Two oxen of three years of age, one of them (ritually) 'pure,' from the fattening stable, (and) two oxen of two years of age, (ritually) 'pure,' of Šamaš-zēru-iqīša, son of Innin-šumu-uṣur, in total four oxen (for the) selection (for offerings) of the 16th day of Ṭebētu.

19 shekels (of silver) of Ištar-šumu-uṣur and Ina-ṣilli-Ayakku, sons of Nabû-īpuš, (for the) selection (for offerings) of 16th day of Ṭebētu.

90 litres (of barley or dates) (have been given to) Arad-Innin, son of Ibni-Ištar.

16th of Ṭebētu, year 15 of Nabonidus, king of Babylon."

(YOS 19, 297, Eanna archive)[19]

A sub-type of the "multiple transaction receipts" is the "list."[20] I define as a list a text which records a number of transactions of the same type. Usually, nearly the entire qualitative information regarding these transactions is given in the heading. The entries which follow are made up only by the amounts of the commodity treated and the name of the person responsible. They are not concluded by a verb. The tablets are nearly always portrait-format ones, and many have subscripts with summations.

---

[19] 3 gur ^{Id}*a-num-ik-ṣur* ^{I}zálag-*e-a, u* ^{I}*ina*-giš.gi$_{6}$-^{d}*taš-met* ^{lú}ḫun.gá^{me} *šá dul-lu, ina* é *a-ki-tu*$_{4}$ *ip-pu-šu,* 2 (pi) 3 bán pad.ḫi.a-*su šá* iti.ab ^{Id}*a-num*-en-ùru *šá* é šu^{II}, 6 *ne-sep* 1 *qa* ì.giš ^{I}mu-ùru a ^{Id}ag-lugal-šeš^{me}-*šú,* ½ ma.na 2½ gín kù.babbar *ka-ra-al-lu šá šá sa-la-mu, še-éb-ru a-na bat-qa ina* igi ^{Id}utu-mu ^{lú}kù.dim, 2 gun 20 ma.na zabar 14 ma.na an.na, *a-na ṣu-uḫ-ḫu-ru,* 1 *pag-ra šá* us.tur^{mušen} ^{Id}inanna-*re-ṣu-ú-a* igi^{ir}, 2 gu$_{4}$ 3me *ina lìb-bi* 1 kù ta ^{é}*ú-re-e,* 2 gu$_{4}$ 2me kù^{me} *šá* ^{Id}utu-numun-ba^{šá} a ^{Id}*in-nin*-mu-ùru, pab 4 gu$_{4}$^{me} *pa-ra-su šá* iti.ab ud.16.kam, 19 gín^{me} *šá* ^{Id}inanna-mu-ùru *u* ^{I}*ina*-giš-gi$_{6}$-é.an.na, a^{me} *šá* ^{Id}ag-dù^{uš} *pa-ra-su šá* iti.ab ud.16.kam, 2 (pi) 3 bán še.bar ^{I}ìr-^{d}*in-nin* a ^{I}dù-^{d}inanna, (rev.) iti.ab ud.16.kam mu.15.kam, ^{d}ag-ní.tuk lugal tin.tir^{ki}

[20] Cf. Da Riva 2002: 23ff.

An example:

> "Estimated yield of dates (of the gardens) of the prebendary gardeners along the canal of Šamaš. 23th of Abu, year 33 of Nebuchadnezzar, king of Babylon.
>
> 8 640 litres: Bēl-aḫḫē-erība
>
> 6 024 litres: Na'id-Marduk
>
> ... (20 more entries of the same kind)
>
> Total: 50 400 litres of dates, (measured) according to the ratio of six *mašīḫu*-measures to 180 litres, (that is, according to) the measure used for estimations of yield." (BM 67096; Jursa 1995 No. 19)

As defined, a list should contain exclusively either entries for income or for expenditures. However, there are cases in which a list of temple income is expanded by the addition of entries for expenditures, that is deductions made from the income recorded. Such texts are combinations of lists and "multiple transaction receipts."

The text types treated so far mostly concern transfers which have been already concluded. In contrast to these, the so-called letter orders, the next group to be considered, exclusively deal with future transfers: they typically convey the central administration's authorisation to effect a payment to an individual on the fringes of the institutional household.[21] Letter orders are usually written on landscape-format tablets (not on the thin, portrait-format tablets typical for real letters), and they are mostly sealed and dated,[22] which normal letters are not.

> "Letter of Muranu, the (royal) supervisor (*bēl piqitti*) of Eanna, and the scribes of Eanna to Tattannu, our brother. Bēl and Nabû may ordain our brother's health and well-being. Give 7 800 litres of dates from his allowance for prebendary service (*maššartu*) to Bēl-kāṣir. Fifth of Nisānu, year 12 of Darius, king [of Babylon], king of the lands."
> (NBC 11498, Eanna archive)[23]

A text category not well studied are memoranda (Akkadian *taḫsistu*), often informal notes drafted by administrators for their own purposes. Their distinctive characteristic is the fact that they are written

---

[21] See MacGinnis 1995 for Ebabbar.

[22] Several exceptions occur in the Eanna archive.

[23] A copy and a transliteration of this text will be included in the forthcoming edition by E. Frahm and myself of the unpublished letter orders and letters from the Eanna archive in the Yale Babylonian Collection.

in the first person singular or plural as if they were letters. The following is an example from the Eanna archive:

> "120 litres of sesame which had been at the disposal of Nabû-balāssu-iqbi from Udannu are (now) at the disposal of Šamaš-šumu-iddin, son of Nabû-balāssu-iqbi. This is disregarding the six shekels of silver, the price of a barge about which Šamaš-šumu-iddin has said as follows: I have delivered the ropes for it.
>
> 3 600 litres of barley (?) (and) 306+ litres of sesame are at the disposal of the man (or: men) from Udannu.
>
> 14 400 litres of barley, the remainder of the tithe of the 33rd year, are at the disposal of Balāssu, son of …
>
> Ina-tēši-ēṭer has delivered the dates thereof (*i.e.*, of the tithe) in the 35th year and they have been booked together with the *sūtu*-rent deliveries of Nabû-ušabši. We shall deduct (this) from (the amount due from) him." (VS 20 71)[24]

This is clearly a memorandum drafted by accountants for internal use at an intermediate stage of the accounting process: it refers to action still to be taken. More often texts of this type simply state that something has been done.[25]

The most complex text group in the present context are lists and accounts which gather and sometimes also summarise information pertaining to several different transactions from a certain viewpoint. These

---

[24] 3 (pi) 2 bán še.giš.ì *šá ina* igi ^{Id}ag-tin-*su*-e, ^{lú}*ú-dan-nu-a-a ina* igi ^{Id}utu-mu-mu, a ^{Id}ag-tin-*su*-e *šá la* 6 gín ⸢kù.babbar⸣, šám 1 ^{giš}má.gíd.da *šá* ^{Id}utu-⸢mu-mu⸣, *iq-bu̥-ú um-ma áš-la-ti-*⸢*šú*⸣ *at-*⸢*ta-din*⸣, 20 ⸢gur$^{?}$ še$^{?}$.bar$^{?}$⸣ 1[+x gu]r 3 (pi) 3 bán še.giš.ì, *ina* igi ^{lú}*ú-dan-nu-a-a*, 80 gur ⸢še.bar⸣ *re-ḫe-et* ⸢*šá*⸣$^{?}$ *eš-ru-ú, šá* mu.33.kam *ina pa-ni*, ^{I}din-*su* a ^{I}⸢x x x⸣ ⸢zú⸣.lum.ma *šá ina lìb-bi* ^{I}*ina-*⸢sùḫ-sur⸣ [*i-na*], mu.35.kam *iš-šá-am-ma it-ti*, ^{giš}bán *šá* ^{Id}⸢ag⸣-gál^{ši} *šaṭ-ru, it-ti-šú ni-nam-ḫi-si*$^{!}$

[25] *E.g.*, from Uruk YBC 9192, a witnessed memorandum dealing with silver expenses, including the phrase: "we have sent the silver via PN_1 and PN_2," YBC 4112, dealing with income of Ebabbar of Larsa ("we have given …"), NBC 4764, dealing with wool ("we have measured …"), or YBC 7434 (to be published by P.-A. Beaulieu); and from Sippar BM 54097, a memorandum (*taḫsistu*) concerning barley deliveries ("I received …, I brought …") or BM 78923 (to be published by S. Zawadzki), dealing with the delivery of bitumen ("we have struck a balance"). See also below on YBC 4028 (note 48). Joannès, TEBR No. 7 and 24 are examples of such texts from later archives from Nippur.

texts, which are not numerous,[26] are overall better represented in the Eanna archive. For the drafting of such accounts, earlier receipts and related documents would have had to be systematically sifted and relevant information extracted. It is however only in rare cases that individual tablets on which later accounts are based can be identified.[27]

Some of these texts focus on certain transaction types and list (all or several?) occurrences of these over a period of time. The long two-column tablet *Cyr* 34+ from the Ebabbar archive, for instance, names probably all barley cultivators of Ebabbar together with the dues expected from them at harvest time in the fourteenth year of Nabonidus.[28] The organising principle of such compilations is however not always so readily apparent.[29] The most impressive example from the Ebabbar archive as far as the quantities treated are concerned is *Cyr* 31. This is, according to the heading, "a settlement of accounts of barley, dates and emmer for the regular offerings of Šamaš, which $PN_{1\text{-}3}$, the scribes of Ebabbar, have established according to (the data on) the (pertinent) writing board."[30] The summary gives a remarkable total of over 2.000.000 litres of staples as expenses over four years for "offering materials (*sattukku*), prebendary income (*pappasu*) and rations." The main part of the text (which is unfortunately damaged) consists of individual entries of high amounts of staples expended for various purposes which however are not exclusively linked to the prebendary system; also rations and fodder for animals are mentioned. Bongenaar has rightly observed that "the heading of a text not always covers its contents."[31] As it stands, *Cyr* 31 seems to be a summary of the main types of expenses of foodstuffs, but there is no way of telling if the listing is complete and what its purpose may have been.[32]

---

26 This is a good indication of the the available material's ephemeral nature; see van Driel 1998:63.

27 For examples see below notes 29, 37 and 49.

28 Jursa 1995:170ff.

29 Note from the early Ebabbar archive the "Sammelurkunden" treated by Da Riva 2002:33ff. These texts collect data from individual debt notes (some of which survive) for an unclear purpose; the only common link the transactions assembled share may be the scribe.

30 See Bongenaar 1997: 143^{+150}.

31 Bongenaar 1997:143.

32 New readings after collation (in addition to those given by Bongenaar): obv. 5: … zí[z*.àm; 6: … *ki**-[…; 9: 15* še.bar …; 10: 16* še.bar … uš.bar$^{\text{meš}*}$ [; 11: … *a-na* $^{\text{d}*}$inanna*-giš*.tuk* […; 12: …^{lú}*ši**-[*ra-ku* …; 14: …]

One of the clearer examples for similar texts from the Eanna archive is YOS 19, 213, a large single-column tablet of 89 lines listing silver arrears owed to the temple resulting mostly from the sale of cattle and sheep. The time period covered is the first to the thirteenth year of Nabonidus.[33] The tablet, which according to its heading is the second of a series, has no summary or conclusion. UCP 9/2, 113ff. No. 60 is a three-column list of silver expenditures, each dated individually to a day in the sixth or seventh year of Nebuchadnezzar II.[34] Some entries may be linked to a (possibly one and the same) building project: they concern baskets, work on a canal, bricks, boat rentals, payment of hirelings for brick-making, straw, firewood or the like for firing of a kiln, naphtha and reeds. Other entries seem unrelated. They concern the purchase of aromatics, wax, quivers, bows, wool, leather gourds and other, unidentified leather objects. The text seems to have neither an explanatory heading nor a concluding summary. Another three-column text of this kind is YOS 17, 360, which lists at least 28 individually dated transactions from the fourteenth year of Nebuchadnezzar involving gold, silver and goats. The information given in the heading, "Gold income which has been sold against silver or given for expenses: Ayyāru, fourteenth year of Nebuchadnezzar," correctly describes only some of the entries. Also this text has no summary. Its overall rationale is unclear.

Texts which intend to cover the temple's entire dealings with a person or a group over a certain period of time by drawing up the balance between debit and credit are referred to as "balanced accounts."[35] Well-preserved examples are again very few, but they are sufficient to show that these texts follow closely the model established by Sumerian administrative practice in the third millennium.[36] Their basic structure is very simple. They consist of three, sometimes four main sections:

⸢pad*.ḫi*⸣.[a …; rev. 2′: pad.ḫi.a ⸣[$^{\text{ú*}}$ …; 3′: … zú.lum.ma _ku*-u_[_m*_ …; 5′: … 3 $^{\text{lú*}}$erín^{meš} …, 7′: … _šá_ é* […; 9′: 3* ME …; 10′: … še.giš.ì _sat*-tuk_ […; 15′: _al_-⸢x⸣ (possibly RU, mistake for _la_?) _er*-bi* šá_ 4 …; left edge 1 (Strassmaier's line 30): … še.bar _u*_ ⸢zú*.lum*.ma*⸣ ta …

33 There are other accounts which cover more than one year, _e.g._, TCL 13, 227 (five years of agricultural income), VS 20, 120 (birds kept or delivered by bird fatteners over six years) and YBC 3990 (materials used by a weaver over five years).

34 The king's name is not mentioned in the preserved part of the text; the date can however be established by means of prosopographical comparisons.

35 The Akkadian technical term is _nikkassu epēšu_ "to strike a balance."

36 See Englund 1990: 13ff.

[1] Debit section (the Neo-Sumerian sag-níg-GA-ra) from which
[2] Credit section (the Neo-Sumerian šà-bi-ta … zi-ga section) is deducted, which yields
[3] Balance: "deficit," if (1)-(2) > 0, "surplus," if (1)-(2) < 0 (LÁ-NI and diri respectively)
[4] date; optional additional information

An example dealing with the activities of a certain tax farmer over one year:

> "[1] (heading:) 91 800 litres of barley, tithes owed to Šamaš by Marduka, son of Bēl-īpuš, and his men for year ten of Nabonidus, king of Babylon.
> [2] (thereof:) 2 700 litres (delivered) to Murānu, for seed, by Šadûnu, the overseer of the bowmen.
> … (more entries of a similar kind)
> [3] In total, he (Marduka) has delivered 78 210 litres. The remainder is 13 590 litres.
> [4] Sixth day of Ṭebētu, year ten of Nabonidus, king of Babylon.
> A balance has been struck. This is in addition to the earlier deficit owed by him."
> (*Nbn* 462 = Jursa 1998: 31ff.; Ebabbar archive)

Any arrears or credits established in such balanced accounts were carried over into the next year, unless of course a final balance was struck which was supposed to settle all accounts.[37]

A variant of these balanced accounts deals with specific sums, documenting the use to which these have been put. Moore Michigan 89 for instance is an account of silver probably sent from Eanna to Babylon in several instalments (lines 1-6) and used (*ina libbi* "thereof") for different purposes, mostly for rations for craftsmen (lines 7-61). This text does not strike a balance between the debit and the credit section. There are several structurally similar texts from the Ebabbar archive, *e.g.*, *Nbn* 658, dealing with flour due as prebendary income for two years, or the fragment BM 54956 concerning silver income from house rentals.

---

37 The arrears mentioned in the present text were carried over into next year's debit. They are referred to in *Nbn* 493 from the beginning of Nabonidus's eleventh year.

The most refined version of the balanced account is the tabulated account. Texts of this type are particularly well attested in the context of animal husbandry. An exceptionally well preserved example has been treated by van Driel and Nemet-Nejat 1994. This is a large eleven-column summary account (bearing the subscript *nikkassū epšūtu*) for an institutional herd of sheep and goats for the period from the 37th year of Nebuchadnezzar II to the first year of Neriglissar. Not only are the different kinds and age groups of animals dealt with, but also their products: wool, goat hair, hides. The general accounting principles, the way one year's result is carried forward to the next year's account, are clear, but the high number of mistakes in the summaries of this text is striking. This casts serious doubt on the overall quality of the book-keeping: "the mistakes occurring in the crucial final section of NBC 4897 again raise the question of how the administration could work with this kind of accounting."[38]

At the end of this typological survey it remains to point out the unresolved—and due to the nature of the evidence unresolvable—issue of the importance of the Aramaic part of the written documentation produced by Neo-Babylonian temples. Neo-Babylonian society was certainly bilingual to a considerable degree, with Akkadian on the decline. It is known that both the Ebabbar and the Eanna employed Aramaic scribes, *sēpiru*. In the Ebabbar, one such scribe at a time even belonged to the top level of the temple administration.[39]

Very few traces of the work of these scribes survive since their parchment and leather scrolls and their wooden writing boards have perished. Aramaic epigraphs on clay tablets are well attested, but they cannot have been indispensable for archival purposes: for this, they are not frequent enough.[40] In most cases they very briefly summarise the contents or at least label the tablet.[41] In one exceptional case from the Eanna archive however the epigraph adds information which is not

---

[38] Van Driel and Nemet-Nejat 1994:57. A forthcoming article by S. Zawadzki will re-examine this text.

[39] See Bongenaar 1997:59f. with further literature.

[40] See most recently Zadok 2003:558ff. Of the 231 epigraphs listed by him, less than 50 come from the large temple archives. Zadok points out however (559) that such epigraphs may in fact have been far more numerous than generally assumed, since notes written in ink and not scratched into the tablet surface may have disappeared.

[41] See Zadok 2003:574ff.

contained in the tablet, probably documenting a later stage of the proceedings. This is a rare glimpse of the interplay of alphabetic and cuneiform writing in the temple administrations.[42] However, cuneiform tablets from temple archives only occasionally explicitly refer to other documentation written in Aramaic,[43] and there are no systematic and structural gaps in the extant documentation which would warrant the assumption that a certain text type was exclusively written in Aramaic. I would at the moment be disinclined to attribute to Aramaic record-keeping more than an ancillary rôle in the temple archives here under discussion.[44]

Primary and secondary records

Piotr Steinkeller (this volume) has argued with good reason that at least in the Ur III archives analysed by him "written records were prepared *post factum* and in locations different than those where the facts in question had actually occurred," drawing far-reaching conclusions regarding the function of the written documentation from this observation. The kind of material on which Steinkeller bases his thesis is not entirely limited to the Ur III period. Possibly a similar claim can be made for the

---

[42] Frame 2001: 100ff., interpreting the Aramaic in the light of the Murašû tablet Ni. 2670: see Frame 2001: 109f.

[43] See CAD S *s.v. sipru* "document in Aramaic."

[44] Unless of course Aramaic was used exclusively or at least predominantly on wooden writing boards. Evidence from Borsippa (BM 26484) proves that Aramaic scribes employed by the Ezida temple were responsible for the accounting pertaining to prebends and prebendaries by keeping lists of payments and service periods on parchment (*niāru*). These must have been lists very similar to those that we know were elsewhere kept on wooden writing boards. But one cannot generalise from this one case. It is known that Akkadian literary texts were also written on such writing boards. So there is definite proof that cuneiform too was used on this medium. —Typological side issues which would merit further treatment are the occasional drawings, hatchings, and archaic signs that appear on the tablets, and the very occasional appearance of case tablets which are not letters—something which according to the general opinion should not exist in Neo-Babylonian. On drawings and the like see Zawadzki and Jursa 2001: 357ff. Two examples of case tablets are known: BM 66261(A) [edited below, appendix 2] and Jursa 1998: 61ff. and 112f. No. 14. There is however a number of (fragmentary) unpublished Neo-Babylonian tablet cases in the British Museum. Further research will, I hope, clarify the text type and archive they belong to.

Middle Babylonian archives from Nippur.[45] The evidence from the Neo-Babylonian institutional archives however does at least not contradict the more traditional view which assumes that the economic transaction and the drafting of the pertinent record were normally not separated by more than a brief period of time at most.[46] This holds true at least for those texts which, following R. Englund, can be called "primary documentation," viz. all those texts which are not themselves based on other written sources but constitute the first or primary record of an economic transaction to be produced by an administration. It may of course be true that some or indeed many records were not written at the very moment a transaction was made,[47] but in general there is no need to definitely dissociate the economic fact from the drafting of its documentation. There are, on the contrary, texts which only make sense if one assumes that they were written more or less contemporaneously with the transactions they refer to. The multiple transaction receipt YOS 19, 297 translated above, for instance, documents the transfer of dates or barley, oil, silver, bronze, tin, some heads of cattle, and a dead duck. Clearly this and similar tablets record activities at a general purpose storehouse. The individual transactions have nothing in common except the fact that they occurred on the same day, certainly in the same place and under the responsibility of the same scribe or accountant. Combining these transactions on one tablet only at a later date would not have been a very sensible thing to do, since at more advanced stages of the accounting process the different commodities would have

[45] This assumption is based on evidence from the so-called storehouse archive studied preliminarily by Sassmannshausen 2001: 187ff. I hope to return to this issue elsewhere.

[46] A separate issue are those tablets which were prepared beforehand by scribes who left blank spaces where (usually quantitative) information was to be filled in when it would become available. These tablets are recognisable whenever such lacunae remain, as *e.g.*, in GCCI 1 60. 79 and 133. Other texts were modified when the need arose: *e.g.*, in a certain group of receipts from the early Ebabbar archive, the notation *ul eṭer* "not paid" was often changed at a later date to *eṭer* "paid" by deleting the negation *ul* with the stylus (Da Riva 2002: 20).

[47] *E.g.*, the issue of travel provisions is routinely noted as having been given to people "who have gone" (*ša … illikū*) to such-and-such a place. This implies that the transaction took place prior to the drafting of the tablet (see for example CT 57 637; CT 56 301. 384; BM 63943. 64043; but note the rarer cases of present tense forms ("who will go") in MacGinnis 1995 No. 4. 12 and *Nbn* 1127).

to be recorded separately anyway on different types of records. The only plausible explanation for the existence of primary records of this type is that scribes compiled these texts to keep track of their daily activities, noting down individual transactions in the sequence they occurred and certainly not long after the fact.

Secondary documentation based on earlier records by contrast could be written days, months or even years after the primary texts.[48] Lists, for instance, may frequently not have been intended to furnish the primary documentation for the transactions concerned. Their compilation rather may be due to some accounting process, such as the summing up of payments made on various occasions by people belonging to a certain group. This is particularly likely in cases in which not only deliveries to the temple are listed and summed up, but also information about the outstanding balance is given.

Summary lists and (balanced) accounts are mostly secondary documents based on earlier written evidence.[49] The way such accounts were drawn up and used is more or less clear; it is however not self-evident how frequently and systematically this was done. This is an important question which at this point can only be answered preliminarily; we will return to this issue below, in the context of the discussion of the wooden writing boards. As we have seen above, in the discussion of YOS 19, 213 and similar texts, the accounting period can be rather long (up to 13 years), and the rationale behind the compilation far from clear. While it is possible and indeed likely that balanced accounts of the type

---

[48] Note YBC 4028 (Beaulieu 2000: 104), a list of barley deliveries: the scribal note accompanying an entry saying "x measures (of barley) the written documentation for which I have not received" (x *mašīḫū ša šaṭāršunu lā amḫur*(*u*)) proves that a) otherwise the scribe used written documentation to draw up the current text and b) he had other sources of information (oral reports?) at his disposal as well on which he could fall back if written records were not available. One can assume that secondary records were meant to be stored with the documentation on which they were based (van Driel 1998:63), but this may not have been the case anymore even in antiquity when these archives were deposited (see below on the issue of the nature of the preserved archives).

[49] A good example is furnished by *Nbn* 350 and 398 (Jursa 1995:96 and 169f). The former text records deliveries of barley which in the latter text are combined with data from other texts and summarised. This text also strikes a yearly balance for individual cultivators' dues by establishing their arrears or, exceptionally, credits. A similar case is the payment referred to in *Nbn* 618:5-8 which is duly mentioned in the pertinent settlement of accounts *Nbn* 656:5.

represented by *Nbn* 462 were drawn up regularly, maybe yearly, for tax or rent farmers or herdsmen, thus forming interlocking chains of accounts similar to those posited by Steinkeller and others for the Ur III period, it seems unlikely that long lists such as YOS 19, 213 (arrears of payments related to the sale of cattle) or YOS 17, 360 (transactions in gold, mostly) were compiled regularly by the temple administrations. Their internal structure is too haphazard, they tend to lack conclusions, and the accounting period occasionally is too long to be really practical. The reason of course is that the temples' business with entrepreneurs—and others on the margin of the temple households—needed constant supervision, whereas activities well within the scope of the normal running of the temple administration, such as gold or silver transactions or the dealings with the temples' craftsmen, were far less problematical. The existing specimens of summary lists and (balanced) accounts for such centrally administrated transactions will be the result of exceptional circumstances. In general, the purpose such summary lists could have served were just as well fulfilled by wooden writing boards, on which see below. This is born out by the attestations of the phrase *nikkassu epēšu* "to strike a balance" (and variants). The expression is used both in connection with real balanced accounts in which debits and credits are compared[50] and lists in which entries of a certain kind are collected and summarised.[51] Usually the texts concern either the dealings of the temples with 'outsiders' of different kinds, for instance tithe farmers, shepherds and generally entrepreneurs, or refer to well-defined, not continuous and sometimes not centrally administered undertakings (building activities, purchases, etc.).[52] The only notable exception to this rule is the issuing of materials for the preparation of

---

50 *E.g.*, *Nbn* 462.

51 *E.g.*, *Cyr* 31.

52 *E.g.*, BM 53913, BM 64080(?), *Nbn* 561, YOS 6, 209, YOS 7, 145, AUWE 11, 221, YOS 17, 328 and GCCI 2, 371 (sheep and cattle), BM 78923 (purchase of bitumen), *Camb* 176 (purchase of sesame), *Nbn* 462, BM 61184, BM 75567 and BM 73522 (tithes and tithe farmers), BM 62587, BM 62339, BM 62634, BM 61782, YOS 3, 17, 31 and 133 (building activities; performance of personnel and/or materials and silver), BM 70197 (transport costs), *Cyr* 180, BM 62000, YOS 3, 40, YOS 6, 159, YOS 7, 131 (agricultural income), BM 63920 (barley delivered to the overseer of the prison for grinding), *Camb* 194 (bird breeding), *Camb* 254, *Bard* 25 and CT 57, 153 (purchase of cattle), BM 72850 (purchase of dates), BM 63823 (dates issued for beer). Exception: *e.g.*, *Nbn* 810, issue of material to a smith.

offerings to prebendaries. In this context the drawing up of summary accounts seems to have been a regular occurrence.[53]

Summing up the typological discussion, we have seen text types pertaining to different levels of the accounting process: primary records, mostly receipts, regularly drawn up more or less at the time the transaction takes place; the lists, some of which certainly are primary records just as the receipts, while others are later compilations based on other written evidence, and finally the accounts for the establishment of which other documentation must have been used regularly.

The relationship between these text types will be discussed in the context of the temples' accounting procedures in more detail later on. The fundamental typological distinctions established have however also important ramifications when one turns to the archives as a whole.

The nature of the Neo-Babylonian institutional archives

The archaeological context, the scope of the preserved textual record and the nature of the Eanna archive as a whole have been thoroughly discussed by van Driel 1998. The main purpose of the institutional administration was on the one hand "assignation of labor and other resources" for productive purposes and on the other hand dealing with "what was produced or bought …, and all the accounting that this implied" (van Driel 1998: 62). He stresses the ephemeral character of the texts: "the clay tablets … are in part the authenticated proofs, like debt notes and receipts, required in the accounting process and in other respects an enormous mass of notes and extracts compiled in the process of accounting. But the real accounts—the ledgers—, are not available …" (van Driel 1998: 63). Van Driel stresses the obvious fact that to serve a purpose, the masses of receipts and debt notes would have had to be kept with the accounts which had been drawn up on their basis. This is however not the case. As was pointed out earlier (above at note 27), it is only in exceptional cases that entries in accounts can be traced back to known individual tablets—a fact which cannot be entirely blamed on partial publication of the textual record and on lack of pertinent research. The Eanna archive may just be a "mass of virtually useless documentation put aside because it has become too cumbersome," van Driel tells us.[54] Current accounts, documentation

[53] *E.g.*, *Cyr* 66 and 118, *Dar* 21, BM 61347, BM 64004, *Camb* 258, *Cyr* 94(?).

[54] Van Driel 1998: 64.

dealing with real estate and similar records of essential importance are mostly missing and seem to have been removed:[55] we are dealing with a "dead" archive (see above at note 11). *Mutatis mutandis* these conclusions hold true also for the Ebabbar archive, as shall now be briefly demonstrated.

What is today called the Ebabbar archive was excavated by Rassam in the 1880s in a few rooms within the precinct of the temple of Šamaš at Sippar, modern Abū Ḥabbah.[56] No detailed archaeological records for these excavations are available. The little that is known has been conveniently assembled by Julian Reade and by Christopher Walker and Dominique Collon.[57] There are no proper excavation records which could help to clarify the issue of the archive's nature. All one can use is the evidence that can be gleaned from the make-up of the British Museum collections containing Sippar material. Tablets were found and shipped in such vast numbers in the 1880s that the assumption is reasonable that at least parts of groups of tablets which had been found together arrived together in the museum and were thus registered in the same collections. Everyone who has worked with the Sippar collections is of course aware of the fact that they contain tablets from different sources and periods all mixed up, but the chaos is not so great that one could not discern at least some patterns.

We are dealing in fact with two larges archives. The smaller group is the "early Ebabbar archive." It consists of at least five thousand tablets and fragments mostly in the 82–3–23 and 81–7–1 collection (most of them unpublished), with strays in other Sippar collections in the British Museum as well as in other museums, such as in the Vorderasiatisches Museum in Berlin. Its temporal range extends from the late Assyrian period to roughly the middle of the reign of Nebuchadnezzar II. The tablets are quite homogenous in content and appearance and clearly distinct from the later Ebabbar tablets. They must therefore be kept apart from the rest of the material. Their unequal distribution among

---

[55] This happened in the second year of Darius. It does not follow that the temple as such was destroyed or even suffered serious misfortunes in this time. It may nevertheless not be totally wrong to assume political reasons for the apparent restructuring and 'clean-up' of the Eanna's administration. See below Appendix 3 on the analogous evidence from the Ebabbar archive, where the documentation ends in the second year of Xerxes.

[56] See the general introduction to the archive in Bongenaar 1997:2ff.

[57] Reade 1986 and Walker and Collon 1980.

the Sippar collections, *i.e.*, the high density of pertinent tablets in 82–3–23 and 81–7–1 must mean that they were found in a group. Apparently they were kept at least partly separate from the second group, the main Ebabbar archive. This "early Ebabbar archive" has been recently treated by Da Riva 2002, I shall therefore not investigate it in any detail. Suffice it to say that there is no reason to believe that this is not a dead archive. The vast majority of tablets is administrative; they must have lost their usefulness long before they were deposited close to the later Ebabbar archive. Furthermore, Da Riva has shown that the distribution of the tablets within the archive's temporal range is as one would expect it to be: the number of tablets peaks during the second decade of Nabopolassar's reign and then drops continuously until about the twentieth year of Nebuchadnezzar II.

The larger and later group is the Ebabbar archive proper. Pertinent tablets appear in all the Sippar collections, although only infrequently within the range of numbers dominated by the early Ebabbar archive. Otherwise their distribution does not seem to follow a discernible pattern. Some collections have unusual numbers of well-preserved tablets, but this is certainly the result of modern selection. The temporal range of the tablets extends from the middle of Nebuchadnezzar's reign until the second year of Xerxes. The beginning and the end of this period are clearly less well represented than the middle; the greatest density of tablets is to be found during the middle of the reign of Nabonidus. This observation is based mostly on the roughly 7 500 tablets from this group which I have read; that is something between 20 and 25 percent of the total. This will be representative; a perusal of the catalogues conveys the same impression. Thus the temporal distribution of the tablets is consistent with the pattern expected in a dead archive.

The distribution of the different text groups will be demonstrated by analysis of two samples: from a chronologically arranged list of Sippar tablets, two groups of two hundred tablets each were selected arbitrarily; one from the fifth to seventh year of Nabonidus, from the middle of the archive's temporal range, the other from the twenty-fourth to thirtieth year of Darius, from the last years (until just eight years before the very end of the documentation).

The unevenness of the texts' distribution expected in a dead archive is immediately apparent: the 200 Darius texts (fig. 2) cover about six years, the 200 Nabonidus texts (fig. 1) just about two—and this although an effort has been made to include more unpublished material from the reign of Darius from the collections of the British Museum.

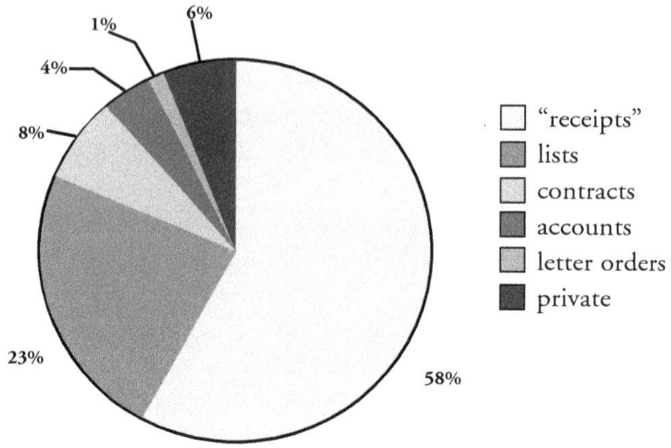

Fig. 1: Ebabbar archive: Text types from Nbn 5-7

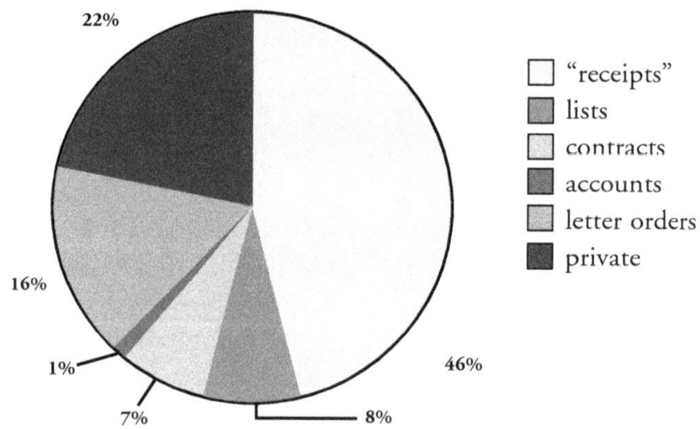

Fig. 2: Ebabbar archive: Text types from Dar 24–30

In both samples, the receipts, that is the ephemeral documents of the day-to-day dealings of the administration, are the largest group. The second largest group in the Nabonidus sample are the lists, the numbers of which however decline sharply under Darius. The same is true for the balanced accounts, of which there is only one in the later group. This means a marked decrease in numbers of those documents which represent more advanced stages of the bookkeeping process and which may have had more than just a passing importance for the administration. The percentage of legal contracts remains more or less the same.

However, nearly all the texts are debt notes for agricultural dues or witnessed receipts, that is texts of probably only temporal importance. Finally, there is a great increase in the number of letter orders in the late period. These texts are of only short-term interest to the administration; it is highly unlikely that they would have been kept for a more than a very limited period. Another feature particular to the reign of Darius is the higher percentage of private contracts mixed among the Ebabbar texts.[58] They come from several archives which need not be treated in detail here. In the present context the main point to make is that they all share one characteristic: none could be considered the archive owners' core archive; all are "dead" in the sense described above.

Altogether, the notable shift in the distribution of text types (fig. 3) comes down to an increase in the numbers of the more marginal text types. We lack for the late period not only property documents and the like, which are already absent earlier, but also most of the evidence for the more advanced stages of the accounting process, which is present in the material for earlier years. The picture is consistent with the dead archive hypothesis. See below Appendix 3 for historical ramifications.

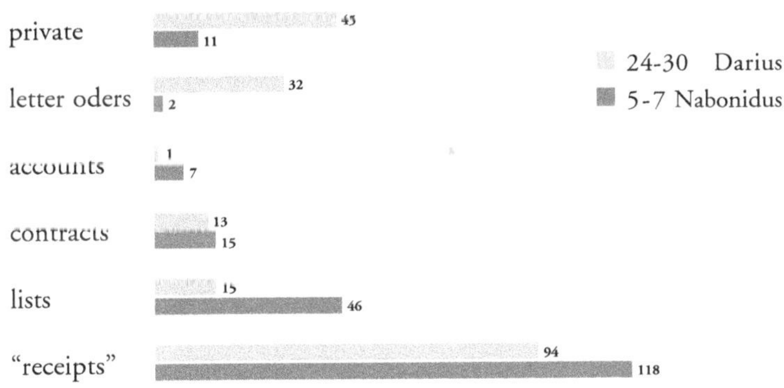

Fig. 3: Comparison of text types

What does the archive document? Fig. 4 shows the subject matter of the receipts.

---

[58] The private texts do not include those belonging to the two recently published large private archives from Sippar (Jursa 1999; Waerzeggers 2001) which have been found mixed up with the main temple archive. If these texts had been taken into account too, the predominance of private texts from the period of Darius would have been even more pronounced.

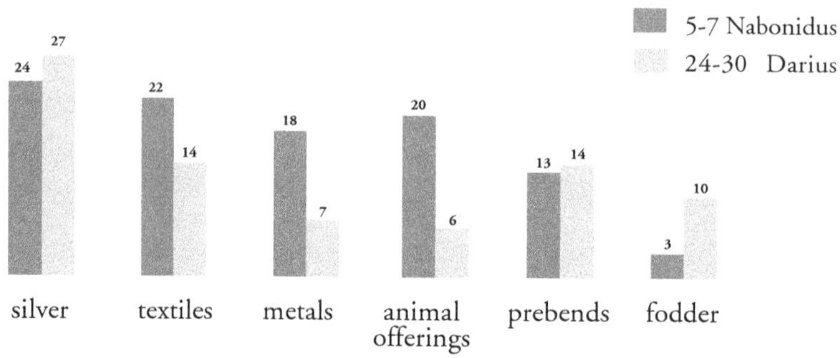

Fig. 4: The "receipts": Main subjects

The six subjects mentioned account for about 90 percent of the texts. Silver texts are of course concerned with outgoing and incoming silver. The majority of the "textiles" texts concern the issue of working materials to the weavers and the receipt of finished goods from them. Similarly, the metals texts concern the activities of the temple's smiths. The animal offering texts are for the most part not real offering lists—these are only frequent in the early Ebabbar archive—but transfers of animals from the outer herds or from other sources into the care of the so-called "shepherds of the regular offerings," who had to prepare the beasts for the offering ceremony. The label "prebends" refers to texts mostly concerned with the issue of working materials to the prebendary bakers and brewers who were responsible for the preparation of the food offerings. The fodder texts concern the issue of barley to the fattening stable.

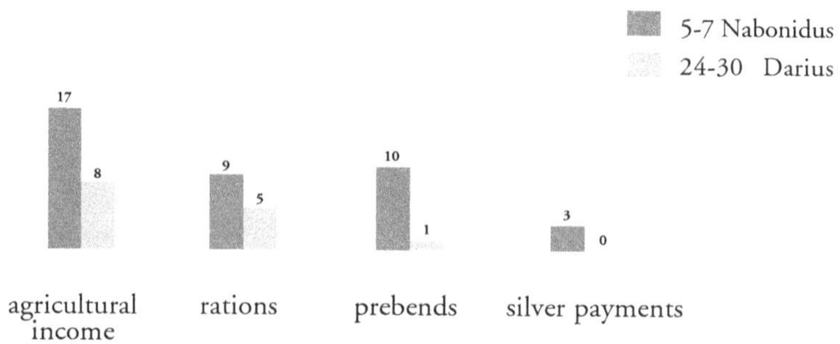

Fig. 5: The lists: Main subjects

The main subjects of the lists given in fig. 5 cover 86 and 93 percent respectively of all the lists in the samples. "Agricultural income" is self explanatory; all the various dues and taxes attested have been lumped together. Ration lists are attested mostly for the personnel working in the inner city of Sippar. The label "prebends" refers again mostly to payments made to bakers and brewers in connection with the food offerings.

Is it possible to identify different departments, workshops or the like, that have generated this material? The Ebabbar archive includes, for instance, hundreds of texts documenting the issue of metals to smiths as working material and the return of finished objects by the smiths. These texts—which have been dubbed the "smith file"—can be compared to the craft archives known from the Ur III and Isin-Larsa periods. So do they come from the smiths' workshop? The answer is no. We don't hear about the smiths' tools, about their internal organisation, their work rosters, their overseers, etc. All that is documented is the smiths' interface with the central temple storehouses. The same is true basically for all the other groups of temple craftsmen, but also for the agricultural personnel and the various entrepreneurs. They normally appear in the sources only when they pay something into the storehouses or receive something from them. The extant documentation is that of an office probably based at the temple storehouses which primarily managed these central storage facilities, but also assigned labor, resources and duties to temple personnel and external entrepreneurs and monitored their performance by keeping track of deliveries to the storehouses.

An example to illustrate this point:

"Barley which has been paid out of the granary of the storehouse for the regular offering prepared by the bakers: fifth of Ṭebētu, year 24 of Darius, king of Babylon, king of the lands.

1 800 litres of barley as payment in part for the regular offerings of Ṭebētu have been given to Ribâta. This is in addition to the earlier (delivery).

90 litres as payment in part for the regular offerings of the shrine of Adad (have been given to) Erībāya. This is in addition to the earlier (delivery).

90 litres as payment in part for the regular offerings of Annunītu have been given to Uballissu-Gula.

45 litres as payment in part for the regular offerings of the shrine of Gula have been given to Iqīšāya.

540 litres of barley have been given as seed grain to Kalbi-Ba'u, Arad-Bunene and Gūzānu, the ploughmen of Bunānu.

180 litres have been given as as payment in part for fodder for the mother birds to Lū-idia. This is in addition to the earlier (delivery).

6 litres ditto (*i.e.*, as fodder) have been given to Nabû-ittannu for the bird house." (BM 64067, Ebabbar archive)[59]

According to the heading, this tablet concerns barley issued from the storehouse to the prebendary bakers. The individual entries document payments to bakers, but also the issuing of barley as seed grain to ploughmen and as fodder for birds to personnel of the bird house. Such tablets make sense only if they are considered to be part of the storehouse's bookkeeping and nothing else.

Writing boards and (selective) gathering of information

The ephemeral nature of the available documentation has already been sufficiently emphasised. There is however yet another limitation: we know not only that we don't have the most important documents, namely the real running accounts—the ledgers—, we even know that we can't expect to find them anywhere, as they were written on waxed wooden writing boards.[60]

These writing boards are of pivotal importance for the bookkeeping, so they will serve as point of departure for the discussion of the main characteristics of the Neo-Babylonian temples' bureaucratic regimes. There are different boards for different purposes. The following uses are attested in the Ebabbar archive:[61]

---

59 ⌜še.bar⌝ *šá* ta ^{é}*ka-lak šá* é gur$_{7}$-⌜*e*⌝$^{?}$, *a-na sat-tuk šá* ^{lú}mu sum^{na} iti.ab, ud.5.kam mu.24.kam ^{I}[*da-ri*]*-mu-šú,* lugal tin.tir^{ki} lugal kur.kur (dividing line), 10 gur še.bar *ina sat-tuk šá* iti.ab *a-na,* ^{I}*ri-bi-a-ta* sum^{na} *e-lat* igi^{tu_4}, 2 (pi) 3 bán *ina sat-tuk šá* é ^{d}im ^{I}su^{a} *e-lat* igi^{tu_4}, 2 (pi) 3 bán *ina sat-tuk šá* ^{d}*a-nu-ni-tu*$_{4}$ *a-na,* ^{I}tin-*su-*^{d}*gu-la* sum^{na}, 1 (pi) 1 bán 3 *qa ina sat-tuk šá* é ^{d}*gu-la, a-na* ^{I}ba^{šá}*-a* sum^{na}, 3 gur še.bar *a-na* še.numun *a-na,* ^{I}*kal-bi-*^{d}ká ^{I}ìr-^{d}ḫar «⌜x⌝», ^{I}*gu-za-nu* ^{lú}engar^{meš} *šá* ^{I}*bu-na-nu,* sum^{na} 1 gur *ina ki-sat-tu*$_{4}$ ama^{meš}, *a-na* ^{I}*lu-ú-di-ia* sum^{na} *e-lat* igi^{tu_4}, 1 bán min *a-na* é mušen.ḫi.a *a-na* ^{Id}ag-*it-tan-nu,* sum^{na}

60 MacGinnis 2002 has assembled most of the pertinent evidence from the Ebabbar archive. See above note 44 for the question of the language and the writing system used on these writing boards.

61 This list is based on MacGinnis 2002: 220f. with some additional references and different interpretations.

1. registers of agricultural land:[62] CT 22, 204
2. registers of temple personnel: BM 64026 (MacGinnis 2002: No. 12) and BM 62587 (temple slaves), BM 83464 (MacGinnis 2002: No. 5; gardeners)
3. accounts of silver: BM 68389 (MacGinnis 2002: No. 10); *Camb* 172
4. accounts of gold: BM 63469 (MacGinnis 2002: No. 4)
5. accounts of rations (for the personnel employed in the inner city): BM 63469 (MacGinnis 2002: No. 4), CT 22, 126 (?), BM 61336 (see note 74)
6. accounts of material issued for the preparation of food offerings (*maššartu*: BM 63469 [MacGinnis 2002: No. 4]; *ginû*: *Cyr* 31)
7. accounts of payments for prebendary income (*pappasu*):[63] BM 74570 (Jursa 1999: 47; MacGinnis 2002: No. 11[64]), *Nbn* 219, *Cyr* 256, BM 63469 (MacGinnis 2002: No. 4)
8. accounts of livestock: CT 55, 482. 596; BM 77960 (Da Riva 2002: 298).
9. accounts of various agricultural dues: MacGinnis 1995: No. 40 and BM 79570 (MacGinnis 2002: No. 9)[65] (*sūtu*), BM 74644 and BM 74564[66] (Jursa 1995: 39+88) (*imittu* of dates), BM 83895 (MacGinnis 2002: No. 6) and BM 61184 (Jursa 1998: 25f. 107f. No. 7) (tithes)
10. accounts of income derived of house rentals: BM 63469 (MacGinnis 2002: No. 4), CT 22, 14

---

[62] Not "seed grain" (MacGinnis 2002: 219 and 220).

[63] See also note 80.

[64] Both treatments cited are partly incorrect; see my forthcoming study referred to in note 80.

[65] Contrary to MacGinnis 2002: 220, the payment made by the *rab sūti* must have been noted on the writing board dealing with the *sūtu* dues.

[66] These texts have now been edited by MacGinnis 2002 as nos. 8 and 7 respectively. MacGinnis 2002: 220 mistakenly takes BM 74644 as referring to a writing board for prebendary income too. Since his understanding of the text differs from mine, a new translation is given here. "5 400 litres of dates, the prebendary income due for bakers' and brewers' service for the temple of Adad, for year thirty of King Darius, owed to Nergal-ēṭer, son of Taqīš-Gula, and Lâbâši, son of Bēl-ittannu, concerning which a letter (order) of the scribes of Ebabbar (has been sent) to Ša-pî-kalbi, the gardener in Laḫarat: Nergal-ēṭer and Lâbâši have received the(se) 5 400 litres of dates from the hands of Ša-pî-kalbi (as part) of the impost (*imittu*) of year thirty owed to the treasury of

Furthermore, there is one attestation of "large" (or major) writing boards, which would seem to imply that there were also smaller or minor ones.[67]

The evidence from the Eanna archive is not quite as rich, but structurally identical:[68]

1. registers of temple personnel, in particular of temple slaves: YOS 3, 17. 59; GCCI 2, 142; TCL 9, 103. 129; UCP 9, 99, No. 36; CRAI 47, 115; YOS 6, 116 (archers conscripted for military service); YOS 7, 167 (registering prebendary service)
2. accounts of rations (for temple personnel): YOS 3, 45. 81. 106;[69] TCL 9, 103
3. accounts of gold: BM 114478
4. accounts of livestock: TCL 12, 119
5. accounts of arrears of livestock: UCP 9, 99, No. 36; YOS 3, 41
6. accounts of various agricultural dues: YOS 3, 147 (barley, no further details given); YOS 3, 199 (barley income of one year); YOS 7, 109 (*imittu* of dates); YOS 7, 113 (dates due, probably *imittu*); NCBT 929 (dates, no further details given)
7. tax lists: NCBT 38 (register of *mār-banê* with *urāšu* obligations)

These lists of writing boards allow some insights into the structure of the temples' bookkeeping. Writing boards were used to keep track of transactions of a single type only. The writing board for prebendary income, for instance, would have included just that, *i.e.*, a list of all

Šamaš. Nergal-ēṭer and Lâbâši will have (the payment) entered in the writing board of Šamaš and give (evidence for this) to Ša-pî-kalbi." Disregarding the question how exactly the *ušazzaz … inamdin* clause is to be translated (Weszeli in Weszeli and Baker 1997: 233ff.; Stolper 2001: 120), it is obvious that Ša-pî-kalbi's payment has to be noted in the temple's books to prove his having discharged his obligation as a gardener, *i.e.*, in the writing board concerning *imittu*.

[67] BM 61336; see note 74.

[68] Note also the *zābil lēʾāni* "carrier of writing boards", possibly a kind of courier, mentioned in an unpublished ration list from the Eanna archive (BM 114533, seventh year of Cambyses).

[69] These letters, from the reign of Cambyses, prove that writing boards were kept for several decades for reference purposes: the writer urges his correspondent to look up such writing boards concerning rations from the times of the Chaldean kings Nebuchadnezzar, Neriglissar and Nabonidus.

prebendaries entitled to payments under that heading together with information on the current state of their individual accounts. It is known that the administration of the Eimbianu temple in Dilbat differentiated broadly between writing boards for income and for expenditures.[70] This is not attested explicitly either in Sippar or in Uruk, but the categories of attested writing boards given in the lists above show that this distinction could have been made there too.

Neither in the Ebabbar nor in the Ebabbar writing boards lumping together all incoming or outgoing amounts of dates or barley would have been kept. Incoming agricultural dues were recorded separately according to their type and certainly also their origin.[71] Likewise, the expenditures were noted on different boards according to type. Comparing the relevant writing boards attested in Sippar, namely those for rations, prebendary income and material for the food offerings, with the subjects of the "receipts" and lists, figs. 4 and 5, it becomes apparent that they cover all the subjects involving payments in kind with exception of the issues of fodder for the animals in the fattening stable. This probably means that one is entitled to postulate the existence of a writing board for fodder too.

Since the days of Mariano San Nicolò[72] it is the common opinion among students of Neo-Babylonian institutional archives that the main

---

[70] VS 6, 331 mentions ^{giš}da *šá er-bi gab-bi*, "writing board(s) for all sources of income," and ^{giš}da *šá te-lit gab-bi* "writing board(s) for all sources of expenditure." Note the expression ^{giš}da *kullu* "to keep (accounts on) a writing board," said of scribes.

[71] Lists like *Nbn* 398 may give a good idea how such a writing board would have been structured: It would have included a list of farmers and the produce expected or delivered, indicating if either a deficit or a surplus had accrued for individuals (cf. *Nbn* 398:9f: ... *a-tar** "surplus" and rev. 13′: ... *re-ḫi* "deficit"). Also the "SWU type" ledgers from Uruk dealing with prebendary payments may be comparable to the writing boards (see van Driel 1998:63).

[72] San Nicolò 1948. Cf. also for example Baker 2003:252f. and van Driel 1998:63. Note also the interesting parallel case of the Middle Assyrian evidence: Freydank 2001:103ff. MacGinnis's material (MacGinnis 2002:223ff.) includes evidence for the following accounting operations involving writing boards: (1) transfer of information from clay tablets to writing boards, (2) transfer of information from writing boards to clay tablets, (3) entering of information on writing boards without its first being entered on a tablet, (4) consultation and (5) scrutiny of writing boards. (I am not convinced by MacGinnis's point (4): information entered simultaneously on both tablet and writing boards.)

ledgers were written on wooden writing boards and that data from cuneiform tablets were routinely transferred onto these ledgers. Therefore, whenever one wanted to strike a balance all that was necessary was to summarise the data on these writing boards. I would subscribe to this opinion too—with some reservations I shall state presently—, but it must be admitted that direct evidence for the procedures involved is not as ample as one could wish. Payments that were entered directly on the writing boards are well attested. For example, a few debt notes and receipts stipulate that the payment in question be entered on the writing board of Šamaš and either a receipt confirming this fact be given to the debtor or his representative or the debtor be shown the entry on the writing board.[73] There is also evidence for the transfer of information from writing boards to clay tablets: Texts occasionally tell us of animals or foodstuffs that are being "withdrawn (*nasāḫu*) from the writing boards." This may mean that the corresponding entry on the writing board was deleted and all the valid information was now to be provided by the tablet at hand, or that the information was simply excerpted from the writing board.[74] But indications for the transfer of data from cuneiform tablets onto writing boards, which was a routine occurrence according to the common hypothesis, are difficult to spot. One can however cite a list of prebendary income which states that the data were *not* entered on the relevant writing board.[75] From this one can infer that the opposite was the rule, but that exceptions were possible. Another text dealing with the same type of subject states that the result of the present settlement of accounts was also noted on the writing board.[76] Furthermore, the hypothesis that data were transferred regularly to the writing boards is supported indirectly, but consistently, by a formal peculiarity of the lists and receipts that hitherto has apparently not attracted any attention. Let us consider

[73] Jursa 1995:39[88]; 1999:47 (on BM 74570). See also note 66 for BM 74644 and literature on the *ušazzaz–inamdin* (or *ukallam*)-formula.

[74] BM 114478 (Eanna archive), CT 55, 596, BM 61336 (Ebabbar archive). The heading of the latter text is as follows: gíd.da *šá muḫ-ḫi* ^{giš}da *šá* mu.4 *u* m[u.5], [*ina mu*]*ḫ-ḫi* ^{giš}da^{meš} gal-*ú-tu na-*⸢*as-ḫu*⸣ iti.diri.še.kin.ku$_5$ mu.5 "receipt excerpted from the writing boards of the fourth and fifth year, (that is), from the large writing boards. Intercalary Addāru, year 5." This is followed by six entries of barley issued to a certain craftsman. Apparently all the information concerning this person was gathered together on this tablet for unclear reasons.

[75] *Nbn* 219.

[76] *Cyr* 256

BM 75567 as one example of many.[77] The text deals with the disbursement of silver for different purposes. Its structure is schematically as follows:

'input':	2 minas, 56 shekels of silver, tithe of the *mašennu*-official Balāṭu
	1 mina, 14 shekels of silver, from the cashbox for income that has accrued in Babylon[78]
therefrom:	
'output':	1 mina for the purchase of cattle
	[…] for work during month […]
date.	

Silver from two sources is expended for two different purposes. The tablet comes from the administration of the storehouse, where all the silver was presumably kept in one place. So why is the origin of the silver important? In a redistributive system, it should be irrelevant for the issuing of commodities where these commodities came from, since everything in principle had to pass through the central storage facilities. Nevertheless, very frequently the origin of commodities disbursed is stated, not only in the case of silver as in the example given, but also in the case of payments in kind.[79]

The explanation must be that this information was important for accounting purposes. One supposes that the data from these receipts and lists were meant to be entered later into the relevant ledgers; and these ledgers of course will have been kept on the writing boards. The typologically oriented subject matter of these writing boards explains why apparently irrelevant information such as the origin of distributed items was included in the primary record: It was meant to enable the accountants to enter the data into the correct running account.

[77] 2 ma.na ⸢56⸣ gín kù.babbar babbar$^{[ú]}$, *eš-ru-ú šá* ^{I}*ba-la-ṭu* ^{lú}⸢agrig⸣, *ù* 1 ma.na 14 gín kù.babbar babbar^{ú}, ta *qu-up-pu er-bi šá* tin.tir^{ki}, pab 4 ma.na 10 gín kù.babbar babbar^{ú}, *ina lìb-bi* 1 ma.na kù.babbar babbar^{ú}, *a-na* ki.lam *šá* gu_4 *a-*[*na*], ^{I}mu^{a} dumu *šá* ^{I}*na-ṣi*[*r* sum^{in}], níg.ka_9 *šá* kù.babbar igi^{ú} [0$^{?}$], [*it-t*]*i* ^{I}*ba-l*[*a-ṭu ép-šu*] (two lines nearly entirely lost; the second must have ended in… kù.babbar]), ⸢*šá*⸣ *ina dul-lu šá* ⸢iti⸣.[x sum^{in}] (two lines uninscribed) iti.bára ud.22.kam mu.25.kam, ^{I}*da-ri-muš* lugal ⸢e⸣$^{[\text{ki}]}$, *u* kur.kur$^{\text{me}[\text{š}]}$.

[78] This entry refers to silver that had been brought to Sippar from Babylon.

[79] One example of many: The barley issued as fodder in CT 57, 37 is said to be partly income derived from tithes (*ešrû*) and partly 'general' income (*erbu*).

The general procedure would seem to be clear.[80] However, texts such as the list of prebendary income mentioned earlier (at note 75) prove that it was not always followed. Documents concerning the rent farmers' bookkeeping provide further evidence to support the hypothesis that not every transaction was automatically transferred to the ledgers on the writing boards. On two occasions one finds that for the settlement of the accounts of the rent farmer Bulṭāya not only his writing boards had to be consulted, but also other types of texts, namely debt notes and receipts.[81] The information on the writing boards was clearly not complete.[82]

It was probably one of the foremost duties of the temples' accountants to collect the data relating to the main types of transactions on writing boards. The processes leading to this result were certainly more complex than we perceive at the moment. To mention just one source of complication, there are several administrative texts—lists of agricultural dues, mostly, but also receipts and large ration lists[83]—which were written in duplicate. Twice one can find textual variants. In one case these are inexplicable[84] and in the other[85] they seem to indicate that the two duplicate tablets in fact belong to different stages of the accounting process, although details escape us. In other cases, individ-

---

[80] Some aspects of the use of writing boards which are not relevant for the present discussion have not been touched upon. Foremost among these is the use of running accounts of individuals (usually prebendary personnel) kept on temple writing boards for cash or giro transfers, *i.e.*, the transfer of funds without any corresponding physical movement of goods (Jursa forthcoming). Among the relevant texts are BM 74570 (see above at note 64) and *Dar* 433, mentioned by MacGinnis 2002: 218 and 220 probably mistakenly as evidence for a writing board dedicated to loans.

[81] *Dar* 451 (Jursa 1995: 107) and *Dar* 368 (see Jursa 1995: 108 for the relevant collation).

[82] One could assume that the debt notes and receipts mentioned together with the writing boards in the texts cited in the preceding note might contain the proofs for individual entries on the writing boards. This may be possible in some cases, but is probably unacceptable as a general rule (this thesis would imply projecting back in time our understanding of 'good' bookkeeping procedures). TCL 9, 98 or Wunsch 1993: No. 157 (Baker 2003: 253[+56]) for instance prove that evidentiary value was attributed to entries on writing boards on their own.

[83] CT 56, 668 and 681, at least as far as the texts preserved on these fragments overlap.

[84] Jursa and Weszeli 2000: 80.

[85] Jursa 1995: 91f.

ual entries from one (summary) account reappear in another without any obvious explanation for this fact suggesting itself.[86]

These are issues of lesser importance, however. The main question is different. As stated earlier, the writing boards cover the main subjects of the "receipts" and lists given in figs. 4 and 5. These in turn represent the majority of payments in kind, but not all of them. Since writing boards were used in the Ebabbar (and, as far as we can tell, Eanna) to collect exclusively one type of transaction each, the existence of writing boards just to cover various odds and ends seems unlikely. For some more unusual payments (loans, purchases paid in kind, etc.), the data would not have been collected in a ledger of their own. The only documentation extant will have been the primary receipt or contract. The same holds true for income in kind, of course. (To give one example: would barley purchased against silver appear anywhere else than in the silver ledger? Probably not. And we know of no writing board at all in which barley purchased against dates could have been noted down.) So even if every receipt or list entry would have been transferred to the appropriate writing board, which, as was pointed out earlier, was not the case, there were areas not covered by this type of documentation. Thus, although it certainly was possible without too much effort to get an overview of the main types of income and expenditure of the temple storehouses by consulting the relevant writing boards, it must have been very difficult and time-consuming, if not outright impossible, to get the whole picture by bureaucratic means.

From all this one can conclude that it is probably no coincidence that no overall yearly account for a Neo-Babylonian temple household comparable to Ur III texts such as 4 NT 197[87] has been found. For such a comprehensive account, a complete set of figures for incoming and expended goods would have been necessary—the availability of which is highly doubtful due to the typologically oriented and incomplete information gathering on writing boards I have described. The few tablets which could be considered to come close to being an overall account of the temples' income and expenditures at least for a certain

[86] S. Zawadzki will edit two such texts dealing with wool. Another case in point may be the pair CT 56, 454 and 599. These are duplicates as far as the entries on the obverse are concerned, but there is no textual overlap on the reverse (this may however be due to the sad state of preservation of these originally quite large tablets).

[87] Zettler 1992: 103ff., 257ff.

commodity and a certain period of time confirm this impression. The somewhat haphazard way in which these texts are often structured has already been pointed out (see above after note 49). *Ner* 70 from the Ebabbar archive, the best-preserved relevant text,[88] collects one year's barley income from the main agricultural settlements and farms as well as the expenditures for offerings, fodder, rations for a certain group of workmen, and payments to two other temples and two officials. This list of expenditures cannot have been complete. The main expenditures for offerings, fodder, and rations would have been easy enough to collect, as they were covered by writing boards, but the documentation for other barley payments was certainly less accessible.

The main objectives of Neo-Babylonian institutional accounting

These are the main features of the bookkeeping documented by the two largest Neo-Babylonian archives. To place these systems into a diachronic context, one can refer to a recent article by J.N. Postgate on "System and Style in Three Near Eastern Bureaucracies" (Postgate 2001). Taking his examples from the Ur III, the Old Babylonian and the Middle Assyrian Period, Postgate distinguishes an archival mode, a legal mode and a commercial mode of bureaucracy. The three systems treated differ with respect to the 'reach' of the administrative network and to the way obligations were phrased.

The general objective of these administrations is supervision of production and redistribution. An institution could attempt to control every single step of the transfer of commodities from the producer to the consumer, or it could withdraw somewhat, restricting itself in the main to checking the flow of commodities through the storehouses and delegating the tasks of production and control to outsiders. If, as is the case in the Ur III period, there exists a tight and hierarchical administrative net, the relevant documentation can consist in the main of 'unilateral' administrative documents (of the kind described above) generated within an institution for this institution's use. In other cases, such as in the Middle Assyrian kingdom, where state control was nearly as far-reaching as in Ur III times, one preferred bilateral contracts for establishing the obligations and liabilities of individuals working within the system. The Old Babylonian period is Postgate's example for a

[88] Jursa 1995:5, 167f.

very restricted 'reach' of state bureaucracy which was supplemented by contractual relationships with private individuals ('entrepreneurs') responsible for the areas of the institutional economy beyond the direct control of the central bureaucracy.

In the terms of this typology, the Neo-Babylonian institutional bureaucracies studied here resemble *mutatis mutandis* Postgate's Old Babylonian example. Within the reach of the tight central administrative network, the predominant bureaucratic mode is archival, beyond that, contractual or legal. The scope of direct supervision is generally restricted to those economic activities that take place in the center of the cities, or, more precisely, in the temples' central workshops and storage facilities. The other, less easily supervisable branches of the temples' economy, notably agriculture and animal husbandry, tend to be run to a large extent or even entirely by entrepreneurs (of very different social status and origin). The temple administrations restrict themselves to determining the income expected from these entrepreneurs and monitoring the corresponding deliveries.

This implies a shift of economic risk from the institutions to the entrepreneurs: At least in principle shortfalls had to be covered by the entrepreneurs' own property. On the other hand, these people were entitled to keep any profits they might manage to achieve over and above the goal set for them by the administrations. This means that the institutional households were willing to accept less than the theoretical maximum income in return for administrative simplification and the shifting of the economic risks to the entrepreneurs. Details, in particular the diachronic development of these arrangements in the different archives, need not concern us here.[89] Suffice it to point out that overall the involvement of private entrepreneurs in institutional economies seems to expand during the course of the first millennium BC. This must have caused an increasing withdrawal of direct institutional management.

Returning now to the issues raised in the introduction to this paper, we need to ask what can be said about the efficiency of the Neo-Babylonian system of institutional accounting by assessing what it was meant to do, what it actually did, and what it potentially could have done. Here the theoretical model developed by Hunt 1991 for the use of bureaucracy in the framework of an ancient (*i.e.*, pre-modern) centralised and urban economy can serve as a guideline for the

---

[89] Jursa 2002.

phenomena and functions one might look for. He envisages an active rôle for bureaucrats at all stages of production, extraction, transport, storage, processing and distribution of foodstuffs. The management of these activities involves either the bureaucratic setting of targets to be met by the producers or the monitoring of actual performances.

Every student of first-millennium accounting will agree that Neo-Babylonian bureaucracy was certainly able to fulfil this second main function, the "police function," to use the term coined by Moses Finley again.[90] It was well suited to keep track of debits and credits, to settle individual accounts, etc. I would argue that the way information was gathered in the central records of the administration, the writing boards, where the different types of dues and expenditures were always kept separate, is indicative of the fact that the main function of these lists was indeed to facilitate the checking of individual obligations, thus enabling the administration to take the necessary measures to ensure that these obligations were met.

What about "global economic prognostication or planning," the main purpose of writing and bureaucracy in third-millennium bureaucracies according to the 'maximalist' position?[91] This is something entirely different from the control function described earlier. Admittedly, in concordance with Hunt's model, even Finley's mere "police function" of bureaucracy implies an outlook to the future which was shaped by bureaucratic means in that the targets the fulfilment of which was to be monitored had to be established first. And of course bookkeeping was necessary for keeping track of supplies and for comparing them to the expected demand. All this could be considered to be "planning." However, the level of sophistication at which this was done needs to be discussed as well as the way targets were set and expected demands were prognosticated.

The issues at stake can be exemplified by reference to the debate among ancient historians mentioned in the introduction to this paper: the question of the limitations of ancient Greek and Roman bookkeeping and its potential for enabling administrators to make economically rational decisions. What precisely is to be understood by this latter expression is obviously not self-evident. W.M. Jongman has recently argued that the term "rationality" has been used in a too nar-

---

90 Above note 4.

91 For the terminology ('minimalist,' 'maximalist') see above at note 4. The quotation is from Steinkeller's contribution to this volume.

row way in this context and that its rôle in modern economics—as opposed to antiquity—has been overemphasised.[92] This notwithstanding, I believe that Assyriology can learn something from this discussion, in particular from the papyrological contributions.

Basing himself on numerous papyri from Roman Egypt, Dominic Rathbone has argued at length that the third-century AD Appianus estate studied by him be considered an economic enterprise managed with a clear consciousness of productivity and profit, that is, "rationally" in a technical sense.[93] For argument's sake I shall accept Rathbone's thesis[94] and use his archive as a yardstick with which I shall briefly compare the Neo-Babylonian evidence regarding the respective bureaucratic systems' potential for enabling comprehensive cost accounting, prognostication and rational, profit-oriented decision-making.

Rathbone's main evidence are monthly accounts of individual estates. These intended not only to furnish data to prove the estate administrators' honesty and accuracy. They present their material in a rigorously structured and synthesised way, and, according to Rathbone, must in fact be considered analytical records of the entirety of the estates' income and expenditures.[95] Many of the estate management's activities were determined of course by natural limitations of some sort. But where it could make its own decisions, a distinct policy aimed at maintaining and increasing productivity in a rational way can be detected.

One can compare the Appianus accounts with the information available regarding the Ebabbar's agricultural administration.[96] For its directly administrated estates, the temple kept track of the amount of land cultivated, estimated the yield, determined the rents to be paid, and ascertained if these had been duly delivered in time. To do so, it needed only very basic information about its domains. Many of the

---

[92] Jongman 2000: 264.

[93] Rathbone 1991; *e.g.*, p. 394.

[94] But see the counterarguments presented by Andreau and Maucourant 1999.

[95] Rathbone 1991: 396ff. The subject matter, presented in a fixed order, of one group of monthly accounts is as follows: **heading—account of cash**: *receipts —expenditures*: cash salaries for permanent staff, taxes, wages for hired personnel—*balance*—**accounts of kind**: wheat (and monthly wages paid in kind)— bread—barley—...—sour wine—equipment (jars, axles, hides)—**list of tools—list of livestock** (Rathbone 1991: table 17b, slightly simplified and abbreviated).

[96] The documentation for the administrative procedures involved can be found in Jursa 1995.

costs that necessarily must have been incurred during the agricultural cycle were of no interest to the bookkeeping. For instance, transportation costs were not systematically taken note of, even though they were an important factor and must have made the cultivation of far-off farms quite expensive.[97] The provisioning of the local work-force and even the issuing of seed grain was either not documented at all in the records of the central administration or appears at best very sketchily. Furthermore, there is no evidence for the renting of outside labor during harvest time, even though this must have been an important issue. These matters were apparently organized locally and not reported back to the central temple administration.

All this is in marked contrast to the Appianus accounts. There is nothing remotely similar at Sippar (or generally in Neo-Babylonian archives) to the interlocking chain of comprehensive estate accounts studied by Rathbone, even though the agricultural production in the various estates and villages in Sippar's hinterland were the backbone of the Ebabbar's economy.[98] I believe that the Ebabbar's bookkeeping (and the Eanna's, for that matter) would have been of little help for rational and cost-conscious management of the kind Rathbone has found in his texts. The administrations probably lacked the information or the means of extracting the information from their records.

There is yet another approach to show that prognostication and planning were not the main objectives of Neo-Babylonian institutional accounting—which anyway would not have been of much help for these purposes on any but a very basic level. I have pointed out above the fact that Neo-Babylonian institutional households tended to delegate to entrepreneurs, usually outsiders, the management of branches of their economy not amenable to permanent and direct control. A large part of the institutional bureaucracy was devoted to checking the performance of these men; we have already seen that most balanced

---

[97] Attested Neo-Babylonian transport costs ranged from 1.3% to 45.8% of the value of the goods transported. In the majority of cases they are somewhat below 10%—certainly not a negligible factor (Weszeli 2002: 202ff.).

[98] *Cyr* 180 comes closest to the Appianus texts. This is a balanced account for the dates owed to the Ebabbar by gardeners working on one of the temple's estates. The accounting period is one year, or one agricultural cycle. In the credit section, not only dates actually delivered to the temple are mentioned, but also some expenses incurred locally, in the countryside, such as certain taxes, the cost of maintenance work on irrigation installations, and costs of transport. The text is isolated, however. Normally the accounting for agricultural income was far less detailed.

accounts deal with such matters. For the present context it is only relevant how the administrations established the future obligations these men were expected to meet.

Already early in the third millennium institutional accountants were faced with the need to define future obligations.[99] They and all their successors up to the first millennium did so in a form that would be easily manageable with the arithmetic and bureaucratic tools available to them. The solutions found for the needs of such different branches of the economy as third-millennium long distance trade, second-millennium animal husbandry, and first-millennium institutional agriculture are in fact quite similar to each other. Very basic arithmetic models were developed to simplify the complex realities considerably to make them appear controllable by the means at the bureaucrats' disposal.

Ur III scribes for example were taught a simple model for predicting the growth of cattle herds—which ostensibly assumes that these animals are immortal: The cattle seemingly are supposed to reproduce indefinitely.[100] Similarly, Neo-Babylonian bird-breeding contracts make no allowances for the inevitable losses of animals, somewhat offsetting this however by postulating rather low reproduction rates.[101] Neo-Babylonian lease contracts for agricultural entrepreneurs often make no distinction for varying soil quality and the like. They posit one expected yield rate for all fields involved. The rents stipulated for extensive tracts of land tend to be unrealistically nice round sums (10 000 *kurru*, 25 000 *kurru*, etc.).[102] The norms for the performance of plough teams and the cost of their maintenance all involve figures which are very easy to handle arithmetically within the metrological and numerical system used. One could continue this enumeration of examples, but the principle is always the same.[103] "Planning" and "prognostication"

---

[99] See Selz 1999.

[100] Englund 1995: 388ff.

[101] Janković (forthcoming).

[102] For rules of thumb in Neo-Babylonian institutional agriculture see for instance YOS 6, 103 and YOS 6, 11 // TEBR 37 and the discussions in van Driel 1987/88 and 1999: 216f.; Jursa 1995: 137f. and the summary in Jursa 2002: 100-18.

[103] More examples and a discussion of the issue of setting "targets" in institutional economies can be found in Jursa 2002. Medieval agricultural handbooks compiled for managers who needed to have guidelines to judge their lessees' performance show a similar kind of thinking: "every two cows on salt marsh pasture will produce every week enough milk to make a stone of cheese and a half-gallon of butter" (Dyer 2003: 123f.).

in Mesopotamian institutional economy always imply to a large degree the use of simplifying models or "rules of thumb."

The degree of approximation to reality reached by these models depended in part of course on the amount and quality of practical experience that went into them. But there were other factors, such as the ever-present temptation to establish models which owed more to wishful thinking on part of the administrators than to practical experience. One might say that in some respects administrative practice was not shaped to conform to reality, but rather reality was made to conform to administrative needs.[104] It is in any case obvious that in such a system accounting was generally not used as an analytical tool to arrive at quantifying prognostications on the basis of records of earlier performance. "Planning" and "prognostication" as described are necessary preconditions for bureaucracy in that they set the targets to be monitored by the administrations. But as such, these activities do not vitally depend on information gathered by bureaucratic means—a corroboration of the "minimalist" position I would like to defend for the Neo-Babylonian evidence here under discussion.

[104]At this point one may well ask how 'efficient' a system based to a considerable extent on such rules of thumb could have been, especially if one recalls that even when the temple administrations did try to keep exact accounts as we would understand them they sometimes were less than successful (see above at note 38). There is no easy answer to this question. Overall one gets the impression that the rules of thumb, which were based on practical experience after all, did work reasonably well, especially for small-scale prognostication. However, entrepreneurs who had entered into contractual relationships with the temples did incur substantive debts regularly—possibly because the temple's demands were occasionally unrealistic (this holds true both for animal husbandry and agriculture). Sometimes these debts had consequences (as in the case of one rent farmer who was forced to take a partner into his business who in return paid off his debts: Jursa 1995: 103ff.). However, the most important of these men had royal backing, which meant that the temples could not easily put pressure on them (as they regularly did in the case of indebted humble shepherds and small-scale agricultural entrepreneurs or share-croppers) and probably had to accept that the ambitious stipulations of the original contracts could not be enforced (see *e.g.*, van Driel 1993: 223f. for animal husbandry). Significantly, it is especially in these cases that the temple administrations seem to make exceptionally high demands: be it that the approximative method of prognostication did not work quite so well for the large scale undertakings involved, or be it that the temples, once they had been forced to enter into a business relationship with a royal protégé, consciously tried to get as much out of this unwanted arrangement as ever they could—while the entrepreneurs might willingly have taken upon themselves impossible obligations knowing they would not be required to keep them in full.

Conclusion

The Neo-Babylonian temple bureaucracies studied here dealt essentially with management of resources and labor. The urban sectors of the temples' economy, that is basically storage and work in the temple workshops, probably also textile production, were supervised by a tight administrative networking in the "archival mode" in Postgate's terminology. Regarding decentralised economic activities taking place in the cities' rural hinterland, such as agriculture and animal husbandry, the central administrations tended to restrict themselves to delegating the management to outsiders and to supervising the performance of these people. Administrative control over institutional property and economic affairs was therefore overall far less direct and strict than for example in the Ur III period. This is reflected also in a possibly changed rôle of bureaucracy. The main purpose of Neo-Babylonian temple bureaucracies was to monitor the temples' debits and credits, that is to exercise a "police function." Their potential use as a tool for an overall analysis of the temples' economic dealings and as an aid for cost control and future planning would have been limited, as information was gathered primarily with the intention to render checking of individual performances as easy as possible. It was probably never intended to achieve a comprehensive overview of a temple's economy by bureaucratic means.[105]

Economic forecasting and prognostication for the setting of targets for production and generally labor, a vital aspect of management, was based to a large extent on (more or less traditional) rules of thumb, which owe much to experience, but were also influenced by non-economic factors such as metrology and sexagesimal arithmetics. Accounting as a source of data with which such rules could have been refined in an objective, 'rational' way seems to have played a minimal rôle at best.

Finally, I would like to draw attention to an instructive parallel to the Neo-Babylonian system described above from later Near Eastern

---

[105]The development of so-called "high farming" in late 12th-century England allows for an interesting comparison. Prior to this period demesnes had most often been rented out, and the landlords' accountants had restricted themselves entirely to what has been called here a 'police function' of collecting the rents and checking that payments were made in full. When this system came under pressure due to the effects of inflation, demesnes were brought under direct management again, and concomittantly, the level of accounting sophistication increased due to efforts to make rational calculations of profitability (Dyer 2003: 119ff.).

history: Ottoman tax farming and fiscal record-keeping.[106] In the Ottoman empire, revenue farming, *i.e.*, the contracting out of the collection of state income of all kinds, was an ubiquitous practice in the 16th and 17th centuries.[107] Just as in ancient Near Eastern rent farming and similar kinds of entrepreneurial involvement in institutional businesses, this meant that the state consented to receive somewhat less than the potential maximum in revenues, trading off this loss for higher security of income (the economic risk having been shifted to the tax farmers) and a facilitation of the collecting process. "The farming of taxes allows for less central control than a fully bureaucratized system of revenue collection by salaried members of a state apparatus."[108] Tax farmers gained their commissions simply by competitive bidding:[109] the state bureaucracy did not prescribe the targets to be met. Budgeting then, or economic prognostication, would have involved simply adding up the successful bids. This, however, was apparently not done. The real rôle of bureaucracy consisted in checking the tax farmers' performance up to the point of drawing up yearly overall balance-sheets—after the fact.[110] The obvious link between contracting out institutional business and a reduced scope for direct bureaucratic control is clearly paralleled by our Neo-Babylonian evidence and suggests the existence of a Near Eastern *longue durée* of institutional management and accounting.

Appendix 1: A Weberian classification of Neo-Babylonian bureaucrats

When attempting to typologically classify the administrators and their bureaucratic ethos, one profitable avenue of approach would be to employ Max Weber's distinction between "legal-rational" and "traditional" domination. The purest form of a "legal-rational" system is a "bureaucratic" regime characterised by the fact that ideally allegiance is owed not to rulers, but to rules: officials are subject to an impersonal order. They are free professionals and assume their positions by their

[106] Note that the Ottoman state has been described by Carter Findley as a Weberian patrimonial household, similar to ancient Near Eastern states (Findley 1989: 46, cited by Schloen 2001: 68). See also İnalcık 1994 for a general survey of Ottoman social and economic structures.

[107] Darling 1996.

[108] Darling 1996: 120.

[109] Darling 1996: 136ff.

[110] Darling 1996: 237ff.

own choice; their public rôle must be kept separate from their private lives.[111] In contrast, in a system characterised by "traditional" domination, "obedience is owed not to enacted rules but to the person who occupies a position of authority by tradition or who has been chosen for it by the traditional master."[112] The classical example for such traditional domination is the patrimonial household system, in which officials are bound by a personal relationship to their superiors (the "master and slave" or "father and child" metaphor is often used). Typically, in such a system the distinction between the public and the private sphere is meaningless. The patrimonial household model has been employed in the past to describe ancient Near Eastern societies. To quote just a few examples, David Schloen used it in his study of the society of Ugarit;[113] Karen Radner referred to this Weberian concept in her analysis of the first-millennium Neo-Assyrian empire;[114] and, most relevant for the present purposes, Piotr Michalowski and Richard Zettler invoked Weber in their respective studies of Ur III evidence.[115] Particularly interesting is Zettler's study of the Inanna temple at Nippur. He shows how one family of administrators "manipulated the resources of the temple ... in a sense to guarantee its ... prosperity and prominence," concluding that this type of organisation should be considered patrimonial rather than bureaucratic.[116] Bongenaar's study of the upper echelons of the temple administration at Sippar has revealed several comparable extended family networks—the top positions however were dependent on royal sponsorship rather than good local connections.[117] There was no clear-cut *cursus honorum*, no strict hierarchy in which an official could ascend by means of training and professional competence. In this sense, Neo-Babylonian administrators certainly do not correspond to the Weberian bureaucrat, but rather to the retainer-type official in a patrimonial system. In other, maybe more important aspects however, the bureaucratic model fits the evidence much better. A main point is that the public and the private sphere

---

[111] Weber 1980: 126ff.

[112] Weber *apud* Schloen 2001:67. German original: "Gehorcht wird nicht Satzungen, sondern der durch Tradition oder durch den traditional bestimmten Herrscher dafür berufenen Person" (Weber 1980: 130).

[113] Schloen 2001.

[114] Radner 1997: 198ff.

[115] Michalowski 1991; Zettler 1991.

[116] Zettler 1991: 114.

[117] Bongenaar 1997 *passim*. Similarly Kümmel 1979 for Uruk and the Eanna archive.

were strictly kept apart. Blurrings between these two do occur of course, but they are invariably considered objectionable and are sanctioned.[118] Judging from their correspondence, I would also be inclined to believe that these administrators were expected to go about their business dispassionately and more or less impersonally. As usual in Mesopotamian administrative practice, these letters are characterised to a certain extent by a terminology congruent with the patrimonial model: equals address each other as brothers, superiors are addressed as fathers. Excepting the introductory formulae however, most letters of Eanna and Ebabbar officials to their colleagues are striking for the near-total lack of any personal reflection. Even urgent requests are in general not phrased in the rhetoric of personal relationships, by promising favours for help received for instance. There is constant reference to dutiful service, obviously the foremost virtue expected from an official.[119] An important issue for which I cannot offer a definitive solution is the question as to whether at least some of these officials were really salaried full-time professional administrators—an important requirement in the Weberian model for an archetypal bureaucratic system. All the top level scribes who are well-known also through their private archives had more than one occupation within the temple household. If there were full-time scribes and accountants, they would have been active on a slightly lower level. But there is evidence for salaries and generally remunerations for administrative activities. At both Sippar and Borsippa the highest temple officials (the *šangû* of Sippar and the *šatam Ezida* respectively) received substantial payments from temple prebendaries.[120] There is one important tablet proving that Borsippean

---

[118]The clearest evidence comes from the Eanna archive's legal files, *e.g.*, the dossier dealing with the malversations of the temple slave and entrepreneur Gimillu (on which see provisionally Joannès 2000:225ff. with further references).

[119]What was expected from a high temple official is succinctly phrased by a letter of a king, probably Nebuchadnezzar, to the highest official of Eanna, Nabû-nādin-šumi: "do not neglect (your) duties for Eanna, the house of my gods. Do your work and pray to the Mistress of Uruk and Nanaya on my behalf" (NCBT 55). The phrase used most often in such a context is the exhortation "do not neglect your work," *ina muḫḫi dullika lā tašelli*; see CAD Š/2, 274. The rhetoric of the Eanna letters will be studied by Eckart Frahm and myself in our forthcoming edition of the relevant unpublished texts from the Yale Babylonian Collection.

[120]For Sippar Jursa 1999:49; for Borsippa BM 29087 and BM 26726.

temple prebendaries had to pay the scribe who kept the accounts for them.[121] Scribes and other specialised personnel, such as surveyors, estimators of yields and 'measurers' (*mandidu*) of staples, were remunerated for their services in the context of the bringing in of the harvest and its distribution.[122] It is not inconceivable that they could have made a living from their profession. Taking of "gifts," or bribes, on the other hand, was deemed unacceptable, according to a royal order quoted in one Eanna letter.[123] The uncompromising, absolute formulation of this order is congruent with the ethos of a genuine "legal-rational" system of domination, whereas it would seem somewhat out of place in a patrimonial system with its much more personalised relationships.

Weber's classification employs ideal types, that is, abstractions. It would be a-historical to expect to encounter them in reality. The intention of the foregoing thoughts was to demonstrate that his models are useful tools to describe the Neo-Babylonian administrator, who by virtue of his affiliation with kin-based networks comes close to the traditional official in a patrimonial system, but who, on the other hand, shares some characteristics with the ideal type bureaucrat due to his impersonal professionalism and the strict division between the official and the private sphere.

---

[121] BM 26484; the recipient of the payment is a *sēpiru*, an Aramaic scribe, which indicates that at Borsippa at least some prebendary accounts were written in Aramaic.

[122] See van Driel 2002: 168ff. At Borsippa, such personnel also received payments from prebendaries in return for similar services (*e.g.*, BM 28880 and BM 29093).

[123] BIN 1, 73. The sender of the letter describes his disagreement with a high official of Eanna concerning a small amount of silver (some details are unclear due to textual damage). He goes on to say: "... when Kudurru rebuked (me), saying: 'it is an order of the king, no-one shall accept a gift,' I relinquished (the silver)." m*níg*.du *ki-i ú-ṭar-ri-du, um-ma a-mat* lugal *šì-i mam-ma,* níg.ba *ul i-ṣab-bat-tu, un-da-áš-šìr* (lines 18-21).

Appendix 2: BM 66261 and BM 66261A, an atypical case tablet from the Ebabbar archive

obv.
i-na 8 gín kù.babbar babb[ar^{ú} šám]
2 túg.kur.ra^{meš} *šá* ^{I}*gu-za-n*[*u*]
a ^{Id}ag-*ni-ip-šá-ri ina lìb-bi*
14 ma.na sík.ḫi.a «sík.ḫi.a»
a-na 4 gín kù.babbar *a-na muḫ-ḫi*
^{I}*gu-za-nu a-na* ^{Id}amar.utu-mu-dù sum^{in}
iti.kin ud.17.kam mu.2.kam
^{I}*kam-bu-zi-ia* lugal e^{ki} lugal kur.kur
10 ma.na sík.ḫi.a ^{I}*ta-at-tan-nu*

BM 66261

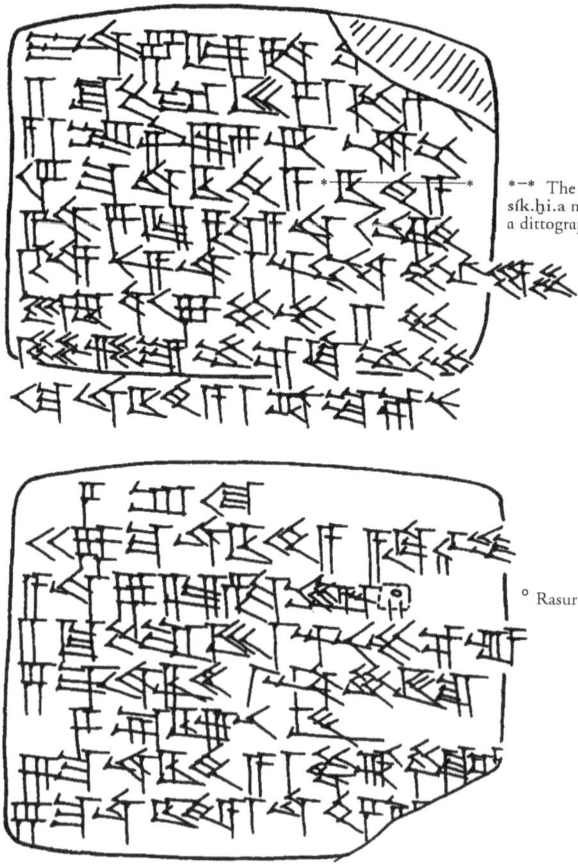

– The second sík.ḫi.a must be a dittography.

° Rasur

rev. *šá* é kisal
28 ma.na sík.ḫi.a *a-di* igi^{tu_4}
a-na 8 gín kù.babbar šám
2 túg.kur.ra^{meš} ^{Id}bad-mu *e-ṭer*
5 ma.na sík.ḫi.<a> ^{Id}utu-šeš^{meš}-su
šá é gur$_7$^{meš}
5 ma.na sík.ḫi.a ^{I}*lib-luṭ* ^{lú}túg.kal.[kal]
5 ma.na sík.ḫi.a ^{I}*na-din šá* ⸢é⸣ [x x]

BM 66261A

Case obv. 1 sík.ḫi.a *šá a-na* túg.kur.ra^{meš}
u ^{lú}un^{meš} é sum^{nu}
5 ma.na sík.ḫi.a ^{I}*šá-pi-i-[kal-bi]*
šá ^{é}*ziq-qur-rat*
(cylinder seal impression)
rev. (two cylinder seal impressions)

I am indebted to Stefan Zawadzki, who brought this text to my attention.

Translation

"Of eight shekels of white silver, [the price] of two KURra textiles of Gūzānu, son of Nabû-nipšari—therefrom 14 minas of wool for four shekels of silver have been given to Marduk-šumu-ibni at the expense of Gūzānu. 17th day of Ulūlu, year two of Cambyses, king of Babylon, king of the lands.

10 minas of wool: Tattannu of the (store-)house in the courtyard.

28 minas of wool, in addition to the earlier (delivery): Ea-iddin has been paid (this) for eight shekels of silver, the price of two KURra textiles.

Five minas of wool: Šamaš-aḫḫē-erība of the store-house.

Five minas of wool: Libluṭ, the clothes mender.

Five minas of wool: Nādin of the [...]-house.

(case)

(Concerning) wool which has been paid for KURra textiles and (given) to temple personnel.

Five minas of wool: Ša-pî-[kalbi] of the ziqqurrat."

This tablet is unique in that a straightforward administrative tablet was enclosed by a case giving a summary of the contents of the tablet, an additional entry and bearing three impressions of the same cylinder seal.[124] Only a future study of the unpublished case fragments mentioned above (note 44) can show if there are more such tablets in the collections of the British Museum.

---

[124] The seal shows a human facing to the left, praying before three pedestals bearing divine symbols, the central of which is a star. It is not among the seals studied by MacGinnis 1995: 164ff.

Appendix 3: The end of the Ebabbar archive

MacGinnis has recently summarised the various explanations that have been offered for the abrupt end of Sippar documentation in the second year of Xerxes.[125] The two most plausible alternatives offered are either destruction of Ebabbar by the Persians, in the context of the upheavals during the beginning of the reign of Xerxes, or the assumption that for unknown reasons the later archives have simply not been found and that in fact no substantial changes occurred in the temple at all.[126] Recent research conducted by C. Waerzeggers on the events during Xerxes's first years[127] proves that the political events in these years definitely did have a marked effect on Northern Babylonia, leading to serious disruption in the lives of the urban elite whose fortunes were intertwined with the fate of the temples, but leaving no traces in the archives of people without such connections. The evidence is consistent with the hypothesis that the temples were a seat of anti-Achaemenid activity, prompting Xerxes to have at least the upper echelons of the temple administrations removed after his victory. There is no evidence for what exactly he did at Sippar. The fact that the Ebabbar archive is manifestly "dead," that is, not cut off by a catastrophic event, but set aside after having been sifted and after important documents had been sorted out and removed, does not support the idea that there was extensive destruction of the temple—no-one would have taken the trouble to go systematically through thousands of clay tablets while a hostile Persian army was at the gates, and there would have been little point in such an operation later, if the Achaemenids had had destroyed the temple and disrupted the cult entirely. The internal evidence argues for a cleanup of the archives under a new administration which definitely intended to continue its work, I believe, and the revolts against Xerxes and their aftermath seem the only plausible scenario for the installation of such a new group of bureaucrats by the Persian rulers.

---

[125] MacGinnis 2002:226f.

[126] The other alternatives discussed by MacGinnis (and partly dismissed) are: abandonment of Sippar due to a change in the course of the Euphrates and switch to record-keeping on writing boards or to record-keeping in Aramaic. Neither of these alternatives is very plausible.

[127] Mostly on the basis of Borsippa material gathered for the project mentioned in the note at the beginning of this article. See Waerzeggers (forthcoming). A forthcoming paper by K. Kessler based on new material from Uruk will present evidence which ties in well with Waerzeggers's findings.

Bibliography

For abbreviations of text editions (which are not included in the following list) see *Archiv für Orientforschung* 48/49 (2001/2002): 311ff.

Andreau, Jean and Jérôme Maucourant (1999), "À propos de la "rationalité économique" dans l'Antiquité gréco-romaine. Une interprétation des thèses de D. Rathbone [1991]," *Topoi* 9/1: 47-102.

Baker, Heather D. (2003), "Record-Keeping Practices as Revealed by the Neo-Babylonian Private Archival Documents," in Brosius 2003: 241-63.

Beaulieu, Paul-Alain (2000) "Ea-dayān, Governor of the Sealand, and Other Dignitaries of the Neo-Babylonan Empire," *JCS* 54: 99-123.

Boiy, Tom (2000), *Laatachaemenidisch en hellenistisch Babylon. Portret van een Mesopotamische stad in een cultureel spanningsveld.* Dissertation, Katholieke Universiteit Leuven.

Brosius, Maria, ed. (2003), *Ancient Archives and Archival Traditions. Concepts of Record-Keeping in the Ancient World* (Oxford: Oxford University Press).

Bongenaar, A.C.V.M. (1997), *The Neo-Babylonian Ebabbar Temple at Sippar: Its Adminstration and Its Prosopography* (PIHANS 80).

— (2000), "Private Archives in Neo-Babylonian Sippar," in A.C.V.M. Bongenaar (ed.), *Interdependency of Institutions and Private Entrepreneurs (MOS Studies 2). Proceedings of the Second MOS Symposion (Leiden 1998)* (PIHANS 87): 73-94.

Da Riva, Rocío (2002), *Der Ebabbar-Tempel von Sippar in frühneubabylonischer Zeit (640-580 v. Chr.)* (AOAT 291).

Darling, Linda T. (1996), *Revenue-Raising and Legitimacy. Tax Collection and Finance Administration in the Ottoman Empire 1560-1660* (Leiden: Brill).

van Driel, Govert (1987/88), "The Edict of Belshazzar. An Alternative Interpretation," *Jaarbericht van hat Vooraziatisch-Egyptisch Genootschap Ex Oriente Lux* 29: 61-64.

— (1989), "The Murašûs in Context," *JESHO* 32: 203-29.

— (1990), "Neo-Babylonian Agriculture, Part III: Cultivation," BSA 5: 219-66.

— (1993), "Neo-Babylonian Sheep and Goats," BSA 7: 219-58.

— (1998), "The "Eanna Archive"," *BiOr* 55: 59-79.

— (1999), "Agricultural Entrepreneurs in Mesopotamia," H. Klengel and J. Renger (eds.), *Landwirtschaft im Alten Orient* (Berlin: Reimer): 213-23.

— (2002), *Elusive Silver. In Search of a Role for a Market in an Agrarian Environment. Aspects of Mesopotamia's Society.* (PIHANS 95).

van Driel, G. and K.R. Nemet-Nejat (1994), "Bookkeeping Practices for an Institutional Herd at Eanna," *JCS* 46:47-58.

Dyer, Christopher (2003), *Making a Living in the Middle Ages. The People of Britain 850-1520* (The Penguin Economic History of Britain; London: Penguin Books).

Edzard, Dietz Otto (1982 [1989]), "Erwägungen zur Typologie der Verwaltungstexte aus Ebla," *Studi Eblaiti* 5:33-38.

Englund, Robert K. (1990), *Organisation und Verwaltung der Ur III-Fischerei.* (Berlin: Reimer).

— (1995), "Regulating Dairy Productivity in the Ur III Period," *Orientalia* 64:377-429.

Findley, Carter V. (1989), *Ottoman Civil Officialdom: A Social History* (Princeton: Princeton University Press).

Finley, Moses I. (1987), *Ancient History. Evidence and Models* (London: Penguin) [first published 1985].

Frame, Grant (2001), "A Neo-Babylonian Tablet with an Aramaic Docket and the Surety Phrase *pūt šēp(i) ... našû*," in P.M.M. Daviau *et al.* (eds.), *The World of the Aramaeans III. Studies in Language and Literature in Honour of Paul-Eugène Dion* (Sheffield: Sheffield Academic Press): 100-33.

Freydank, Helmut (2001), "*lēʾāni* „(Holz)tafeln"—eine Grundlage der mittelassyrischen Verwaltung," in Th. Richter *et al.* (eds.), *Kulturgeschichten. Altorientalische Studien für Volkert Haas zum 65. Geburtstag* (Saarbrücken: Saarbrücker Druckerei und Verlag): 103-11.

Gibson, McG. and R.D. Biggs, eds. (1991), *The Organization of Power. Aspects of Bureaucracy in the Ancient Near East* (Chicago: Oriental Institute).

Hudson, Michael and Baruch A. Levine (1996), *Privatization in the Ancient Near East and Classical World.* Peabody Museum Bulletin 5 (Cambridge, Mass.: Peabody Museum, Harvard University).

Hunt, Robert C. (1991), "The Role of Bureaucracy in the Provisioning of Cities: A Framework for Analysis of the Ancient Near East," in McG. Gibson and R.D. Biggs 1991:141-68.

İnalcık, Halil (1994), *An Economic and Social History of the Ottoman Empire. Volume One. 1300-1600* (Cambridge: Cambridge University Press).

Janković, Bojana (forthcoming), *Vogelzucht und Vogelfang in Sippar im ersten Jahrtausend vor Christus* (AOAT).

Jongman, W.M. (2000), "Hunger and Power: Theories, Models and Methods in Roman Economic History," in Bongenaar 2000:259-84.

Jursa, Michael (1995), *Die Landwirtschaft in Sippar in neubabylonischer Zeit* (AfO, Beiheft 25).

— (1998), *Der Tempelzehnt in Babylonien vom siebenten bis zum dritten Jahrhundert v. Chr.* (AOAT 254).

— (1999), *Das Archiv des Bēl-rēmanni*. PIHANS 86.

— (2002), *Prywatyzacja i zysk? Przedsiębiorcy a gospodarka instytucjonalna w Mezopotamii od 3 do 1 tysiąclecia przed Chr.* [Polish; Privatisation and Profit? Entrepreneurs and Institutional Households in Mesopotamia from the Third to the First Millennium BC] (Poznań: PTPN).

— (forthcoming), "Banken im hellenistischen Babylonien."

Jursa, Michael and Michaela Weszeli (2000), "Der ‚Zahn des Schreibers'. Ein aramäischer Buchstabenname in akkadischer Transkription," *ZA* 90:78-84.

Kümmel, Hans M. (1979), *Familie, Beruf und Amt im spätbabylonischen Uruk.* Abhandlungen der Deutschen Orient-Gesellschaft 20 (Berlin: Gebr. Mann).

MacGinnis, John (1995), *Letter Orders from Sippar and the Administration of the Ebabbara in the Late-Babylonian Period* (Poznań: Bonami).

— (2002), "The Use of Writing Boards in the Neo-Babylonian Temple Administration at Sippar," *Iraq* 64:217-36.

Michalowski, Piotr (1991), "Charisma and Control: On Continuity and Change in Early Mesopotamian Bureaucratic Systems," in McG. Gibson and R.D. Biggs 1991:45-57.

Van De Mieroop, Marc (1997), "Why Did They Write on Clay," *Klio* 79:1-18.

Pedersén, Olof (1999), *Archives and Libraries in the Ancient Near East 1500-300 B.C.* (Bethesda: CDL Press).

Postgate, J. Nicholas (2001), "System and Style in Three Near Eastern Bureaucracies," in S. Voutsaki and J. Killen (eds.), *Economy and Politics in the Mycenaean Palace States. Proceedings of a Conference Held on 1-3 July 1999 in the Faculty of Classics, Cambridge*, Cambridge Philological Society Supplementary Volume no. 27 (Cambridge): 181-94.

Powell, Marvin A., ed. (1987), *Labor in the Ancient Near East* (AOS 68).

Radner, Karen (1997), *Die neuassyrischen Privatrechtsurkunden als Quelle für Mensch und Umwelt.* (SAAS 6; Helsinki: The Neo-Assyrian Text Corpus Project).

Rathbone, Dominic (1991), *Economic Rationalism and Rural Society in Third-Century A.D. Egypt. The Heroninos Archive and the Appianus Estate.* (Cambridge: Cambridge University Press).

Reade, Julian (1986), "Introduction," in E. Leichty, *Catalogue of the Babylonian Tablets in the British Museum. Volume VI: Tablets from Sippar 1* (London: British Museum Publications): xiii-xxxvi.

San Nicolò, Mariano (1948), "Haben die Babylonier Wachstafeln als Schriftträger gekannt?," *Orientalia* 17: 59-70.

Sassmannshausen, Leonhard (2001), *Beiträge zur Verwaltung und Gesellschaft Babyloniens in der Kassitenzeit* (Mainz: Philipp von Zabern).

Schloen, J.David (2001), *The House of the Father as Fact and Symbol. Patrimonialism in Ugarit and the Ancient Near East* (Winona Lake: Eisenbrauns).

Selz, Gebhard J. (1999), "Vom "vergangenen Geschehen" zur "Zukunftsbewältigung". Überlegungen zur Rolle der Schrift in Ökonomie und Geschichte," in B. Böck *et al.* (eds.), *Munuscula Mesopotamica. Festschrift für Johannes Renger* (AOAT 267): 465-512.

Steinkeller, Piotr (1987), "The Foresters of Umma: Toward a Definition of Ur III Labor," in Powell 1987: 73-115.

— (1996), "The Organization of Crafts in Third Millennium Babylonia: The Case of Potters," *Altorientalische Forschungen* 23: 232-53.

— (2003), "Archival Practices at Babylonia in the Third Millennium," in Brosius 2003: 37-58.

Stolper, Matthew W. (2001), "Fifth Century Nippur: Texts of the Murašûs and from Their Surroundings," *JCS* 53: 83-132.

Waerzeggers, Caroline (2000/2001), *Het archief van Marduk-rēmanni.* Dissertation, University of Ghent.

— (forthcoming), "Xerxes and the End of Archives," *AfO* 50.

Walker, C.B.F. and D. Collon (1980), "Hormuzd Rassam's Excavations for the British Museum at Sippar in 1881-1882," in L. de Meyer (ed.), *Tell ed-Dēr. Sounding at Abū Ḥabbah (Sippar)* (Leuven: Peeters): 93-114.

Weber, Max (1980), *Wirtschaft und Gesellschaft. Grundriß der verstehenden Soziologie. Fünfte, revidierte Auflage besorgt von Johannes Winckelmann* (Tübingen: Mohr Siebeck) [First edition 1921].

Weszeli, Michaela (with a contribution by H. D. Baker) (1997), "Eseleien II," *WZKM* 87: 231-47.

— (2002), *Textzeugen zu Schiffen und Schiffern im zweiten und ersten Jahrtausend v. Chr.: Die Schiffahrt im Süden Mesopotamiens und in Mari.* Dissertation, University of Vienna.

Wunsch, Cornelia (1993), *Die Urkunden des babylonischen Geschäftsmannes Iddin-Marduk. Zum Handel mit Naturalien im 6. Jahrhundert v. Chr.* (Cuneiform Monographs 3; Groningen: STYX).

Zadok, Ran (2003), "The Representation of Foreigners in Neo- and Late-Babylonian Legal Documents (Eighth through Second Centuries B.C.E.)," in O. Lipschits and J. Blenkinsopp, *Judah and the Judeans in the Neo-Babylonian Period* (Winona Lake: Eisenbraus): 471-589.

Zawadzki, Stefan and Michael Jursa (2001), "Šamaš-tirri-kuṣur, a Smith Manufacturing Weapons in the Ebabbar Temple at Sippar," *Wiener Zeitschrift für die Kunde des Morgenlandes* 91: 347-63.

Zettler, Richard L. (1991), "Administration of the Temple of Inanna at Nippur under the Third Dynasty of Ur: Archaeological and Documentary Evidence," in McG. Gibson and R.D. Biggs 1991: 101-14.

— (1992), *The Ur III Temple of Inanna at Nippur. The Operation and Organization of Urban Religious Institutions in Mesopotamia in the Late Third Millennium B.C.* (Berlin: Reimer).

7.

Weight Systems and Trade Networks in the Old World (2500-1000 BC)

Alfredo Mederos and C.C. Lamberg-Karlovsky
Harvard University

The presence of raw materials imported from the Indus Valley, Persian Gulf, Mesopotamia, Egypt and the eastern Mediterranean reflect the existence of commercial exchanges throughout the Bronze Age. In each of these regions independent weight systems were developed. Our study demonstrates that commercial relationships developed conversion systems that enabled the different weight systems to be equated with mutual confidence. This convertibility facilitated international trade and exchange.

Introduction

In the last three decades it has become increasingly clear that an abundance of imported artifacts, discovered from Egypt to the Indus Valley and from Central Asia to the Arabian Peninsula, attest to the existence of a lively international trade that was already in place by 2500 BC.

Settlement at Ugarit (Syria), the most important port of the eastern Mediterranean throughout the Late Bronze Age (Courtois 1990), or the shipwreck of Uluburun (Turkey), dated to around 1300 BC (Pulak 1997, 1998), demonstrate the coexistence, within the same city, and on a single ship, the co-occurrence of multiple weight systems. Whether it was within a city or on a ship, merhants were able to convert the standard weight system of the region they were visiting to that of other regions. Needless to say, the existence of conversion systems was particularly important to a ship such as the Uluburun, for it carried a rich load of merchandise to be sold in eastern Mediterranean ports, where a number of different weight systems prevailed.

Foreign trade and long-distance exchange permitted communities to obtain resources which they lacked from distance places, such as lapis lazuli from Afghanistan. Exotic and precious materials also played an important role in conferring status and prestige upon the community and/or the individual capable of commanding such resources.

Additionally, the presence of imports and exports integrated distant regions into commercial and social networks, further conveying prestige and status upon individuals and communities. Patterns of production, consumption and redistribution were transformed by the expanding networks of trade and gift exchange that characterized the Bronze Age Near East.

Weight systems

The principal function of a given weight system was to guarantee that the buyer and the seller exchanged a standard quantity of goods. The principal function of the conversion system, permitting one weight system to be converted into another, was to guarantee the mutual confidence of their equivalence between buyer and seller.

The need for conversion systems was of paramount importance in dealing with transactions involving precious metals, gold and silver, or aromatic essences of great value such as incense. In order to facilitate the conversion of the weight of an object, *i.e.*, an ingot, the object was "packaged," that is produced to weigh a specific amount. The Uluburun ingots weighed about 1 Syrian talent, allowing for a ready conversion into other weight systems (see Chart 1).

A Sumerian text c. 1800 BC addresses the convertibility of different weight systems: "... they had given to us 5.5⅔ minas of copper according to the standard of Dilmun. Its weight is in total 611 talents 6⅔ minas according to the standard of Ur ..." (Roaf 1982: 137-38).

The Uluburun ship was transporting a rich inventory of merchandise, including 354 oxhide copper ingots, of which 317 were four-handled and 31 two-handled, each weighing c. 1 Syrian-Ugaritic talent equal to 28 kg 200 gr, 5 were pillow-shaped of ca. 10.75 kg and 1 was a small four-handled ingot (Pulak 1998: 193-94). The standardization of shape was complemented by that of weight, so that upon arrival in port one needed only to weigh one ingot of a given shape to note the similar weight of all others of that shape.

We know that rare resources such as lapis lazuli were reaching Mesopotamia, Egypt and the Aegean from the closest and indeed only known source, in Afghanistan (Hermann 1968). In Egypt lapis lazuli is present already in predynastic contexts c. 3200 BC (Davis 1983:25), while in Mesopotamia it is a relatively common item in the Uruk period c. 3500 BC (Moorey 1994), while its presence is noted in tomb A of Ayia Triada on Crete c. 2200 BC (Lambrou 1990:192). A Mesopotamian text of Gudea, c. 2130 BC, is explicit with regard to these imports: "Copper and tin, blocks of lapis lazuli, (...) bright carnelian from Meluhha [India]" (Rosen 1988:39). Laboratory analysis of lapis lazuli artifacts recovered from archaeological contexts confirms the fact that the lapis lazuli in the above regions was coming from the Sar-i-Sang mines, located in the Badakhshan region of Afghanistan (Delmas and Casanova 1990:502, 504; Casanova 1992:56).

To date a comprehensive study of the numerous weight systems within the Indus Valley, Egypt, the Near East, and the eastern Mediterranean, together with their conversion rates, has not been undertaken. The significant contributions of Parise (1981, 1986) and Zaccagnini (1986a, 1986b) have offered a foundation for this study.

Previous studies

Four trends exist within studies pertaining to the analysis of weight systems. The first has sought to demonstrate the interrelationship between most of the metrological systems (Lehmann-Haupt 1918) as well as their continuity into the weight systems of the modern era (Berriman 1953; McDonald 1992).

A second trend attemps to relate metrological norms that connect distant regions. An example of this approach connects the Dilmun weight of c. 1371 grs to its shared use in distant regions, *i.e.*, the Indus Valley, Persian Gulf and Mesopotamia. It should come as no great surprise that these three regions, connected by more or less regular commercial exchanges (Ratnagar 1981; Edens 1992), were all aware of and used a common, but not exclusive, weight system (Bibby 1970). A second example is provided by the Hyksos invasion of Egypt in the Second Intermediate Period (Dynasty XV c. 1640-1530 BC). The Hyksos introduced to Egypt from Syria/Palestine the Syrian shekel of c. 9.4 (8.8-10) grs. This became the standard weight of the XVIII Dynasty in Egypt (Weigall 1908:ix).

A third current is extremely conservative. It argues that an insufficient metrological data base prohibits one from formulating comparative weight systems and their equivilances. In spite of a relatively rich textual and archaeological data base, especially in Mesopotamia, this school believes that only with the recovery of more substantive evidence can one resolve the nature of comparative metrological systems (Weisbach 1907; Powell 1979, 1983, 1990).

Finally, a fourth trend, concerned with unraveling the nature of the economic systems that brought the Indus Valley, the Persian Gulf, Mesopotamia, Egypt and the eastern Mediterranean into contact throughout the third and later millennia, considers the fact that independent weight systems were developed in each of the above regions and efforts were made to allow for the conversion of these different standard weights in order to facilitate trade and exchange. The commercial relationships that tied these different regions together demanded the development of conversion systems (Liverani 1972, Parise 1981 and 1986, Roaf 1982; Archi and Klengel-Brandt 1984; Petruso 1992; Zaccagnini 1986a, 1986b and 1991; Courtois 1990; Cour-Marty 1990; Eran 1996). Within the context a model approach is offered by Parise (1981), who attempts to relate the Hittite, Ugarit and Karkemish weight systems.

A new view

Our proposal demonstrates the interrelationship and conversion of the different weight systems. For example, a Syrian-Ugaritic talent has 28.2 kg=28.200 grs. This can be subdivided by 60 minas of 470 grs, 60 × 470 grs = 28.200 grs. At the same time, each mina can be subdivided to 50 shekels of 9.4 grs, 50 × 9.4 grs = 470 grs. Consequently, 3000 shekels of 9.4 grs formed a talent of 28.2 kg, 3000 × 9.4 grs = 28.200 grs (see Chart 1).

This Ugaritic shekel (US) of 9.4 grs can be correlated with all the weight systems of the Near East and eastern Mediterranean. It is equal to the Egyptian *kdt* (EK) which also is 9.4 grs. At the same time it equals ¾ of the Egyptian gold *dbn* (ED) of 12.83 grs. Furthermore, four Ugaritic shekels (4 × 9.4 grs = 37.6 grs) is roughly equivalent to three Egyptian gold *dbn* (3 × 12.83 grs = 38.49 grs). We doubt that the weight measurements in the third or second millennium BC were accurate enough to detect an error of less than 1 gram in 38, or 2.6%.

These equivalences permitted one to make use of weights that were generally multiples of 2 and 5. For example, two weights with the value of 2 Ugaritic shekels, 18.8 grs (9.4 grs × 2) + 18.8 grs = 37.6 grs. In turn, one could equate the 37.6 Ugarit weight with weights having the value of 1 and 2 Egyptian gold dbn, 12.8 grs + 25.6 grs = 38.4 grs. Thus, 2 + 2 Ugaritic shekels = 1 + 2 Egyptian gold *dbn* = c. 38 grs.

Taking other examples, 9.4 grs of the Ugaritic shekel equals ⅘ of the Hittite shekel (HS) of 11.75 grs. Therefore, 5 × 9.4 grs = 47 grs, at the same time 4 × 11.75 grs = 47 grs, thus allowing for the equivalences of a weight of 5 Ugaritic shekels to be the equivalent of two weights of 2 Hittite shekels, 5 Ugaritic shekels = 2 + 2 Hittite shekels = 47 grs.

The Ugaritic shekel equals 9.4 grs while the Mesopotamian shekel (MS) equals 8.55 grs. The difference between the two is 0.95 grs. (rounded off to 1 gram). Thus 10 Ugaritic shekels should equal 11 Mesopotamian shekels. A weight of 10 Ugaritc shekels (10 × 9.4 grs = 94 grs) equals 11 Mesopotamian shekels (11 × 8.55 grs = 94.05 grs). In commercial terms, a merchant would add 1 Mesopotamian shekel to a weight of 10 Mesopotamian shekels to equal a weight of 10 Ugaritic shekels, 10 US = 10 + 1 MS = 94 grams (Chart 1).

Second, on Chart 2 we offer the continuous conversion of a fixed weight of 1370 grams of lapis lazuli and 4700 grams of tin. The hypothetical weights of these objects are chosen from our own weight system. The chart indicates how this weight could be readily converted into the nine different weight systems registered on the chart in a hypothetical route East-West. For example, 1370 grs. would be equal to 100 Dilmun "shekels" (13.68 grs—Dilmun shekel— × 100 = 1368 grs), 160 Mesopotamian shekels (8.55 grs × 160 = 1368 grs), 175 Eblaitic-Karkemish shekels (7.83 grs × 175 = 1370 grs), etc.

Third, the port of Ugarit in North Syria was the principal commercial node in the eastern Mediterranean throughout the second half of the second millennium BC. At least five different weight systems coexisted in the city: Aegean, Hittite (Anatolia), Ugaritic (coastal Syria), Karkemish (inland Syria) and Mesopotamian. All these weight systems shared the predominance of weights measuring 1, 2, 5 and 10-shekel units. The use of these weights, in any manner of combination, allowed one to determine the weight of any object (Chart 3). The good correlations that we propose for the different weight systems, utilized in the different regions, are presented on Chart 4.

An analysis of the different weight systems that prevailed from the Indus Valley to Mesopotamia and Egypt suggests a very considerable complexity. Yet, we note that behind this complexity there exists a relative simplicity of structure that allows for the conversion of the different weight systems. Our investigation proves not only the fundamental structure of the rules of weight conversion but demonstrates that there was no confusion within the trade networks in dealing with comparable units of weight between far distant regions. As Adam Smith noted there is a propensity for man to "truck and barter," but that propensity is greatly enhanced when merchants are able to speak a related language. Weight conversion was a paramount component of that language. From the third millennium BC it formed the foundation for the economic interrelationship that connected the regions from the eastern Mediterranean to Egypt, Mesopotamia and the Indus Valley (Lamberg-Karlovsky 1972 and 1985; Zaccagnini 1986a and 1986b; Sherratt and Sherratt 1991; Cline 1994; Mederos 1997 and 1999), and as Colin Renfrew (1992: vii) has noted, was "one of the most significant early developments of the human intellect."

Writing and weights: A cognitive transformation and/or a technology of control

Writing, as well as standard weights and measures, first appears in Mesopotamia, Egypt, and the Indus Valley in the context of the first cities. A half century ago V.G. Childe (1950), in his classic study, recognized writing and weights and measures as two of the ten attributes that he defined as hallmarks of the "urban revolution." Their seminal role in the transformation of human society continues to play on center stage (Senner 1989).

Over a decade ago the psychologist Merlin Donald published his influential *Origin of the Modern Mind* (1991). In this work the author offers an overview of the human behavioral and cognitive evolution. His emphasis upon the cognitive phases of evolution interests us here. Specifically, the transition to the last stage of cognitive development; what he terms the emergence of "theoretic culture." This stage is characterized by the invention of systems of "external symbolic storage" by which is meant the development of a store of knowledge located outside of the human brain. In this regard the appearance of written texts, as well as the invention of standard weights and measures, is believed to attest to the emergence of "theoretic culture." The emergence of "external symbolic storage" systems "changed cognitive architecture completely" (Donald 1991:306).

> An entirely new memory structure was needed for readingand writing, including highly specialized skills, such as scanning and analyzing the written image. There was a rapid increase in the number of logograms, alphabetic items, words and graphic images in use; these had to be encoded in biological memory. One requirement for successful use of the ESS (external symbolic storage) is a *map* of its contents. Thus, biological memory must contain information about the structure and access routes of the ESS, as well as its retrieval codes. These skills are necessary, above and beyond the decoding skills needed to understand ESS entries, in order to find the appropriate information when needed. A significant percentage of the knowledge contained in the literate brain falls into this category; this is particularly true of scholars and administrators, whose familiarity with "field" or the "levers of power" usually translates into the possession of a good cognitive map of the ESS entries relevant to some highly specific pursuit..." (Donald 1991:320-21).

Alexander Marshack (1972) was among the first to discuss the importance of cognitive evolution in his treatment of the first decorated and "notational" objects recovered from the Paleolithic period of tens of thousands of years ago. Twenty years ago Colin Renfrew (1982:17) asked whether one could examine the operation of the mind from archaeological evidence. He offered an affirmative answer and one of his examples was in the unraveling of the Indus weight system (0.836 grs) multiplied by integers such as 1, 4 or 8 up to 64 then 320 and 1,600. The development of a unit of measure is taken as an important step in the procedure of mapping the world—a cognitive mapping. More recently Jacques Cauvin (2000) and David Lewis-Williams (2002) attempted to probe the cognitive structures of the mind evident in the first farming communities and of those that produced some of the earliest rock art. Donald (1991) considers the transformations of our cognitive abilities within a long evolutionary perspective, taking us from the Paleolithic to the computer age. The appearance of written texts, as well as weights and measures, attest to the emergence of what he terms "theoretic culture." Donald (1991:340) states, "Until writing could be combined with other visual symbolic media, the *theoretic attitude*, that is, the deliberate analytic use of symbolic thought, had little chance to develop" (emphasis in original). The most important attribute in the emergence of the theoretic stage is the invention of "external symbolic storage" systems, *i.e.*, writing and symbols of meaning, as with weights and measures. Thus, a weight bears no relationship to what is weighed and a number has no perceptual relationship to what is represented. Within an evolutionary context the increasing recognition that goods (property) could be, or were allowed to be, systematically exchanged led to an increasing significance of commodity and value. This, in turn, demanded units of measure and a permanence of memory, namely, the development of writing. Donald's second evolutionary cognitive transformation, the emergence of a "theoretic culture," privileges the development of writing as a powerful tool for "external symbolic storage."

Donald argues that writing played a major role in transforming the cognitive processes of the mind by introducing new systems of symbolic storage. If, however, one looks upon the function and nature of the earliest writing, as well as standard weights and measures, one finds them to be new and powerful technologies of social control. Thus, the transforming of cognitive processes in conjunction with a new technology of social control were co-evolutionary processes that transformed both brain and culture.

Writing, whether in ancient Egypt, Mesopotamia, China or the New World, is frequently portrayed as allowing for the collective management and distribution of staple products, controlling the organization of labor and crafts, glorifying the deeds and genealogy of the rulers, and eventually permitting for the codification of law, taxes, interest rates, etc. Within an evolutionary perspective writing is seen as an event-like invention, a powerful tool controlled by the elite in processes leading to the centralization of power. It is self-evident that bureaucratic control does not necessarily serve the interests of the community; it is as likely to serve specific segments of society in their quest for economic privileges. In like manner standardized weights and measurements serve not only to facilitate trade but to control that trade. Thus, toward the end of the third millennium a well-known archaeological artifact is the duck-weight with inscription. The inscription attests to the validity of the weight as authorized by the state. Typically, archaeologists working in the Near East relate writing, cylinder seals, and the standardization of weights and measures as tools of administrative bureaucracy that came into being in the Uruk Period (c. 3500 BC) in the contexts of the first states. A transforming cognitive world within a context of a technology of invented writing should come as no surprise.

With the invention of a writing technology comes an unprecedented rate of cultural change and technological innovation. The co-evolution of writing, monumental architecture, rapid urbanization, standard weights and measurements, the expansion of the crafts, extensive long-distance trade, and an evermore elaborate bureaucracy cannot be a coincidence. All of the above features appear in concert and although occurring in different places at different times, they appear in each instance rather rapidly, whether it be in China, Egypt, Mesopotamia, or Mesoamerica. One can see in this synergistic process the evolution of cultural complexity, a complexity that Robert McC. Adams (2000: 101) correctly perceives as "essentially technological," a movement toward greater centralization and integration. If writing allowed for the beginnings of a system of "external symbolic storage" permitting for a permanence of memory through the written word, it also permitted for a communications revolution through the emergence of an administrative bureaucracy. Cognitive transformation and technologies of social control went hand-in-hand, bringing about a new social and mental map of the world.

Standard Weight Systems	Mass	Talents	Minas	Shekels	Equivalences	**Weights**
Syrian talent	•	**28.200**				
mina	kgs.	**470**×60				
Hittite shekel (HS)	grs. grs.	11.75	×40	×2400	5/4 of 9.4 3/2 of 7.83 12/7 of 6.84 9/5 of 6.58	(HS) 2+2=5 (US-EK) (HS) 2=2+1 (EKS) (HS) 5+2=10+2 (IS) (HS) 5=5+2+2 (AS)
Ugaritic shekel (US)	grs.	9.4	×50	×3000	7/10 of 13.68 3/4 of 12.83 4/5 of 11.75 11/10 of 8.55 6/5 of 7.83 11/8 of 6.84 10/7 of 6.58	(US) 10=5+2 (DS) (US) 2+2=2+1 (ED) (US) 5=2+2 (HS) (US) 10=10+1 (MS) (US) 5=5+1 (EKS) (US) 5+2=10 (IS) (US) 5+2=10 (AS)
Egyptian kdt (Dynasty XVIII...) (EK)	grs.	9.4		×3000	7/10 of 13.68 3/4 of 12.83 4/5 of 11.75 11/10 of 8.55 6/5 of 7.83 10/7 of 6.58	(EK) 10=5+2 (DS) (EK) 2+2=2+1 (ED) (EK) 5=2+2 (HS) (EK) 10=10+1 (MS) (EK) 5=5+1 (EKS) (EK) 5+2=10 (IS)
Eblaite-Karkemish shekel (EKS)	grs.	7.83	×60	×3600	4/7 of 13.68 8/13 of 12.83 2/3 of 11.75 5/6 of 9.4 12/13 of 8.55 8/7 of 6.84	(EKS) 5+2=2+2 (DS) (EKS)10+2+1=5+2+1 (ED) (EKS 2+1=2 (HS) (EKS) 5+1=5 (US-EK) (EKS)10+2+1=10+2 (MS) (EKS) 5+2=5+2+1 (IS)
Mesopotamian talent	kgs.	**30.800**				
Mesopotamian mina		**513**×60				
Mesopotamian shekel (MS)	grs.	8.55	×60	×3600	5/8(10/16) of 13.68 3/2 of 12.83 10/11 of 9.4 13/12 of 7.83 5/4 of 6.84 13/10 of 6.58	(MS)10+5+1=10 (DS) (MS) 2=2+1 (ED) (MS) 10+1=10 (US-EK) (MS) 10+2=10+2+1 (EKS) (MS) 2+2=5 (IS) (MS) 10=10+2+1 (AS)
gold Egyptian dbn (Dynasty VI-XVII) (ED)	grs.	12.8(3)		×2400	15/16 of 13.68 4/3 of 9.4 2/3 of 8.55 13/8 of 7.83 2/1(15/8) of 6.84 2/1 of 6.58	(ED) 10+5+1=10+5 (DS) (ED) 2+1=2+2 (US-EK) (ED) 2+1=2 (MS) (ED) 5+2+1=10+2+1 (EKS) (ED) 1=2(5+2+1)=(10+5) (IS) (ED) 1=2 (AS)
Dilmun mina		1368		×22.5		
Dilmun shekel (DS)	grs.	13.68		×2250	16/15 of 12.83	(DS) 10+5=10+5+1 (ED)
Indus "shekel" (IS)	grs. grs.	6.84		×4500	10/7 of 9.4 8/5(16/10) of 8.55 7/4 of 7.83 2/1 of 6.84 2/1(25/12) of 6.58	(DS) 5+2=5+5 (US-EK) (DS) 10=10+5+1 (MS) (DS) 2+2=5+2 (EKS) (DS) 1=2 (IS) (DS) 10+2=10+10+5 (AS)
Ashdodite talent		**23.700**				
Ashdodite mina	kgs.	**474**×50				
Ashdodite shekel (AsS)	grs. grs.	7.9(7.83)	×60	×3000	4/7 of 13.68 8/13 of 12.83 4/1(12/3) of 11.75 5/6 of 9.4 12/13 of 8.55 6/5 of 6.58	(AsS) 5+2=2+2 (DS) (AsS) 10+2+1=5+2+1 (ED) (AsS) 2+1=10+2 (HS) (AsS) 5+1=5 (US-EK) (AsS) 10+2+1=10+2 (MS) (AsS) 5=5+1 (AS)
Aegean talent		**31.600**				
Aegean mina	kgs.	**480**×65.8				
Aegean "shekel" (AS)	grs. grs.	65.8 6.58	 ×72	 ×4800	1/2(12/25) of 13.68 1/2 of 12.83 5/9 of 11.75 7/10 of 9.4 10/13 of 8.55 5/6 of 7.9 1/1(75/28) of 6.84	(AS) 10+10+5=10+2 (DS) (AS) 2=1 (ED) (AS) 5+2+2=5 (SH) (AS) 10=5+2 (US-EK) (AS) 10+2+1=10 (MS) (AS) 5+1=5 (EKS) (AS) 10+10+5+1=10+10+5 (IS)

Chart 1: Weights systems between the third and first millennia BC.

SOURCE AFGHANISTAN	RAW MATERIAL example 1	SOURCE AFGHANISTAN	RAW MATERIAL example 2
ROUTE EAST-WEST	LAPISLAZULI ' INGOT' 1370 grs.	ROUTE EAST-WEST	TIN INGOT 4700 grs or 4.7 kg.
Dilmun-Indus "shekel" INDUS-GULF	100 "shekels"	Dilmun-Indus "shekel"	344 "shekels" 3.5 minas
Mesopotamian shekel MESOPOTAMIA	160 shekels 100+50+10	Mesopotamian shekel	550 shekels
Eblaite-Karkemish shekel SYRIA	175 shekels 100+50+20+5	Eblaite-Karkemish shekel	600 shekels 10 minas
Ugaritic shekel SYRIA	145 shekels 100+20+20+5	Ugaritic shekel	500 shekels 10 minas
Hittite shekel ANATOLIA	117 shekels 100+10+5+1+1	Hittite shekel	400 shekels 10 minas
Ashdodite shekel PALESTINE	175 shekels 100+50+20+5	Ashdodite shekel	600 shekels 10 minas
gold Egyptian dbn EGYPT	107 dbn 100+5+1+1	gold Egyptian dbn	366 dbn
Egyptian kdt EGYPT	145 kdt 100+20+20+5	Egyptian kdt	500 shekels 5 sep
Aegean "shekel" CRETE-GREECE	208 "shekels" 100+100+5+2+1	Aegean "shekel"	71 "shekels" 4.5 M*

Chart 2: Two examples of the continuous conversion of a fixed weight: 1370 grams of lapis lazuli, weight in grams according to the current standard, with the different prevalent weight systems between the third and the first millennia BC in a east-west route, from the mines in Afghanistan.

ARTIFACTS USED AS WEIGHTS IN THE DIFFERENT WEIGHT SYSTEMS					
Value in shekels	Mesopotamia n	Ugaritic	Karkemish	Hittite	Aegean
1		39	2	8	
2	3	47	3	–	
5	5	29	2	–	
10	7	46	4	–	2
20	15	25	2	–	
50	13	10		3	
100	8	7			
200	7	3			
1000	4	5			

Chart 3: Correlation of archaeological artifacts used as weights with their value in shekels to the different weight systems of the Near East and the Aegean at the port of Ugarit (Syria) during the second half of the second millennium BC, where is observed the coexistence of at least 5 weight systems in the city, and the predominance in all of them of weights of 1, 2, 5, 10 and 20 shekels, which facilitate the transactions (Courtois 1990: 120-122).

Source	Hittite	Ugarit	Kdt Egypt	Ebla	Akkad Babylonia	Dbn Egypt	Dilmun Indus	Ashdod	Aegean
Mederos-Karlovsky, 01	11.75	9.4	9.4	7.83	8.55	12.83	13.68	7.83	65.8
Archi 87	11.75		9.4	7.8-7.83					
Bibby 70							1371.5-1376.8		
Cour-Marty 90			8.8-9.8		7.9-8.8	12-13		7.52	
Courtois 90	11.2-11.8	9-9.9		7.83	8-8.5				61.25-64
Eran 96					8.18-8.41	13.65	13.65		
Heltzer 96	11.75		9.1-9.4	7.8-7.9	8.0			7.52	
Hemmy 35					8.22		13.62		
Hendrickx-Baudot 72							13.69		
Liverani 72	11.75	9.4		7.83					
Parise 81	11.75	9.4		7.83					
Parise 86	11.75	9.4		7.83				7.83	65.27
Parise 91	11.75	9.4	9.4	7.83	8.42			7.83	65.27
Petruso 92									61
Powell 79					8.13-8.6		1370		
Powell 90					8.33			7.8-7.9	
Roaf 82			9.7				1350		
Segre 28					8.37	12.77-14.17			65
Weigall 08			8.8-10			13-14.2			
Zaccagnini 86			9.4	7.9	8.42		1350	7.9	6.5-6.8
Zaccagnini 91	11.75	9.4		7.83	8.5				6.5-6.8

Table 4: Current proposals about the weight systems in grams between the third and the first millennia BC.

BIBLIOGRAPHY

Archi, A. and Klengel-Brandt, E. (1984), "I pesi provenienti da Zincirli," *Studi Micenei ed Egeo Anatolici* 24:245-61.

Berriman, Algernon Edward (1953), *Historical Metrology. A New Analysis of the Archaeological and the Historical Evidence Relating to Weights and Measures* (London: J.M. Dent & Sons).

Bibby, T.G. (1970), "...Efter Dilmun Norm," *P. V. Glob På 60 Årsdagen. Kuml* 1970:345-53.

Casanova, Michèle (1992), "The Sources of the Lapis-lazuli Found in Iran," in C. Jarrige, J.P. Gerry and R.H. Meadow (eds.), *10th South Asian Archaeology 1989 (Guimet, Paris, 1989)* (Monographs in World Archaeology, 14; Madison: Prehistoric Press):49-56.

Cauvin, Jacques (2000), *The Birth of the Gods* (Cambridge: Cambridge University Press).

Childe, V. Gordon (1950), "The Urban Revolution," *Town Planning Review* 21:3-17.

Cline, E.H. (1994), *Sailing the Wine-Dark Sea. International Trade and the Late Bronze Age Aegean* (British Archaeological Reports, International Series, 591; Oxford: Tempus Reparatum).

Cour-Marty, M.A. (1990), "Les poids égyptiens, de précieux jalons archéologiques," *Sociétés urbaines en Egypte et au Sudan. Cahier de Recherches de l'Insitut de Papyrologie et d'Egyptologie de Lille* 12:17-55.

Courtois, J.C. (1990), "Poids, prix, taxes et salaires, à Ougarit (Syrie) au IIe millénaire," in R. Gyselen (ed.), *Prix, salaires, poids et mesures. Res Orientales* 2:119-27.

Davis, W. (1983), "Cementery T at Nagada," *Mitteilungen des Deutschen Archäologischen Instituts, Abteilung Kairo* 39:17-28.

Delmas, A.B. and M. Casanova (1990), "The Lapis Lazuli Sources in the Ancient East," in M. Taddei and P. Callieri (eds.), *9th South Asian Archaeology 1987 (Venice, 1987)* (Serie Orientale, Roma, 66 (1); Rome: Istituto Italiano per il Medio ed Estremo Oriente):493-505.

Donald, Merlin (1991), *Origins of the Modern Mind: Three Stages in the Evolution of Culture and Cognition.* (Cambridge: Harvard University Press).

Edens, C. (1992), "Dynamics of Trade in the Ancient Mesopotamian 'World System'," *American Anthropologist* 94 (1):118-39.

Eran, A. (1996), "Weights and Weighing in the City of David: The Early Weights from the Bronze Age to the Persian Period," in D.T. Ariel and A. de Groot (eds.), *Excavations at the City of David 1978-1985*. IV, (Qedem 35; Jerusalem: The Hebrew University of Jerusalem): 204-56.

Heltzer, Michael (1996), "The 'Unification' of Weight and Measure Systems in Foreign Trade in the Eastern Mediterranean (1500-700 BCE)," *Michmanim* 9: 31-38.

Hemmy, A.S. (1935), "The Statistical Treatment of Ancient Weights," *Ancient Egypt and the East* 1935 (1): 83-93.

Hendrickx-Baudot, M.P. (1972), "The Weights of the Harappa-Culture," *Orientalia Lovaniensia Periodica* 3: 5-34.

Hermann, G. (1968), " 'Lapis lazuli'. The Early Phases of Its Trade," *Iraq* 30 (1): 21-57.

Lamberg-Karlovsky, C.C. (1972), "Trade Mechanisms in Indus-Mesopotamian Interrelations," *JAOS* 92: 222-29.

— (1985), "The Longue Durée of the Ancient Near East," in J.L. Huot, M. Yon and Y. Calvet (eds.), *De l'Indus aux Balkans, Recueil Jean Deshayes*, (Éditions Recherche sur les civilisations; Paris): 55-72.

Lambrou-Phillipson, C. (1987), *Hellenorientalia: The Near Eastern Presence in the Bronze Age Aegean ca. 3000-1100 B.C. plus Orientalia: a Catalogue of Egyptian, Mesopotamian, Mitannian, Syro-Palestinian, Cypriot and Asia Minor Objects from the Bronze Age Aegean*, (Studies in Mediterranean Archaeology, Pocket Books; Göteborg: Paul Åströms Förlag).

Lehmann-Haupt, Carl Friedrich (1918), "Gewichte," in G. Wissowa and W. Kroll (eds.), *Paulys Real-Encyclopädie der Classischen Altertumswissenschaft*. Supplementband 3 (Stuttgart: J.B. Metzlerscher Verlag): 587-654.

Lewis-Williams, David (2001), *The Mind in the Cave*. (London: Thames and Hudson).

Liverani, Mario (1972), "Il Talento di Ashdod," *OrAn* 11 (3): 193-199.

Marshack, Alexander (1973), *The Roots of Civilization: The Cognitive Beginnings of Man's First Art, Symbol, and Notation*. (New York: McGraw-Hill).

Mederos Martín, A. (1997), "Cambio de rumbo. Interacción comercial entre el Bronce Final Atlántico ibérico y el micénico en el Mediterráneo Central (1425-1050 A.C.)," *Trabajos de Prehistoria* 54 (2): 113-34.

— (1998), "Ex Occidente Lux. El comercio micénico en el Mediterráneo Central y Occidental (1625-1100 AC)," *Complutum* 10: 229-66.

— and Lamberg-Karlovsky, C.C. (2001): "Converting Currencies in the Old World. Simple Arithmetic Underpinned Trading throughout the Near East during the Bronze Age," *Nature* 411 (6836): 437 + 2 tables in http://www.nature.com.

Moorey, P. R. S. (1994), *Ancient Mesopotamian Materials and Industries* (Oxford: Clarendon Press).

Parise, Nicola F. (1981), "Mina di Ugarit, mina di Karkemish, mina di Khatti," *Dialoghi di Archeologia* N.S. 3: 155-59.

— (1986), "Unità ponderali Egee," in M. Marazzi, S. Tusa and L. Vagnetti (eds.), *Traffici Micenei nel Mediterraneo. Problemi storici e documentazione archeologica (Palermo, 1984)* (Taranto: Istituto per la Storia e l'Archeologia della Magna Grecia): 303-14.

— (1993), "Unità ponderali e circolazione metallica nell'Oriente mediterraneo," in T. Hackens *et alii* (eds.), *A Survey of Numismatic Research 1985-1990*, I (International Association of Professional Numismatics 12; Brussels): 28-34.

Petruso, Karl M. (1992), *Ayia Irini: The Balance Weights. An Analysis of Weight Measurement in Prehistoric Crete and the Cycladic Islands*, in J. L. Caskey (ed.) (Keos VIII; Mainz: Philipp von Zabern).

Powell, Marvin A. (1979), "Ancient Mesopotamian Weight Metrology: Methods, Problems and Perspectives," in M.A. Powell and R.H. Sack (eds.), *Studies in Honour of T. B. Jones* (AOAT 203): 71-201.

— (1983), "The Standard of Dilmun," in D.T. Potts (ed.), *Dilmun. New Studies in the Archaeology and Early History of Bahrain* (Berlin: Dietrich Reimer Verlag): 141-42.

— (1990), "Maße und Gewichte," in D.O. Edzard (ed.), *Reallexikon der Assyriologie und Vorderasiatischen Archäologie*, 7, (Berlin — New York: Walter de Gruyter): 457-517.

Pulak, C. (1997), "The Uluburun Shipwreck," in S. Swiny, R.L. Hohlfelder and H. Wylde Swiny (eds.), *Res Maritimae. Cyprus and the Eastern Mediterranean from Prehistory to Late Antiquity (Nicosia, 1994)*, (American School of Oriental Research, Archaeological Report 4; Atlanta: Scholars Press): 233-62.

— (1998), "Uluburum shipwreck: an overview," *The International Journal of Nautical Archaeology* 27 (3): 188-224.

Ratnagar, Shereen (1981), *Encounters. The Westerly Trade of the Harappan Civilization* (New Delhi: Oxford University Press).

Renfrew, Colin (1992), "Foreword," in C.J. Scarre (ed.), *The Origins of Metrology* (Cambridge: McDonald Institute for Archaeological Research, University of Cambridge): vii-viii.

Roaf, Michael (1982), "Weights on the Dilmun Standard," *Iraq* 44:137-41.

Rosen, L. von (1988), *Lapis lazuli in Geological Context and in Ancient Written Sources*, (Studies in Mediterranean Archaeology and Literature, Pocket-book 65; Partille: Paul Åströms Förlag).

Scarre, Christopher J. (1992), "Accuracy of Extant Sumerian Weights," in C.J. Scarre (ed.), *The Origins of Metrology. Collected Papers of Dr. Daniel McLean McDonald* (Cambridge: McDonald Institute for Archaeological Research, University of Cambridge):41-47.

Segrè, Angelo (1928), *Metrologia e circolazione monetaria degli antichi*, (Bologna: Nicola Zanichelli).

Sherratt, A. and S. Sherratt (1992), "From Luxuries to Commodities: The Nature of Mediterranean Bronze Age Trading Systems," in N.H. Gale (ed.), *Bronze Age Trade in the Mediterranean*, (Studies in Mediterranean Archaeology 90; Jonsered):351-86.

Weigall, Arthur E.P. (1908), *Weights and Balances. Catalogue Général des Antiquités Égyptiennes du Musée du Caire, n° 31.271-31.670* (Le Caire: Institut Français d'Archéologie Orientale).

Weissbach, Franz Heinrich (1907), "Über die babylonischen, assyrischen und altpersischen Gewichte," *Zeitschrift der Deutschen Morgenländischen Gesellschaft* 61 (2):379-402 and 61 (4):948-50.

Zaccagnini, Carlo (1986a), "Aspects of Copper Trade in the Eastern Mediterranean during the Late Bronze Age," in M. Marazzi, S. Tusa and L. Vagnetti (eds.), *Traffici Micenei nel Mediterraneo. Problemi storici e documentazione archeologica (Palermo, 1984)* (Taranto: Istituto per la Storia e l'Archeologia della Magna Grecia):413-24.

— (1986b), "The Dilmun Standard and Its Relationship with Indus and Near Eastern Weight Systems," *Iraq* 48:19-23.

— (1991), "'Nuragic' Sardinia: Metrological Notes." *II Congresso Internazionale di Studi Fenici e Punici* (Roma, 1987), I (Roma: Consiglio Nazionale delle Ricerche):343-47.

8.

Accounting Practices and Economic Planning in Ancient Egypt before the Hellenistic Era*

Ogden Goelet, Jr.
New York University

Introductory remarks

Given the long duration and stability of ancient Egypt's civilization, this great social edifice must have rested on the solid foundation of a well-run economy. Of course, the very phrase "well-run" immediately leads one to wonder about the level of planning that was necessary to ensure such long-standing success. But which Egypt does one have in mind? No history of Egypt's economy and its political system can approach that society as an unchanging entity. There were significant changes in direction at several junctures.

The greatest transition in Egypt's economic history occurred over the course of the Twenty-sixth or Saite Dynasty (664-525 BC), as Egypt turned to the outside world as never before and began to integrate its economy with that of the entire Eastern Mediterranean. A major force behind that change, if not the initial impetus that started Egypt on the path from its largely autarchic economy to a major trading nation, was the appearance of Greek colonists as permanent settlers at the western Delta town of Naucratis during the early years of the Twenty-sixth Dynasty. Another major change came at the end of the same dynasty, when the Persians conquered Egypt (525 BC) and turned it into their Sixth Satrapy.[1] The Persian administration brought in the first use of coinage—the start of the monetization of the Egyptian economy—in addition to completing a ship canal linking the

* All dates in this article follow those appearing in the chronological tables in Shaw 2000: 479-83.

[1] This is according to Herodotos, *Histories* III, 91, but it is not known whether the Persians had a fixed numbering system for their satrapies.

eastern branch of the Nile to the Red Sea, a project probably begun under the Saites. With these changes in its political and economic structure, Egypt emerged as a maritime power in both trade and warfare. As a result, Egypt's economic center of gravity shifted northwards to the Delta. Although even greater changes were to come under the rule of the Ptolemies, it is safe to say that together the period of Saite and Persian rule marked a watershed in Egypt's economic history.[2]

However, at no time during these great transitions, or even during the Ptolemaic regime that followed, did the mechanisms of the old and somewhat obsolete native economy entirely disappear, especially in connection with agricultural practices and temple staffing. Certain "home truths" based on the old economy remained in place and were used effectively by both the Persians and the Greeks. Accordingly, this paper focuses on planning before the Twenty-sixth Dynasty in order to understand some of the fundamentals of Egypt's early economy and the degree to which it was managed.

This is a vast, yet elusive topic. Despite an abundance of textual references to plans of one kind or another, there is considerably more evidence of foresight as an ideal than information concerning the plans themselves. There has been little treatment of planning in Egyptological literature, but in light of the potentially enormous size of this topic, one can easily see why this is so. I cannot hope to fill this gap within the constraints of a paper as short as this, so I shall concentrate on a few instances, primarily from one archive, and then make some generalizations from these examples. The following paper is in many respects the foundation for a more extensive treatment at a future date.

I. The concept of planning in Ancient Egypt

It would be unrealistic to expect that economic planning could have existed in ancient Egypt in the sense that one thinks of the concept today. The essential tools of planning—centralized, timely collection and communication of nation-wide economic data followed by its statistical analysis and development of policy—were either rather rudimentary or nonexistent. One might further raise the fundamental

[2] Other major economic innovations such as the introduction of the practices of long-term debt and interest may have been initiated as early as the late Third Intermediate Period, but the facts surrounding these changes are rather elusive. On these questions, see Goelet 2002: 277-84.

question of whether long-term planning on a national level could have been useful or effective given the largely unmonetized system that prevailed before Hellenistic times. Due to the almost exclusively agricultural basis of the economy throughout most of its history, Egyptian economic planning was necessarily more reactive than proactive. The most essential forces of nature were and still are unpredictable and beyond human control. Still, the picture was never completely uncertain. Compared with their contemporaries in the Mesopotamian heartland, who were at the mercy of irregular rainfalls and erratic rivers, the Egyptians lived in a distinctly more predictable environment. They were blessed with some ability to predict crop yields according to the current year's flood level. There is ample evidence to show that they used this information as the basis for some degree of short-term planning both on the national and local level, so that Egypt's institutions ran smoothly and were not entirely at the mercy of the vagaries of climate.

Planning and foresight as ideals in Ancient Egyptian sources: Theoretical and metaphorical aspects of the economy

In the ancient world people believed that climate was controlled by the gods and was part of the divine order. When studying any aspect of ancient Egyptian political and economic structure, it is therefore important not to underestimate the power that religion had over the ways the Egyptians conceptualized the relationship between many aspects of their daily life and the creation of the world—the relationship between the actual and the mythical, if you will. In a remarkable passage in the Coffin Texts which Egyptologists have dubbed "The Four Great Deeds of the Creator," the demiurge states that he created nature's bounty for all mankind to share in equally.[3]

Another of the creator's benefactions was that he alerted humanity to their need to plan for the afterlife. Successful passage into a blessed afterlife required people not only to tailor their earthly behavior according to an exacting moral code, but also to create an estate in this world that would ensure a comfortable existence beyond the grave. These are all wonderful sentiments, but the Egyptians, being realists, understood that such great standards could be met only through careful management of their natural resources. It should come as no surprise, then,

[3] Coffin Texts 1130, CT VII 462d-464f. There are many translations of this important text available, see, for example, Lichtheim 1973:131-33, esp. 132 and Allen 2002:26-27.

that Egyptian texts are filled with words for knowledge, plans, and related concepts. In light of the vast scope of the vocabulary, only a few words from a wide selection can be examined here.[4]

The Treaty between Ramesses II and the Hittite king refers to another type of plan which could affect all aspects of life, including the economy: the plans of the gods.[5] In fact, an occasional *topos* in the construction of royal ideology was that the king had been chosen by divine foresight, the deities realizing ahead of time that the monarch would manage the land excellently on their behalf. In the *Blessing of Ptah*, another of Ramesses II's lengthier texts, we learn that a god could even engender a king with enlightened self-interest in mind, since a successful ruler would also be a prosperous one and thus bring the gods even greater benefactions in return for theirs. Perhaps the most common of all motifs in Egyptian temple reliefs depicts the monarch and his deity facing each other and exchanging favors. These scenes express the concept that kingship was based on a pattern of such reciprocal gift-giving, either in the form of *do ut des* "I (the god) give in order that you (the king) give" or *do quia dedisti* "I (the king) give because you (the god) have given." These concepts were by no means merely pious lip-service, but rather reflect the theoretical underpinning of Egyptian kingship and additionally served as the basis of much of their economic activity in actual practice.

One might say, then, that the king was the nexal point between humanity and the gods, the ultimate source of all benefactions from nature. Due to his intimate association with the gods, the king was also especially endowed with the quality of *śỉꜣ*, roughly "Perception," a divine hypostasis. Being well-provided with *śỉꜣ* meant that the monarch was more aware of plans of the gods and more able to intuit the correct course of action than anyone else. But, for the average Egyptian, divine intentions were largely hidden and probably unknowable. For instance, the great Ramesside didactic text, *The Instruction of Amenemope* warns:[6]

[4] For valuable overviews of many lexicographical problems connected with Egyptian economics, see Warburton 1997.

[5] On the theme of a divine plan in the Hittite Treaty and other Egyptian inscriptions, see Goelet and Levine 1998:266-75.

[6] Lichtheim 1976:159-60. In this respect, it is significant that in *The Tale of Sinuhe*, that great Middle Kingdom narrative tale, the hero should attribute his flight into foreign lands as a "plan of god," which he did not understand, see Loprieno 1996:406, fn. 18.

"Indeed, you do not know the plans of god /and should not weep for tomorrow."

At the same time there was a somewhat contrary line of thought among the royal and non-royal elite alike.[7] Throughout Egyptian history an essential element in the ideological self-presentation of any official, from the highest to the lowliest, was his ability to plan and to carry out the plans of others. This requirement extended even to the king, for the standard royal ideology demanded that the king portray himself as a ruler who faithfully executed the commands of the gods. The pharaoh was a good shepherd, that is to say, he was both a protector and manager of his flock, the Egyptian people. Not all plans, however, were simply divine commissions for the king to execute. Rulers frequently boasted of their own initiative and great foresight in the projects they initiated, not only because these propitiated the deities, but also because their plans had brought prosperity to the land. At the heart of most such descriptions was the term *sḫr*,[8] a portemanteau word with a vast range of meanings, most of which ultimately amount to a combination of the English words "plan" and "arrangement." Occasionally, this word appears in parallel with *nt-ˁ*, both terms referring to foresight and ordered arrangements. *Nt-ˁ* perhaps expressed a more formal and regular type of arrangement than did *sḫr*.

Lower down the social and political scale, officials patterned many aspects of their biographies after royal inscriptions. Accordingly, among the most treasured of all virtues an administrator could possess were his abilities as a manager. To be sure, these skills required his faithful execution of orders, either from the king or a superior official. Yet what would set an official apart from his peers, according to official self-presentations, was his knowledge of human behavior. During the Middle Kingdom the ability to plan was associated with an official's effectiveness and guidance, especially with his ability to administer independently of any guidance from above. As it was even for the king himself,

---

7 These "biographies" were to a certain extent ideological and literary exercises. For an overview of these qualities and the nature of the genre, see Gnirs 1996:191-241.

8 For a lexicographical sketch of the term *sḫr* and the related concept *nt-ˁ*, see Goelet and Levine 1998:262-71, with references. The two words appear together in several key passages in the treaty between Ramesses II and the Hittite Hattusili III.

a functionary's initiative was a mark of his effective governance.[9] More than anything else, the ideal official had to be able to manage other men and to stand out amongst his peers—important qualities, to be sure, but perhaps not what we need to know if we are interested in planning as an economic activity. Terms such as *sḫr* and *nt-ʿ* may play a paramount role in Egyptians' ideology of governance, but, ironically, these words rarely occur meaningfully in actual administrative documents.

Planning: Central administration and inspections

Planning and accounting practices are intimately related subjects. All effective systems of management require controls such as accounting and inspections to ensure that resources are being allocated and consumed according to plan. This would be especially necessary in Egypt where, according to the evidence from private individuals, temples, and royal decrees, endowments tended to be dispersed over hundreds of miles along the Nile River and its Delta.[10] Some early textual evidence alludes to the methods of oversight the early government may have employed. Some of the earliest readable Egyptian inscriptions mention a group of high-ranking officials called "the Following of Horus" who apparently accompanied the king, the earthly embodiment of the god Horus, on an annual progress across his dominion. The exact purpose of these tours and the intervals at which they took place are not known, but it is probably safe to view this custom as an early attempt at the fact-finding essential to any central control over the land. In a similar vein the earliest records also mention an annual or bi-annual cattle count that eventually developed into the system of recording regnal years. These counts were probably more wide-ranging than a census of cattle alone.

---

[9] In official self-presentations of the Middle Kingdom, the majority of the epithets employing the word *sḫr* imply that the plan originated with the official, not with a higher authority see the discussion and the table in Doxey 1998:51.

[10] For instance, in private tombs of the Old Kingdom, the estates providing income for an official's funerary establishment could be very widely dispersed, see Jacquet-Gordon 1962 and Gödecken 1976. Similarly, the institutions supporting royal funerary temples in the same period may have been largely concentrated in the vicinity of the king's temple, but many properties were located far away as were other institutions contributing income. See the overview in Posener-Kriéger 1976:611-34 and Roth 1991:177-86.

Equally important and at the heart of both customs was the king's role as Egypt's *theoretical* landlord. Perhaps one can view both customs as the first steps towards information gathering as the king's interests increasingly required a complex and wide-spread administration. The Egyptian monarchy seems to have realized at an early stage that it had to interact directly with its widely dispersed holdings, either through the king's personal inspections or through delegation of authority. Yet, in the end run, these observations amount to the banality that property requires management, which in turn must rest upon accurate information.

Already by the Archaic Period and the Old Kingdom (First through Sixth Dynasties c. 2686-2181 BC), there was a highly centralized administration located at the king's residence, a natural result of an often repeated notion in religious texts that the gods had given Egypt to the king to manage on their behalf. The Residence soon evolved into what we would consider as a capital city, or more accurately, an administrative capital. The central administration there supervised a great number of smaller, local institutions scattered across the country, which in turn handled the bulk of Egypt's planning and resource management for most of its existence as an independent nation.

A necessary part of what would make any administration "central" in the Egyptian context would be its control over activities in both Upper and Lower Egypt. How the royal institutions at the residential city evolved into what we might consider a proto-state managing these subsidiary organizations is a much debated question among historians and lies far beyond the scope of this paper. Nevertheless, one aspect of that development is fairly clear. Unlike the more urbanized path direction the early civilizations of Mesopotamia took, Egypt did not become much of an urban society until fairly late in its history. The existence of only two or three major royal administrative cities is a situation that probably persisted until the advent of the Persian period.

The vizierate and the central administration

One of the most informative of all texts pertaining to management and planning in ancient Egypt with regards to how the central administrations at the capital may have interacted with royal house, the temples, and other subsidiary institutions is *The Duties of the*

Vizier.[11] If the king can be described as the nexus between the world of the gods and humanity, then the vizier was the link between the king and the entire governmental apparatus. Metaphorically, he was the executive officer on the Egyptian Ship of State. The vizieral inscription dates to the early part of the Eighteenth Dynasty (c. 1550-1295 BC), when the Egyptian government had reached a rather high level of complexity and the overall governmental organization had changed considerably from its form under the Old and Middle Kingdoms. Putting aside the thorny questions about its actual compositional date, it is likely that this inscription describes basic operating principles which had been in place since the earliest days of the Egyptian state.

The Egyptians employed two basic, if somewhat obvious, methods of long-distance management: regular transmittal of orders and inspections from "headquarters" in the administrative capital. Local authorities in turn responded by regularly reporting back to the vizier's office either by letter or, more often, traveling to the capital to report to him personally.

The vizier's office apparently had archives of considerable size. From the tomb inscription of a Nineteenth Dynasty official named Mes or Mose, we know that, in a few cases, it may have been possible to trace some details back for several centuries.[12] These principles of reporting, archives, and inspections were more than mere theoretical ideals—they were the foundation of procedures that figure prominently in some administrative documents discussed below.

The vizieral inscription is quite lengthy and has already been the subject of a number of extensive studies. Accordingly, I shall discuss only a few passages that seem particularly good illustrations of the main themes of the text—the vizier's strong control over the central administration and his delegation of authority to his agents or various sorts of local officials.

---

[11] Three Eighteenth Dynasty and one Nineteenth Dynasty copies of this text are known. The most complete and best preserved is that of the Vizier Rekhmire, see *Urk*. IV 1103, 14–1117, 5; Davies 1944, Pls. 119-122. A monograph-length analysis of this inscription appears in van den Boorn 1988. For a discussion of whether this text might be based on a Middle Kingdom original and other of its aspects, see van den Boorn 1982:369-81 and the review article by Lorton 1991:291-316.

[12] Gardiner 1905. For a more recent study and collation of this text, see Gaballa 1977. Also informative are Allam 1989:103-12 and Haring 1997:19, n. 3; Eyre 1994:116-19.

The first of the three excerpts I have chosen for discussion occurs near its beginning in a description of the vizier's responsibility over the *ẖnw* "Residential City" and the *pr-nśw*(*t*) "Royal Estate,"[13] the latter term comprising both the king's residence in addition to all legal and economic activity associated with the monarch. These aspects of the vizier's responsibility were an outgrowth of his title "Overseer of the City," which originally referred to his oversight of the king's pyramid city and construction there during the Old Kingdom. Since managing the *ẖnw* and the *pr-nśw* together entailed control over a considerable proportion of the entire state's administrative and economic activities, the title "Overseer of the City" obviously involved far more than acting as the local mayor at the administrative capital.

As early as the Old Kingdom, there was a striking, and most significant, orthographic peculiarity in the writing of those departments that the vizier and other high-ranking officials managed at the *ẖnw*, now the administrative capital. These organizations, particularly the Treasury and the Granary, were frequently written out with two *pr*-determinatives (Sign-list O1 "house, department"), indicating that they dealt with the affairs of both Upper and Lower Egypt.[14] These institutions had thus acquired the characteristics of what we would consider as

[13] In a major departure from van den Boorn's otherwise masterful treatment of this highly intricate inscription, I would tend to agree with Lorton (and several others) in assigning a more significant role to the *pr-nśw*(*t*) than that of primarily being the king's residence. The *pr-nśw*'s activities were far too wide-ranging to be connected with just a palace as residence. However, in all fairness, it should be pointed out that the Egyptians often blurred the distinction between the king's residence and the royal estate, both terminologically and practically. The problem springs from the extended meaning of the element *pr* "house, estate," for which, see Haring 1997:26-29, 32-33, and 199-200. Perhaps the terminological ambiguities in English can be resolved by rendering *pr-nśw* as "royal household," see Warburton 1997:32, 67, 178, and 180.

For a provocative examination of the same metaphorical problem of the house as both residence and estate in the Ancient Near East, see Schloen 2001. Of course, the very word "economy" derives from the Greek word οικος "house."

[14] There has been no comprehensive study of this orthographical feature which appears most often in the writing of official titles, but is encountered in offering lists and narrative inscriptions as well. Some information on this subject appears in Helck 1954:61, 73 and 105, with fns. 114-115 and Goelet 1989/90: 77-90. By the Middle Kingdom, such writings with two *pr*-signs also began to occur regularly with the term *pr-ꜥꜣ* "the Great House, pharaoh," a striking indication of the king's close association with the central administration.

"central offices." According to this passage, the vizier's day started with a combination of ceremony and official business, which, significantly, involved the reporting (*śmi*) of all the royal estates' income and expenses. Needless to say, such reporting certainly must have been accompanied by record-keeping for future reference:[15]

> ... Any dispersal that must go out (*pr prrt nbt*) from the royal estate (*pr-nśw*) is reported to him. Any income entering (*ʿḳ ʿḳt nbt*) into the royal estate is reported to him. As to anything which must be dispersed or received by the grounds of residential city (*ẖnw*), when they enter or they (are) dispersed, it is his (the vizier's) agent (*wpwty*) who causes the entry or dispersal.

The second excerpt describes the vizier's powers of appointment and the duties of reporting that naturally were charged to the local officials whom he chose:[16]

> It is he who appoints (*irr*) the (leading) member(s) of the magistracy (*nty m ḫt śrwt*[17]) [... in?] Upper and Lower Egypt, in the Thinite Nome (in) the Head of the South. It is to him that they report (*śmi*) the matters accomplished under their charge (at) the beginning of every four months. It is to him that they bring the pertinent documents (*zẖ3w iry* lit. "pertinent writings") in their charge together with their councils (*ḏ3ḏ3t*).

The key term here is *śmi* "report," a word that is so common in this text and van den Boorn's commentary that he references it with "*passim*." Although *śmi* can be used of both oral and written communication,[18] the intent of the passage is certainly clear—the physical

---

[15] Urk. IV 1105, 5-9; van den Boorn 1988: 42-43. In this case the translation is mine, rather than that of van den Boorn. Like Lorton and other commentators, I have decided that the nominalized forms of the verb *pr* and *ʿḳ* in this text have a more specific administrative meaning as "income" and "outgo, expenses" despite the absence of a monetized economy. For example, in an overwhelmingly agricultural society like Egypt, a shipment of grain leaving the capital would almost be the equivalent of a delivery of money in our modern usage.

[16] *Urk.* IV 1112, 9-11, following the translation of van den Boorn 1988: 208, with some minor additions and revisions.

[17] The term *śrwt* is a designation of a class of officialdom who operated all over Egypt, but who were frequently associated with the *ẖnw* or royal residential city; see van den Boorn 1988: 24, fn. 80 and 209-212.

[18] The verb *śmi* occurs in many royal inscriptions, particularly those of military or diplomatic import. The significance of the term is that it meant that the king was not omniscient. Unlike the gods who truly know everything, the

presence of the subordinate officials was required in either case. The nature of the phrase *zẖ3w iry*, on the other hand, ensures that local officials were required to report to the vizier in person along with their written reports and at regular intervals—*i.e.*, at the beginning of each of the three seasons of the Egyptian calendar. Also, like most Egyptian means of governance there was always a degree of reciprocity involved.

In a similar vein, the third example notes that the vizier often dispatched personal deputies or commissioners (*wpwty* lit. "he who pertains to a mission/task"; *wpwtyw* plur.) from his offices out to the local administrators in order to ensure that the commands of the central government were being carried out: [19]

> It is he who dispatches every messenger (*wpwty nb*) of the palace sent to the mayors and the settlement-leaders. It is he who dispatches everyone who will circulate all messages (*wḏyt*) of the palace (*pr-nśw*).

The "messengers" mentioned here were far more than mere dispatch- or letter-carriers. Other parts of this text make it abundantly clear that a *wpwty* of the king, the vizier or any other high official was to be treated with the utmost respect and be obeyed virtually as if that official himself were present.[20]

The excerpts above are but three among many others that underscore an obvious but important principle of Egyptian management that was to remain constant over the centuries despite whatever structural changes the state underwent. Administration was based on the regular interchange of orders and accounts. This arrangement theoretically required the local administration, be they local governors or priests at a temple, to account for every activity and every bit of income at the local level. In both examples there is little unusual or unexpected in the procedures, but as obvious as they may seem, it was important to show that they were formal requirements that emanated from the highest level of the administration.

---

monarch had to be informed of events. Obviously, the same must hold for the king's subordinates such as the vizier. For a study of the motif of informing the king in Egyptian military narratives, see Spalinger 1983: 1-33.

[19] *Urk.* IV 1112, 5-6; van den Boorn 1988: 202. The word *wḏyt* used here could be translated either as "command, order" or as "letter," both of which alternatives would fit the present context.

[20] *Urk.* IV 1107, 11–1108, 14; van den Boorn 1988: 88-89. The *wpwtyw* were important as delegates in administrative and diplomatic activity; they also had an important role as divine emissaries. For an extensive study of these "messengers," see Valloggia 1976.

For all the discussions of specifics here, it is important to realize the main importance of this inscription in setting forth the broad operating principles of the Egyptian bureaucracy and its role in the economy. For instance, even though the vizieral text never uses the precise word *śip* "inspection," we can nevertheless be sure that this was the underlying sense of all the transactions described in the passages above. A scene elsewhere in the vizier Rekhmire's tomb depicts him viewing (*m33* "seeing")—*i.e.*, inspecting—various officials who have traveled to the capital in order to present their *ipt* "accounting" to him,[21] just as *The Duties of the Vizier* envisaged. Similarly, many other details in this key text can be confirmed from a wide variety of sources across the full extent of Egyptian history, but a full exposition of that vast subject cannot be accomplished here.

Planning, expectations and the inundation

One dimension that goes unmentioned in the vizieral text was the factual information on which the vizier and other high officials could base whatever expectations they had of "disposable income" from year to year. Even with a rudimentary level of planning such data would be highly desirable. As Egypt was an agricultural economy, all the government's income derived ultimately from a widely dispersed network of land holdings and locally based institutions. It seems unlikely that these officials had to wait for hundreds of reports of the actual harvest to arrive at the capital late in the year. Here again we must proceed more on inference than actual evidence and some of that inference, unfortunately, must be based on practices dating to millennia after the Greco-Roman era.

Luckily, not all information is of a late date. In the late Eleventh or early Twelfth Dynasty (c. 1985-1773 BC),[22] a private farmer named Hekanakht away on business in the Memphite region sent a number of letters to his family at Thebes instructing them in great detail as to how they should manage his interests. In the opening line of the first of these letters, he calls his readers' attention to the event on which all the rest of his affairs will flow, both figuratively and literally—the inundation:[23]

[21] Davies 1944, Pl. 29, with van den Boorn 1988: 103.

[22] Allen and Arnold have recently offered a combination of palaeographic and archaeological arguments for dating the Hekanakht archive to the early Twelfth Dynasty, see Arnold 1991: 5-48, esp. 36-38.

[23] Wente 1990: 58.

> Communication by the mortuary priest Hekanakht to Merisu. As for whatever gets soaked by the inundation in our farmland, it is you who should cultivate it with attention on the part of all my people including yourself, since I am holding your responsible for this.

As we know from Hekanakht's letters as well as from many other sources on Egyptian agriculture and land management, the amount of water reaching a plot of land during the inundation determined the yield of the property and even what crops should be grown.[24] It is significant that the Palermo Stone, one of the earliest of all Egyptian historical documents to survive, recorded the height that the inundation had reached for nearly every year. In fact, the inundation was such a central factor in Egyptian economic life that the three seasons of the civil calendar began with *ꜣḫt* "Inundation." Only after the flood had come could one make a reasonable estimate of what the subsequent seasons, *prt* "Growing" and *šmw* "Harvest," might bring. In fact, in later times under the Fatimids, the annual Nile height was of such critical importance that it was sometimes kept as a state secret until it had reached a certain level.[25]

It would have been relatively easy for an official at the capital who possessed a reasonable amount of agricultural expertise to extrapolate from past years and estimate the size of the crop, providing, of course, he knew how much land was under cultivation in each district. Yet, the size of the population and labor available seem to have been two remarkable, yet consistent, blindspots among those who managed the economy. Lack of information on the population would certainly present a considerable obstacle to any attempt by the Egyptians to put their planning on a rational basis. After all, as Eyre has pointedly remarked, "land was valueless without people."[26] At the same time, though, the surviving royal decrees of all periods are very much concerned with protecting the labor force of a given institution from encroachments by other institutions and organizations. Even so, there is no record of a census of any kind until well after pharaonic civilization had passed from the scene.[27]

---

[24] For a commentary on the agricultural aspects of this passage and their implications for lease holding in Egypt in later times, see Eyre 1999:48-53. Failure to take into consideration various categories (and qualities) of land was a difficulty that frequently confronted both local administrators and central government officials throughout pharaonic rule.

[25] Bowman and Rogan 1999:2-3. [26] Eyre 1994:46.

[27] Although it might be possible to estimate the population of a number of urban settlements in ancient Egypt, we have no accurate idea of the size of the far greater mass of rural inhabitants; see Eyre 1994:36-37, with references.

II. An introduction to Egyptian archival and scribal practices

For the second part of this paper I intend to shift my attention from theoretical and ideological considerations to more practical matters by examining a few actual administrative documents for evidence of planning as well as what the accounting practices used can tell us about the mechanisms of economic governance. Needless to say, these are two unwieldy topics and some sharp limitations must be imposed at the beginning for the sake of manageability. Accordingly, I have decided to focus this paper primarily on the Fifth and Sixth Dynasties of the Egyptian Old Kingdom—the period roughly between 2500-2150 BC—bringing in some comparitiva from later periods where I feel they illuminate certain points. Although the nature of the government and the institutions changed, sometimes considerably, over the centuries between the Old Kingdom and the Late Period, much of the underlying mechanisms of economic management on the local level probably remained relatively unchanged. It should not come as a surprise that the examples I have chosen for discussion derive almost entirely from temples, which had the greatest need to plan the management of their various resources, at least over the short term. At the same time, however, Egyptian temples, either divine or royal, normally derived a substantial portion of their income from outside sources and could hardly be considered independent entities.[28]

Administrative documents can reveal much about the approach to resource and income management, providing one understands their nature from the start. We should remind ourselves that in the case of ancient Egypt, our difficulties in discerning the purpose of a document often goes to the very heart of the matter. Frequently documents are ill-preserved and the part of a papyrus most apt to suffer damage are the beginning sections of a roll where its title and a description of its purpose would likely be written. As we have noted, the Wilbour Papyrus is an example of these difficulties. Most of the discussion to follow will be based on papyri from a relatively limited source—the so-called Abusir archive—where the descriptive portions of many of the documents have survived.

---

[28] Haring 1997: 389-96 paints a mixed picture. It is fair to say that, as a group, New Kingdom memorial temples formed a relatively independent segment of the economy, but at the same time they were intimately involved with each other as well as some elements of the "state," particularly the ruling pharaoh.

An objective here will be to show what scribal and accounting practices can reveal about the organization of work and the management of income at an early Egyptian institution. These are subjects which will require examination of the way in which Egyptian documents were made, how they were drawn up, and the general manner in which institutions accounted for their income and labor.

In order to address these issues adequately, it is necessary first to describe some important technical details about Egyptian papyri in general. These were more than mere technicalities; they had a profound impact on documentary practices generally and influenced how scribes handled different genres of texts—economic / legal materials as opposed to literary texts. To be sure, many fundamental details about the Egyptian economy and its administration are preserved on stone stelae and temple inscriptions as well, but nearly all those texts are royal decrees and thus reveal less about the day-to-day practicalities of managing the intricate network of supporting institutions.

Unfortunately, for all its versatility, papyrus was a distinctly more fragile and perishable medium than the clay tablets of Mesopotamia. Conservative estimates are that less than 1% of all Egyptian papyri have survived, and those that have are often rather damaged. In the case of documentary papyri, the survival rate is even smaller, since these were likely to be stored close to where they were needed, *i.e.*, in the damp environment of everyday life in the Nile valley. Funerary or religious materials, by contrast, are largely derived from the arid environment of the desert necropoleis.

Papyrus was manufactured by placing the two layers of fibrous strips from the plant's core horizontally and vertically upon each other and then pressing them together, juices in the plant stem apparently serving as a natural binder.[29] After bleaching the sheets in the sun, the sheets were pasted together and a roll was thus formed. Due to the manner in which the sheets would naturally curl, rolls were formed so that the sides with the fibers running horizontally were placed on the inside portion of the roll. Generally speaking, when the need arose, sheets would be cut off the main roll and used in the amount necessary for the task at hand. In cases of particularly lengthy documents such as certain judicial or administrative records, the entire roll could be kept intact.

---

[29] Much of the following discussion of the manufacture of papyrus and papyrus rolls is drawn from two sources: Parkinson and Quirke 1995 and Černý 1947.

Egyptologists conventionally call the side of a papyrus sheet having the horizontal fibers uppermost the recto of a papyrus, regardless of which side the writing may have actually begun. Overwhelmingly, the scribes preferred to begin a document upon the recto of the papyrus and, in a few cases involving lengthier matters, they would then continue writing on its verso. Two options were available when a sheet or roll were reused for some reason or another. On the whole, scribes seem to have preferred to efface the previous writing by wiping it off with a damp cloth; less often, they simply began the new text on the verso of the papyrus. Remarkably enough, scribes had a distinctive manner of distinguishing between literary and documentary texts (*i.e.*, letters, accounts, and legal records). For reasons still unknown to us, the Egyptians tended to write literary materials so that the writing went on horizontal lines in the same direction as the fibers, whereas documentary papyri (*i.e.*, accounts and legal texts) were inscribed so that the text ran at right angles to the fibers (fig. 1).

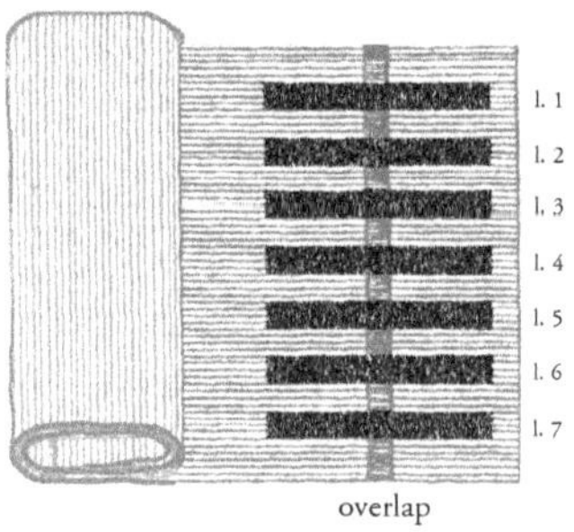

Fig. 1a: The fiber and text arrangement on a typical literary papyrus of the Old Kingdom

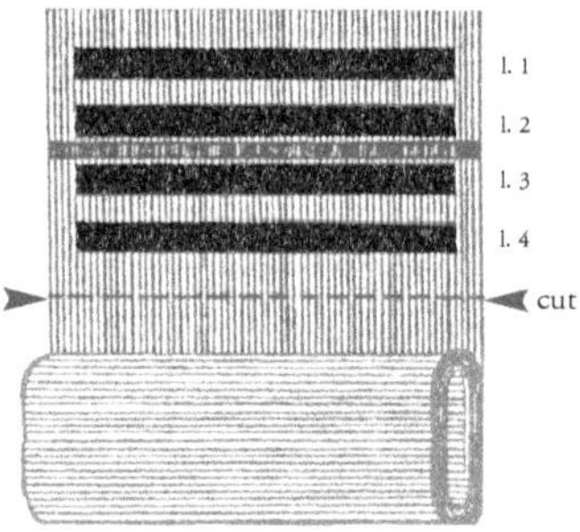

Fig. 1b: The fiber and text arrangement on a typical documentary or official papyrus of the New Kingdom

Script form and register: The relationship between monumental texts and writing on papyrus

Three other factors normally played important roles in how Egyptian texts were written—sign orientation, text format, and linguistic register. In my opinion, the influence of such technical aspects in the formal layout of Egyptian documents tends to be sorely underestimated by scholars. Unlike the cuneiform scripts of Mesopotamia and the Levant, the hieroglyphic form of the script could be written from left to right or from right to left, the latter direction being the canonical, most prevalent form. Texts could be written in columns or in rows using either text orientation. There are cases, such as royal and funerary materials or the *Book of the Dead* papyri, for instance, where the texts can occur in all four modes at once: columnar and linear, left-to-right and right-to-left.

Also unlike the situation in Mesopotamia where the forms of cuneiform encountered in stone monumental inscriptions were not markedly different from writing used on clay tablets, the Egyptians developed script forms within their writing system that were considerably more abstract than the ornate Egyptian hieroglyphs. These abstract script forms, known as hieratic and demotic, could only be written in the right-to-left direction and were reserved largely for texts on papyri. In addition to these styles there was a "book script" of semi-cursive hieroglyphs that occupied a position half-way between the hieroglyphs and hieratic. These cursive hieroglyphs were employed mostly for private tomb inscriptions and religious manuscripts such as the *Book of the Dead*, whose manuscripts are history's first illustrated books (fig. 2).

These writing styles interacted in a number of ways when it came to deciding the style of both script and presentation of Egyptian written materials, even in the case of the simplest matters of daily life. Often the register of the text and the expense of creating it could dictate the script form to be used. The most prestigious and most expensive texts employed the hieroglyphs; the cheapest and most widely used script form was hieratic, the "documentary" hand. By contrast, the hieroglyphic signs retained much of their explicitly pictorial and decorative nature throughout their history. Since papyri often imitated the format of monumental texts, both the script hierarchy and the manner in which stone inscriptions were executed exercised a profound and often overlooked influence upon the scribal practices employed on papyri. All these factors came into play in the Abusir archive that we shall discuss shortly. In these documents one can encounter a few instances where the style of royal monumental inscriptions has had a pronounced effect on how records were maintained on papyrus. However, this relationship between sheet fibers, text orientation, and genre did not become the standard until the late Middle Kingdom due to another development in Egyptian documentary practices—the shift from predominantly vertical texts to predominantly horizontal ones. The two most likely reasons for the preference for horizontal texts were the greater ease of writing and the more efficient use of space.

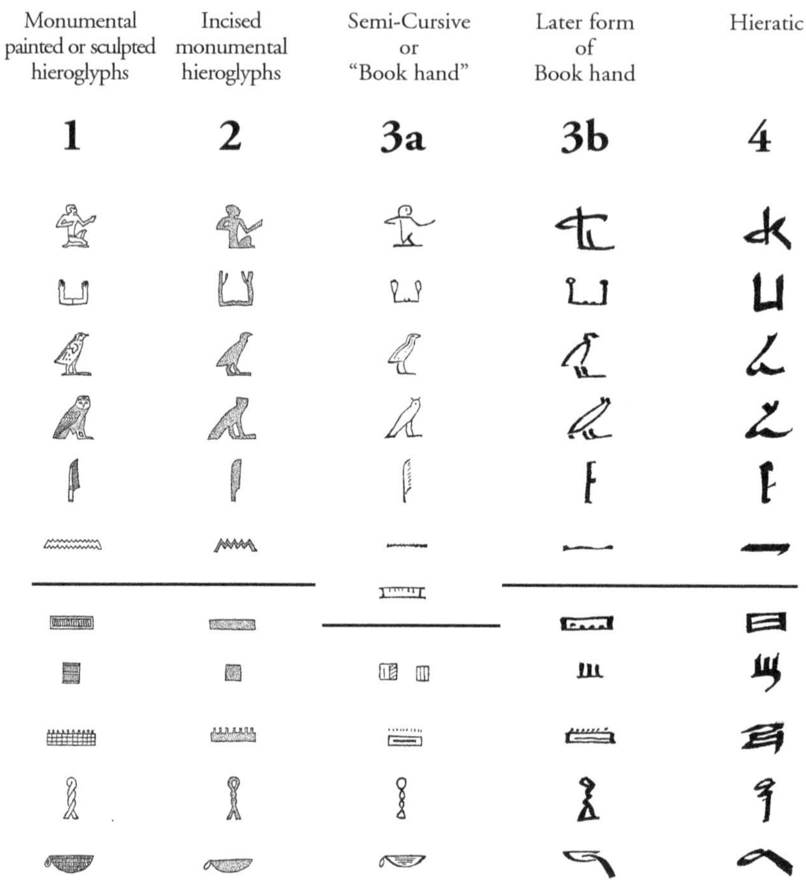

Fig. 2: Incised hieroglyphs (3a) compared with less cursive forms (1-2) and more cursive (3b-4).

Fischer 1976: 41, fig. 4 with the following references (p. 40):

1. All based on P. Lacau and H. Chevrier, *Une Chapelle de Sésostris I*[er], Plates (Cairo 1969), except , which is from Blackman, *Meir* III, Pl. 3 (restored).

2. Mostly based on an early Twelfth Dynasty stela: Anthes, *ÄZ* 65 (1930), 108ff. and Pl. 7 (Berlin 22820).

3a. Mostly based on the late Twelfth Dynasty box shown in Earl of Carnarvon and H. Carter, *Five Years' Explorations at Thebes* (London 1912), Pl. 49: hieroglyphs incised in wood and ivory (MMA 26.7.1438). The sign is from Nagib Farag and Zaky Iskander, Discovery of Neferwptaḥ, p. 15, Fig. 10. The left-hand form of □ is from a plaque from the pyramid of Sesostris I at Lisht: *BMMA* 28 (April, 1933, Section II), Fig. 10, p. 12.

3b. All from the Twelfth Dynasty coffin of *Ḫty* from Lisht, MMA 32.1.133, except , which is from Gardiner, JEA 41 (1955), 9ff. and Pl. 5.

4. All from Möller, *Hieratische Paläographie* I.

The nature of administrative papyri: Working copies or final compilations?

Many years ago S. Allam raised an interesting (and fundamental) question about legal and economic ostraca from Deir el-Medina. Were these texts intended as final archival documents, or did they represent informal, yet legally valid, intermediate memoranda that would be later used as the basis for a more formal transcription of the transaction involved?[30] Among other things, Allam's reasons for posing this question lay in the often lapidary, sketchy nature of texts on ostraca when compared with the far more detailed and descriptive material on their papyrus counterparts. Certainly, the combination of the normal script form (hieratic) and the material used (limestone flake or potsherd) would place such an ostracon in a rather low position along the hierarchical scale of prestige of the script and the expense of the recording medium. Indeed, one can easily see the implication Allam's question would have on the nature of many Egyptian legal and economic document on papyri, especially accounts papyri—are we dealing with a scribe's working notes, or does the document represent a "clean copy," *i.e.*, a transcription from an intermediate source with additions and corrections. Allam's article did not discuss in any detail two important terms often found in Egyptian legal-documentary material that might bear significantly on this question—*śip* "to inspect, inventory" and *mitt* "copy."

In addition to the royal progresses and cattle counts mentioned earlier, there is other textual evidence that the royal house and/or the central administration regularly appointed and dispatched commissioners on inspection tours. The words that most frequently appeared in this context were the verb *śip* and its related noun *śipt*, both derived from the root *ip* "to count." In many cases the *śip* or *śipt* seems to have amounted to little more than an inventory of institutional property or goods on hand,[31] the concepts "inspection" and "inventory" being

30 Allam 1968: 121-28. A related question is whether some literary ostraca might represent the ancient Egyptian equivalent of "paperback editions" of their classics; see Janssen 1992: 81-94.

31 The very title of the main section in the Harris Papyrus I was *śipt wr* "great inventory." The most detailed study of the terms *śip* and *śipt* appears in Grandet 1994: 95-101, with 129-130, n. 23. A valuable contribution to this question is the discussion of *śipty*, a variant of the same term, by Redford 1981: 92-94.

basically coterminous in the Egyptian point of view.[32] This term appears on numerous occasions in the main descriptive sections of the so-called "tomb robbery" papyri of the late Twentieth Dynasty. Their purpose was to record items stolen from royal tombs and temples at Thebes, in which case both inspections and inventories would be performed at the same time.

In most instances, then, those papyri involving a *śip* in its sense of "inventory" almost always represented what might be called a post-factum work, transcribed from an intermediate document containing the working notes. Given the great rarity of ostraca dating to the Old Kingdom, it seems more likely that sketch notes were made first on papyrus scraps or writing boards.[33] However, this is largely speculative as no likely examples of such a preliminary stage has yet come to light in the earlier periods.

Another term which alludes to intermediate stages of official records is *mitt/mity*, normally translated as "copy," but in many instances meaning more generally "summary." To begin with, the Egyptian concept of what constituted a copy was considerably looser than ours today. *Mitt* could refer to an excerpt from a longer document and could involve considerable editing of the original.[34] Even records of court proceedings could be called *mitt*, because such documents often summarized only those facts most salient to the matter at hand rather than preserving transcripts of entire cases. An especially pertinent example occurs on the Abbott Papyrus, one of the most important of the "tomb robbery" papyri. The short name lists, or dockets, at the end of documents were called there *mitt n zḫ3* "copy/summary of the document."

---

32 Posener-Kriéger1976: 226-27. In her discussion of Fragment 71B, (1976): II 443, an account dealing with various building(?) blocks which had not been put in place, she also offers "contrôle" as a translation. In that instance the sheet also contains a remark beneath the names of some low-ranking personages that these blocks had been "found conforming to the verification of the phyle," a clear indication of an inventory procedure. For the record of the findings of an actual inspection performed on a divine barque, see Posener-Kriéger 1976: II 429-39. The word *śip* does not appear on this document, but its absence proves little.

33 A number of such "brouillons" have actually been found on the versos of some of the assignment rosters among the Abusir archive; see Posener-Kriéger 1976: I 1-2 and below pp. 250f.

34 For the use of this term in official documents, see Helck 1974: 129 and Goelet 1996: 112 with n. 3, 119.

In other words, *mitt* does not imply an exact reproduction of a document, yet it can be sufficient for legal purposes. Since the term *mitt* tends to be associated with lists of objects or personal names rather than with accounts proper, perhaps the Egyptians sometimes intended it as a contrast to the more numerically oriented *sip*. The occurrence of the word *mitt* in a document, therefore, might be a good indication that the scribe was working from some manner of archival record. In later materials such as ostraca from the Ramaesside workmen's village at Deir el-Medina, one occasionally encounters the notation *spẖr* "transcribed, transferred" (lit. perhaps "caused to move around") written boldly across the surface as a note to the scribe that the text had been revised and copied onto a final clean copy, most likely a papyrus.[35] In the discussion of specific papyri from the Old Kingdom and some Ramesside examples below, I shall discuss evidence of such a two-stage process of preparing records for future reference.

III. The Abusir Papyri: Examples from an Old Kingdom administrative archive

Ironically, one of the most informative sources on the operation of Egyptian "state" institutions comes from the early part of Egyptian history. Excavations at Abusir of royal funerary complexes belonging to the Fifth Dynasty kings, Neferirkare (c. 2474-2455) and Neferefre (c. 2448-2445), have yielded two closely related documentary archives that cast light on many aspects of the day-to-day administration of those royal institutions. These archives, found nearly a century apart at the same site, are known collectively as the Abusir Papyri.[36] Although there are longer and better-preserved documents from later periods in Egyptian economic history—the Wilbour Papyrus, for example—these later papyri, by and large, clearly comprise a much more limited range of records from what must have been a wide stock of the document types necessary for the management of these and similar institutions as well as the complicated network of their supporting organizations.

[35] Helck 1974:62 *s.v. spẖr*, referring to Černý-Gardiner Ostracon 22, 1.

[36] Actually, only the papyri connected with the funerary complex of Neferirkare have been published thus far; those associated with Neferefre are still in the early stages of conservation and publication; see Posener-Kriéger 1991:167-76. Not much is known about how the Egyptians maintained documentary archives. For a discussion of the question vis-à-vis literary materials, see Quirke 1996:379-401.

Thus, it is fair to say that the overwhelming majority of ancient Egyptian administrative records usually provide us with a more episodic, anecdotal view of their administrative practices. In the case of the very lengthy Wilbour Papyrus, in fact, it is not certain as to what its ultimate purpose was—the recording of taxes or of rental imposts—nor do we know for whose benefit the document was composed.[37]

The Abusir Papyri, by contrast, addressed a wide variety of managerial needs, such as equipment inspections, inventories, duty lists, letters, and monthly accounts.[38] For economic and administrative historians, the Abusir Papyri offer two additional advantages—they comprise a relatively closed archive and derive from a relatively limited period of approximately two and a half centuries—hardly contemporaneous, yet sufficiently enough so for the sake of this study. In fact, the time period involved is effectively much shorter than that. Although datable documents and cylinder seal impressions recovered at Abusir indicate that the royal funerary establishments there were active during the period from the reign of Shepseskare Izi to Pepi II,[39] the more important of these documents relate to a shorter period—the great majority dating within an interval of approximately seventy years in the Fifth Dynasty, from Djedkare Isesi to Unas (c. 2414-2345 BC).[40] These figures testify to the endurance of many of similar quasi-state institutions that apparently could function long after the decease of the founding monarch. During the Old Kingdom, the most striking example of this phenomenon were the exemption decrees which Pepi I made in favor of the two pyramid cities of Snofru, who had reigned some 300 years previously.[41]

---

[37] Katary 1989:6-7.

[38] For a good sketch of the operation of the royal funerary temples at Abusir and the significance of the archive, the author recommends the highly readable popular book by Verner 1994, esp. 157-170.

[39] According to Posener-Kriéger 1976:II 483, the dates found on some of the documents in addition to seal impressions found at Abusir indicate that the funerary establishments there were active in the period between the reigns of Shepseskare Izi and Pepi II, or approximately 250 years, long after the political and economic center of gravity had shifted southwards to the region near Saqqara.

[40] Posener-Kriéger 1976:II 490-491.

[41] This is the so-called Dashur Decree, *Urk.* I 209-213, see Goedicke 1967:54-77. Donations from long-deceased kings also played a role in the funerary cult of Neferirkare at Abusir; see Posener-Kriéger 1976:II 622-23. For some similar examples of institutional longevity during the Eighteenth and Nineteenth Dynasties, see Haring 1997:392-94.

In another instance, a title on a statue from Giza shows that at least the memory of Neferirkare's cult still existed as late as the Middle Kingdom.[42]

The evidence from all periods shows that officials in charge of these organizations were aware how valuable accurate document-keeping was for future administrators, as they themselves undoubtedly constantly needed to consult and compare past records. The existence of such temple archives is in itself evidence of an impressive degree of planning, at least on the local institutional level. However, practically speaking, the Abusir Papyri do not represent an archive in the strict sense of the word. Many of these documents are palimpsest,[43] meaning that a good number of sheets may have been kept primarily as scrap paper for eventual reuse rather than for consultation or as models for drawing up similar records. It is unclear how much time had to elapse before a given sheet might be considered obsolete and available for recycling.[44] The appearance of the term *mit(t)* in a broken context on one papyrus is one of several indications that the scribes at Abusir may have extensively consulted and copied texts from archives.[45]

Papyrus format and accounting procedures in the Abusir archive

The document that I have been discussing is a prime example of one of the most striking features of the Abusir archive. Many of the larger documents were ruled both horizontally and vertically, giving them the

[42] Posener-Kriéger, *Les archives* II 641.

[43] Posener-Kriéger 1976: I 2. One papyrus from the archive even mentions a box containing sheets designated as *ˁ-wˁb* which would translate roughly as "cleaned / washed document."

[44] The problem of papyrus reuse and the relationship, if any, between texts on palimpsests is a complex one; see the conflicting points of view of Caminos 1986: 43-61 and Janssen 1987: 33-35.

[45] Posener-Kriéger and de Cenival 1968: Pl. 73E, with commentary and corrections in Posener-Kriéger 1976: 479, where she translated the phrase as *mit(t) n zẖ3w* as "écrit semblable." Since the papyrus mentioned in this document had apparently been found or kept in a box, she saw this "forte modeste" papyrus fragment as confirmation not only that archives in our sense of the word were maintained at Abusir, but also that some of those papyri were used as models for other documents and copied.

appearance of modern spread sheets.[46] The ruling and formatting were quite intricate having numerous subsections in both red and black inks. The entries themselves likewise employ both colors.[47]

Oddly enough, subsequent to the creation of this archive, this eminently practical means of presenting complex numerical data all but disappeared, ruling henceforth appearing mostly in religious and didactic papyri.[48] The intricate layout of the papyri and the careful entry of the data attest to the regularity of both the temple's operations and the professionalism of the upper level of its management. This level of complexity was not confined to the accounts papyri, but is equally present in the elaborate duty rosters among the archives. Papyri such as these are proof that the Egyptians' ability to plan, at least on a short-term basis, was not just empty an boast. The compartmentalized presentation of data offers the modern observer many opportunities to see how the Egyptians organized and categorized both labor and income—the fundamental processes of management.

Activities such as the distribution of temple income, for example, required a rather detailed sequence of steps, each of which required careful accounting. These papyri, therefore, prove that the men who prepared these documents must have had similar sheets available as

---

[46] The papyri from the Abusir archive are perhaps the most heavily formatted group of all Egyptian documentary papyri. For a survey of the use of ruling in Egyptian documents, see Simpson 1963: 18-19. A wide-ranging treatment of the format of both ruled and unruled documents, on stone as well as papyrus surfaces, appears in Helck 1974: 10-52.

[47] Red ink was used primarily in situations where the scribe wished to emphasize a point or in titles—rubrics in the most literal sense of the word. Sometimes red ink was employed to make corrections; see, for instance, Posener-Kriéger 1976: I 297. However, there were a number of other factors, religious and magical, that were taken into consideration as well; see the summary in Parkinson and Quirke 1995: 44-47. For a brief discussion of the use of red ink within the Abusir accounts papyri, see Posener-Kriéger 1976: I 209-11.

[48] Although ruled or lined text was a standard practice on stone surfaces such as stelae, it remained relatively uncommon on papyri, see note 28 above. In later times, the predominantly columnar format of *The Book of the Dead* was the most frequent context for ruled lines on papyri. Interestingly enough, religious texts such as these employed the increasingly archaic cursive hieroglyphs. The combination of this antique script format and ruled columns first appears on non-documentary papyrus in two religious texts of the Middle Kingdom, the Hymns to Sobek (see Gardiner 1957: 43-56) and the Ramesseum Dramatic Papyrus (see Sethe 1928).

models—hardly surprising, since the economic and ritual life at funerary temples was based on the continual rotation of the priestly staff within a framework of duties and income that was theoretically eternally unchanging. Accordingly, a number of the documents show evidence of being prepared ahead of time, in particular those papyri containing duty assignments. Despite such appeals to eternal continuity, the reality was that all activities were framed within the far more limited scope of a single month, namely the tour of duty for a *zꜣ* "phyle," or monthly division of the priestly staff.[49] At the beginning of each monthly shift, the head of the phyle going off duty needed to attest to his counterpart in the incoming division that he was handing over all the temple affairs and property in the same condition in which he had received them—a form of internal control of assets.[50] Each phyle did its own accounting independently of the others; the temple had no general manager who handled the accounts overall. An important implication of this system was that nearly all the personnel at the Old Kingdom funerary temples were part-time staff only, with the result that no manager could operate successfully without access to records provided by his counterparts in the other phyles.

One of the largest and best preserved of the Abusir Papyri also serves as one of the best witnesses to the complexity of the accounting required (figs. 3 and 4 on the following pages). This large papyrus has many interesting features and shall be the centerpiece of much of my discussion of Egyptian documentary and accounting practices. The papyrus originally consisted of several sheets pasted together and, even though portions of it are currently located in no less than four different

---

[49] The Egyptian word *zꜣ* was pretty close in meaning to our nautical term "watch," *i.e.*, the basic division of a boat crew. But some distinctions were made between that term and its use in connection with groups of priests; see Roth 1991b:9, 41-59, providing the best exposition to date of the phyle system during the Old Kingdom. The Greek rendering *phyle* for the word *zꜣ* literally means "tribe," reflecting Hellenistic social and religious practices. It is employed as the translation of the Egyptian term in the Greek text of bilingual and trilingual decrees during the Ptolemaic period.

[50] There is a convenient example of the documentary procedure of transferring duties from one phyle to another among the Middle Kingdom Kahun Papyri that appears as a reading exercise in Gardiner 1957b:255f. Over the course of history, the number of priestly divisions in Egyptian temples varied from four to six; during the Old Kingdom most temples probably had five phyles active. At Abusir these each comprised roughly 50 people.

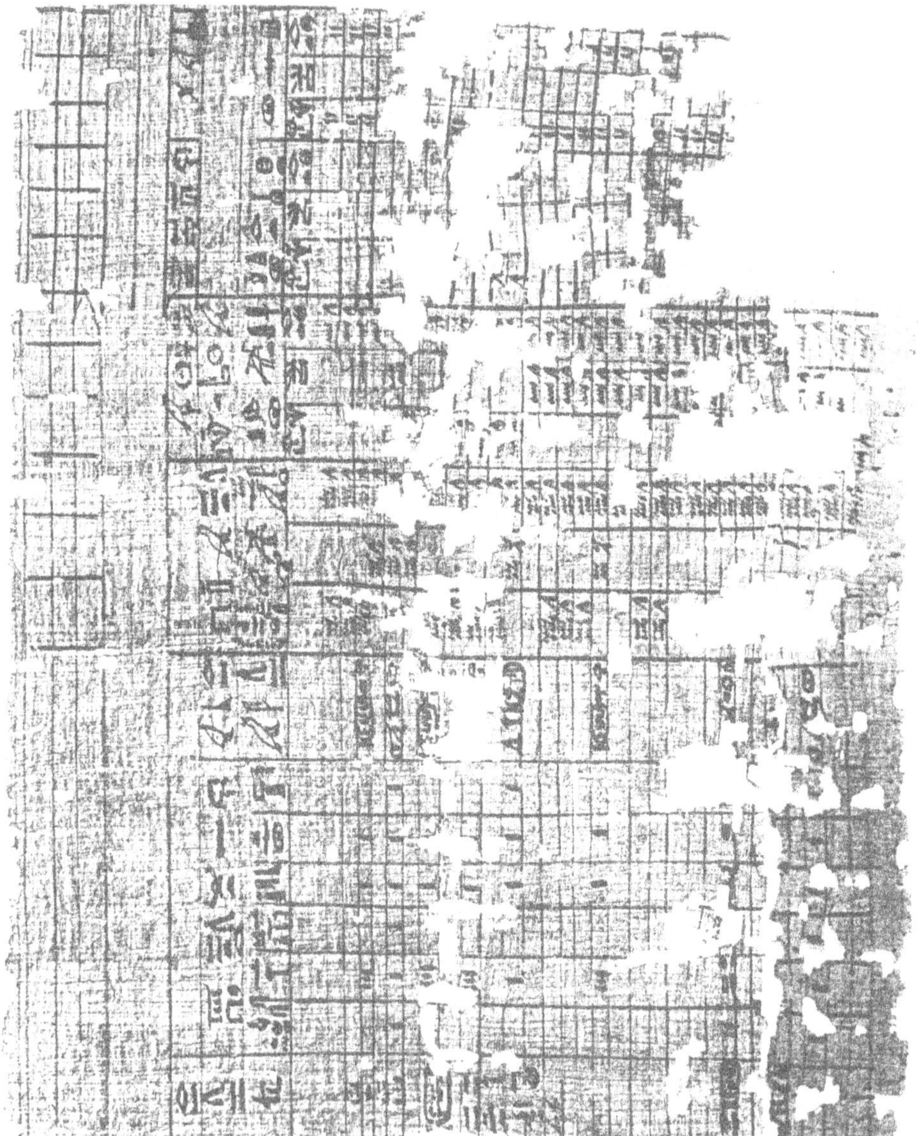

Fig. 3a Hieratic original of the first section of an accounts papyrus from the Abusir Archive: Louvre E. 2.415C recto + Cairo 602, frame XI + BM EA 10735, frame 10 + University College Sheet C (here rotated 90° counterclockwise).

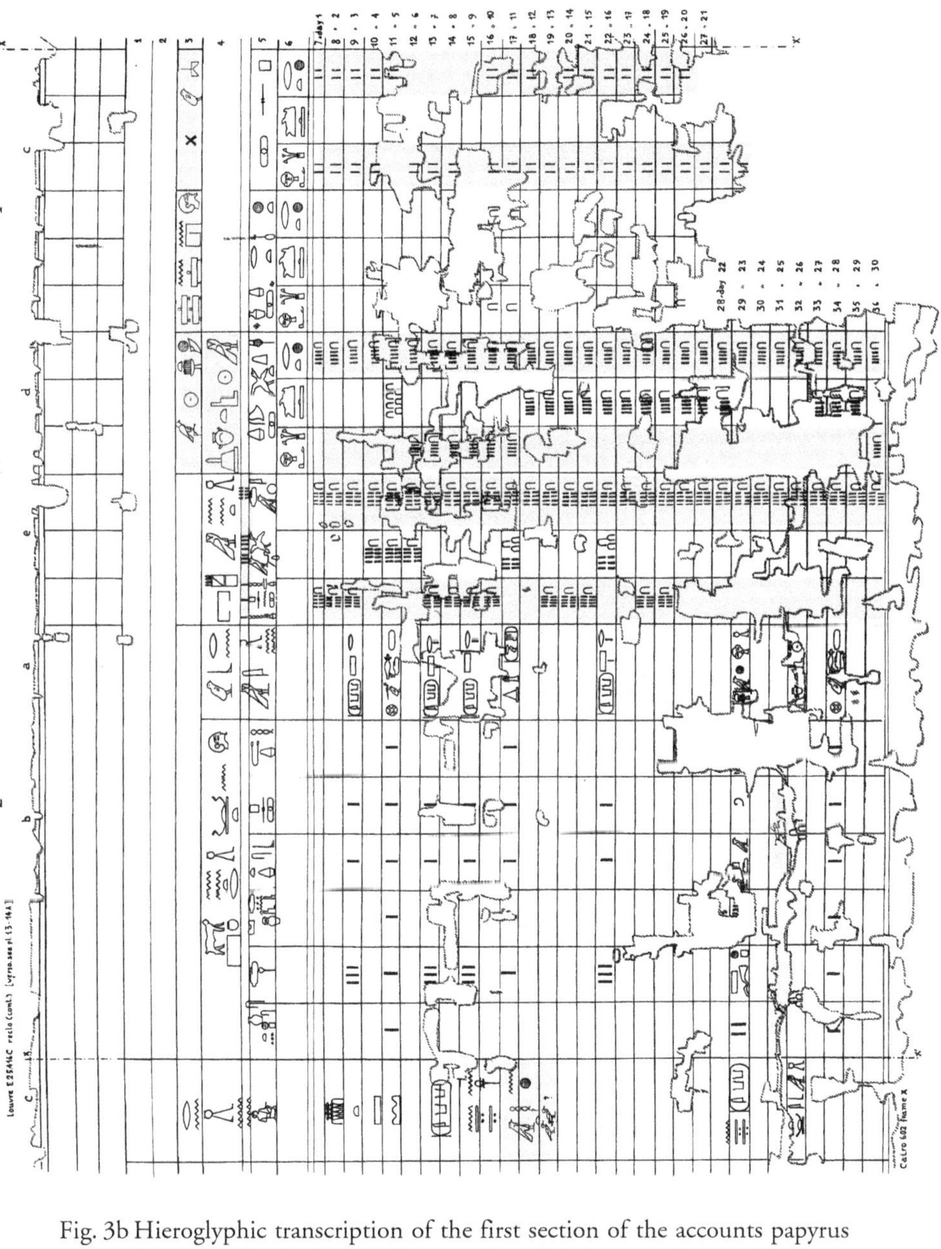

Fig. 3b Hieroglyphic transcription of the first section of the accounts papyrus from the Abusir Archive Louvre E. 2.415C recto + Cairo 602, frame XI + BM EA 10735, frame 10 + University College Sheet C (here rotated 90° counterclockwise, areas with hieroglyphics in red ink are greyed-in).

Fig. 4a Hieratic original of the second section of an accounts papyrus from the Abusir Archive: Louvre E. 2.415C recto + Cairo 602, frame XI + BM EA 10735, frame 10 + University College Sheet C (here rotated 90° counterclockwise).

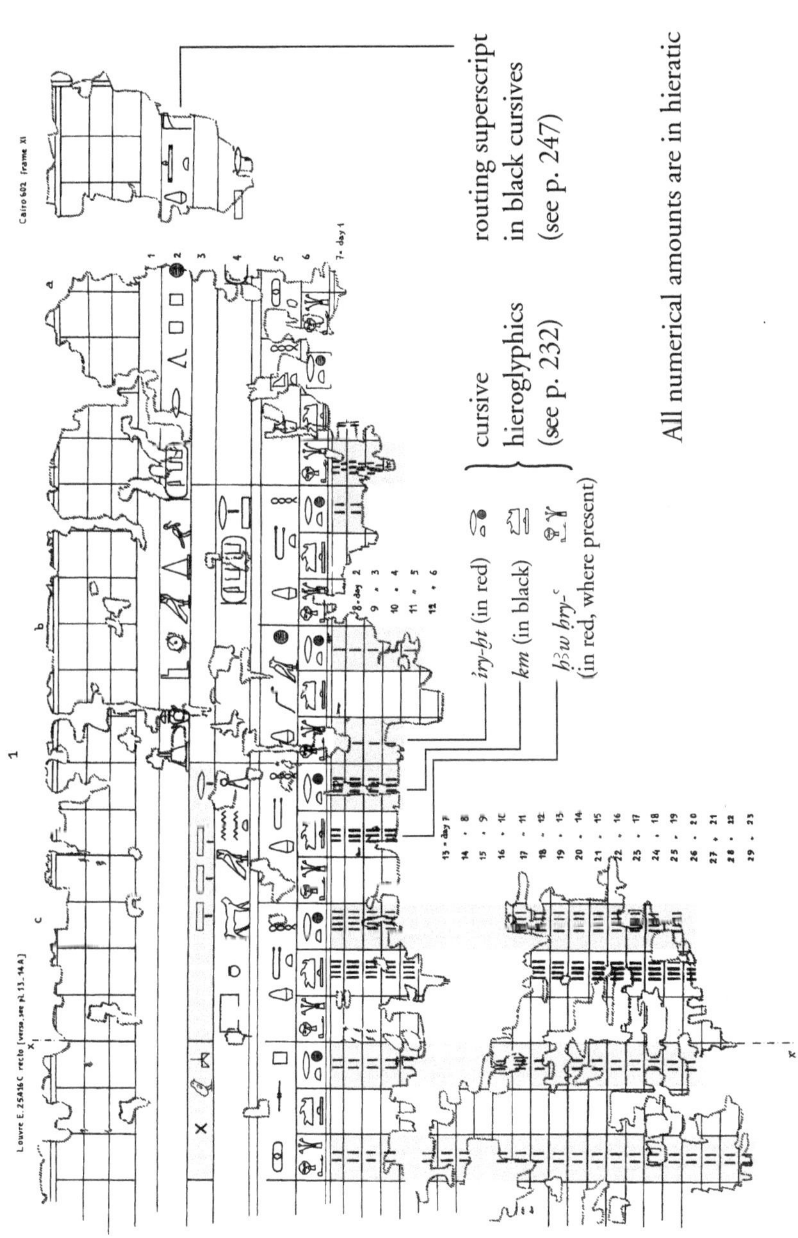

Fig. 4b Hieroglyphic transcription of the second section of the accounts papyrus from the Abusir Archive Louvre E. 2.415C recto + Cairo 602, frame XI + BM EA 10735, frame 10 + University College Sheet C (here rotated 90° counterclockwise, areas with hieroglyphics in red ink are greyed-in).

museum collections, the entirety is preserved in reasonably good condition, considering that it dates roughly to 2350 BC.[51] As with many of the larger documents from Abusir, the scribes had economized by using both the recto and verso of this papyrus. The verso, almost certainly written slightly later in the same year,[52] contains unrelated records concerned with duty assignments for the Sokar festival. The brief interval between the two uses of the sheets—perhaps only a matter of a few months—gives us an indication of how short the "shelf life" of papyri could sometimes be in this so-called archive.

As with a number of the other larger papyri from Abusir, this document employs a curious mixture of cursive hieroglyphs and hieratic script. The cursive hieroglyphs in part represent an association with a higher register of script forms,[53] but mostly they are simply a means of marking the most important organizational divisions within the accounts by means of an ancient Egyptian equivalent of "capital letters."[54] In either case a hierarchy of script forms and subject matter was intended. Hieratic script, by contrast, was employed for the less formal recording of the actual materials received and disbursed. This papyrus records the distribution of the *ḥtp-nṯr* "divine offering," or temple income, that was delivered from a variety of sources over an entire month, that is, a phyle's tour of duty. The daily records that appear at the bottom portion of the document are subdivided according to the three decades (ten-day weeks) of an Egyptian thirty-day month. These subdivisions are indicated by three red horizontal lines; the days, each marked by a black line, are listed at the right margin running down-

---

[51] Louvre E. 25.416C recto + Cairo 602, frame XI + BM EA 10735, frame 10 + University College Sheet C, see Posener-Kriéger and de Cenival 1968: Pls. XXXIII-XXXV. The document as a whole is discussed in Posener-Kriéger 1976: I 257-72, who describes it (p. 257) as "une section compete d'un rouleau de comptabilité." She dates it (1976: II 490) to the 27th regnal year of Djedkare Isesi.

[52] Posener-Kriéger and de Cenival 1968: Pls. 13-14 and Posener-Kriéger 1976: I 59-76; the text on the verso apparently dates to somewhat later in the same 27th year of Isesi.

[53] On the use of cursive hieroglyphs and their place within the hierarchy of Egyptian script forms, see Fischer 1976: 39-46, esp. 40; and Goelet 2003: 10-18.

[54] On occasion, the size of the cursives can be very large in proportion with the rest of the text in the case of date lines or other protocol elements, *e.g.*, Posener-Kriéger and de Cenival 1968, Pls. 1 and 2.

wards so that each horizontal line pertains to a single day across the page. The accounts papyri employ both columnar and horizontal text, whereas the few letters and other non-economic documents among the archives are nearly exclusively written in the normal columnar format that is characteristic of Old Kingdom texts generally.

The divine offering was the temple's regular income in the form of edible provisions, nearly all of which seem to be processed foodstuffs—special breads and beverages. Some meats also appear, but more irregularly. Quite significantly, the accounting for each variety of income is presented in three columns below each category of foodstuff. The first column is headed by the word *iry-ḫt* "registered amount," lit. "that which pertains," perhaps even "book value" in red; the next column bears the title *km* "total (scil. received)" in black; the third column records the *ḥ3w ḥry-ˁ* perhaps "remainder outstanding" in red, which, in this case, is reminiscent of the way we today mark deficits in red ink.[55] The last of these figures always represents the difference between the first two quantities.

The situation is clear and remarkable. Although the temple was theoretically supposed to receive the amount listed as *iry-ḫt*, the *km* represented the actual (and often distinctly smaller) amount that was actually delivered from the supporting institutions. The disparity between the expected and the actual (the *ḥ3w ḥry-ˁ* figures) shows us that just one hundred years after the death of the founder, Neferirkare (Kakai), his cult's effective income had dwindled to roughly one-half of the original value at its establishment and endowment.

The Egyptians were quite aware that even though royal endowments were made "for the full extent of eternity," the reality was that funerary institutions would eventually slowly fade away through neglect.[56]

---

[55] For a discussion of these words and the relationship between them, see Posener-Kriéger 1976:211-14 and 255-57. Her suggested translations for each are: *km* "montant effectif"; *rḫt* (her transliteration of *iry-ḫt*) "quantités effectivement en possession de l'administration du temple"; *ḥ3w ḥry-ˁ* a composite term whose two components she rendered as "excédent" and "qui reste sur la main," neither of which quite fits the circumstances, since this figure certainly represents goods which were *not* available. Helck 1974:28 has suggested that the three terms be rendered as follows: *rḫt* "Soll"; *km* "Haben"; and *ḥ3-ḥr-ˁ* "ausstehender Rest." Significantly, the term *km* is often modified by the passive participle *gmy* "found," without doubt in the sense of being "verified."

[56] Haring 1997:1-3.

Truly, the accountant-scribes at Neferirkare's temple were not so deluded as to expect that the deficits they carefully recorded would suddenly be made whole in the future. Neither, in all likelihood, was it likely that these scribes maintained the accounts in this manner solely because of a mechanical adherence to tradition. Instead, the *ḫ3w ḫry-ʿ* entries most likely reflected a need to be able to show any outside inspectors the temple's actual income, expenses, and how goods had been dispersed. Among other things, such inspections could protect against the possibility of irregular diversions of goods by those charged with their delivery.[57] By providing for checks by an outside authority, this document, not incidentally, provides indirect evidence that there was some level of revenue control by the central administration during the Egyptian Old Kingdom, a "paper trail" in the modern parlance.

A more direct confirmation of the role of outside authorities at Abusir occurs in a document that mentions a *wpwty* "messenger," a type of delegate-functionary whom I discussed above in connection with the New Kingdom vizieral text. Posener-Kriéger's reading and interpretation of the circumstances surrounding this papyrus fragment led her to interpret these particular *wpwtyw* as "représentants de l'administration."[58] The presence of such functionaries in the Abusir Papyri seems to show that the underlying principles of control and confirmation that play so prominent a role in the New Kingdom *The Duties of the Vizier* were already practiced during the Old Kingdom, even if both the central and local administrative structures were quite different.

---

[57] For an example of such a peculation in the Ramesside period, see the Turin Indictment Papyrus (P. Turin 1887), Gardiner 1948a:73-82, with *idem* 1941:19-73; and more recently, Vernus 1993:123-40. For a recent English translation of the papyrus, see Peden 1994:109-16, with the discussion 69-72. Significantly, some of the material diverted from the Khnum temple at Elephantine came from estates as far north as the Delta. For a summary of outright thefts of temple property during the Twentieth Dynasty, see Haring, 1997:275-78, to which add the case discussed in Goelet 1996. The subject of much of the so-called "tomb robbery" papyri was actually thefts from temples.

[58] Posener-Kriéger and de Cenival 1968:Pls. 80 A and Posener-Kriéger 1976:II 453 with the discussion on p. 460, note (k). Another, but more damaged, document may have also mentioned such *wpwtyw*; see Posener-Kriéger 1976:II 471, note (i).

Script hierarchy and document format

If we were to judge by the hierarchy of script forms alone, then the texts at the top of the sheets I have been discussing must have recorded the most significant details of all. These notations were written horizontally in a slightly larger handwriting and used cursive hieroglyphs instead of the hieratic for the numerical entries below. These superscripts in effect served as the papyrus's title, informing the scribe as to the document's general purpose and tracing the routing of various goods at the funerary temple—yet another indication that temple scribes consulted archives. Identifying titles such as these were necessary in accounts papyri, but such differentiation in script is unusual. In this manner, the larger scripts added an extra degree of formality to the document overall by imitating royal decrees.

On a more immediate, practical level, the enlarged text, placed as it is near the beginning of the document, allowed a scribe to identify a papyrus's subject matter quickly without having to unroll or read much of the document. Later in the Ramesside period legal papyri occasionally had summarizing titles in hieratic script written on the outside of the scroll for yet easier referencing in storage.[59] Among the Abusir archives, cursive hieroglyphs also appear instead of hieratic on a few royal decrees from the Neferefre funerary temple.[60] Once again, the intent seems to have been to increase the prestige of the documents by imitating their counterparts on stone stelae.[61]

The superscripts in cursive hieroglyphs serve two main purposes. They effectively divide the accounts into three principal sections and they trace the route and sources of a substantial portion of the temple's entire income, the *ḥtp-nṯr* "divine offering." The main subject of the document is given on the first of the sheets: *ḥtp-nṯr śḫpp r Bꜣ-Kꜣkꜣi͗ m Śt-i͗b-Rꜥ* "Divine Offering which delivered to *Ba-Kakai* (Neferirkare's funerary temple) from *Set-ib-Re* (Neferirkare's sun-sanctuary)." This

[59] See Parkinson and Quirke 1995:57-58. Similar practices are known from Mesopotamia.

[60] See Parkinson and Quirke 1995:41; compare a similarly formatted, but probably non-royal *wḏ* "command" from the Neferirkare temple, Posener-Kriéger and Cenival 1968:Pl. 72A with Posener-Kriéger 1976:477-78.

[61] Line drawings of all the royal decrees of the Old Kingdom can be found in Goedicke 1967. The presentation of the content can be every bit as complex on the papyri; the framing of the texts by means of the royal protocol is similar in both instances.

was the first stopping point in the distribution route. The latter heading, in turn, has been broken down into three sub-categories, moving from right to left—*r3-š* KN "the *ro-she* (a type of temple land endowment) of KN [king's name lost, but perhaps Djedkare Isesi]"; *r3-š K3k3i* "the *ro-she* of Kakai (a similar and nearby block of land endowment attached to Neferirkare's temple) and *innt m ẖnw* "income (lit. what was brought) from the Residence." The breakdown of the main sources of the temple's *ḥtp-nṯr* continues with the final major category in the adjacent section: *innt m ꜥḥ* "income from the (ceremonial) palace."[62] There may be a nuance intended in the distinction between the verb *sẖpi* "to deliver," lit. "to cause to travel" in the document's top heading and the verb *ini* "bring" in the subheadings, but since the sun-sanctuary may have been within walking distance of the funerary temple,[63] the difference in terminology probably has little significance.

The complex layout of the papyrus offered several different points at which someone could check, compare, and thus control the temple's income. In all fairness, the brief synopsis of the document I have provided does justice neither to the complexity of document's format nor to the convoluted route taken by some of the smaller contributions sent to Neferirkare's funerary temple. I have not, for instance, mentioned a number of possible subdivisions within the income sources, nor have I discussed how these might relate to the rest of the accounts. More important for our present purposes is that the upper part of the document was rendered graphically distinct by the highly formatted gridwork working in conjunction with the large cursive hieroglyphic characters—a demonstration of the sophistication of Egyptian accounting practices.

62 The term *ꜥḥ* is a toponym or administrative department often translated as "palace," but actually seems less residential than ceremonial or, more broadly, religious in nature during the Old Kingdom. In all likelihood, the *ꜥḥ* in question was located in the residential city or *ẖnw*, even if the two institutions were administratively distinct.

63 Oddly enough, Posener-Kriéger did not comment on the unparalleled use of the verb *sẖpi* rather than *iwt*/*iit* "to come" or *ini* "to bring" in this context. Ironically, for all its importance in Neferirkare's mortuary cult at Abusir, his sun-sanctuary has not been found yet; see Verner 1994: 110-12. It is likely that Neferirkare's sun temple was likewise close to Abusir, judging from the location of the remains of two sun sanctuaries at nearby Abu Gurob.

Nevertheless, one brief observation concerning an aspect of the routing might be in order here. The prominent role that the sun-sanctuary, *Set-ib-Re*, a divine temple built by Neferirkare and possibly located less than a mile away, seems to have played in the economy of the funerary temple may seem puzzling at first glance.[64] However, a certain religious, rather than practical, logic was in force. The deity worshipped at *Set-ib-Re* was in reality not simply Re, but more likely he was the deceased king subsumed into the sun-god. In the system of "Reversion Offerings" that prevailed throughout Egyptian history, a portion of the total offering was first made to the chief god at a temple, then the remainder was distributed among the other participants, be they gods, deceased mortals, or the cult's priests. Nefirirkare-as-god, *Set-ib-Re*, first received a portion of the *ḥtp-nṯr* at the sun-sanctuary, then the rest was transmitted to Neferirkare-the-(deceased)-king at *Ba-Kakai*, his funerary temple at nearby Abusir. This document, therefore, should remind us how important seemingly unrelated religious concepts were for the practical workings of the Egyptian economy.

Less puzzling are the contributions from the *ẖnw* and the *ʿḥ* recorded on these sheets.[65] Although, the *ẖnw* ultimately may have been the main routing point through which much of the mortuary cult's income ultimately flowed,[66] our brief study of the complex vizieral inscription should have alerted us to how the affairs of the central administration, the king's residence, and his estate, largely construed, tended to be blurred. The present accounts papyrus demonstrates that the funerary temple supplemented the income derived from its own holdings with donations from both the king personally and the government at large. The proportions assigned to each source and the reasons behind their assignment are subjects too complicated to examine here and ultimately not germane to our discussion.

---

[64] The relationship between these two institutions is summarized in Posener-Kriéger 1976: II 519-26. Remarkably enough, it is not clear whether the sun-sanctuary had its own staff or whether it might have been drawn largely or entirely from that of Neferirkare's funerary temple.

[65] For a summary of the relationship between the various institutions including the royal residence and the capital city in the supply of offerings sent to the funerary temple, see Posener-Kriéger 1976: II 631-34 and the temple's economy more generally, 611-641.

[66] On this point, see Posener-Kriéger 1976: II 621-22.

The Abusir Papyri as archives: Pre-formatted blanks, intermediate documents, and final copies

When it comes to accounting practices, the ways in which papyri were prepared, stored, and (re)used can sometimes be almost as informative as the records they contain. For example, the papyri treated in the previous section of this paper confirm the existence of managerial practices known primarily from texts throughout Egyptian history—inventories and inspections. In the Abusir archive the verb *śíp* usually appears in the passive meaning "to entrust (something to a person)," normally with the intent that the official in question should redistribute enumerated materials to his subordinates.[67] Quite a number of the papyri appear to be inventory lists of temple equipment and furnishings, which have supplied scholars with much useful vocabulary. Most inventories were formatted by ruled lines, so that the number on hand and the state of the objects could be recorded in a regular manner.[68] Because some sheets have the object names written in large semi-cursive hieroglyphs with outline drawings below, these papyri seem once again to be deliberate imitations of more prestigious stone inscriptions, in this instance the offering lists incised on tomb walls.[69] A few of these inventories even appear to have additional checkmarks next to the items as one might expect when re-employing the document during a later inspection,[70] a practice which by definition is an archival usage.

The practice of regular inventories raises an interesting question about the nature of the large Abusir accounts papyrus discussed above. Was this elaborate papyrus a working document or does it represent a *post factum* copy prepared for official examination? My immediate impression of these sheets is that, despite their evident complexity, the accounts have been handled with an unusual, even suspicious, degree of certainty, without any indication of erasures or other hesitancies. In the case of unexpected circumstances in the delivery, an extra donation, or the like, it does not seem to have been necessary to squeeze the extra information into some awkward space on the document. On these grounds alone it seems unlikely that this document represents a set of working records.

---

[67] Posener-Kriéger 1976:I 227, with fn. 3.

[68] *Ibid.* 1976:I 125-208.

[69] For example, *ibid.* 1976:I 142 (Fig. 6a).

[70] *Ibid.* 1976:I 127f.; 145 (Fig. 9).

Sometimes descriptive terminology in a document can answer such questions by itself. In the main section of the great Harris Papyrus I, one of the longest of all Egyptian papyri that was prepared shortly after the death of its ostensible author, King Ramesses III, we encounter the descriptive title *šip wr* "great inventory." In our discussions below we shall produce paleographic evidence confirming that this work is undoubtedly a transcribed final compilation copy, rather than the product of a site-by-site inspection.

In addition to *post-factum* documents, there is much evidence among the Abusir archives that certain types of documents were prepared *prior* to their use. These papyri were the monthly personnel assignments, the more detailed of which sometimes contained what Posener-Kriéger described as "brouillons" for similar documents on their versos.[71] The latter type of document in effect offers proof that many papyri did move through an intermediate stage before a final copy was produced. Unfortunately, we have not been able thus far to link definitively any such set of notes to a finished product.

Turning now to completely prefabricated documents, we encounter a bit of operational reality. In the daily life of an organization like a funerary temple, many of its functions were simply routine, as should be expected of institutions that operated around a calendar of religious rituals. It therefore was relatively easy for a scribe to know well in advance the type of documents that he would have to fill out over the course of a month's tour of duties. In fact, due to the rotating responsibilities inherent in the phyle system, the scribes who kept the accounts were in effect given a set of model papyri by their counterparts going off duty.[72] Posener-Kriéger, the chief editor and translator of the papyri, remarked that certain documents were so formulaic in nature that a scribe going through the archive would have to unroll only a small portion of a papyrus in order to ascertain its content.[73]

In a few cases, such as the large accounts papyrus discussed above, a blank sheet could be ruled out in advance, but in other cases the

---

71 Posener-Kriéger 1976:I 1-2.

72 For a brief discussion of the revolving responsibility, see the discussion above, p. 239.

73 Posener-Kriéger 1976:I 2-4. Strikingly enough, although none of the monthly duty rosters was preserved in its entirety, their formulaic nature allows those working today with these damaged documents not only to gather the nature of a fragment quickly, but also to make restorations more easily.

preparations could go far beyond that. Some of the clearest and most interesting examples among the prepared documents are the duty rosters that phyle administrators drew up in advance.[74] Like the accounts papyri, these large sheets were formatted into a complex arrangement of vertical and horizontal lines. The format of such documents was fairly standard. First, the date of the festival and/or the royal protocol would appear in a column at the right hand margin of the sheet, often in large cursive hieroglyphs, as would befit the king, the most prestigious person mentioned in the document. The hieratic script of everyday life would be employed for the rest of the document. The large-scale and excessive attention to what are essentially purely formal elements have little to do with practicalities of normal documentation. Scribes must have added in such largely decorative elements in anticipation either of inspections or of eventual presentation to some manner of outside authority (fig. 5).

After the dateline, the document would switch to a predominantly horizontal direction of text. The name of the festival would appear across the top, then below that, separate ritual acts or religious tasks appeared as a superscript title below that in rectangles across the top; finally, there was a column below the task description which detailed the office or offices that were to be performed. In a few cases, two columns were used for different and presumably equivalent functions listed side by side. Each such column, single or double, was subdivided into thirty small rectangles corresponding to the days of the month. Judging from the uniformity of script and ink, it is immediately obvious from the appearance of such sheets that the names of the individuals selected to perform the required duties had been filled in a single session at the beginning of the phyle's tour of duty. The phyle members listed on such sheets were presumably performing tasks in return for the properties which they held in usufruct from the funerary temple. It is uncertain as to what proportion of their total obligation the duties on such sheets represented. In this respect, one might consider such duty rosters as a means of accounting for the temple's labor costs, such as they were. One can easily imagine how the head of a phyle or some other supervisor would choose men to perform certain

---

[74] In some instances the prepared nature of the documents is further signaled by the use of future tense constructions; see Posener-Kriéger 1976:I 11-12.

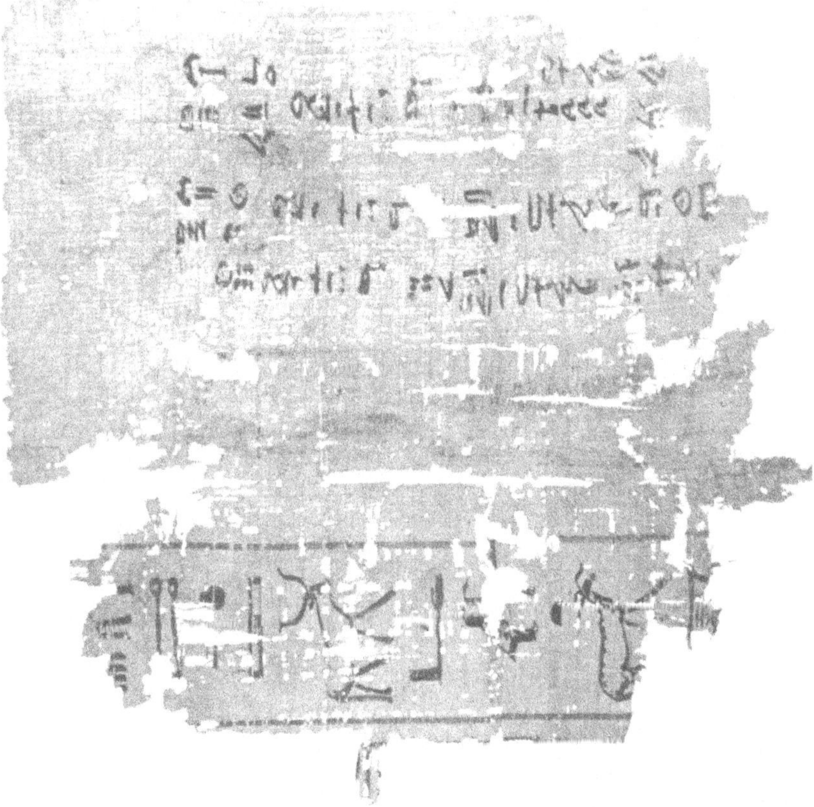

Fig. 5: The first sheet of a duty-roster from the Abusir Archive, showing the dating and titulary protocol in large cursive hieroglyphs (here rotated 90° counterclockwise). At the right (here: top) are some additional, less formal notations in hieratic.
BM 10735, frame 10 © The British Museum. See also fig. 6.

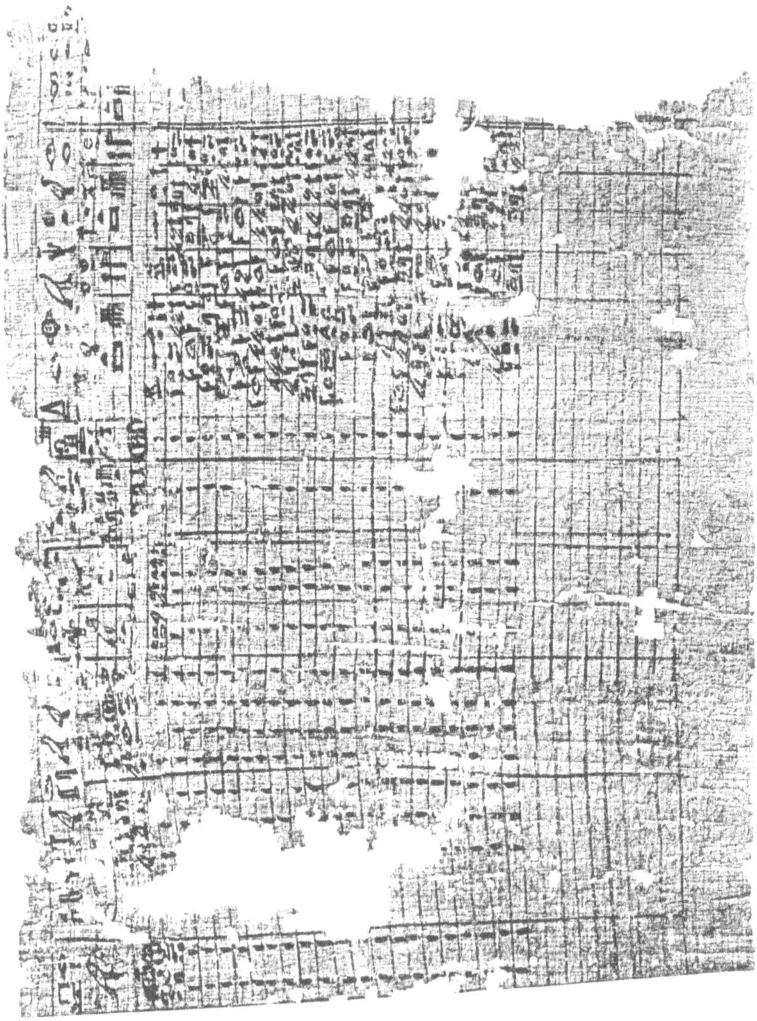

Fig. 6: The second sheet of the monthly duty-roster (see fig. 5, here rotated 90° counterclockwise), showing the ceremonial function to be performed, the titles of the officials who are to perform that duty, and finally the actual names of the individuals who were assigned according to each day of the month.
BM 10735, frame 7 recto © The British Museum.

tasks either because of their special competence, or through favoritism, if the work involved was easily done. It would be tempting to assume that such assignment sheets would be posted publicly to allow the staff to read them, but the generally low level of literacy even among Egyptian priesthoods would seemingly preclude this possibility.

On one of the best preserved of these monthly rosters, specific individuals were assigned tasks in connection with a festival (fig. 6).[75] Interestingly enough, since their actual names were used, we learn that it was possible for a person to alternate between two different ritual functions from day to day: *ḫnty-š* and *ḥm-nṯr* in this instance. This shift is remarkable and quite unexpected. Before the discovery of the Abusir archive, the general opinion among scholars of the Old Kingdom was that the title *ḫnty-š* was essentially connected with a functionary's land-holdings and entailed no ritual duties—certainly none on a par with a moderately high-level priestly office such as the *ḥm-nṯr* , lit. "god's servant," who generally ranked higher than the average *wʿb*-priest or "pure one."[76] In addition, rosters of this sort give substance to the term usufruct, showing that it was a working principle in the operation of temples. Whether the foodstuffs a phyle member received while on duty should be considered "payment" or whether the performance of ritual service was considered an obligation that had to be discharged in return for land tenure, unfortunately, are both subjects beyond the scope of the present study. Such papyri may not have been concerned with accounts, strictly speaking, but they do have broad implications for how and why the Egyptians maintained records of all types, especially if they were connected with institutional affairs.

---

[75] Louvre E. 25279 recto, see Posener-Kriéger and de Cenival 1968: Pls. 2-3 with Posener-Kriéger 1976: I 14-57, where various aspects of this particular document are discussed and compared with similar papyri.

[76] The exact nature of the title *ḫnty-š* continues to be the subject of much discussion. For a detailed examination of the title generally during the Old Kingdom and specifically within the context at Abusir, see Posener-Kriéger 1976: II 577-81. These individuals most likely have some connection with the type of temple endowment known as the *rꜣ-š* "*ro-she*," but this relationship is not quite understood yet. That and other questions about this important title have been studied at length by Roth 1991a: 177-86 and *idem* 1987: 133-40; Stadelmann 1981: 153-64; Eyre 1994: 111-12.

Post-factum documents in the Ramesside period: The Wilbour Papyrus and Papyrus Harris I

Although the present study has focused largely on the Abusir archive, I would like to discuss briefly some evidence from a much later date that demonstrates that the Egyptians did maintain what one might call running accounts in which a scribe or scribes recorded data continuously. In these examples, my interest in these documents lies not so much in what they contain as it lies in how the papyri came to be written out. Scribal practices can sometimes be as informative as the contents of a papyrus, as we saw above with some of the Abusir archive. Both Papyrus Harris I and the Wilbour Papyrus represent a different sort of post-factum document—the group effort. Both rolls were physically integral, yet, at they same time, several scribes wrote upon the papyrus large roll at different times.

The Wilbour Papyrus, dating to the reign of Ramesses V (c. 1147-1143 BC) and one of the lengthiest of all surviving Egyptian papyri—it is 10.33 m. long—has long fascinated and frustrated the economic historians who have studied it.[77] The papyrus overall might be described as a cadastre, or registry of land-holdings for an approximately 90 mile stretch of Middle Egypt between the modern towns of Atfih and el-Minya. The names of the land surveyors are not preserved, but instead represented by an ancient Egyptian version of a "ditto" mark.[78] As a cadastre, the Wilbour Papyrus was concerned with the ownership, size, and location of plots and rather than with what was planted or with the estimated crop yield. In a recent article on this document, S.L.D. Katary, who also is the author of a book length study,[79] notes that the large roll presents scholars with some problems that are, regrettably, often encountered when working with original papyrus sources:[80]

---

[77] Brooklyn Museum E 34.5596; the original publication is Gardiner 1948b. It was purchased in Cairo around 1929 and has no provenance.

[78] Haring 1997:283. Marks of this sort are particularly common in personnel lists.

[79] Katary 1999:61. In addition to Katary's work, there have been numerous other studies of this document. A selection of the more recent and productive bibliography can be found in Warburton 1997:165-69. Other important discussions are: Janssen 1975:139-47; Janssen 1986:351-66 (a review and discussion of the work of I.A. Stuchevsky); Eyre 1999, esp. 119-125; Haring 1997:282-345 (Chap. X, "The Administration of Temple Fields").

[80] Katary 1989:61. Presumably the surveyors' names would have appeared on the document's introductory sheet.

> ... the Wilbour Papyrus poses considerable difficulties since the text as we have it does not identify either the authority under which the data were compiled or the purpose for which the survey was made. These particulars were possibly contained at the beginning of the document, which is lost.

Unlike most other documentary papyri, the Wilbour Papyrus had entries on both sides of the roll, as often is the case for very large rolls. Given its great length and detail, it is not surprising that this papyrus often serves as the centerpiece in the discussion of many aspects of New Kingdom economy and society: land tenure, the relationship between state and temple institutions, demographics and ethnicity, agricultural yields, etc. The loss of the front section of the scroll, however, prevents us from being able to understand a fundamental question—to what end were its 5,223 entries made? For our present purposes, therefore, I shall concentrate primarily on the layout and other physical features of the document.

The papyrus appears to be palimpsest to a small degree—there are traces of effaced writing in between the two sections of the verso, sometimes called Text C in the literature[81]—and essentially bipartite. Depending on which of the four scribes entered the data, the script varies from a somewhat formal hieratic to a hand which is so cursive that it is almost reminiscent of demotic.[82] Text A, containing the so-called apportioning paragraphs or *posh* entries,[83] consists of 81 columns of text on the recto, running in the canonical direction from right to left and takes up the entire recto, continuing for an additional 20 columns on the verso, for a total of 101 columns. Text B, the non-apportioning paragraphs, consists of 25 columns of text, beginning at the left hand margin of the verso, and running from left to right, a direction rarely encountered in documentary papyri. (The paragraphs were entered in this direction, but the hieratic script retained its right-to-left direction.) Text C probably comprised a few lines of Text A that were effaced in order to provide room for Text B. Text B was written by one scribe; a single scribe wrote out the great majority of entries in

---

81 *E.g.* Haring 1997: 283f.

82 For the identification of the various scribes and a discussion of the degree of cursiveness in their script, see von Bomhard 1998: 10-20.

83 The term *posh* derives from Gardiner's proposed vocalization of the modifier *p(ś)š*, from a root meaning "divide, share." The term "paragraph" is slightly misleading since Gardiner was really speaking of lines of text.

Text A, with a few shorter portions added later by two other individuals. The "tête-bêche"[84] arrangement of the two main texts on the verso is highly unusual for an administrative document, especially since the two sections were clearly associated (fig. 7).

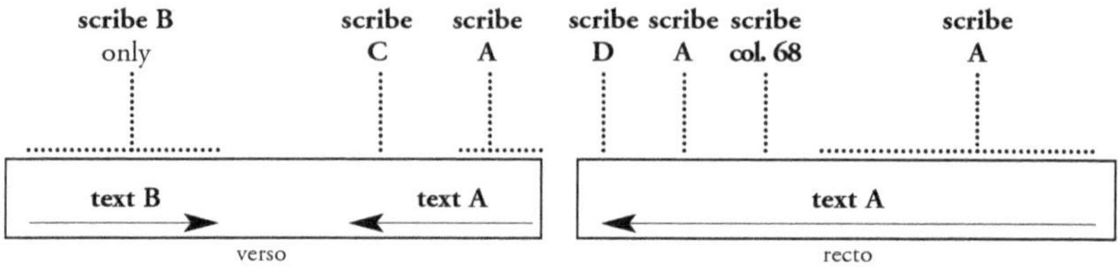

Fig. 7: The complex interaction of texts, direction of texts, and scribal hands on the Wilbour papyrus

These observations lead me to some observations on the layout of the verso and how the scribes may have worked as a team. As evidence from the Abusir archive clearly indicates, scribes normally entered upon a task with an informed estimate of how much papyrus the records would require. In the case of the Wilbour Papyrus, it is not unreasonable to assume either that one or more of the scribes had gathered the same data previously, or that the individual in charge of the work could retrieve a previous year's records from the archives. Text A was written in first, then Text B followed slightly later,[85] but the data for both was almost certainly acquired at the same time. Normally a scribe entering a second text on a papyrus would begin his portion directly after the first text's end and then continued onto the verso, if necessary. However, Text A was so large that it already consumed a considerable part of the verso, so the second scribe, not completely sure of how long his part of the document would be, began working at the left margin and worked rightwards towards the center. By this method, any potential overlap would be minimized and no additional sheets would have to be affixed to the papyrus. Nonetheless, someone overestimated how

[84] The term is that of von Bomhard 1998:7.

[85] The dates preserved in Text A range from II *ꜣḫt*, 15 to II *ꜣḫt*, 28; Text B is undated but was clearly written afterwards, since some erasures in Text A were made to insure that the second text would have enough room, see von Bomhard 1998:8.

much space Text B would require, which led to the erasure of some material near the end of Text A. Oddly enough, twice after Text B had been completely inscribed, two other scribes added a few columns of data to Text A's new end point. Both texts are sprinkled with minor emendations, additions, and corrections inserted at later dates. In short, not only was the Wilbour Papyrus a group effort, it also was not just quickly finished, then stored; it must have been unrolled and re-rolled at several points, clear indications of archival use.

The special treatment given Text B clearly indicates that it contained the more important of two sets of records. The outward appearance and text arrangement on this papyrus thus afford us with another example of how important the physical layout of documents can be for their overall interpretation. In fact, when one examines the text itself, one quickly learns that, unlike the people mentioned in Text A, the land-holders in Text B were relatively higher-level functionaries—*i.e.*, higher-status individuals meriting a higher-status text. These non-apportioning fields were said to be "under the authority" ((*r*)-*ḫt*) of an official. Their higher status is also implicit in the fact that many of them seem to have placed parts or all of their holdings "in the hand" (*m-ḏrt*) of a subordinate who seems to be managing the property on their behalf. I can do no better than to present here Haring's skillful summary of the situation:[86]

> The officials in charge as indicated by both (*r*) *ḫt* and *m sr.t* were not local personnel: many of them worked in places widely separated, and some of them acted on behalf of different institutions. The agents and deputies were probably the regular inspectors of the work on the fields, who reported their findings to their superiors on the *ḫt*-level. The later were generally high functionaries, and often attached to institutions other than the one holding the fields they supervised … … In this way, they seem to represent a form of *external control on a high level of institutional management* [my italics]. To the officials themselves, the supervision of agricultural domains may have been an extra task, as well as an extra source of income: we do not know how they were remunerated for their (nominal) service, but perhaps we may regard the fields under their supervision as the 'prebendal domain'.

[86] Haring 1997:286, with fn. 1.

Although it would be unwise to project all the details of this system back in time to the Abusir archive,[87] one can sense that the Wilbour Papyrus reveals several important operating principles that had long enabled a vast network of institutions to manage widely-scattered holdings. From this and other evidence, scholars estimate that a "management fee" amounting to approximately 7.5% of the crop may have been in force for much of Egypt's history.[88]

Judging from the few incidental dates, this enormous field-registry was made while the inundation had reached or was reaching its peak, a critical moment in economic life, especially if crop yields needed to be estimated.[89] As Hekanakhte's letter reminds us, all agricultural activity, and hence, all economic life, was based what effect the inundation would have on the individual plots—this was the implicit base of all planning.

Papyrus Harris I is a somewhat different case.[90] It purportedly records a lengthy series of statements made by Ramesses III (c. 1184-1153 BC), but was certainly written early in the reign of his successor, Ramesses IV (c. 1153-1147 BC). Like the Wilbour Papyrus, both the recto and verso were used. In a previous discussion of the prevalence of inspections as an Egyptian administrative practice, I briefly remarked that the presence of the term *śỉp wr* "great inventory" reveals this document's special nature. On one hand, the document records the result of extensive inventories. But when were these performed? The answer to that question emerges from the handwriting on this enormous and beautifully calligraphed document, listing in the most minute detail the benefactions which the pharaoh had made on behalf of the gods of Thebes, Heliopolis, and Memphis. An examination of the handwriting reveals it to be the work of no less than four different scribes, in addition to a scribal artist who drew the vignettes.[91]

---

[87] Eyre 1994: 123. The social status of people working institutional or "private" holdings was probably quite different during the Old Kingdom. The types of 'shares,' furthermore, changed from period to period, see Eyre 1994: 119-27.

[88] Eyre 1994: 119f.

[89] Haring 1997: 284.

[90] The most modern and complete treatment of the text is that of Grandet 1994/99. A recent study of this text has been done by Haring 1997: 156-91 (Chap. VI: "Pap. Harris I (P. BM 9999)").

[91] On this point, see Grandet 1994/99: 91f. It is uncertain whether the vignette scribe might not have also been among the scribes who wrote out the main entries.

Considering its size, Papyrus Harris I has only a few corrections or erasures. Furthermore, the papyrus was not pasted together, but written out continuously, probably with each scribe writing his section out immediately after the previous one, and most likely transcribing his work from some manner of an immediate document. We are looking at a final report, not a working document. Like the Wilbour Papyrus, then, Papyrus Harris I was clearly a collaborative effort, not a literal pastiche of documents.

Before leaving the subject of *post-factum* documents, I would like to note that the practices whereby several scribes worked on the same papyri or produced pre-fabricated documents were hardly confined to the realm of documentary materials. During the New Kingdom and Ramesside period, the huge West bank necropolis at Thebes was the site of what might be called a lively "funerary industry," that produced grave goods of all kinds for the burial of the high and low elite at the southern administrative capital. Among the most popular of all such funerary materials were copies of *The Book of the Dead.* In some cases, these works were produced ahead of time, leaving blank spaces for the name and titles of the deceased, much as we do today with standard leases or wills. The British Museum's famous and beautiful *Book of the Dead* belonging to a certain Nineteenth Dynasty official name Ani, is such a work.[92] In fact, the funerary workshop that produced this lovely manuscript took the process of prefabrication one step further by pasting together sheets that had been previous inscribed by no less than four separate scribes possibly including a specialist in vignette illustrations – a pastiche in the true sense of the term.

Concluding remarks

The purpose of this paper has been to survey two closely interrelated topics in relation to Egyptian administrative documents—intimations of planning and how it may be reflected in the papyri produced by actual institutions. Of course, a study of this length can hope only to present a brief survey of two vast areas in Egyptian economic and administrative history. I concentrated my efforts on the Abusir archive, since it does represent a widely disparate, yet related, group of docu-

[92] For a description of such practices and how the Ani papyrus was created, see Goelet 2003: 13-18. To a certain degree, this technique represents the transfer of tomb-building practices to the scribal workshop.

ments that offered a picture of Egyptian administration from the point of view of an organization operating in conjunction with a centralized authority. Unfortunately, I had to omit discussion of many important and highly informative sources and collections of documents such as the Reisner Papyri, the Kahun Papyri, Louvre E. 3226, the Theban Necropolis Diary, and Gardiner's *Ramesside Administrative Documents*, to say nothing of the vast number of economic and legal ostraca from Deir el-Medina—small, yet often most productive. Likewise, discussion of such related subjects as leases, taxation, and land tenure, personnel and absentee lists, ration lists, the use of check marks, as productive as all these might be, could not be handled here. Above all, I have only been able to present a sketch of what the very notion of "plan" meant within Egyptian royal and private ideological texts.

Nevertheless, I believe I have been able to present some evidence for the existence of a basic sense of planning and control within the Egyptian state or proto-state—a limited degree of planning, to be sure. The Egyptians seem to have arrived at a system for checking and controlling a rather extended network of institutions from a distant central point. One of the hallmarks of good managerial practice is that a mechanism should be in place for insuring that orders are carried out and that goods and income dispersed to subordinates are actually used for the purposes intended. In the case of ancient Egypt, whose geography forced a wide dispersal of institutions, these administrative ideals became an administrative necessity. The "Duties of the Vizier" shows that the means the Egyptians developed for controlling such a widely dispersed network were the simple, but effective, methods of on-site inspections and compelling administrators to report regularly to the central authorities at the royal administrative capital. The discussion of a few documents from the Abusir archive seem to confirm that these methods were actually employed, even at a rather early date.

Sometimes the evidence was rather direct—for instance, when *wpwtyw* "agents, emissaries" were mentioned or the existence of records containing the results of an inspection and/or inventory of temple equipment. In other cases, the evidence was more inferential in nature, such as the implication of large-scale formal protocols or the provisions for checking dispersals at numerous junctures in other documents. The Abusir Papyri which we studied certainly exhibit that Egyptian accounting practices afforded many ways in which an outside agency could trace and check income and outgo against other documents. The

Harris Papyrus I and the Wilbour Papyrus confirm the ability to perform highly detailed data collection on behalf of the authorities, even if that information does not appear to have been eventually used for large-scale planning. If such data were preserved in archives, then the central authorities could be quite well informed about some important local conditions outside the administrative capitals. Finally, I hope I have shown that close examination of the format and presentation of texts, even those on papyrus, can be employed as a powerful interpretive device in determining the rationale behind many Egyptian accounting practices.

ILLUSTRATIONS

Fig. 1: After F. Junge, *Late Egyptian Grammar. An Introduction*, transl. D. Warburton (Oxford: The Griffith Institute 2001): 25.

Fig. 2: Fischer 1976: 41 with permission by The Metropolitan Museum of Art, New York.

Fig. 3a, 3b, 4a, 4b: Reproduced from Posener-Kriéger and de Cenival 1968: XXXIII, XXXIIIA, XXXIV, XXXIVA with permission by The British Museum Press. Annotations on Fig. 3b/XXXIIIA are by the author.

Fig. 5, 6: © The British Museum.

Fig. 7: After von Bomhard 1998: 10.

Bibliography

Abbreviations

ÄA	Ägyptologische Abhandlungen, Wiesbaden
ÄF	Ägyptologische Forschungen, Glückstadt
BdÉ	Bibliothèque d'Étude, Cairo
BES	*Bulletin of the Egyptological Seminar*, New York
BIFAO Suppl.	*Bulletin de l'Institut Français d'Archéologie Oriental, Supplement*, Cairo
BSAK	*Beiträge, Studien zur altägyptischen Kultur*, Hamburg
DE	*Discussions in Egyptology*, Oxford
JEA	*Journal of Egyptian Archaeology*, London
MÄS	Münchener Ägyptologische Studien, Munich and Berlin
MMJ	*Metropoltan Museum Journal*, New York
OBO	Orbis Biblicus et Orientalis, Fribourg and Göttingen
Or.	*Orientalia, N.S.*, Rome
RdÉ	*Revue d'Égyptologie*, Paris
SAK	*Studien zur altägyptischen Kultur*, Hamburg
SAOC	Studies in Ancient Oriental Civilization, Chicago
UGAÄ	Untersuchungen zur Geschichte und Altertumskunde Ägyptens, Leipzig

Allam, S. (1968), "Sind die nichtliterarischen Schriftostraka Brouillons?" *JEA* 54:121-28.

— (1989), "Some Remarks on the Trial of Mose," *JEA* 75:103-12.

Allen, J.P. (2002). "From Coffin Texts 1130," in W.W. Hallo, ed., *The Context of Scripture*, vol. I: *Archival Documents from the Biblical World* (Leiden, Boston, and Cologne: Brill):26-27.

Arnold, D. (1991), "Amenemhat and the Early Twelfth Dynasty at Thebes," *MMJ* 26:5-48.

von Bomhard, A.S. (1998), *Paléographie du Papyrus Wilbour. L'écriture hiératique cursive dans les papyri documentaires* (Paris: Cybele).

van den Boorn, G.P.F. (1982), "On the Date of 'The Duties of the Vizier'," *Orientalia* 51:369-81.

— (1988), *The Duties of the Vizier. Civil Administration in the Early New Kingdom* (London and New York: Kegan Paul International).

Bowman, A.K., and E. Rogan (1999), "Agriculture in Egypt from Pharaonic to Modern Times," in A.K. Bowman and E. Rogan, eds., *Agriculture in Egypt from Pharaonic to Modern Times*. Proceedings of the British Academy 96 (Oxford: Oxford University Press): 1-32.

Caminos, R.A. (1986), "Some comments on the reuse of papyrus," in M.L. Bierbrier, ed., *Papyrus: Structure and Usage*. British Museum Occasional Papar 60. (London: The British Museum): 43-61.

Černý, J. (1947), *Paper and Books in Ancient Egypt* (London: H.K. Lewis & Co).

Davies, N. de G. (1944), *The Tomb of Rekh-mi-Reᶜ at Thebes*. Publications of the Metropolitan Museum of Art 11 (New York: Metropolitan Museum of Art).

Doxey, D.M. (1998), *Egyptian Non-royal Epithets in the Middle Kingdom. A Social and Historical Analysis*. Probleme der Ägyptologie 12 (Leiden, Boston, and Cologne: Brill).

Eyre, C.J. (1994), "Feudal Tenure and Absentee Landlords," in S. Allam, ed., *Grund und Boden in Altägypten (Rechtliche und Sozio-ökonomische Verhältnisse). Untersuchungen zum Rechtsleben im Alten Ägypten 2. Akten des internationalen Symposions Tübingen 18.-20. Juni 1990* (Tübingen: Selbstverlag des Herausgebers): 107-33.

— (1999), "Village Economy in Pharaonic Egypt," in A.K. Bowman and E. Rogan, eds., *Agriculture in Egypt from Pharaonic to Modern Times*. Proceedings of the British Academy 96 (Oxford: Oxford University Press): 33-60.

Fischer, H.G. (1976), "Archaeological Aspects of Epigraphy and Palaeography," in H.G. Fischer and R.A. Caminos, eds., *Ancient Egyptian Epigraphy and Palaeography* (New York: Metropolitan Museum of Art): 29-50.

Gaballa, G.A. (1977), *The Memphite Tomb Chapel of Mose* (Warminster: Aris & Phillips).

Gardiner, A.H. (1905), *The Inscription of Mes. A Contribution to the Study of Egyptian Judicial Procedure*. UGAÄ 4, 3 (Leipzig: Hinrichs).

— (1941), "Ramesside Texts Relating to the Taxation and Transport of Corn," *JEA* 27: 19-73.

— (1948a), *Ramesside Administrative Documents* (Oxford: Oxford UP).

— (1948b), *The Wilbour Papyrus*, four vols. (Oxford: Oxford UP).

— (1957a), "Hymns to Sobek in a Ramesseum Papyrus," *RdÉ* 11: 43-56.

— (1957b), *An Egyptian Grammar*, 3rd ed. rev. (Oxford: Oxford UP).

Gödecken, K.B. (1976), *Eine Betrachtung der Inschriften des Meten im Rahmen der sozialen und rechtlichen Stellung von Privatleuten im ägyptischen alten Reich*. ÄA 29 (Wiesbaden: Harrassowitz).

Goedicke, H. (1967), *Königliche Dokumente aus dem Alten Reich*. ÄA 14 (Wiesbaden: Harrassowitz).

Goelet, O., (1996), "A new 'Robbery' Papyrus: Rochester MAG 51.346.1," *JEA* 82: 107-27.

— (1989/90), "The Nature of the Term *pr-ꜥꜣ* during the Old Kingdom," *BES* 10: 77-90.

— (2002), "Fiscal Renewal in Ancient Egypt: Its Language, Symbols, and Metaphors," in M. Hudson and M. Van De Mieroop, eds., *Debt and Economic Renewal in the Ancient Near East* (Bethesda: CDL): 277-326.

— (2003), "Ancient Egyptian Scripts—Literary, Sacred, and Profane," in L.H. Schiffman, ed., *Semitic Papyrology in Context. A Climate of Creativity. Papers from a New York University conference marking the retirement of Baruch A. Levine.* Culture and History of the Ancient Near East (Leiden, Boston, and Cologne: Brill 2003): 1-21.

Goelet, O., and B. Levine (1998), "Making Peace in Heaven and on Earth: Religious and Legal Aspects of the Treaty between Ramesses II and Hattušili III," in M. Lubetsky, *et al.*, eds., *Boundaries of the Ancient Near Eastern World. A Tribute to Cyrus H. Gordon.* Journal for the Study of the Old Testament, Supplement Series 273 (Sheffield: Sheffield Academic Press): 252-99.

Gnirs, A.M. (1996), "Die ägyptische Biographie," in A. Loprieno, ed., *Ancient Egyptian Literature: History and Forms.* Probleme der Ägyptologie 10 (Leiden, New York, and Cologne: Brill): 191-241.

Grandet, P. (1994/99), *Le Papyrus Harris I (BM 9999).* BdÉ 109, I-III (Cairo: Institut Français d'Archéologie Orientale).

Hallo, W.W., ed. (2002), *The Context of Scripture,* vol. I: *Archival Documents from the Biblical World* (Leiden, Boston, and Cologne: Brill).

Haring, B.J.J. (1997), *Divine Households. The Administration and Economic Aspects of the New Kingdom Royal Memorial Temples in Western Thebes.* Egyptologische Uitgaven 12 (Leiden: Nederlands Instituut voor het Nabije Oosten).

Helck, W. (1954), *Untersuchungen zu den Beamtentiteln des ägyptischen Alten Reiches.* ÄF 18 (Glückstadt, Hamburg and New York: Augustin).

— (1974), *Altägyptische Aktenkunde des 3. und 2. Jahrtausends v. Chr.* MÄS 31 (Munich and Berlin: Deutscher Kunstverlag).

Jacquet-Gordon, H. (1962), *Les noms des domains funéraires sous l'Ancien Empire.* BdÉ 34 (Cairo: Institut Français d'Archéologie Orientale).

Janssen, J.J. (1975), "Prolegomena to the Study of Egypt's Economic History during the New Kingdom," *SAK* 3: 127-85.

— (1986), "Agrarian Administration in Egypt During the Twentieth Dynasty," *BiOr* 43: 351-66.

— (1987), "The Price of Papyrus," *DE* 9:33-35.

— (1992), "Literacy and Letters at Deir el-Medîna," in R.J. Demarée and A. Egberts, eds., *Village Voices.* CNWS Publications 13 (Leiden: Centre of Non-Western Studies): 81-94.

Katary, S.L.D (1989), *Land Tenure in the Ramesside Period* (London and New York: Kegan Paul International).

— (1999), "Land Tenure in the New Kingdom: The Role of Women Smallholders and the Military," in in A.K. Bowman and E. Rogan, eds., *Agriculture in Egypt from Pharaonic to Modern Times.* Proceedings of the British Academy 96 (Oxford: Oxford University Press): 61-105.

Lichtheim, M. (1973), *Ancient Egyptian Literature* I: *The Old and Middle Kingdom* (Berkeley: University of California Press).

— (1976), *Ancient Egyptian Literature* II: *The New Kingdom* (Berkeley: University of California Press).

Loprieno, A. (1996), "Loyalist Instructions," in A. Loprieno, ed., *Ancient Egyptian Literature. History and Forms.* Probleme der Ägyptologie 10 (Leiden, Boston and Cologne: Brill): 403-14.

Lorton, D. (1991), "What Was the *pr-nśw* and Who Managed It? Aspects of Royal Administration in 'The Duties of the Vizier'," *SAK* 18:291-316.

Parkinson, R.B., and S.G. Quirke (1995), *Papyri.* The Egyptian Bookshelf (London: British Museum Press).

Peden, A.J. (1994), *The Reign of Ramesses IV* (Warminster: Aris & Phillips).

Posener-Kriéger, P. (1976), *Les archives du temple funéraire de Néferirkarê-Kakaï* (*Les papyrus d'Abousir*). BdÉ 65, 1 and 2 (Cairo: Institut Français d'Archéologie Orientale).

— (1991), "Aspects économiques des nouveaux papyrus d'Abousir," *BSAK* 4:167-76.

Posener-Kriéger, P., and J.L. de Cenival (1968), *The Abu Sir Papyri.* Hieratic Papyri in the British Museum. Fifth Series (London: British Museum Press).

Quirke, S.G. (1996), "Archive," in A. Loprieno, ed., *Ancient Egyptian Literature. History and Forms.* Probleme der Ägyptologie 10 (Leiden, Boston and Cologne: Brill): 379-401.

Redford, D.B. (1981), "A Royal Speech from the Tenth Pylon," *BES* 3:86-102.

Roth, A.M. (1987), "The Organization and Functioning of the Royal Mortuary Cults of the Old Kingdom in Egypt," in M. Gibson and R.D. Biggs, eds., *The Organization of Power: Aspects of Bureaucracy in the Ancient Near East.* SAOC 46 (Chicago: University of Chicago Press): 133-40.

— (19991a), "The Distribution of the Old Kingdom Title *ẖntj-š*," *BSAK* 4: 177-86.

— (1991b), *Egyptian Phyles in the Old Kingdom*. SAOC 48 (Chicago: University of Chicago Press).

Schloen, J.D. (2001), *The House of the Father as Fact and Symbol. Patrimonialism in Ugarit and the Ancient Near East*. Studies in the Archaeology and History of the Levant 2 (Winona Lake: Eisenbrauns).

Sethe, K. (1928), *Dramatische Texte zu altägyptischen Mysterienspielen*. UGAÄ 10 (Leipzig: Hinrichs).

Simpson, W.K. (1963), *Papyrus Reisner I. Transcription and Commentary. The Records of a Building Project in the Reign of Sesostris I* (Boston: Museum of Fine Arts).

Spalinger, A.J. (1983), *Aspects of the Military Documents of the Ancient Egyptians*. Yale Near Eastern Researches 9 (New Haven and London: Yale University Press).

Stadelmann, R. (1981), "Die *ẖntjw-š*, der Königsbezirk *š n pr-ꜥꜣ* und die Namen der Grabanlagen der Frühzeit," *Bulletin du Centenaire. BIFAO Suppl.* 81: 153-64.

Valloggia, M. (1976), *Recherche sur les 'messagers' (wpwtyw) dans les sources égyptiennes profanes*. Centre de Recherches d'Histoire et de Philologie de IVe Section de l'École pratique des Hautes Études. Hautes Études Orientales 6 (Geneva and Paris: Librairie Droz).

Verner, M. (1994), *Forgotten Pharaohs, Lost Pyramids. Abusir* (Prague: Academia Škodaexport).

Vernus, P. (1993), *Affaires et scandales sous les Ramsès. La crise des valeurs dans l'Égypte du Nouvel Empire*. Bibliothèque de l'Égypte (Paris: Pygmalion/Gérard Watelet).

Warburton, D.A. (1997), *State and Economy in Ancient Egypt. Fiscal Vocabulary of the New Kingdom*. OBO 151 (Fribourg and Göttingen: University Press Fribourg and Vandenhoek & Ruprecht Göttingen).

Wente, E.F. (1990), *Letters from Ancient Egypt*. SBL Writings from the Ancient World Series 1 (Atlanta).

9.

Mycenaean Accounting Methods and Systems and Their Place within Mycenaean Palatial Civilization

Thomas G. Palaima
University of Texas at Austin

1. Introduction

My purpose here is to discuss the effects of Linear B accounting on the economic and social life of the Mycenaean palace period (c. 1500-1200 BC) and to give some sense of the integration of record-keeping administration into the activities of daily life in the well-documented Mycenaean palatial territories. Right up front I would like to say that it is easy to overemphasize the degree to which centralized palatial administration permeated or controlled the working lives of the 50,000-100,000 inhabitants of a palatial territory like Pylian Messenia in southwestern Greece. We should keep in mind that from the well-preserved destruction horizon of the palatial center we have c. 1,000 clay tablets attributed to just over thirty 'scribes' (Palaima 1988 2l and 2003 2i below). The tablets from Pylos indicate an administrative reach that covers the entire region of two geographically natural provinces divided into 16 (and two alternative) districts and that encompasses c. 240 sites.

Nonetheless, the tablets also only reference about 4,000-5,000 individuals and many of them anonymously as members of collective groups (smiths, wall-builders, herdsmen, specialized crafts personnel, women cloth production workers, rowers, infantry soldiers) (Hiller 1988 2b below). Religious and political officials, some with clear administrative functions, are mentioned in the texts, too. But many of these, *e.g.*, the local village big man or *basileus*, occur on the texts only as their areas of rather independent interests coincide with some specific need of the palatial center, *e.g.*, regarding the control of specific groups of smiths in outlying areas who would be used for palatial bronze production (Morpurgo Davies 1979 2b below). The influence of the palatial center would be felt by most inhabitants of the territory only intermittently and indirectly. Most inhabitants would be directly affected by clan chieftains, local big men (*basileis* in the plural), or even socially and economically prominent 'aristocrats' who occur in the tablets without any title, by personal name only, and are known as 'collectors' from their involvement with sheep and wool/cloth production. The 'collectors' also have relations with the palace centers (Killen 1995 2p, Olivier 2001 2p below), but they do not seem to be exclusive agents of the palatial centers out in the landscape.

Five major sites have yielded substantial to modest numbers of Linear B clay tablet records. In descending order of documentation these are: Knossos (c. 3300 tablets), Pylos (c. 1000 tablets), Thebes (c. 200 tablets once likely aggregates of fragments from the same tablets are taken into account), Mycenae (c. 75 tablets) and Tiryns (c. 24 tablets) (for typology of tablets, cf. Palaima 1990 2i and 2003 2i below). These tablets are minimalistic in their overall information contents and in their purposes. They are all focused on registering information that would be useful, most likely later in a mnemonic way, to those involved in monitoring the materials, economic interests and activities of sites, groups and individuals linked, directly or tangentially, dependently or almost independently, into the palatial system of regional organization.

Pylos and Thebes clearly exploit, without necessarily totally controlling, the resources of well-defined regions, known for this reason as palatial territories. The scale of these territories and the palatial centers will strike Near Eastern textual scholars as rather small, not to say petty (the Pylos region is 2,000 square kilometers and it is large for a palatial territory). The records from these two sites give us good evidence for yet smaller localities whose materials and human resources came under the view of the central administrations (cf. below Sergent 1994 2m and Piteros, Olivier and Melena 1990 2m).

The Pylos records, most of which come from the single administrative year that marked the end of the palatial center's existence c. 1200 BC (Palaima 1995 2l below), give us our best view of the relationships that existed among the palatial center proper, two natural geographical 'provinces', districts within those provinces, regional centers within those districts, and an array of other minor sites, social, political, and economic organizations, and human agents involved in the economic activities that made the entire complex system viable. Mycenological understanding of these relationships is constantly under revision. We are now seeing that almost all the simple models of organization proposed in the first two decades after the decipherment of Linear B in 1952 were reductionist.

This does not mean that they were *wrong*. Their binary-ism, partly adapted from what Mycenological linguists, Aegean archaeologists, Homerists and Greek economic historians thought of as Near Eastern models (*e.g.*, for temple vs. palatial economy, centralized economic control, workshops, scribal status) helped us to see different facets of the overall economic and political organizational scheme (for an overview of trends in history of scholarship in the last century, cf. Palaima 2003 2a). But where, in the 1950s into the 1970s, we were likely to interpret the whole of things in the light and darkness of single on-off switches, we now use dimmer controls and panels of switches to focus lighting and shading on areas of evidence in subtler ways. This also means, of course, that we are less categorical about the general scheme of things. Most of the words that I will necessarily use here, *e.g.*, 'scribes', 'administration', 'agents', 'regional economy', 'monitor', 'palatial center' and 'control', have specific or even vague meanings in a Mycenaean context that do not transfer readily to non-Mycenaean cultures.

The Knossos Linear B records have a difficult chronology, and the administrative system of which they are part has a longer and more complicated history, with antecedents reaching back into Minoan palatial society. The extant Linear B tablets of the so-called Mycenaean phase (c. 1450-1200 BC) give us a broad view of how the palatial center interacted with regional centers of different orders throughout the central and western parts of the island. They also attest to the importance on the island of Crete in this period of several of the conspicuous social, political and economic organizations and one main class of human agents, those prominent individuals, already mentioned, known as 'collectors' (Olivier 2001 2p, Bennet 1992 2k below), documented also at Pylos.

The sparser Thebes, Mycenae and Tiryns material gives us glimpses of some of the same patterns of organization we see elsewhere. The Thebes material is especially critical in providing us with a set of nodules, *i.e.*, clay devices with sealing impressions molded around the knot in a looped fine string, by which single transactions among agents and institutions involving specific commodities, in this case animals destined for ritual slaughter and commensal ceremonial consumption (Killen 1994 2f, Piteros, Olivier and Melena 1990 2f), were authenticated, authorized and/or verified as fulfilled (Palaima 2000a and 2000b 2o below).

All in all, then, Mycenaean accounting within Mycenaean palatial civilization looks markedly different from record-keeping in cuneiform cultures. Here I shall try to give some sense of how Mycenologists interpret the evidence we now have. I shall do this first by providing some guidance to what I consider accessible works of scholarship on particular sub-topics relating to economic and administrative interests. Then I shall describe the Mycenaean situation in broad outline. Finally I shall offer a few detailed examples, or test cases, of how particular kinds of records or recording formats affect social life within Mycenaean palatial civilization, specifically through the physical and conceptual organization of accounts and how they enable the control of labor and the provision of goods and services.

Regarding scholarship, I am being highly selective. The works I cite can be viewed as convenient portals for outsiders into the distinctive world of Mycenaean script and administration. Based on my own experience with intensive hyper-specialization in the many sub-disciplines of Mycenology (for example, epigraphy, palaeography, archival studies, sphragistics = sealing systems, linguistics, archaeology, anthropology, iconography, general prehistory, Indo-European studies, Homeric studies and so forth) I doubt whether any of us can become more than generally informed non-accidental tourists in scholarly realms that are not our own. For this reason, it is crucial that we refer to well-documented and well-argued scholarly interpretations and reconstructions.

I start with scholarship because briefly surveying key publications will also indicate what topics are of critical concern to leading specialists at this time and therefore are, as I implied above, in interpretive flux. In other words, these are areas where readers cannot rely on whatever general information about Myceneaean record-keeping seeps out through mostly outdated handbooks or the occasional 'outside' article into the domain of scholarship on ancient Near Eastern economies. I concentrate on scholarship relating to the Linear B inscribed tablets and sealings and Linear B paint-inscribed transport stirrup jars as records within economic administrative and accounting systems. All these works are relevant to understanding how records and record-keeping were integrated into what we rather artificially still separate, primarily for analytical purposes, into Mycenaean social, political, economic and religious systems of organization.

2. *Succinct scholarly review*

2a. The Mycenaean palatial system: Context, general overview and scholarly trends

Shelmerdine, C.W. (1997), "Review of Aegean prehistory VI: The palatial Bronze Age of the southern and central Greek mainland," *American Journal of Archaeology* 101:537-85.

Chadwick, J. (1976), *The Mycenaean world.* Cambridge: Cambridge University Press.

Dickinson, O. (1994), *The Aegean Bronze Age.* Cambridge: Cambridge University Press.

Palaima, T.G. (2003), "Archaeology and text: Decipherment, translation and interpretation," in *Theory and practice in Mediterranean archaeology: Old world and new world perspectives*, edited by J.K. Papadopoulos and R.M. Leventhal, 45-73. Cotsen Advanced Seminars 1. Los Angeles: The Cotsen Institute of Archaeology.

Driessen, J. and C. MacDonald (1997), *The troubled island. Minoan Crete before and after the Santorini eruption.* Aegaeum 17. Liège and Austin: Histoire de l'art et archéologie de la Grèce antique Université de Liège and PASP UT Austin.

Wright, J.C. (1994), "The Spatial configuration of belief: The archaeology of Mycenaean religion." In *Placing the gods. Sanctuaries and sacred space in ancient Greece*, edited by Susan E. Alcock and Robin Osborne, 37-78. Oxford: Clarendon Press.

2b. The General structure of society

Palaima, T.G. (1995), "The nature of the Mycenaean wanax: Non-Indo-European origins and priestly functions," in *The Role of the ruler in the prehistoric Aegean*, edited by P. Rehak, 119-39. Aegaeum 11. Liège and Austin: Histoire de l'art et archéologie de la Grèce antique Université de Liège and PASP UT Austin.

— (1997), "Potter and fuller: The royal craftsmen," in *Tekhne*, edited by R. Laffineur and P.P. Betancourt, 407-12. Aegaeum 16. Liège and Austin: Histoire de l'art et archéologie de la Grèce antique Université de Liège and PASP UT Austin.

Lindgren, M. (1973), *The People of Pylos* vols. 1-2. Boreas 3:1-2. Uppsala: Almqvist & Wiksell.

Morpurgo Davies, A. (1979), "Terminology of power and terminology of work in Greek and Linear B," in *Colloquium Mycenaeum. Actes du sixième colloque international sur les textes mycéniens et égéens tenu à Chaumont sur Neuchâtel du 7 au 13 Septembre 1975*, edited by E. Risch and H. Mühlestein, 87-108. Geneva: Libraire Droz.

Hiller, S. (1988), "Dependent personnel in Mycenaean texts," in *Society and economy in the eastern Mediterranean (c. 1500-1000 B.C.)*, edited by M. Heltzer and E. Lipiński, 53-68. Orientalia Lovaniensia Analecta 23. Leuven: Uitgeverij Peeters.

—— (1981), "Mykenische Heiligtümer: Das Zeugnis der Linear B-Texte," in *Sanctuaries and cults in the Aegean Bronz Age*, edited by R. Hägg and N. Marinatos, 95-126. Acta Instituti Atheniensis regni Sueciae, series in 4°, 28. Stockholm: Paul Åströms Förlag.

Chadwick, J. (1988), "The women of Pylos," in *Texts, tablets and scribes*, edited by J.-P. Olivier and T.G. Palaima, 43-95. Suplementos a *Minos* 10. Salamanca: Ediciones Universidad de Salamanca.

Lupack, S. (2002), *The Role of the religious sector in the economy of Late Bronze Age Mycenaean Greece*. Ph.D. dissertation, University of Texas at Austin.

Lejeune, M. (1972), "Le damos dans la société mycénienne," in *Mémoires de philologie mycénienne* volume 3. Incunabula Graeca 41. Rome: Edizioni dell' Ateneo: 137-54.

Carlier, P. (1984), *La royauté en Grèce avant Alexandre*. Études et travaux (Université des sciences humaines de Strasbourg. Groupe de recherche d'histoire romaine) 6. Strasbourg.

2c. Economy: Overall and representative spheres

Killen, J.T. (1985), "The Linear B tablets and the Mycenaean economy," in *Linear B: A 1984 survey*, edited by A.M. Davies and Y. Duhoux, 241-305. Bibliothèque des Cahiers de L'Institut Linguistique de Louvain 26. Louvain-la-Neuve: Cabay.

Olivier, J.-P. (1996-97), "El comercio micénico desde la documentación epigráfica," *Minos* 31-32:275-92.

Duhoux, Y. (1976), *Aspects du vocabulaire économique mycénien (cadastre–artisanat–fiscalité)*. Amsterdam: Adolf M. Hakkert.

Halstead. P. (1992), "The Mycenaean palatial economy: making the most of the gaps in the evidence," *Proceedings of the Cambridge Philological Society* 38:57-86.

Voutsaki, S. and J. Killen (2001), *Economy and politics in the Mycenaean palace states*. Cambridge Philological Society Supplementary Volume no. 27. Cambridge 2001.

Carlier, P. (2001), Journées égéennes Nanterre, 8-10 mars 1999 *KTEMA Civilisations de l'Orient, de la Grèce et de Rome antiques* 20:5-159.

2d. Representative agricultural commodities (land, grains and wine)

Palmer, R. (1989), "Subsistence rations at Pylos and Knossos," *Minos* 24:89-124.

— (1992), "Wheat and barley in Mycenaean society," in *Mykenaïka*, edited by J.-P. Olivier, 475-97. *Bulletin de Correspondance Hellenique* Supplement 25. Paris: Diffusion de Boccard.

— (1999), "Perishable goods in Mycenaean texts," in *Floreant studia mycenaea*, edited by S. Deger-Jalkotzy, S. Hiller and O. Panagl, vol. 2:463-85. Österreichische Akademie der Wissenschaften Philosophisch-Historische Klasse Denkschriften Band 274. Vienna: Verlag der Österreichischen Akademie der Wissenschaften.

— (2002), "Models in Linear B landholding: An analysis of methodology," in *Economy and politics in the Mycenaean palace states*, edited by S. Voutsaki and J. Killen, 223-50. Cambridge Philological Society Supplementary Volume no. 27. Cambridge 2001.

Halstead, P. (1995), "Late Bronze Age grain crops and Linear B ideograms *65, *120 and *121," *Annual of the British School at Athens* 90:229-34.

— (1999b), "Surplus and share-croppers: The grain production strategies of Mycenaean palaces," in *Meletemata*, edited by P. Betancourt, V. Karageorghis, R. Laffineur and W.-D. Niemeier, 319-26. Aegaeum 20. Liège and Austin: Histoire de l'art et archéologie de la Grèce antique Université de Liège and PASP UT Austin.

— (2001), "Mycenaean wheat, flax and sheep: Palatial intervention in farming and its implications for rural society," in *Economy and politics in the Mycenaean palace states*, edited by S. Voutsaki and J. Killen, 38-50. Cambridge Philological Society Supplementary Volume no. 27. Cambridge 2001.

Palmer, R. (1994), *Wine in the Mycenaean palace economy*. Aegaeum 10. Liège and Austin: Histoire de l'art et archéologie de la Grèce antique Université de Liège and PASP UT Austin.

Wright, J.C. (1995), "Empty cups and empty jugs: The social role of wine in Minoan and Mycenaean societies," in *The origins and ancient history of wine*, edited by P.E. McGovern, S.J. Fleming and S.H. Katz, 287-309. Philadelphia: Gordon and Breach Publishers.

2e. Wool products and sheep management

Killen, J.T. (1964), "The wool industry of Crete in the late Bronze Age," *Annual of the British School at Athens* 59:1-15.

Luján, E.R. (1996-97), "El léxico micénico de las telas," *Minos* 31-32:335-69.

2f. Livestock and their use in commensal ceremonies and for other purposes

Killen, J.T. (1994), "Thebes sealings, Knossos tablets and Mycenaean state banquets," *Bulletin of the Institute of Classical Studies* of the University of London 39:67-84.

— (1998), "The Pylos Ta tablets revisited," *Bulletin de Correspondance Hellenique* 122:421-22.

— (1999a), "Mycenaean *o-pa*," in *Floreant studia mycenaea*, edited by S. Deger-Jalkotzy, S. Hiller and O. Panagl, vol. 2:325-41. Österreichische Akademie der Wissenschaften Philosophisch-Historische Klasse Denkschriften Band 274. Vienna: Verlag der Österreichischen Akademie der Wissenschaften.

Piteros, C., J.-P. Olivier and J.L. Melena (1990), "Les inscriptions en linéaire B des nodules de Thèbes (1982): La fouille, les documents, les possibilités d'interprétation," *Bulletin de Correspondance Hellenique* 104:103-84.

Palaima, T.G. (1988), "Perspectives on the Pylos oxen tablets: Textual (and archaeological) evidence for the use and management of oxen in Late Bronze Age Messenia (and Crete)," in *Studia Mycenaea (1988)*, edited by T.G. Palaima, C.W. Shelmerdine and P. Hr. Ilievski, 85-124. *Živa Antika* Monographies No. 7. Skopje.

Speciale, M. Stella. (1999), "La tavoletta PY Ta 716 e i sacrifici di animali," in *ἐπὶ πόντον πλαζόμενοι. Simposio italiano di Studi Egei dedicato a Luigi Bernabò Brea e Giovanni Pugliese Carratelli*, edited by V. La Rosa, D. Palermo and L. Vagnetti, 291-97. Rome: Scuola Archeologica Italiana di Atene.

Nikoloudis, S. (2001), "Animal sacrifice in the Mycenaean world," *Journal of Prehistoric Religion* 15:11-31.

2g. Perfumed oil production and trade

Van Alfen, P. (1996-97), "The LMIIIB inscribed stirrup-jars as links in an administrative chain," *Minos* 31-32:251-74.

Shelmerdine, C.W. (1998), "The perfumed oil industry," in *Sandy Pylos: An archaeological history from Nestor to Navarino*, edited by J.L. Davis, 101-09. Austin: University of Texas Press.

Hallager, E. (1987), "The Inscribed Stirrup-Jars: Implications for Late Minoan IIIB Crete," *American Journal of Archaeology* 91:171-90.

Palaima, T.G. (1991), "Maritime matters in the Linear B texts," in *Thalassa. L'Égée prehistorique et la mer*, edited by R. Laffineur and L. Basch, 273-310. *Aegaeum* 7. Liège.

2h. Literacy, orality and the use of written documents

Palaima, T.G. (1987), "Comments on Mycenaean literacy," in *Studies in Mycenaean and Classical Greek presented to John Chadwick*, edited by J.T. Killen, J.L. Melena, J.-P. Olivier, 499-510. *Minos* 20-22.

— (1988), "The Development of the Mycenaean writing system," in *Texts, tablets and scribes: Studies in Mycenaean epigraphy and economy in honor of Emmett L. Bennett, Jr.*, edited by J.-P. Olivier and T.G. Palaima, 269-342. Suplementos a Minos 10. Salamanca: Ediciones Universidad de Salamanca.

— (1994-95), Review of Kevin Robb, *Literacy and paideia in ancient Greece* (New York, Oxford University Press 1994). *Minos* 29-30:392-97.

2i. Overview of Mycenaean record-keeping and archival accounting systems

Palaima, T.G. (1990), "The purposes and techniques of administration in Minoan and Mycenaean society," in *Aegean seals, sealings and administration*, edited by T.G. Palaima, 83-104. *Aegaeum* 5. Liège: Histoire de l'art et archéologie de la Grèce antique Université de Liège.

— (2003), "'Archives' and 'scribes' and information hierarchy in Mycenaean Greek Linear B records," in *Ancient archives and archival traditions*, edited by M. Brosius, 153-94. Oxford: Oxford University Press.

Driessen, J. (1994-95), "Data storage for reference and prediction at the dawn of civilization? A Review article with some observations on *Archives before writing*," *Minos* 29-30:239-56.

Bennet, J. (2001), "Agency and bureaucracy: thoughts on the nature and extent of administration in Bronze Age Pylos," in *Economy and politics in the Mycenaean palace states*, edited by S. Voutsaki and J. Killen, 25-35. Cambridge Philological Society Supplementary Volume no. 27. Cambridge.

Pluta, K. (1996-97), "A reconstruction of the Archives Complex at Pylos: Preliminary progress report," *Minos* 31-32:231-50.

Shelmerdine, C.W. (1999), "A comparative look at Mycenaean administration," in *Floreant studia mycenaea*, edited by S. Deger-Jalkotzy, S. Hiller and O. Panagl, vol. 2:555-76. Österreichische Akademie der Wissenschaften Philosophisch-Historische Klasse Denkschriften Band 274. Vienna: Verlag der Österreichischen Akademie der Wissenschaften.

Carter, A.L. (2003), *Ancient inventories: A Comparative study of temple inventories from Athens and Delos and the Linear B inventories from Pylos and Knossos.* M.A. Thesis. The University of Texas at Austin.

2j. Linear A and Linear B

Palaima, T.G. and Sikkenga, E. (1999), "Linear A > Linear B," *Meletemata. Studies in Aegean archaeology presented to Malcolm H. Wiener as he enters his 65th year*, edited by P. Betancourt, R. Laffineur, V. Karageorghis and W.-D. Niemeier, 599-608. Liège and Austin: Histoire de l'art et archéologie de la Grèce antique, Université de Liège and PASP UT Austin.

Duhoux, Y. (1985), "Mycénien et écriture grecque," In *Linear B: A 1984 Survey*, edited by A. Morpurgo Davies and Y. Duhoux, 7-74. Louvain-la-Neuve: Cabay.

Chadwick, J. (1987a), *Linear B and related scripts.* Berkeley: University of California Press.

Schoep, I. (1996), *Minoan administration on Crete. An interdisciplinary approach to documents in Cretan Hieroglyphic and Linear A.* Ph.D. Dissertation. Katholieke Universiteit Leuven.

— (2002a), "Minoan administration at Haghia Triada: A multi-disciplinary comparison of the Linear A tablets from the *Villa* and the *Casa del Lebete*," in *A-NA-QO-TA. Festschrift for J.T. Killen*, edited by J. Bennet and J. Driessen. *Minos* 33-34:205-22.

— (2002b), *The administration of Neopalatial Crete. A critical assessment of the Linear A tablets and their role in the administrative process.* Suplementos a Minos 17. Salamanca: Ediciones Universidad de Salamanca.

Specific regional Mycenaean record-keeping economies and archival accounting systems

2k. Knossos and Crete

Driessen, J. (1997), "Le palais de Cnosos au MR II-III: Combien de destructions," in *La Crète mycénienne*, edited by J. Driessen and A. Farnoux, 113-34. *Bulletin de Correspondance Hellenique* Supplement 30. Paris: Diffusion de Boccard.

— (2000), *The scribes of the Room of the Chariot Tablets: Interdisciplinary approach to the study of a linear B deposit.* Suplementos a Minos 16. Salamanca: Ediciones Universidad de Salamanca.

Bennet, J. (1985), "The structure of the Linear B administration at Knossos," *American Journal of Archaeology* 89:231-49.

— (1990), "Knossos in context: Comparative perspectives on the Linear B administration of LM II-III Crete," *American Journal of Archaeology* 94:193-211.

— (1992), "'Collectors' or 'owners'? An examination of their possible functions within the palatial economy of LM III Crete," in *Mykenaïka*, edited by J.-P. Olivier, 65-101. *Bulletin de Correspondance Hellenique* Supplement 25. Paris: Diffusion de Boccard.

Hallager, E., M. Vlasakis and B.P. Hallager (1992), "New Linear B tablets from Khania," *Kadmos* 31:61-87.

2l. Pylos and Messenia

Shelmerdine, C.W. (1998), "The palace and its operations," in *Sandy Pylos: An Archaeological history from Nestor to Navarino*, edited by J.L. Davis, 101-09. Austin: University of Texas Press.

Palaima, T.G. (1988), *The Scribes of Pylos*. Incunabula Graeca 87. Rome Edizioni dell' Ateneo.

— (1995), "The last days of the Pylos polity," in *Politeia: Society and state in the Aegean Bronze Age*, edited by R. Laffineur and W.-D. Niemeier, 623-33. Aegaeum 12. Liège and Austin: Histoire de l'art et archéologie de la Grèce antique Université de Liège and PASP UT Austin.

Bennet, J. (1998), "The Linear B archives and the kingdom of Nestor," in *Sandy Pylos: An archaeological history from Nestor to Navarino*, edited by J.L. Davis, 111-33 and 134-38. Austin: University of Texas Press.

Davis, J.L., and J. Bennet (1999), "Making Mycenaeans: Warfare, territorial expansion and representations of the other in the Pylian kingdom," in *Polemos*, edited by R. Laffineur, vol. 1, 105-20. Aegaeum 19. Liège and Austin: Histoire de l'art et archéologie de la Grèce antique Université de Liège and PASP UT Austin.

Galaty, M.L., and W.A. Parkinson (1999), *Rethinking Mycenaean palaces: New interpretations of an old idea*. The Cotsen Institute of Archaeology University of California, Los Angeles Monograph 41. Los Angeles.

Davis, J.L. (1998), "The palace and its dependencies," in *Sandy Pylos: An archaeological history from Nestor to Navarino*, edited by J.L. Davis, 53-68. Austin: University of Texas Press.

De Fidio, P. (1987), "Palais et communautés de village dans le royaume mycénien de Pylos," in *Tractata Mycenaea*, edited by P.H. Ilievski and L. Crepajac, 129-49. Skopje: Macedonian Academy of Sciences and Arts.

2m. Thebes

Sergent, B. (1994), "Les petits nodules et la Grande Béotie," *Revue des Études Anciennes* 96:365-84.

Piteros, C., J.-P. Olivier and J.L. Melena (1990), "Les inscriptions en linéaire B des nodules de Thèbes (1982): La fouille, les documents, les possibilités d'interprétation," *Bulletin de Correspondance Hellenique* 104:103-84.

Inscribed sealings as a component of Mycenaean economic administration

2n. The Minoan background

Hallager, E. (1996), *The Minoan roundel and other sealed documents in the Neopalatial Linear A administration.* Aegaeum 14. Liège and Austin: Histoire de l'art et archéologie de la Grèce antique Université de Liège and PASP UT Austin.

Palaima, T.G. (1994), "Seal-users and script-users / Nodules and tablets at LM I B Hagia Triada" and "Response to Paper of G. Fissore," in *Archives before writing,* edited by P. Ferioli, E. Fiandra, *et al.*, 307-37, 355-61. Pubblicazioni del Centro Internazionale di Ricerche Archeologiche Antropologiche e Storiche I. Turin.

2o. The Mycenaean system of inscribed sealings

Palaima, T.G. (1987), "Mycenaean seals and sealings in their economic and administrative contexts," in *Tractata Mycenaea,* edited by P.H. Ilievski and L. Crepajac, 249-66. Skopje: Macedonian Academy of Sciences and Arts.

— (1996), "Sealings as links in an administrative chain," in *Administration in ancient societies,* edited by P. Ferioli, E. Fiandra and G.G. Fissore, 37-66. Turin: Centro Internazionale di Ricerche Archeologiche Antropologiche e Storiche.

— (2000a), "Transactional vocabulary in Linear B tablet and sealing administration," in *Administrative documents in the Aegean and their Near Eastern counterparts,* edited by M. Perna, 261-76. Turin: Centro Internazionale di Ricerche Archeologiche Antropologiche e Storiche.

— (2000b), "The palaeography of Mycenaean inscribed sealings from Thebes and Pylos, their place within the Mycenaean administrative system and their links with the extra-palatial sphere," in *Minoische-mykenische Glyptik: Stil, Ikonographie, Funktion.* V. internationales Siegel-Symposium, Marburg, 23.-25. September 1999, edited I. Pini and W. Müller, 219-38. *Corpus der minoischen und mykenischen Siegel* Beiheft 6. Berlin: Gebr. Mann Verlag.

Killen, J.T. (1992), "Observations on the Thebes sealings," in *Mykenaïka,* edited by J.-P. Olivier, 365-80. *Bulletin de Correspondance Hellenique* Supplement 25. Paris: Diffusion de Boccard.

Pini, I., ed. (1997), *Die Tonplomben aus dem Nestorpalast von Pylos.* Mainz: Philipp von Zabern.

2p. Work, production, taxation and economic control

Melena, J.L. (1983), "Further thoughts on Mycenaean *o-pa*," in *Res Mycenaeae*, edited by A. Heubeck and G. Neumann, 258-86. Göttingen: Vandenhoeck and Ruprecht.

Killen, J.T. (1984), "Last year's debts on the Pylos Ma tablets," *Studi Micenei ed Egeo-Anatolici* 25:173-88.

— (1995), "Some further thoughts on Mycenaean 'collectors'," in *Politeia: Society and state in the Aegean Bronze Age*, edited by R. Laffineur and W.-D. Niemeier, 213-24. *Aegaeum* 12. Liège.

— (1999), "Mycenaean *o-pa*," in *Floreant studia mycenaea*, edited by S. Deger-Jalkotzy, S. Hiller and O. Panagl, vol. 2:325-41. Österreichische Akademie der Wissenschaften Philosophisch-Historische Klasse Denkschriften Band 274. Vienna: Verlag der Österreichischen Akademie der Wissenschaften.

Olivier, J.-P. (2001), "Les 'collecteurs': leur distribution spatiale et temporelle," in *Economy and politics in the Mycenaean palace states*, edited by S. Voutsaki and J. Killen, 139-59. Cambridge Philological Society Supplementary Volume no. 27. Cambridge.

Palaima, T.G. (2001), "The modalities of economic control at Pylos," in *KTEMA Civilisations de l'Orient, de la Grèce et de Rome antiques* 20:151-59.

Deger-Jalkotzy, S. (2002), "Working for the palace: Some observations on PY An 261," in *A-NA-QO TA. Festschrift for J.T. Killen*, edited by J. Bennet and J. Driessen. *Minos* 33-34:65-82.

2q. Identification of scribes and their spheres of activity

Palaima, T.G. (2002), "Special vs. normal Mycenaean: Hand 24 and writing in the service of the king?" in *A-NA-QO-TA. Festschrift for J.T. Killen*, edited by J. Bennet and J. Driessen. *Minos* 33-34:205-22.

— (2000), "The Pylos Ta series: from Michael Ventris to the new millennium," *Bulletin of the Institute of Classical Studies* 44:236-37.

Thompson, R.J.E. (1996-97 [1998]), "Dialects in Mycenaean and Mycenaean among the dialects," *Minos* 31-32:313-33.

2r. Mycenaean evidence for legal terminology

Palaima, T.G. (2000), "θέμις in the Mycenaean Lexicon and the Etymology of the Place-Name **ti-mi-to a-ko*," *Faventia* 22/1:7-19.

3. Features of Mycenaean palatial civilization and record-keeping

The primary feature to highlight is that the Mycenaean regional palatial system and forms of record-keeping administration within it were late developments in the nearly 2000-year history of Aegean Bronze Age culture. Bennet (1998 2l) and Davis and Bennet (1998 2l) make clear that at least in Messenia on the Greek mainland, the stage where the central palatial complex of Pylos and its surrounding community were fully integrated into and in some sense in control of an overall unified territory consisting of two provinces and pyramidally organized districts and centers likely lasted little more than a century. Even a generous estimation of the longevity of the Linear B script gives it no more than c. 300 years, its invention either taking place at 15th-century Knossos or roughly coinciding with the point in the same century at which mainland palatial society had advanced enough to necessitate the keeping of records on clay and perhaps now lost less-permanent materials (Palaima 1988 2h).

This is important because it limits the degree to which written administration would have had to insinuate itself into long-standing traditional modes of economic control and operation involving clans and other kin group and pseudo-kin groups, villages, groups of elders, local chieftains, and land collectives (Deger-Jalkotzy 2002 2p, de Fidio 1987 2l). The Minoan system of record-keeping, so far as we can tell from our even more limited attested evidence (Hallager 1996 2n, Palaima 1987 2h, 1990 2i, Driessen 1994-95 2i, Schoep 2002b 2j), never fully replaced traditional arrangements for handling economic activities. Its system of uninscribed or single-sign countermarked sealings is much more complex than the Mycenaean (Hallager 1996 2n, Palaima 1994 2n). The most likely reason for this is that many of the sealings (with the exception of the flat-based packet sealings used to transmit folded parchment documents long distances) were used within the confines of individual regions. On such a 'local' level, the sealings accompanied a standard range of transactions which were known to the parties involved and for which there was no need to draw up lengthy written documents (Palaima 2000a and 2000b 2o). The limited information recorded on Linear A tablets also gives the impression of being very focused on regional centers. The Linear A tablets were used rather sparingly at that, even at the end of a four-century process of development within Minoan Cretan palatial civilization (c. 1850-1450 BC) (Schoep 2002b 2j).

The Mycenaean system adapted, rather than adopting, concepts, procedures, materials, forms and techniques of record-keeping and accounting from Minoan culture (Hallager 1996 2n, Palaima 1990 2i). Even from the earliest attested period for Linear B, the so-called Room of the Chariot Tablets inscriptions from Knossos (Driessen 2000 2k), we have clear differences from Minoan practices in tablet shapes and sizes, formatting elements such as the use of standardized ruling, a brand new system of metrical ideograms and, of course, a repertory of phonetic signs tailored to the needs of representing the closed-syllable structure of the Greek language (Palaima and Sikkenga 1999 2j, Chadwick 1987 2j, Palaima 1990 2i).

The Mycenaean Linear B system has signs for standard increments of weight and measure in contrast to Linear A, which uses, so far as we can tell, a combinatory 'aliquot' fractional system to specify aggregate parts of a larger whole unit. The metrical signs in these two different systems do not seem to be related, *i.e.*, the Linear B system would imply the imposition of new public standards for handling goods and commodities that had to be weighed and measured. Lastly the Linear B system is universal, with no valid proof of significant regional or chronological variation within the attested history of the use of the script. Thus we can speak of a use of writing and inscriptions which is culturally specific and tooled to the needs of Mycenaean palatial territories. Here, however, standardization appears not to be the result of some form of imposition by any overarching Aegean-wide authority.

Although we do not have a full diachronic picture, what we have suggests the following. Within the mainly homogeneous Mycenaean palatial culture, a prominent class of individuals, known conventionally as 'collectors' and perhaps related by ties of birth and family, acted as important economic agents (Killen 1995 2p, Olivier 2001 2p, Bennet 1992 2k). Their presence within different palatial territories alone would have exerted a conservative influence upon economic structures, making it more efficient to do things the same way region to region. Given the absence of any pressing need for radical experimentation or expansion of the uses of written recording, the concepts, procedures, materials, forms and techniques of record-keeping and accounting remained static within Mycenaean civilization for over two centuries. Small traces of variation come at the outset, transitional 'Minoanized' features being detected in the earliest extant documentation at LM II Knossos (Driessen 2000 2k).

The Linear B script had then a relatively brief *floruit* (c. 1450-1200 BC) and was used, so far as current evidence allows us to see, for limited purposes within territories of limited scale and scope. These palatial territories exist within the natural regions more familiar to us from the later Greek *poleis*. The sole exception here is the attested administrative reach of Knossos over the central and western two-thirds of the island of Crete, where a larger hierarchical extra-regional scheme operated with Knossos as the main organizational center (Bennet 1985 and 1990 2k). This appears to be, in some way, a carry-over from the status of Knossos in the Minoan period (Driessen and MacDonald 1997 2a).

The mainland regions, too, may well have had their own idiosyncrasies relating to the histories of their formation (Shelmerdine 1997 2a). But Pylos alone offers us inscriptional and archaeological evidence sufficient to put its accounting methods into context. Pylos in the latter half of LH III A and in LH IIIB (roughly the late 14th and 13th centuries BC) extended its dominance over a natural territory of c. 2,000 km^2 in Messenia in southwestern Greece. It is estimated that c. 4,000-5,000 individuals are recorded in the extant Pylos tablets. Just over a thousand of these individuals are supported by direct rations, others by palatially 'monitored' landholdings (Hiller 1988 2b). Thus a rather small percentage of the regional population, estimated at various times as between 50,000 and 100,000, made it into the extant central records (Shelmerdine 1997 2a and 1998 2l, Davis and Bennet 1999 2l, Davis 1998 2l). Depending on how we classify the status of the western Cretan site of Khania (Hallager, Vlasakis and Hallager 1992 2k) in the Mycenaean period, we have no evidence from anywhere in the Mycenaean world of Linear B administrative documents being found at what we consider second-order centers. This may change with further excavation.

The most stunning difference between patterns of economic accounting in cuneiform cultures and in Mycenaean culture is the lack of any evidence so far that written records were used in private households (*e.g.*, contracts and deeds or titles are missing) or at habitation sites other than palatial centers (albeit few second-order sites have been excavated). Economic administrative literacy, then, seems to have been limited to and have been monopolized—or viewed as useful—by the palatial centers where the complexity of operations and activities had outstripped simpler means of tracking economic data. To repeat, this must be related to the relatively late overlaying of the palatial system upon existing social and political structures (Bennet 1998 2l; Palaima 1995 2b).

The Mycenaean palatial system required intensive economic exploitation of regional resources (Killen 1985 2c, Morpurgo Davies 1979 2b). Sudden expansion of the power of a single palatial center to control broader regional resources and production would have created new hierarchies of power, work and socio-political networks (Bennet 1998 2l, Davis 1998 2l, Davis and Bennet 1999 2l, Galaty and Parkinson 1999 2l, Killen 1985 2c, Wright 1995 2d, Palaima 1990 2i). This led to intensive labor specialization with necessary systems of support, to traditional and new arrangements for reward and obligation (and related vocabulary within the texts: Palaima 2000a 2o), and to control structures (Hiller 1988 2b, Chadwick 1988 2b, Palaima 1987 2o, 1996 2o, 2000b 2o) that combined pre-existing and continuing procedures and relationships with new, super-imposed palatial elements.

The palatial system required maximal exploitation of regional resources within specific industries (*e.g.*, wool and flax and dye substances for cloth production: Killen 1964 2e, Lujan 1996-97 2e; olive oil, scent substances, and related pottery manufacture for perfumed oil: van Alfen 1996-97 2g, Shelmerdine 1998 2g, Hallager 1987 2g). The finished products of such specialized industries were traded in order to obtain necessary products (everything from exotic wood inlay materials to vital resources like copper and tin: Palaima 1991 2g). Subsistence rations were allotted to totally dependent (aka 'slave') women labor groups (Palmer 1989 2d, Chadwick 1988 2b). Land was carefully managed (Palmer 2002 2d) within religious sanctuaries and by agents for local land-management collectives known as *da-mo* (Lejeune 1972 2b) for the support of those who were dependent, directly or indirectly, upon the palatial system or who drew benefits from forms of service for the palatial authority or the sanctuaries (Lupack 2002 2b).

This led to steep pyramids of distributed economic and political power, with hierarchies consisting, in individual regions, of the palatial center, secondary centers, 'villages' (de Fidio 1987 2l), and collectives in outlying locales (Bennet 1985 2k and 1998 2l, Palaima 1995 2b and Morpurgo Davies 1979 2b). The Pylos Linear B records refer to c. 240 place names (including 16 districts or district capitals that function as second-tier centers). When we include the site of Pylos itself and the two alternative names that are used occasionally as substitutes for two of the canonical district capitals, we are left with 220 minor places in the Pylos tablets that are somehow involved in the economic interests of the center in the final year of its existence. Only 150 sites are so far traceable on the ground during the III B period (Bennet 1998 2l), many quite small. In terms of scale the Pylos palatial center with its surrounding town now measures c. 20 hectares. From our looks at a few second-order centers we estimate that their size would be c. 5-7 hectares. There are then clusterings of yet smaller sites.

The surviving written records, as we have mentioned, attest to a highly limited literacy and dominant orality (Palaima 1987 and 1994-95 2h). Much of the economic activity must have relied upon traditional transactional arrangements between individuals and among social organizations (Palaima 1990 and 2003 2i, Driessen 1994-95 2i, Bennet 2001 2i, and especially Deger-Jalkotzy 2002 2p). Conspicuous is the traditional use of sealings, inscribed and more frequently uninscribed, at the interface between the palatial sphere and outlying individuals and communities (cf. especially Palaima 2000b 2o and Pini 1997 2o). We should also emphasize the absence of written texts relating to history (including propagandistic pronouncements), literature, ritual and cult (hymns, ceremonial prescriptions), compilations of legal precedent (contrast the Hittite law codes), and, as we have mentioned, contracts (for economic goods and services, deeds and titles to landholdings and possessions) (Palaima 2003 2i).

4. *Record-keeping administration*

The special nature of the Linear B documentation arises from the peculiar features of Mycenaean social, political and economic organization. At every Mycenaean site or locus within a site where Linear B is attested, records come from a single administrative period of not more than a year. The Knossos records contain c. 7 month names. The Pylos records preserve at most 5 month names. These few month names are brought into play only in 'religious' offering contexts, where the specification of the performance of the economic actions connected with rituals and ceremonies defined within the ritual calendar is clearly important. No specification of days or periods within months (Palaima 1995 2l) is known. There is no designation of long-term chronology by means of dating mechanisms, for example, no designation of year according to regnal lists or by archon or magistrate or priesthood dates, as are familiar from later Greek history. This in itself indicates either that records were not kept for long-term planning purposes, or, if they were, that they would have been kept on ephemeral materials like parchment (attested clearly on Minoan flat-based nodules) or papyrus.

The signs of the Linear B script, in fact, contain many complex patterns and curvilinear elements which are not very well-suited to writing on clay, although the blade-like writing tip of the Mycenaean stylus helps in this regard. They are much easier to execute, as I have recently privately experimented, with the ancient equivalent of an A-5 size calligraphic pen.

With regard to planning of economic activity, there is some indication of carry-over information in accounting terminology. The words 'last year', 'this year', 'next year', and 'yearly' are found sparingly, mainly in regional 'taxation' records (Killen 1984 2p, Palaima 1995 2l) wherein standard proportional quotas of products are recorded as expected from the sixteen canonical second-order districts and the two alternative places. 'Payments', short-falls, exemptions and carry-overs are listed for these districts.

The records that we have are intensively focused on the concerns of the palatial centers. The palatial centers in turn pursue their interests in their regions through human agents—palatially appointed, co-opted, or quasi-independent of the palatial centers—and through secondary centers. These agents and centers mobilize and orchestrate economic activity of benefit to the palatial centers. We always have to keep in mind that our view depends on the hazards of archaeological investigation. As we shall see below, certain tablets (for example, Pylos Jn 829 and the Pylos Ma series) offer clear evidence for major second-order centers (where we assume some kinds of extensive 'administrative accounting' took place: Bennet 1985 and 1990 2k) and others attest to the existence of separate religious territories (Hiller 1981 2b) with their own institutions (*na-wo* = 'dwelling place of a deity', later Greek 'temple'; *do* and *wo-ko* = 'house' or 'home' of deities; *i-je-ro* 'holy place', later Greek 'sanctuary'; and sanctuary designations in noun forms relating to individual deities). But no outlying sanctuary area of the period has yet been archaeologically identified within Messenia (Wright 1994 2a), and very few second-order centers have been investigated (cf. *ti-mi-to a-ko* = Nichoria: Palaima 2000 2r).

There is some evidence provided by the palaeography and the 'language' of the tablets that palatial tablet-writers were influenced by contact with individuals and institutions outside the palatial orbit (Palaima 2002 2q, Thompson 1996-97 [1998] 2q). Still we have no known 'private' records.

The tablet records in and of themselves do not seem to have 'legal' status, and so it is somewhat misleading to refer to them as 'documents', given what this term implies. However, the tablets do record transactions and conditions that are dependent on relationships among individuals and institutions. Such transactions must have relied upon notions of legal proof and legal arbitration as known from other societies, including Greek historical culture (Palaima 2000 2r). There is scanty evidence within the Linear B records of 'disputes', and absolutely no indication of how they were settled (Palaima 2000 2r). In the most famous case (on Pylos tablet Ep 704, see below) the status of a landholding is disputed between the priestess who is named *e-ri-ta* and the collective organization, known as the *da-mo* (later Greek *damos*), that monitors local land apportionment (Lejeune 1972 2b).

At individual palatial sites the administrative systems attested in clay records preserved from destruction phases were written by a good number of tablet-writers. Pylos has c. 33 identifiable 'scribes'. These tablet-writers are anonymous. We do not even have a word for 'scribe'. It is still disputed whether 'scribes' are 'hidden' among the many titles for officials listed within the tablets or are 'petty functionaries', subordinate to such officials (Palaima 2003 2i, Driessen 1994-95 2i, Bennet 2001 2i). The most intensive focal point for this question is the Pylos Ta tablets (Carter 2003 2i). The header tablet (Ta 711) indicates that the documents were drafted *o-wi-de* pu_2*-ke-qi-ri o-te wa-na-ka te-ke au-ke-wa da-mo-ko-ro*, *i.e.*, on a ceremonial occasion that required *Phugebris* to make a visual 'inventory' inspection when the *wanaks* ('king') appointed an individual named *Augewas* to the office of *damokoros*. The tablets then list cult paraphernalia and furniture in a document structure that is the result of 'experienced improvisation' (again seeming to reinforce the idea that the main purpose of such documents is 'system-internal' documentation and 'memory-aid' for the officials in charge: Palaima 2000 2q).

In such circumstances, with barely over 5,000 minimalist tablets and fragments from eight archaeological sites, it is understandable that the definitions of key terms are still being discussed. Among these are 'archives', 'pre-archives', 'tablet deposits', 'offices', 'departments', 'bureaus' and the internal relationships among these and such concepts as 'workshops' and 'storage areas' (Palaima 1987 2o, Palaima 2003 2i, Driessen 1994-95 2i).

5. *Particular cases of resource mobilization and economic planning*

As should be clear from the foregoing, we have a good sense of the complex hierarchies and relationships that were woven into the regional economic, social and political systems during the Mycenaean palatial period. Our ability to understand what long-term planning, if any, the central authorities used is severely limited by the nature of our data. But the data themselves, as I have argued above, may reflect how the Mycenaeans of the palatial period organized and used their resources.

My own belief is that many elements of economic production had histories that preceded, in whole or part, the establishment of the palatial centers atop regions. If this is so, the ways in which processes were controlled and managed may well also have large pre- and proto-literate components. Such traditional arrangements and procedures would never have required setting information out in written form, either temporarily or for longer periods. Written planning and tracking of execution and fulfillment is called into play when the scale and scope of a system far outstrip traditional methods of organization and control. In my opinion, the Linear B texts, especially those from Pylos, reveal that the palatial system of organization was exploiting labor and resources as much as possible through traditional channels. We might in fact do better to view economic mobilization simultaneously as both a top-down imposition upon and a bottom-up siphoning off of resources.

Although some of the following details are still subject to discussion among Mycenologists, what I offer here is a view of a few test cases of the Mycenaean regional system of economic mobilization and planning that study of the Linear B tablets reveals.

Mycenaean palatial centers and their rulers (the Mycenaean 'king' or *wanaks*: Carlier 1984 2b, Palaima 1995 2b) legitimize and maintain their authority partly through control and management of resources. The tablets contain terminology for 'obligation' and 'benefit' and indicate how obligations were fulfilled and benefits were dispensed. The frustrating aspect of the Linear B tablets is that very few tablets and series contain descriptive headers that would inform us who is not privy to what is going on inside the administrative system, why particular data are being recorded and how they are being used.

Let us start with a tablet (Pylos tablet Jn 829) that does contain a header with an extravagant, by Mycenaean standards, amount of information. The tablet is written by Hand 2, who is a high-ranking 'scribe' of the first palaeographical class at Pylos (often viewed as the main 'pupil' of the 'master scribe' of the site Hand 1: Palaima 1988 21) and is responsible for a number of high-level economic records. These include: (1) the Ta 'banquet-paraphernalia' inventory discussed above; (2) some of the Jn records of allotments of copper (traditionally translated as 'bronze') to groups of smiths at outlying locales; (3) the Ma regional taxation records, which, as we have mentioned, list quantities of six items due in proportional amounts from the sixteen (plus two) major districts or second-order centers and also list shortfalls, exemptions and carry-overs.

PYLOS Jn 829

.1 Thus will give the *ko-re-te-re*, and *du-ma-te*,
.2 and *po-ro-ko-re-te-re*, and *ka-ra-wi-po-ro*, and *o-pi-su-ko*, and *o-pi-ka-pe-e-we*
.3 temple bronze for light javelins and spears as points

.4	at pi-*82^{PL}	*ko-re-te*	BRONZE 2 kg.	*po-ro-ko-re-te*	BRONZE 0.75 kg.
.5	at me-ta-pa^{PL}	*ko-re-te*	BRONZE 2 kg.	*po-ro-ko-re-te*	BRONZE 0.75 kg.[ ] *blank*
.6	at pe-to-no^{PL}	*ko-re-te*	BRONZE 2 kg.	*po-ro-ko-re-te*	BRONZE 0.75 kg.
.7	at pa-ki-ja-ne^{PL}	*ko-re-te*	BRONZE 2 kg.	*po-ro-ko-re-te*	BRONZE 0.75 kg.
.8	at a-pu$_2$^{PL}	*ko-re-te*	BRONZE 2 kg.	*po-ro-ko-re-te*	BRONZE 0.75 kg.
.9	at ạ-ke-re-wa^{PL}	*ko-re-te*	BRONZE 2 kg.	*po-ro-ko-re-te*	BRONZE 0.75 kg.
.10	at ṛọ-ụ-so^{PL}	*ko-re-te*	BRONZE 2 kg.	*po-ro-ko-re-te*	BRONZE 0.75 kg.
.11	at ḳạ-ra-do-ro^{PL}	*ko-re-te*	BRONZE 2 kg.	*po-ro-ko-re-te*	BRONZE 0.75 kg.
.12	at ri-]j̣ọ^{PL}	*ko-re-te*	BRONZE 2 kg.	*po-ro-ko-re-te*	BRONZE 0.75 kg.
.13	at ṭị-mi-to-a-ko^{PL}	*ko-re-te*	BRONZE 2 kg.	*po-ro-ko-re-te*	BRONZE 0.75 kg.
.14	at ra-]wa-ra-ta$_2$^{PL}	*ko-re-te*	BRONZE 2.75 kg.	*po-ro-ko-re-te*	BRONZE 0.75 kg.
.15	at sa-]ma-ra^{PL}	*ko-re-te*	BRONZE 3.75 kg.	*po-ro-ko-re-te*	0.75 kg.
.16	at a-si-ja-ti-ja^{PL}	*ko-re-te*	BRONZE 2 kg.	*po-ro-ko-re-te*	0.75 kg.
.17	at e-ra-te-re-wa^{PL}	*ko-re-te*	BRONZE 2 kg.	*po-ro-ko-re-te*	0.75 kg.
.18	at za-ma-e-wi-ja^{PL}	*ko-re-te*	BRONZE 3.75 kg.	*po-ro-ko-re-te*	0.75 kg.
.19	at e-ro^{PL}	*ko-re-te*	BRONZE 3.75 kg.	*po-ro-ko-re-te*	0.75 kg.
.20-.23			*blank*		

Jn 829 is a rare 'prospective' text, *i.e.*, its verbal form is in the future and it records that the amounts of metal here 'will be given' by the designated parties. One can, therefore, view the entire text as setting out an anticipated 'target' for the delivery of an important refurbished raw material. The third line of the heading designates that the 'recycled' bronze/copper to be contributed all falls under the heading of 'temple bronze' and will be used for spears and javelins. It has recently been shown that the word 'points' was added as a fine point of *post hoc* clarification to rule out its use for other metallic elements of spears and javelins.

On the actual tablet two changes were made as the scribe Hand 2 was entering the words in the heading. These changes reveal the concern he had to set up a syntax that will make clear most, but not all, of the actions involved here. The reader of the translated heading here should be aware that the scribe has taken special pains, after erasure, to group the *ko-re-te-re* with the *du-ma-te* and the *po-ro-ko-re-te-re* with the *ka-ra-wi-po-ro* and the following two 'officials' (the *o-pi-su-ko* and the *o-pi-ka-pe-e-we*).

These clusterings are meaningful. As can be deduced from the actual entries in lines .4-.19, the *ko-re-te-re* are officials (the noun-termination here, singular *-te*, plural *-te-re*, is agentive) and the *po-ro-ko-re-te-re* are associated subordinate officials. They are charged with seeing to it that the required 'bronze' from each of the sixteen second-order centers/districts listed is eventually 'given'. In each case the officials, who I believe are palatially appointed agents for palatial interests in each of these districts, are nameless. The tablet writer at the palatial center is only concerned on this 'prospective' text with indicating that responsibility for collection in each second-order district lies with the *ko-re-te* and the *po-ro-ko-re-te* in that district. Note that there are no data for where and when the deliveries are to be made or the underlying reasons, regular or irregular, that give rise to this prospective collection. Lines .4-.12 give the 'donations' from the Nearer Province communities: 24.75 kg. Lines .13-.19 record the 'donations' from the Further Province communities: 25.25 kg. Both total amounts are within the general weight range of single copper ingots.

The *ko-re-te-re*, the syntax suggests, are to interact with religious officials of considerable standing in the tablets known as *du-ma-te*. The subordinate associates of the *ko-re-te-re*, *i.e.*, the *po-ro-ko-re-te-re*, are to interact with lesser religious officials known as the 'key-bearers' (*ka-ra-wi-po-ro*) and agricultural officials (perhaps with some connection to agricultural activity in sanctuary areas, but that is here unspecified) known as 'fig-supervisors' (*o-pi-su-ko*) and 'overseers of digging' (*o-pi-ka-pe-e-we*). Both of these latter officials occur only here in all of Linear B, so their identification is purely 'etymological', conditioned slightly by the context on Jn 829.

There is no concern with indicating how, *i.e.*, by what authority or means, the palatial officials (*ko-re-te-re* and *po-ro-ko-re-te-re*) are to collect the bronze/copper. Nor does the tablet indicate why the religious and agricultural officials should feel obliged to contribute. Finally the text does not indicate whether this 'collection' and 'donation' kingdom-wide of essentially two ingots' worth of scrap metal is a regular procedure, and if so, how often it would recur, or an extraordinary event, and if so, what circumstances gave rise to it. We assume all this information was known to the administrators who were involved in writing the text and overseeing its eventual fulfillment.

We should also note that we do not know how the orders to do all this reached the officials involved in the sixteen districts. But Jn 829 indicates that the palatial center had the ability to mobilize regional resource collection and in something of a micro-managed way. Given that Jn 829 is a unique text, our questions will be answered only by further human ingenuity or by the discovery of new tablets. Unfortunately that is often the case in Linear B even when we have fuller or multiple 'sets' of tablets relating to a given economic concern.

The Ma records, however, appear to be part of ongoing and regular yearly 'taxation' recorded in terms of district-by-district proportional targets of six different commodities/raw materials. Of these six, we only know that **146* is a kind of cloth and **152* is 'oxhide'. It is assumed that the other commodities/raw materials are of a similar sort. For *KE* 'beeswax' has been proposed. I here give a selection of five texts sufficient to indicate their variety.

For each district the proportional relationship among the six listed items is the same: 7:7:2:3:1.5:150. This implies that the central administration is not trying to squeeze maximum amounts of these items out of the different districts. Given the variation in human and natural resources that must have existed district to district, such proportions would only work if the quantity of any item produced by the proportional formula was well within the capacity of each district. That whole districts had to donate 8, 10, 12, 22 and even up to 30 oxhides seemingly on a yearly basis does not seem to be hyper-exploitation. Once again, however, we should point out that cloth production workshops, herders and slaughterers and tanners, and specialized workers and crafts personnel associated with the other four commodities/raw materials recorded in these tablets would not have been occupied throughout the year manufacturing these numbers for the central palatial authority. Within the context of their work, perhaps for the *basileis* or prominent clans and other social groups of their localities, the quantities of materials siphoned off by the palatial center at Pylos might not have been recognized locally as a significant exploitation of labor or resources.

PY Ma 124
.1 a-pu$_2$-we **146* 23 *RI* M 23 *KE* M 7 **152* 10 *O* M 5 *ME* 500
.2 o-da-a$_2$, ka-ke-we , o-u-di-do-si **146* 1 *RI* M 1 **152* 1 *ME* 20

PY Ma 365
.1 ro-u-so **146* 17 *RI* M 14[ ] *KE* M 5 **152* 8 *O* M 4 *ME*
.2 o-da-a$_2$, ka-ke-we , a$_2$-te-ro , we-to , di-do-si **146* 1 *RI* N 2 *ME* 10

PY Ma 346
.1 ka-ra-do-ro **146* 18 *RI* M 18 *KE* M 4 **152*[8 *O* M 4] *ME* 4̣00
.2 a-pu-do-si **146* 14 *o* **146* 4 *RI* M 16 *o* 2 *KE* Ṃ 4 **152* 8 *O* M 4 *ME* 440

PY Ma 123
.1 ti-mi-to-a-ke-e *146* 24 *RI* M 24 *KE* M 7 **152* 10 *O* M 5 *ME* 500
.2 a-pu-do-si *146* 21 *o* 2 *RI* M *KE* M **152* *O* M *ME*
.3 o-da-a$_2$, ka-ke-we , o-u-di-do-si **146* 1 *RI* M 1 *ME* 10

PY Ma 378
.1 sa-ma-ra **146* 24 *RI* M 24 *KE* M 7 **152* 10 *O* M 5 *ME* 500
.a **152* 2̣ *ME* 60
.2 o-da-a$_2$, ka-ḳẹ-we , o-u-di-do-si **146* 3 *RI* M 3 *KE* M 1 pe-ru-si-nu-wo ,
o-pe-ro **146* 1 **152* 2 *ME* 100

PY Wr 1457
.α **152*
.β *a-pu-do-si*
.γ uninscribed

I have arranged the texts according to the canonical order of the secondary districts/centers as listed on Jn 829. Here official human agency does not enter into the written records, *i.e.*, the scribe, again Hand 2, does not stipulate in writing who is responsible at the palatial center or in the outlying districts for seeing to the ordering, collection, shipment, receipt and verification of the 'taxed' items. All of that is left invisible, most likely because these activities and responsibilities and networks had long been set in place. The fullest text is Ma 123 for the site of **ti-mi-to-a-ko*, the first main center of the Further Province. Oddly enough the place-name is listed in the dative/locative (*ti-mi-to-a-ke-e*), which at least syntactically indicates that the scribe conceived of these materials as being 'at' the regional center at the time he was writing the text. Whether this is in fact the case is impossible to tell, because, again, we are not given any details in this or any related series about the where and when and how and why of these 'deliveries'/'payments'.

The scribe here does record in line .2 of Ma 123 the amounts rendered in 'payment' (Mycenaean Greek *a-pu-do-si*, a noun abstract in the nominative case, literally 'a giving away'). Twenty-one out of the 24 cloth units (*146) have been delivered; 2 are still 'owing' or due (abbreviation *o* = *o-pe-ro* 'owed'). In line .3, Hand 2 explains the discrepancy. The final one unit 'the smiths [in **ti-mi-to-a-ko*] are not giving.'

This last entry acknowledges an exemption that this group of specialists has and which accordingly lowers the overall tax payment actually due from the district. This in itself gives us some insight into resource mobilization through textual administration, since it implies that within the districts collective groups were responsible for deliveries of specific items and that adjustments could be made, as need arose. It is assumed that some special activities in the bronze production realm consumed the time that the collective smiths would otherwise have put into obtaining and providing the listed commodities/raw materials. Consequently they were exempted from same. This kind of decision meant that information about the work activities of the collective group of smiths was reported to and assessed by the central palatial administration or its agents in the districts (in my opinion the *ko-re-te-re* and *po-ro-ko-re-te-re*) perhaps in consultation with the local big men or *basileis*.

In ten out of the eleven cases where such excused 'non-payments' are listed on the eighteen extant Ma tablets, the group involved is the smiths (Mycenaean Greek *ka-ke-we*). The one exception is Ma 393 ,where the exemption is listed against a collective masculine group, here designated by the ethnic adjectival form (*ma-ra-ne-ni-jo*) of a minor place name that occurs in the dative/locative on a rower-mobilization text (Pylos An 610). Smiths are designated in Jn bronze/copper allotment texts by place-name adjectives (ethnics) so it is not impossible that the *ma-ra-ne-ni-jo* group of men are in fact smiths designated by the sub-locality where they live within the district of *za-ma-e-wi-ja* (the second-order district recorded on Ma 393).

Such variation in reference is well enough attested in Linear B and speaks to the degree of flexibility and improvisation permitted the 'scribes' during the course of their work. It also reflects the essential fact we stressed at the outset, namely that these clay tablet records functioned as mnemonics for administrators who understood the context of whatever economic activities were reported on them. The tablets therefore can be telegraphic and minimalist and still be very useful.

Ma 378 gives us a different variant for the site of *sa-ma-ra*. The targeted quantities are again listed in line .1. But here line .2 (and line

.2a) lists what smiths in the district do not give and also some quantities of cloth, oxhide and *ME* that are carried over as 'owing from last year' (*pe-ru-si-nu-wo* , *o-pe-ro* **146* 1 **152* 2 *ME* 100). We therefore know that administrative memory went back at least one calendar year.

Ma 365 for the site of *ro-u-so* lists the target quantities, but then on line .2 some amounts of the commodities that 'smiths are giving next year' (*ka-ke-we* , a_2*-te-ro* , *we-to* , *di-do-si*), apparently a form of postponement rather than exemption or pure 'write-off'. Again we are given no means of knowing why one group of smiths was handled one way, and another group another way. We just know now that they were.

Ma 124 gives the district targets with the smith dispensation already subtracted (unlike Ma 123 and Ma 378 with which it shares the same total taxation quantities). On Ma 124 no actual delivery has yet been recorded. Ma 346 is the simplest text, listing the target in line .1 and the 'payment' in line .2. In line .2 it specifies any still 'owed' quantities of **146* and *RI* by the abbreviation *o* = *o-pe-ro* and writing of the appropriate quantities following the entered paid amount.

An additional datum for resource mobilization of these commodities/raw materials comes from the central Archives Complex at the site of Pylos. Here was found an impressed sealing, counter-inscribed by the scribe of the Ma series, Hand 2, with the added information: oxhide 'payment' (**152 a-pu-do-si*). Unfortunately we do not have precise information about find-spot for this sealing. But the sealing does indicate that a delivery of oxhides or of records about oxhide deliveries had been registered at some point by the central record-keeping authorities.

How such inscribed sealings function in the control of economic activities is best exemplified by the following small selection of sealing inscriptions from Thebes (Piteros, Olivier and Melena 1990 2f, Killen 1994 2f, Palaima 2000a and 2000b 2o). The purpose of inscribed sealings is to document that a transaction regarding single items or single groups of items was authorized by the user/holder/owner of the seal that impressed the sealing. The inscribed sealings from Thebes were found collected in a group in a work room at the palatial center. Their assembly accounted for the individual contributions, under different conditions of obligation, of animals for a commensal sacrificial ceremony such as is known from fuller tablets recording animals and other foodstuffs, especially from Pylos (Killen 1994 2f, Nikoloudis 2001 2f).

THEBES Wu 46	.α	SHE-GOAT *written over* **seal impression** C [5]
	.β	of Praus^{PERSON}, *o-pa* work
	.γ	*cyperus*-fodder 30
THEBES Wu 56	.α	HE-GOAT *written over* **seal impression** C [5]
		surface above damaged
	.β1	Ophelestas^{PERSON}
	.β2	*o-pa* work
	.γ	*cyperus*-fodder 30
THEBES Wu 58	.α	PIG *written over* **seal impression** C [5]
	.βa	*o-pa* work
	.βb	of Therios^{PERSON}
	.γ	(at) Amarynthos^{PLACE}
	.βb	Written (and thus read) before .βa.
THEBES Wu 76	.α	COW^{f} *written over* **seal impression** C [5]
	.β1	a-e-ri-qo^{PERSON}
	.β2	*empty space*
	.γ	*o-pa* work *cyperus*-fodder 30
THEBES Wu 88	.α	GOAT^{x} *written over* **seal impression** C [5]
		surface below damaged
	.β	ra-mi-jo^{PERSON}, *o-pa* work
	.γ	*facet missing*

The brief inscriptions on the three facets of each nodule (the technical name for the small lump of clay, ending up in rough 'triangular' shape, which is wrapped around fine knotted string and then impressed while resting between an individual's fingers) identify the kind of animal, the conditions governing the contribution of the specific animal, and individuals and places involved with the contribution. In three of the example sealings given here (Thebes Wu 36, 56 and 76) the animals were accompanied by fodder in quantities sufficient for their maintenance over a thirty-day period, obviously until the particular ceremonial occasion came around on the ritual calendar.

In many cases the syntax of these brief entries is not clear. Accordingly, it is hard to know sometimes why an animal is listed as 'at' a locality when the sealing is found at the palatial center. It seems likely that the sealings were in fact manufactured at the place of origin of the animals. Otherwise the genitive of source or even a 'case less' use of the 'nominative of rubric' might be in order. The sealing would then accompany the animal en route, as a kind of document of authorization that the individual bringing the animal had the right to be transporting it from one point to the other.

On Wu 58, the locality is probably located on the island of Euboea across a sea strait from the mainland region of Boeotia that Thebes dominated in prehistoric and historical times (Sergent 1994 2m). It thus attests to the outreach of the palatial center at least in connection with whatever ceremonial event gave rise to this contribution. The term '*o-pa* work' indicates that the animals have been 'finished off', *i.e.*, brought to a state of readiness for ritual slaughter and consumption (Melena 1983 2p, Killen 1999 2p). The term can also be used of work with pieces of armor or chariot equipment that are brought into a state of readiness for their use.

The degree to which the palatial centers controlled or interacted with sanctuary locales and their officials and other personnel is a topic of considerable debate right now (convenient full discussion in Lupack 2002 2b). The Pylos E-series texts demonstrate that the palatial center had an interest in monitoring landholdings in the religious district known as *Sphagianes* (the name seems to mean 'the place of ritual slaughter'). These are measured by quantities of seed grain. The terms under which the land is held (from the collective land-organization known as the *da-mo*) are stipulated. The most frequent term is *o-na-to*, literally 'land for beneficial use'. In one interrelated series of tablets, these land allotments are listed as held by individuals with cult titles. Another series is specifically connected with personnel and specialists associated with the 'military leader' (or *ra-wa-ke-ta* = *lawage(r)tas*). The most frequent terms are *do-e-ro* and *do-e-ra* (servant, masculine and feminine) of the deity. We do not know whether the terms *do-e-ro* and *do-e-ra* are to be taken in a ceremonial, honorific or literal sense. But other cult titles and even occupational titles occur: priest, priestess, 'key-bearer' (as on Jn 829), and the potter, fuller, and perhaps armorer of the *wanaks* (Palaima 1997 2b).

PY Ep 704

.5 *Eritha*^{PERSON} the priestess has and claims to have *etonijo* land for the god, but the *damos* says that she has a beneficial plot of land from the communal land shares so much seed grain BARLEY 3 9⁄10 maximum dry units

.7 *Karpathija*^{PERSON} the key-bearer has two communal shares and is supposed to perform service on the basis of two shares, but she does not perform service so much seed grain BARLEY [quantity missing]

The entry on line .5 of Pylos tablet Ep 704 is *the* example of a dispute over the terms of landholding between the priestess and the local collective land organization known as the *da-mo*. What is at stake seems to be the degree to which she, or the deity she represents, will be obliged later to contribute some portion of production from the plot here registered. That is to say, this is a dispute over 'tax status'. The 'key-bearer' in line .7 is obligated, at least from the perspective of the central administration, to perform service (the actual word is *wo-ze-e* 'to work') for the two communal shares. She has not done so. This is recorded, and there the matter rested when the palatial center was destroyed.

In these land documents we see the palatial center being very precise, just as on the Thebes sealings, to specify the exact terms under which resources were being somehow acted upon. We can extrapolate and say that persons of sufficient status to come within the orbit of the central administration would have aspects of their roles within the overall economy monitored and recorded. But, again, the impression one gets is that this is done on a selective basis and in accordance with traditional arrangements of long-standing. I would imagine that the partitioning of landholdings had long histories and was for centuries under control of the local *damos* organizations. The palatial center at Pylos records those particular holdings that were of concern to it.

The final example of resource mobilization that we will discuss concerns the mobilization of men, here as rowers and most likely in a military context.

PY An 610

.1	me-za-[wo?-]ne , rowers [ ]		*blank* [	
.2	*traces of text* [ ] , settlers	MEN 46	[	
.3	'later settlers'(?)	MEN 19	[	
.4	]wa , settlers]	MEN 36	[	
.5	'later settlers'(?) [ ]	MEN 3	[	
.6	e-wi-ri-po^{PLACE}	MEN 9	'refugees' [	
.7	a-ke-re-wa^{PLACE}	MEN 25	wo-qe-we$^{?}$ [	
.8	ri-jo^{PLACE}	MEN 24	wi-nu-ri-jo$^{?}$[	
.9	te-ta-ra-ne^{PLACE}	MEN 31	'later settl[ers'(?)	
.10	a-po-ne-we^{PLACE}	MEN 37	'later [settlers'(?)	
.11	ma-ra-ne-nu-we^{PL}	MEN 40	po-ti-ja-ke-e$^{PLACE?}$	MEN 6[
.12	ẓạ-ku-si-jo^{PLACE}	MEN 8̣	za-e-to-ro^{PLACE}	MEN 3
.13	da-mi-ni-jo[ ]	MEN 40	of e-ke-ra$_2$-wo^{PERSON}	MEN 40[
.14	of we-da-ne-u^{PERSON}	MEN 20	ko-ni-jo$^{PL?}$126 'later settlers'(?)	MEN 26
.15	po-ku-ta	MEN 10	we-re-ka-ra, te-qa-ta-qẹ	MEN 20
.16-.19		*blank*	[	

By now the minimalist nature of such texts is familiar. An 610 (written by 'master scribe' Hand 1) lists groups of men specified in the heading, unfortunately fragmentary, as 'rowers' and as somehow being overseen or under the control of an individual named *me-za-wo. me-za-wo* recurs on an important banqueting food provision text (Un 138) of the kind mentioned just above as being the end recorded result of collections of materials associated with sealings. The men are listed by the localities where they are, or, given the use of ethnics in lines .12 and .13 (*za-ku-si-jo* and *da-mi-ni-jo*), most likely are 'from'. They are also specified by their status as either 'settlers' or 'later settlers'. This, combined with the ethnics, indicates that these groups of men were compensated for their service as rowers by whatever rights and privileges, and perhaps landholdings, were accorded to their designated status. The numbers of men vary considerably, giving the impression that this is not a 'target' list, or at least not an 'end-result' 'target' list. It is possible that these numbers represent how many men are still required to meet the needs of the rower force. Five hundred and sixty-nine men are recorded in the preserved entries. The total number would be even greater, given the missing entries on lines .6-.10.

e-ke-ra$_2$-wo (line .13) is the personal name that 'takes the place of' the *wanaks* ('king') on commensal offering text Pylos Un 718.2. This arguably implies that he is the *wanaks* and is here personally responsible for providing men as rowers, men who would be attached to him as an individual 'aristocrat' rather than through his office as *wanaks*. This view is supported by the very next entry. *we-da-ne-u* (line .14) is an important person who has cultic associations in the Pylos Es series and is in charge of sacrificial bulls and other animals in Cn 418. Again these twenty men on An 610 might well be affiliated with *we-da-ne-u* as an individual of prominence, rather than because of any office he holds within the central administration. It must be significant that these two figures are recorded together near the end of this lengthy text.

po-ku-ta (line .15) is an occupational term. It was traditionally interpreted as 'pourers' *vel sim.*, but recently the suggestion has been made that it is related to Latin *pecus* and refers to herdsmen of some sort. The contextual association here of *po-ku-ta* and *we-da-ne-u*, who elsewhere is connected with herd animals, lends some support to this new etymology. The place names of *ri-jo*, *te-ta-ra-ne*, and *a-po-ne-we* (lines .8-.10) recur in the same order on An 1, a tablet that lists 30 rowers total (the size of a single ship) going to the site of Pleuron and coming from five different localities.

Hand 1 within the central administration was able to access and record this information about the military use of manpower. It is difficult to know exactly how the data on An 610 were ultimately used. But using the Ma exemptions granted to smiths as a parallel, it is possible that the service of these specific individuals from these localities as rowers had to be factored into whatever 'payments' had to be made to them for their service and whatever demands the central administration would otherwise make of these localities. Again we have no knowledge of whether any of these individuals would ever have interacted with an official of the central record-keeping administration, who would have taken the head counts of these contingents of men, or who would have verified those counts.

Given the facts that we have no deep chronology of written administrative records from any Mycenaean palatial center, it is difficult to know the extent to which economic planning occurred, how it was managed, and the degree to which written administration permeated the lives of inhabitants of Mycenaean palatial territories. It is worth repeating that the two most accomplished 'scribes' identifiable within the Pylos central 'archives' were responsible for just over 200 tablets (Hand 1) and just fewer than 90 tablets (Hand 2) (Palaima 1988 2l). Hand 2's work covers 5 or 6 economic subject areas (bronze allotments and collection, regional taxation, banqueting paraphernalia inventorying, perfumed oil allotments to sanctuaries, the transfer of unguent oil between individuals and the specification of the number of stirrup jars [containers] involved, and allotments of wheat or barley to sanctuaries, deities and religious personnel). Hand 1 deals with landholdings, rations to women work groups, flax production, commensal ceremonial texts, livestock and many kinds of personnel. We have seen representative texts of both scribes here above.

By modern information accessing and processing standards, such an output of tablets over a five-month period seems meager. I once asked (Palaima 2001 2p) what the scribes did in the rest of their time, since these few tablets could be written out, at least mechanically and physically, in a matter of days. I now think that if we take into account all the information that had to be accumulated concerning the goods, materials, places, responsible parties, nuances of obligation, fulfillment or non-fulfillment of same, and so forth, we might rather wonder how these particular scribes could be so productive in so little time. The data we do see amassed in the tablets of our thirty or so identifiable scribes indicate a great concern on the part of the palatial center for economic activities and manpower use in the territory it dominates. At the same time, there is good reason to believe that the late developing palatial system extracted resources from pre-existing networks of labor and production, targeting a few areas for its own benefit.

10.

The Development of Money-of-Account in Sumer's Temples

Michael Hudson
University of Missouri (Kansas City)

Controversy over how money came into being has raged for over a century. Inspired by Adam Smith's description of individuals "trucking and bartering," most economists assume that money emerged from barter exchange. Silver and other metals are said to have emerged as the most convenient forms of money, thanks to their compact store of value, their durability, their ready divisibility into small denominations, and (so it would appear at first glance) their uniform quality.

This "metallist" origin myth holds that money was created at the outset of civilization without a need for temples, palaces or other public institutions. Governments are said to have gotten into the act belatedly, causing instability by irresponsible money creation, and then making matters worse by imposing bureaucratic price controls in a vain attempt to contain the resulting inflation. The inference is that governments should be kept out of the financial picture, having no positive role to play—ever.

A countervailing approach was mounted by the German economist Georg F. Knapp's *State Theory of Money* (1905, translated into English in 1924 at the urging of John Maynard Keynes). Criticizing metallist theories for trying to deduce the genealogy of commodity money "without the idea of a State," he defined money as whatever governments "accepted at the public pay offices" for taxes, fees or the sale of public services.[1] The policy conclusion is that when monetary order has been destabilized, it is likely to result from weakening public oversight and taxing power as creditors gain undue power.

---

1 Knapp 1924:vii-viii. Wray 1998 provides a review and bibliography of the State Theory of money. I trace the ideological and political motivations behind metallist theories of money and the state theory in Hudson 2003 and 2004. See also Goodhardt 2003.

Knapp's basic approach had a long pedigree. Around 325 BC, three centuries after the first electrum coins (an amalgam of gold and silver) were struck in Lydia, Aristotle described money as a creature of the state, and hence of law (Greek *nomos*). Observing that money had no "natural" value independent of its legal and political context, he provided the earliest documented statement of the rationale for minting coins. Money is called *nomisma*, he explained (*Ethics* 1133), "because it exists not by nature, but by law (*nomos*), and it is in our power to change it and make it useless," as Sparta did when it issued iron slab-money treated with vinegar to make it brittle and hence economically useless except as money. The metallic content was largely incidental. Its value was set by public institutions.

Keynes wrote in his *Treatise on Money* (1930) that the principles underlying the State Theory of Money could be traced back twice as far as Aristotle, to Mesopotamia some two thousand years earlier. Although having only a cursory familiarity with Sumerian records, he saw enough to deduce that money must have originated there as a unit of account. "Money itself, namely that by delivery of which debt-contracts and price-contracts are discharged, and in the shape of which a store of General Purchasing Power is held, derives its character from its relationship to the Money-of-Account, since the debts and prices must first have been expressed in terms of the latter." Such money, he explained, "comes into existence along with Debts, which are contracts for deferred payment, and Price-Lists, which are offers of contracts for sale or purchase."[2]

What Knapp outlined in theorizing about modern finance and Keynes intuited for the origins of money can now be filled in with much more historical detail and informed reconstruction. In the 1950s, Karl Polanyi (1957a and 1957b) described a three-stage evolution of markets and prices. In between the "reciprocity" stage of gift exchange and modern price-setting markets came a centralized "redistributive" system of administered prices. The past half-century has seen anthropologists, French structuralists and classical scholars elaborate on the role played by temples, palaces and civic authorities in establishing monetary and coinage systems.

Assyriologists, including the contributors to this volume, have described money-of-account as emerging out of the price grids by

---

[2] Keynes 1930:3-7.

which the large institutions valued the rations distributed to their work force, the flow of raw material to their workshops, and the redistribution or consignment of their finished output.

These early developments are so familiar that it is easy to overlook how deeply they challenge the accepted fables of how money and markets originated. Economists have long agreed on the four basic functions of money: (1) money-of-account to serve as a measure of value and (2) of debt, (3) "legal tender" to serve as a means of payment, and (4) a store of value. But there is disagreement with regard to how these functions developed.

The controversy between metallists and "state theorists" is essentially between opponents of government and advocates who see public institutions as playing a positive role. Mesopotamia's role in introducing money and monetary standards is thus a topic that bears on a controversy that has become increasingly intense over the past century: Did money arise out of barter among individuals, or was it created by public institutions and spread to the rest of the economy by the palace and temples selling goods and services, leasing their land, mines and workshops, charging fees and levying taxes?

The present paper begins by reviewing the theories developed to replace the myth that money arose out of individuals bartering commodities. I then discuss the role of temples in refining, weighing and later minting silver and gold, and trace the origin of money back to the Sumerian temples and palaces in the third millennium BC. I examine silver's emergence as the main monetary metal and the role of debt management in overall monetary equilibrium, and conclude by comparing the Near Eastern experience to that of classical Greece and Rome.

The individualistic anti-government approach

Economics students are indoctrinated with a fable about how money might have emerged out of the process of exchange among individuals if public institutions never existed. The tacit assumption is that labor could not have specialized without markets to provide a "demand" for each specialist's products. Markets in turn are held to have required money. Otherwise, how could bakers and smiths have paid each other? There is no idea of bakers and smiths belonging to a single large institutional household supplying them all with food while distributing their output administratively.

The modernist approach goes back to Aristotle, who believed that money emerged out of the barter process even though he also described it as the product of law. The reason why individuals invented money, he explained, was to make possible a division of labor so that everyone could specialize in what they were best in producing.

When the inhabitants of one country became more dependent on those of another, and they imported what they needed, and exported what they had too much of, money necessarily came into use. For the various necessaries of life are not easily carried about, and hence men agreed to employ in their dealings with one another something which was intrinsically useful and easy to handle in general life, for example, iron, silver, and the like. Of this the value was at first measured simply by size and weight, but in the process of time they put a stamp upon it, to save the trouble of weighing and to mark the value.[3]

This explanation assumed that the specialization of labor already had occurred at the time money was introduced. But if this were the case, what performed the "money" function *before* there was money? Having assumed that the division of labor already had come about, Aristotle seems to explain it by introducing the monetary breakthrough and attributed this to the individualistic exchange that characterized his own day.

Modern economists have not made matters much clearer. Without money to provide a convenient medium of exchange, states Paul Samuelson in his textbook on *Economics* (1973: 274f.), "every man had to be a jack-of-all-trades and master of none," for without money, how could people exchange what they produced? Barter would have presupposed a seemingly vast array of cross-product equivalencies. "If we were to construct history along hypothetical, logical lines," he concludes, "we should naturally follow the age of barter by the age of commodity money."

It did not occur either to Aristotle or to modern individualistic theorists that specialization developed mainly within single large households of chieftains in tribally organized communities, or what Sumerians called the "large house," é.gal, the palace that emerged out of temple precincts c. 2750 BC. Such households supported non-agricultural labor with rations rather than obliging each profession to market its output in exchange for food, clothing and other basic neces-

[3] *Politics* I.9 at 1257a, trans. B. Jowett (Oxford 1921). Perhaps by the word "value" Aristotle meant "purity," except that as noted above, he also saw coinage as *nomisma*, a legal creation.

sities. Administrators allocated rations and raw materials in keeping with what was deemed necessary for production and for ceremonial and other institutional functions rather than resorting to private-sector markets, which had not yet come into being.

Neither Samuelson nor Aristotle addressed how the monetary metals were supplied to individuals, and how they were weighed and denominated. Writing in economies much less centralized than had been the case in the Bronze Age Near East, they assumed that the social context of the past was like that of their own day. Yet long before coins were minted, it was the temples that sanctified and oversaw the weights, measures and quality of metallic money. Greek monetary weights did not evolve spontaneously but reflected much earlier practices brought from the Near East at a time when the Mediterranean was still in a Dark Age.[4]

The problem is that instead of taking notice of Mesopotamia's catalytic commercial and monetary role, economists tend to speculate about money abstractly, assuming a starting point of individuals exchanging commodities made by themselves rather than in a complex institutional context. This logic fails to acknowledge the role of Mesopotamia's large institutions in developing money-of-account as a bookkeeping unit to administer their resources and denominate the debts owed to them. The Mesopotamian reality was more complex than the abstract generalities of modern economics. Smiths and other specialized professionals did not have to buy their grain in a market. They either had their own self-support family land or were supplied with rations as part of the temple or palace work-force.

It was the temples that carried the specialization of labor furthest, and financed long-distance trade by supplying merchants with textiles and other handicrafts from their workshops, and even provisioning and outfitting them in the early centuries. The temples also regulated weights and measures, and sanctified the purity of the monetary metals. But most economic historians have averted their eyes from the public sector's commercial and monetary innovations—and hence, Assyriological studies generally—apparently because this history contradicts rather than reinforces their general antipathy to government planning.

In attributing the value of monetary metals to their raw bullion value, metallists neglect to observe that this value was set initially by the public institutions. Sumer's account-keeping systems designated the

---

4 I provide the details in Hudson 1992 .

value of a shekel of silver relative to barley and other commodities, as part of their system of administered prices. The large institutions promoted the use of silver by insisting that it get paid in that metal. This involved creating the weights in which it and other metals were denominated, and this was done initially to schedule, coordinate and forecast—in a word, to *plan*—the circulation of raw materials and rations within their own households.

The State Theory of Money and its offshoots

In describing how modern money derived its value from the state's acceptance of it in payment for taxes and other fees, Knapp traced how this official role established money as the dominant medium of exchange. He applied his theory mainly to governments issuing paper money and supporting banking systems to supply credit on the basis of national debts. Even in the case of early coins or bullion, it was their acceptance by public institutions that set their value.

Knapp's approach inspired Bernard Laum to suggest in 1924 that money originated in contributions to the temples that sponsored antiquity's communal festivals. The main examples he cited were the Greek *oboloi* ("spit-money") and *drachmae* ("handfuls") derived from the food contributions to public feasts. In subsequent writings he elaborated how fish money and other edibles fit into this category. In time, Laum theorized, monetary tokens were used as exchange equivalents for the contribution or purchase of such food.[5] This would explain the public oversight of weights and measures, of which money was a logical extension.

A generation after Laum wrote, Polanyi established a research group centered at Columbia University. Criticizing modernist economic approaches as being abstract and "disembedded," he analyzed the evolution of markets and exchange as occurring in three stages: reciprocity (gift exchange), redistributive economies with administered price equivalencies, and modern market economies with prices responding flexibly to shifts in supply and demand.[6] Mesopotamia and other

---

[5] Laum 1924 and 1952:211-35, esp. 216. An English-language summary of Laum's ideas appears in Desmonde 1962.

[6] See Polanyi 1957 and 1977:40ff. His approach is elaborated by Renger 1984. Economists like to use their own jargon. John Hicks referred to the transition from "customary" to "command" pre-market societies (see Grierson 1977:19; for a general discussion see Wray 2004).

Bronze Age economies were "redistributive," dominated as they were by the large institutions.

Assigning prices to the major commodities made them co-measurable and hence mutually convertible with each other. Establishing a stable grid of price equivalencies enabled payments to be made in terms of any commodity listed on such a schedule. It was out of this overall set of proportions that monetary commodities emerged, headed by barley and silver. Shifting price equivalencies would have destabilized the large institutions by making their accounting systems unmanageable.

Leo Oppenheim was the major Assyriologist in Polanyi's group. One of his articles described how sacred statues were adorned with golden ornaments that could be melted down in times of need to pay mercenaries (or perhaps ransom or tribute), much as were the Winged Victory statues of Athens during the Peloponnesian War.[7] These forms of saving reflect the fact that throughout antiquity the public sector was in a surplus position, not the deficit position that it is in today. There was no public debt to provide a monetary base in the form of government obligations to banks or other financial institutions.

Among other member of Polanyi's group, Moses Finley described how the idea of commercial and financial gain-seeking was not deemed respectable in classical Greece and Rome. Usury stood at the bottom of the moral pyramid, often conducted by slaves (although dealing with funds supplied by their masters) or by resident aliens such as the metics in Athens (whose ranks included the famous banker Pasion). Nearly the only form of money-lending at interest that met with approval were shipping loans, which were largely in the form of maritime insurance to spread risks by organizing trade ventures as partnerships. By this time commercial and much other lending had become thoroughly privatized. Temples still made loans, but mainly for social-welfare purposes such as to enable slaves or other unfree labor to buy their liberty.

Along similar lines the French structuralist school has been joined by a widening range of classicists taking an anthropological and sociological approach emphasizing the role of religion and politics.[8] Yet free-market monetarists dismiss such considerations as non-economic, finding the public-sector nexus of early monetary development to be an anomaly.

---

7 Oppenheim 1949. His 1959 article first suggested that early clay tokens were accounting devices and the inscriptions on their envelopes proto-cuneiform. See Schmandt-Besserat 1992:8f.

8 Among the leading French studies are Edouard Will 1975a and 1975b.

The role of temples and their sanctification of monetary silver

It is by no means natural on purely abstract logical grounds for prehistoric communities to have agreed to adopt silver as the preferred means of denominating loans, settling payments, and holding savings. What is likely to have led individuals to adopt a metal so little associated with the production process?

Evidently the explanation does not lie in any inherent necessity dictated by the mode of production. What social role did silver play that imbued it with its monetary desirability? For that matter, how did they maintain a standard of purity and prevent adulteration?

Individualistic barter theories of money's origins depict silver and other valuable metals as being chosen spontaneously by popular acclaim to serve as monetary commodities. One problem with this notion is its assumption that silver is uniform in quality. Silver and other metals need to be refined and alloyed—and may be adulterated. Although its alloy could be tested fairly easily, it cannot have been easy for individuals acting by themselves to find metal minted to a standard purity, given the exhortations from Babylonian down through biblical times against merchants using false weights and measures.

Commercial sale and debt documents from the second and first millennia BC typically specify that monetary silver should be of ⅞ purity (.875 fine, the equivalent of 21 carats). Down through classical Greece and Rome, temples oversaw the refining of metal in order to sanctify its purity and weight. This was part of their role in overseeing weights and measures. In third-millennium Mesopotamia the temples supplied silver as a byproduct of their role in foreign trade, being paid for their consignments of goods in silver as the most general and abstract (and hence, the highest) measure of obligations. Marketplaces normally were located in the vicinity of temples, whose authority helped sanctify commercial exchange.[9]

Kolin Kraay's history of Greek coinage concludes: "The issuer in all identifiable cases proves to be the supreme political power in each city or state; there is no evidence in the Greek world for the private issue of coins by bankers or merchants."[10] The monetary historian C.J. Howgego agrees. "There is no certain case in the whole of antiquity of coins being produced by individuals."[11] As far west as Greece, temples over-

[9] See Powell 1999.

[10] Kraay 1966:12.

[11] Howgego 1995:3.

saw the refining of metals and organized smithing and metal-working into guilds. The mint in classical Athens was located in the Stephanophore temple devoted to Theseus. The word "money" itself derives from the temple of Juno Moneta, where Rome's first silver and gold coins were struck during the Punic Wars with Carthage in the closing years of the third century BC. The term "Moneta" meant "warner," referring to Juno's sacred geese, which were said to have squawked to warn the Romans that marauding Germanic tribes were about to invade their city.

Why silver? For one thing, it was the epoch's most widespread prestige commodity, used for the sacred objects that adorned the temples as well as for personal wealth in the form of jewelry. Silver and gold traditionally were sanctified as religious contributions,[12] whose value attested to the open-handed and public-spirited character of their givers. In an epoch when social ideology opposed undue wealth concentrated in the hands of individuals and social philanthropy was the main way to obtain public status, donating a share of new wealth to the community's temple helped legitimize gain-seeking. Examples include votive donations such as the ceremonial tripods in Greece and the customary *dekate* set aside by victorious generals out of the booty they seized. Grateful merchants presented offerings upon the successful completion of their voyages.

By sanctifying commercial relations, taking the lead in coordinating foreign trade and adjudicating mercantile disputes, temples promoted the fair dealing and continuity that were preconditions for market exchange to develop. Placed at the center of worldly economic affairs as economic catalysts and innovators, Sumer's temples were the first formally commercial corporate "households," and developed most of the financial practices that subsequently passed into private hands. They and the palace became the natural vehicles by which the monetary metals were circulated to the population at large, although the means by which this circulation occurred are not fully understood.

At first silver fulfilled the money-of-account function interchangeably with copper, tin, gold and other commodities, but gradually it emerged as the dominant monetary medium. Its emergence as the dominant monetary metal stemmed in large part from its desirability as

---

12 Many anthropologists have discussed the sacred associations of these metals, gold being identified with the sun and silver with the moon. Hocart 1927 deals with early money from this perspective.

temple contributions as noted above, and from merchants who obtained it in the course of their trade and used it to repay their suppliers—initially the temples—that had consigned handicrafts to them. By the third millennium it therefore was natural for silver to be designated as the standard monetary medium to value these commodities. In modern terminology the temples and palace served as "buyers of last resort" by accepting it for their output and for public payments.

Gold was rarer, and also was difficult to test in its alloyed form. The fact that it was the most expensive metal also deterred it from serving as general-purpose money. It typically was used c. 1900 BC for large-scale investment in the Assyrian trade to the north, where trade contracts called for an advance of 2 minas of gold, with the merchant-debtor to return 4 minas in five years. Even here, actual payment typically was made in silver.

In subsequent economic documents throughout the Levant gold appears most often in the form of jewelry for dowries. (Today, world gold reserves are estimated to be a block the size of 10 cubic meters, of which about two-thirds take the form of jewelry, largely by Asians who use gold as the main dowry metal.)

There has been some suggestion that gold was a *nouveau riche* metal. The ornate grave goods of Ur have been interpreted this way, and gold's dominant monetary role under Kassite rule (14th-12th centuries BC) likewise may have reflected the preference of military warlords. By classical antiquity, however, the main occasion when Athens coined gold was when it melted down its statues of Winged Victory to pay mercenaries during its war with Sparta, much as Rome coined gold in the closing years of its war with Carthage.

The sexagesimal monetary system

A further hint to the public-sector genesis of monetary silver comes from the sexagesimal system in which minas and shekels were weighed. How did people decide on the units to weigh metals and their appropriate fractional denominations?

Silver originally came in pieces (*Hacksilber*, Latin *ponderata*) as coinage would not emerge until the 7th century BC. But its price needed to be expressed in terms of quantity. After all, a monetary commodity hardly can exist by itself without being plugged into a broad array of commodities to form an interconnected system. This system initially was—and indeed, needed to be—organized under public sponsorship.

The earliest quantitative measure appears to have been a volumetric one to measure grain and barley. It was the Sumerian equivalent of a bushel, the gur, which was divided into multiples of 60 sila—at first 300, later 180 (and at times only 144). These measures appear to have been calendrical in character, or at least were well suited to the accounting needs of the temples and palace allocating a barley ration of two measures to be consumed daily, distributed in bulk each standardized 30-day administrative month.

The earliest weight was the mina, divided into 60 shekels to quantify silver and other metals. If my interpretation is correct regarding the calendrical function of volumetric measures, these sexagesimal weights were designed to dovetail into the fractional system used to measure barley, grain and other crops. Weights and measures, silver and barley were integrated along with other major commodities in a way that enabled the large institutions to track their economic position with a unified set of accounts. Amounts expressed in terms of barley also could be expressed readily in terms of silver, in round numbers for easy calculation. This integrated the commercial system involving foreign trade with the food-supply system.

Administering such a grid of price equivalencies enabled Mesopotamia's temples and palaces to value their output, calculate their flow of rations and schedule their resource flows in terms of a common denominator. Commodities on the price grid were readily convertible into labor time as measured by the rations that were dispersed, while interest and land charges also could be readily factored into the calculations. Long before markets developed, silver, barley and other monetized commodities served as measures of value, denominators of debt, means of payment and vehicles for saving—the four functions of money.

It was natural for the monetary measures that the large institutions designated for their own account-keeping to become the preferred medium of payment for goods and services, fees and taxes by the population at large. These institutions gave value to the key commodities by accepting them in payment for fees and taxes, and for the goods they produced on their own land and in their own workshops, especially inasmuch as most of the earliest obligations by families living on the land were owed to these institutions. Evolving out of their own money-of-account, general-purpose money made economic transactions fungible, that is, mutually convertible.

The experience of Sumer, Babylonia and their neighbors thus bears out the basic principles of the State Theory of money. Rather than taxing the private sector, the palace and temples were direct producers of economic surpluses or at least the major vehicles for their production. They related to their communities as creditors not as debtors, and as sellers of goods and services, leasers of land, and consigners of goods to merchants. Families on the land produced most of their own means of support, exchanging surplus barley or other crops for metal tools, utensils and prestige goods from the large institutions.

Payment by settling debt balances

Early societies economized on actual cash payments. Most transactions, including those between the large institutions, their collectors or merchants and families living on the land were not paid for at the time of purchase but took the form of running debt balances. Rental agreements, the supply of raw materials to craftsmen to work up, investment in trade ventures and even the purchase of beer were arranged on credit.[13] This solved the problem of the lack of a convenient small medium of exchange and the tendency of scales to become more prone to error as the weight of silver or other means of payment got tinier, making cash payments for small transactions less accurate. Actual payment was made as infrequently as possible. Small buyers ran up accounts much like customers at a modern retail shop to be settled on payday. Obligations were settled on seasonal occasions such as harvest time for crop debts (the "payday" in Mesopotamia) or, in the case of commercial silver debts, on the return of the sea voyage or overland caravan.

The way a Babylonian typically would buy a beer, for instance, was to run up a tab with the local ale woman, who evidently obtained vats of beer from the palace, paying its collector after her customers paid her at harvest time. The debt probably was settled on the threshing floor, where an official would collect the debts that had been run up to the palace and its agents, starting with the crops designated as a share on temple and palace fields, followed by various charges for what had been bought during the year.

---

[13] For a review of the many kinds of transactions treated as debt, see Wunsch 2002.

Public institutions and the supply of silver

What must strike any economic historian as remarkable about the ancient Near Eastern economies is how stable their prices and interest rates remained decade after decade, and even century after century. Free-market theorists deny that governments can control prices for long. How then was this price stability maintained?

Modern economists explain price shifts by changes in the money supply. They therefore would start by asking how the population obtained silver and how much there was. But this kind of question is too modernist. As for other modern modes of monetary management, tax policy also was out of the question. Governments today rely on taxing the private sector (or borrowing from it when their ability to tax is eroded), but Mesopotamian temples and palaces were endowed with land, dependent labor, herds of livestock and other resources of their own, enabling them to run a surplus vis-à-vis the rest of the economy. Commercial interest rates were not raised or lowered, but remained stable. There were no "banks" or bank reserves, nor market intervention in government debt, which did not exist.

No concept of the money supply would have been relevant in any event. Hammurapi's laws and those of other rulers decreed that scheduled payments denominated in silver could be made in barley at the official price equivalence. This meant that it was not necessary to get silver into the hands of the population in order for transactions to take place. Stabilizing the barley-silver conversion rate enabled exchange to occur without a monetary deflation when families lacked silver to pay debts or buy metal tools and other products needed for their daily life.[14]

Apart from selling their crops, it is not clear just how the population obtained silver, although the large institutions played a key role in providing it. Their workshops advanced textiles and other handicrafts to merchants who traded them abroad and paid the temples in silver or goods that had a silver-equivalent. Some families may have obtained extra barley from working as sharecroppers on palace land and sold it to the palace and temples. Military conquest no doubt also played a

14 Vargyas 2001:9f. finds that "the expression of prices in terms of silver did not necessarily require actual reserves of the metal." It follows that "there was always a sufficient amount of silver in circulation, and that a rise or fall in supply did not influence prices *in the long term*." Even the looting by Sargon II and Alexander "never had as substantial an effect on price changes as the influx of American gold and silver into Europe in the 16th century" (fn. 19).

role. Charioteers and mercenaries were paid, and victorious cities levied tribute on defeated populations. In classical antiquity generals brought minters on their campaigns to melt down booty and share it within the ranks of their victorious armies and with their home-city temple. The anthropologist Hocart has suggested that rulers may have distributed silver, coins or other money on ceremonial occasions, or perhaps following victories that led to an influx of tribute.

How royal debt management maintained early price stability

Financial instability did arise, to be sure, and rulers dealt with it. Backed by religious values, they recognized a dynamic that modern monetary theorists have all but neglected. The major source of instability was debt, headed by the inability of cultivators to pay crop debts in the face of bad harvests, floods or other natural disasters, or military disruption. Arrears mounted up at compound interest. Centrally managed economies coped by canceling debts when they became overgrown. This is what gave the Bronze Age its remarkable price stability.

Matters hardly could have been otherwise in an epoch when cultivators had only land rights and a few animals to support their families. The main balance aimed at was that of land tenure so as to maintain a self-supporting armed force. To have demanded payments and debt service beyond the ability of cultivators to meet would have reduced these families to dependency. Stabile property relations thus were part of the system that promoted price stability.

Was coinage all that important a breakthrough?

It once seemed that economies could not be monetized until silver and other metals were provided in the form of coins, whose weight and purity were attested. Today, coinage appears less important. For thousands of years weighed pieces of metal of standard purity had served the commercial and economic functions formerly attributed exclusively to coins.[15] Vargyas (2001:31, fn 161) points out that "in the Hellenistic

[15] On the general use of silver see Vargyas 2001. Balmuth 1967 and 1971 has pointed to literary suggestions of earlier Babylonian rulers ordering the casting of coin-like tokens. See most recently Joannès 1989 regarding proto-coinage already under Hammurapi. As Powell 1999:22 put matters: "Like markets, coinage was there before the Greeks. Neither are mentioned, because it was not necessary to state the obvious. Besides, the only significant difference that

period when the same symbols (*e.g.*, the anchor) were used on Seleucid coins and weights. The fact that weights marked as standard had been in use for over a thousand years must have made the introduciton of coined money easier. In fact, nothing was new, as money continued to be measured by weight."

Economic historians in the 19th century noticed that in the turbulent 7th century BC when coinage first was introduced, debt struggles were sweeping the Greek-speaking world. It seemed reasonable to infer that the century's rural distress, land forfeitures and debt bondage were caused by the transition from payments-in-kind to cash payments. However, Mesopotamia's monetary experience shows that the origins of money far predate coinage. It was debt, not money as such, that had been causing the forfeiture of land and liberty for some two thousand years prior to the striking of coins. It is now clear that the debt crises of Greece and Rome were not caused by coinage but by Syrian and Phoenician traders in the 8th century BC bringing the silver money, weights and interest-bearing debt that had become common throughout the Levant into lands where military chieftains had taken control during the Dark Age that followed the collapse of the Mycenaean palace economies around 1200 BC.

Modern scholarship dates coinage to c. 650-625 BC in Lydia (in Asia Minor), spreading westward across the Aegean to the Greek mainland to around 550, nearly a half-century after Solon cancelled the debts of Athenians in 594. As far as market efficiency was concerned, coinage was no more convenient than weighing standardized pieces of metal. As one historian of coinage has observed: "Through most of the Middle Ages, many individual coins of the same issue differed substantially in weight and fineness. Indeed, prior to the 13th century, coinage methods hardly permitted less than a 5 to 10 percent variation in weight between individual coins struck from the same plate."[16] It thus would be in error to assume that coinage was a natural technical invention to minimize transaction costs. A more social and political explanation is required.

---

coinage makes in money transactions is the guarantee of quality; in Babylonia, as elsewhere, silver coins were cut up just like other silver and put in the balance pan."

[16] Mélitz 1974:71, cited in Goodhardt 2003, fn 1. Professional weighing was required to avoid the risk of variation between face value and actual bullion content. This deviation was aggravated by wear, clipping and sweating of coins.

Democratic reforms and the origins of Greek coinage

Around 750 BC, a century before the first coins were struck, Syrian and Phoenician traders brought Near Eastern commercial and debt practices which Greek and Italian chieftains and local warlords adopted in the context of their own control of the land and trade. Neither Greece nor Italy had public institutions for specialized production on anything like the scale of Mesopotamian temples or palaces, or even those of the Mycenaean period. Nor were there local traditions of "divine kingship" to apply a political and religious ethic promoting economic balance and liberty from debt bondage. Religious cults were under the hereditary control of a few aristocratic families who combined sacred, civic and economic power in their own hands—the role that temples and palaces had played in the Near East. Under these conditions the growth of commercial and financial wealth at the top of the social pyramid found its counterpart in the spread of interest-bearing debt, bondage and land forfeitures for families living on the edge of subsistence.

Given this economically polarized character of Greece in the 7th and 6th centuries BC, the "individuals" whom free-market theorists credit with inventing money would have been the powerful families that monopolized the land and held its cultivators in debt. But modern scholarship has found that they were not the class responsible for minting coins in the early cities. Credit for that achievement belongs to the populist reformers known as tyrants who overthrew them.

The evolution of military technology and tactics favored the infantry and naval recruits relative to the cavalry. The ensuing social warfare was waged over the source of the aristocracy's economic power: lending at interest and the appropriation of land. As the *demos*-infantry rose in importance, popular leaders arose to drive the dominant families into exile, redistribute their lands and cancel the debts that had deprived so many clients of their liberty.

These reformers were called "tyrants" by writers unsympathetic to democracy who gave the word an autocratic connotation. The term is better translated as "demagogue," which retains the populist *demos* root of their policies. Or they can simply be called reformers. What the emerging oligarchies found so tyrannical was the assertion of public power over creditors by annulling agrarian debts, liberating indebted bond-servants and redistributing the land as Mesopotamian rulers had done—the three features of earlier Near Eastern Clean Slates, whose final echo is found in the Levitical Jubilee Year.

What the Greek reformers added that was new was the civic minting of coins. Sparta, for instance, is reported to be the first to experience a major social revolution. One of the most prosperous and also economically polarized city-states on the Greek mainland at the start of the 7th century, its Lycurgan reforms c. 680 set it on a radically different path from other city-states. An important part of its program was to reject the use of silver and even copper as money, and to promote a schematized equality by introducing a token coinage of iron. Plutarch reports that this metal was treated with vinegar so as to make it too brittle to have a useful value on its own, explicitly to prevent money from having value as savings. In addition to discouraging monetary forms of wealth, Sparta made the land inalienable so that it could not be forfeited through debt foreclosure. At least that was the original plan.

A generation later, in Corinth, Kypselos gained power and did what many other reformers would do. He exiled the wealthy families that had monopolized the land. He cancelled the debts, redistributed the land and reorganized exchange by striking coins. Polykrates did much the same on the island of Samos. Later in the 7th century Pittakos was elected "tyrant" of Mytilene, and was denounced by aristocratic writers in terms that suggest that he emulated the policy of other reformers and drove out the old aristocracy, redistributed their lands and cancelled the debts that had kept rural families in bondage. His contemporary Cleobulus of Lindos may have done the same.

When a similar financial and land crisis developed in Athens as its wealth began to grow, the reform process culminated in Solon's comparatively moderate "shedding of burdens" which freed cultivators from their debts, banned debt bondage for Athenians and made subsistence land unalienable to outsiders. This latter ruling blocked aliens from foreclosing on the land of indebted Athenians. Solon also reformed the monetary weights and measures in which debts were denominated and trade was conducted.

The first Athenian coins are now dated a half-century after Solon, by the reformer Peisistratos or his son Periander. The aim was to standardize economic relations and thereby lay the groundwork for Athenian democracy by means of a public currency that standardized payments and denominated prices for trade in the *agora*, the public marketplace in which merchants rented stalls from the city. Other elements of this civic program included extensive public building and the staging of dramatic festivals to replace the old religious cults whose priesthoods were controlled by the aristocratic families.

It should be noted that this period of Greek history is so poorly documented, and so overlayered with the political pamphleteering of later periods, that reconstructions can be sketchy at best. Nonetheless, enough is indicated to show that much as occurred two thousand years earlier in Mesopotamia in monetizing the precious metals, the motive for coinage was to establish civic control over the standard of value as a precondition for creating standardized and orderly markets. This uniformity of money and prices was part and parcel of early political democracy.

Four reformers who played a major role in monetary affairs—Solon, Periander, Pittakos and Cleobulus—were placed among the Seven Sages. In addition to promoting civic coinage to govern the valuation, supply, refining and weighing of silver and other metals—along with "debt management" by annulling rural debts—these reformers acted as "straighteners,"[17] the same metaphor used by Babylonian rulers who proclaimed *misharum*, "straight order" with connotations of economic justice.

Sitta von Reden notes that the French scholar "Edouard Will argued some time ago that in the Greek polis *nomisma*, coinage, had strong associations with fair distribution; it described the relationship between citizens and the city. Not accidentally *nomisma* and *nomos*, law, had the same roots: both were the result of rightful distribution, a conventional standard, something used by custom or convention among a political community."[18] Following Will's interpretation, Kurke observes that the term Aristotle used, *nomisma*, means "currency"—not necessarily money, for which the usual term was *chremata*. In addition to meaning law or rule, the root *nem-* meant "to allot, to

[17] Kurke 1999:67f. observes that "The association of tyrants or rulers with coinage is made in the cases of Pheidon king of Argos; the Phrygian king Midas's Kymaian wife; Hippias of Athens [the son of Peisistratos]; Polykrates of Samos." The first mention of coinage in a Greek text (Alkaios fr. 69 V) links "the 'staters of the Lydians' to the 'cunning-minded fox' who is presumably the tyrant Pittakos." From Herodotus and other biographers, one can distil a "portrait of the tyrant as champion of egalitarian justice and opponent of aristocratic overreaching. ... James McGlew (1993:81-86) has recently teased out the traces of a representation of the tyrant as *euthunter*, 'straightener,' the bringer of justice and law ..."

[18] von Reden 2002:53, citing Will 1975a and 1975b.

distribute."[19] She accordingly views the development of coinage as an expression of distributive justice. "Whether we etymologize it (with Will) as 'process or result of lawful distribution' or (with Laroche) as 'convention,' the term *nomisma* points to the political function of coinage, either as a means of effecting retributive justice or as an institution of consensus."[20] Conversely, she believes that early oligarchies refrained from creating public coinage, price and market regulation because they preferred to conduct exchange opportunistically, not standardized but on a personal basis favoring their own powerful status according to circumstances.

Randall Wray summarizes the implications of this public origin of coinage. "As the polis used coins for its own payments and insisted on payment in coin, it inserted its sovereignty into retail trade in the agora. Mainstream economists frequently assert that growth of the local market was associated with expansion of democracy, but Kurke stands the Austrian argument on its head by noting the critical role played by the polis in wresting control away from the elite."[21] The numismatist Kraay confirms that Greek coinage was introduced to standardize payments made to and by the state.[22] Like money in Mesopotamia, it was developed not by individuals bartering silver and other metals for commodities but by the public sector, starting with its fiscal transactions vis-à-vis the rest of the community.

Athens was unique in having its own silver mines at Laurion, owned by the city-state and leased out to private operators much as Babylonian enterprises had been leased. The Athenian "owls" became an added reason for the city-state to give silver the leading monetary role, whereas in Mesopotamia its use derived from the public sector's role in foreign trade.

---

[19] Kurke 1999:332, 13f.,

[20] Kurke, *ibid.*:41, citing von Reden 1995:173f.

[21] Wray 2001.

[22] Kraay 1964:76-91. Kurke describes Lydia as having issued its early coinage in conjunction with organizing regional games as public festivals that provided an occasion for markets and payment to prostitutes (*porne*) as the democratic counterpart to the courtesans who served the wealthy in exchange for gifts rather than fixed monetary payments.

How coinage altered the character of money

The lesson of Greek coinage is much the same as that which can be drawn from Mesopotamian monetary development. Far from representing an individualistic instrument of barter, coinage asserted the principle of civic authority in determining the nominal value of coins. Metallic value was not the key, as Sparta's token coinage shows.

Kurke suggests that this democratic coloration of civic coinage is a major reason why the practice spread only slowly outside of the Greek sphere. For despite the flowering of trade in this period, Egypt, Phoenicia and Carthage did not strike coins for many centuries, nor did Mesopotamia until Alexander the Great looted its temples and melted down their statues, ornaments and other savings into bullion and put it into circulation.[23]

Why was the geographic sphere of coins so localized if they were invented to facilitate trade? For that matter, why were their early denominations so large?

A pragmatic reason is that coins did not really provide much help in reducing the cost of transactions. Trade had been conducted readily for thousands of years with uncoined money. Rather than simplifying payments, the proliferating variety of coins complicated matters, especially as their face value diverged from their metallic value.[24]

How fiscal insolvency led to barter

This disparity, known as seignorage, was highest near the outset of coinage with Sparta's iron money, and became even wider at the end of antiquity when Rome debased its coinage and dragged the Empire into monetary chaos. The collapse into a subsistence-based economy with payments "in kind" replacing monetary demand occurred at the end of antiquity, not at the outset.

To understand how different the origins of money were from its modern development, it is crucial to recognize that antiquity's public institutions were creditors not debtors, and ran fiscal surpluses rather than deficits. There was no public debt, and hence no paper money

---

[23] Kurke 1999: 7, 12. Her book includes an up-to-date bibliography on the history of coinage in the ancient world and on the modern ideological debate over the political character of early coinage.

[24] See Cohen 1997:18 and Vargyas 2001:31.

such as exists in today's world. This meant that when Rome un-taxed its landed wealth, the path of least resistance was to adulterate the coinage. Paper credit and the monetization of public debts would have to await the epoch of central banks, starting with the Bank of England in 1694.

Metallists blame Rome's inflation on the government debasing the coinage in order to issue too much money. Adherents of the State Theory of money blame the collapse on the state's fiscal inability to tax wealth that was becoming increasingly concentrated. Upon gaining control of Rome's Senate in the 2nd century BC, the oligarchy abolished taxes on its land and opposed—with violence and political assassination—any central authority that sought to check its power.

By the fifth century of the modern era the western half of the Roman Empire was reverting to barter as fiscal breakdown led to monetary collapse. The "metallist" view postulated by individualists to be the original and natural form of money is found only at the end of a long process of economic polarization. Instead of Europe's Dark Age being caused by the government stifling private wealth, the breakdown resulted from a financial oligarchy gaining control of Rome and shifting the tax burden onto the cultivators whose liberty and land-tenure rights had been protected by earlier regimes throughout the Mediterranean and Near East.

"In the beginning" Mesopotamian rulers (and later, Greek reformers) maintained monetary and price stability by annulling rural tax arrears and other personal debts. This mode of restoring economic balance prevented indebtedness from impoverishing and disenfranchising the citizen-army. The effect was to adjust the volume of debt to the economy's ability to pay—that is, to pay without debtors having to forfeit their homesteads to creditors on a broad a scale.

The idea of economic and monetary balance narrowed after the families of warlords and chieftains gained power by acting as merchants and creditors in their own personal interest, depriving cultivators of their liberty and the land rights that formed the basis of their citizenship status in the infantry. Many cultivators who lost their means of support found their best option to lie in fleeing. The effect was to depopulate their communities, leaving them prone to be conquered.

Debt deflation occurred as local oligarchies gained wealth and power. As creditors, they did not recycle their revenue but pushed the bottom layers of society into bondage. By imperial Roman times usury and the levy of imperial tribute had become inexorable. The state lost its fiscal and monetary power,[25] breaking the traditional circular flow of revenue between the public and private sectors and hence drying up the means of issuing coinage. Monetary collapse ensued as taxing power was stripped away by the creditor oligarchy whose dominance Mesopotamian rulers had blocked by Clean Slate proclamations and early Greek reformers had driven into exile.

A Dark Age descended as entire populations as well as governments were stripped of monetary metal by the unchecked growth of individualism leading to a concentration of financial and landholding power at the top of the economic pyramid. This set the stage for a new monetary ethic to emerge in medieval Europe. As commerce recovered, bankers and other creditors advocated metallic "government-free" bullion-money whose issue and exchange value was independent of public control. When paper credit and currency developed, it was issued mainly by private bankers. This "metallic" stage of monetary and credit evolution signaled a victory of personal wealth over the central government authority that originally had assigned value to money.

Conclusion

The essential function of Mesopotamia's money-of-account, measuring the value of goods and services, remained that of money in classical Greece. The bibliophile Athenaeaus reports that when Anacharsis, a Scythian 6th-century BC prince renowned for his admiration of Greek culture, was asked for what purposes the Greeks used money, he answered, "For reckoning."[26] As Aristotle explained in his *Ethics* (1133), "all things that are exchanged must be somewhat comparable. It is for this end that money has been introduced, and it becomes in a sense an intermediate; for it measures all things ...—how many shoes are equal to a house or to a given amount of food." In sum, he concluded: "Money, then, acting as a measure, makes goods commensurate and equates them" by enabling them to be co-measured.[27]

---

[25] I describe the dynamics in Hudson 1998. On the tax system's reliance on the land, see Hudson 2001.

[26] Athenaeus, *Banquet of the Scholars* (I.iv.49). Marx quotes this in his chapter on money in *Capital* (1887:73).

[27] Aristotle explains rather awkwardly: "Let A be a house, B ten minae, C a bed, A is half of B, if the house is worth five minae or equal to them; the bed, C, is a tenth of B; it is plain, then, how many beds are equal to a house, *viz.* five."

Money-of-account initially was created by Mesopotamia's temples and palaces to administer prices. These were adopted by society at large via the sale and consignment of products, credit arrangements and fiscal transactions. Barley and silver evolved into a means of payment by being accepted by the public institutions for their trade, credit and fiscal operations that supplied and drew in these commodities.

Although the preconditions for modern credit-money were developed in antiquity—credit, debt and money—three novel ingredients of modern money were lacking. First, there was no deposit banking. Temples acted as depositories for grain, and as lenders of last resort, but did not lend out deposits, much less engage in "fractional reserve" banking by creating a credit pyramid. The normal rate paid for holding people's money was the same as for lending money—20 percent annually. This left no margin between borrowing and lending rates, and hence no incentive for banks to become financial intermediaries taking in deposits at a low rate (or even charging their depositors for safekeeping) and lending them at a higher rate.

The second factor deterring creation of a modern credit superstructure was the fact that debt tablets were not transferable as means of payment to third parties. Assyrian traders occasionally used such clearing transfers, but only among close associates. Neither temples nor private parties intermediated credits and debts. Transferability begins only in medieval Europe, when it was developed by Knights Templars during the Crusades and soon was adopted by private Italian bankers. Private bankers, however, had a much narrower interest than that of early Mesopotamia's temples and palaces. The new objective was to make money from their clients, without regard for broad social considerations such as saving debtors from being expropriated to become a landless underclass.

The third new factor that transformed matters was governments running deficits. In antiquity this was done only in times of war, and it was financed by monetizing the savings of the temples. As Rome's fiscal position fell into chronic deficit, emperors debased the metal content of coinage, and subsequent European rulers "cried down" the coinage, redefining the face value of coins. But only in medieval times did kings begin to borrow from private bankers, mainly to finance their wars.

This borrowing created a new *modus operandi* between palaces and their creditors. Private credit was institutionalized outside of government, under arrangements where it was backed to some degree by the purchase of government bonds as reserves.

Governments issued their own paper money in times of major war, suspending convertibility into bullion. It was largely to deter this option—and to reverse war-induced inflationary monetary issues of currency—that bankers developed a nostalgic myth of money as having a metallist origin independent of public institutions. By the end of the 19th century this myth was spliced onto a parallel mythology of individualism to depict money and commercial innovation as developing without public institutions having to act as catalysts and regulators.

It has taken the discovery of Sumerian economic origins over the past century, along with a re-evaluation of the politics of Greek coinage, to provide the needed empirical corrective to this false "parallel universe" mythology, and to put the many twists and turns in monetary development in its proper long-term perspective.

BIBLIOGRAPHY

Aristotle, *Politics* trans. B. Jowett (Oxford 1921).

Athenaeus, *Banquet of the Scholars* (Loeb Classical Library; London–New York).

Balmuth, Miriam (1967), "Monetary Forerunners of Coinage in Phoenicia and Palestine in Antiquity," in A. Kindler (ed.), *The Patterns of Monetary Development in Phoenicia and Palestine in Antiquity* (Jerusalem).

— (1971), "Remarks on the Appearance of the Earliest Coins," in David Gordon Mitten, John Griffiths Pedley, and Jane Ayer Scott (eds.), *Studies Presented to George M. A. Hanfmann* (Cambridge, Mass.): 1-7.

Cohen, Edward E. (1997), *Athenian Economy and Society, a Banking Perspective* (Princeton: Princeton University Press).

Desmonde, William H. (1962), *Magic, Myth and Money* (New York: Free Press of Glencoe).

Goodhardt, Charles (2003), "The Two Concepts of Money: Implications for the Analysis of Optimal Currency Areas," in Nell and Bell 2003: 1-25.

Hocart, Arthur M. (1927), *Kingship* (London; Reprint 1969, Oxford University Press).

Howgego, Christopher J. (1995), *Ancient History from Coins* (London *etc.*: Routledge).

Hudson, Michael (1992), "Did the Phoenicians Introduce the Idea of Interest to Greece and Italy—And if So, When?" in Günter Kopcke (ed.), *Greece Between East and West: 10th–8th Centuries BC* (Mainz: von Zabern): 128-43.

— (1998), "Land Monopolization, Fiscal Crises and Clean Slate 'Jubilee' Proclamations in Antiquity," in Robert C. Hunt and Antonio Gilman (eds.), *Property in Economic Context* (University Press of America, Monographs in Economic Anthropology 14): 139-69.

— (2001), "Land Taxation in Mesopotamia and Classical Antiquity," in Robert Andelson (ed.), *Land-Value Taxation Around the World* (London: Blackwell's): 17-35.

— (2003), "The Cartalist/Monetarist Debate in Historical Perspective," in Nell and Bell 2003: 39-76.

— (2004), "The Archaeology of Money: Debt versus Barter Theories of Money's Origins," in Wray 2004: 99-127.

Joannès, Francis (1989), "Médailles d'argent d'Hammurabi?" *NABU* 1989/108.

Keynes, John Maynard (1930), *Treatise on Money* (London: Macmillan).

Knapp, Georg F. (1924), *The State Theory of Money* (London) [first published in German, Leipzig 1905].

Kraay, Kolin (1964), "Hoards, Small Change and the Origin of Coinage," *Journal of Hellenic Studies* 84:76-91.

— (1966), *Greek Coins* (New York: Harry Abrams).

Kurke, Leslie (1999), *Coins, Bodies, Games, and Gold* (Princeton: Princeton University Press).

Laum, Bernard (1924), *Heiliges Geld* (Tübingen: J.C.B. Mohr).

— (1952), "Geschichte der öffentlichen Finanzwirtschaft im Altertum und Frühmittelalter," in Wilhelm Gerloff and Fritz Neumark (eds.), *Handbuch der Finanzwissenschaft*, 2nd ed. (Tübingen): 211-35.

Marx, Karl (1887), *Capital* (London: Swan Sonnenschein).

McGlew, James (1993), *Tyranny and Political Culture in Ancient Greece* (Ithaca: Cornell University Press).

Mélitz, Jacques (1974), *Primitive and Modern Money: An Interdisciplinary Approach* (Reading, Mass.: Addison-Wesley).

Nell, Edward and Stephanie Bell, eds. (2003), *The State, The Market and The Euro: Chartalism versus Metallism in the Theory of Money* (Cheltenham: Edward Elgar).

Oppenheim, A. Leo (1949), "The Golden Garments of the Gods," *JNES* 8:172-93.

— (1959), "On an Operational Device in Mesopotamian Bureaucracy," *JNES* 18:121-28.

Polanyi, Karl (1957), *Primitive, Archaic, and Modern Economies: Essays of Karl Polanyi*, ed. George Dalton (New York: Doubleday).

— (1977), *The Livelihood of Man* (New York).

Polanyi, Karl, Conrad M. Arensberg and Harry W. Pearson (1957), *Trade and Markets in the Early Empires* (New York: The Free Press).

Powell, Marvin (1999), "*Wir müssen alle unsere Nische nuzten*: Monies, Motives, and Methods in Babylonian Economics," in J.G. Dercksen (ed.), *Trade and Finance in Ancient Mesopotamia* (= MOS Studies 1; Proceedings of the First MOS Symposium [Leiden 1997]; PIHANS 84): 5-23.

von Reden, Sitta (2002), "Demos' *Phialê* and the Rhetoric of Money in Fourth-century Athens," in Paul Cartledge, Edward E. Cohen and Lin Foxhall (eds.), *Money, Labour and Land: Approaches to the Economies of Ancient Greece* (London *etc.*: Routledge).

— (1995), *Exchange in Ancient Greece* (London: Duckworth).

Renger, Johannes (1984), "Patterns of Non-Institutional Trade and Non-Commercial Exchange in Ancient Mesopotamia at the Beginning of the Second Millennium B.C.," in Alfonso Archi (ed.), *Circulation of Goods in Non-Palatial Context in the Ancient Near East* (Incunabula Graeca 82, Rome): 31-123.

Schmandt-Besserat, Denise (1992), *Before Writing: From Counting to Cuneiform* (Austin, Texas: University of Texas Press).

Vargyas, Peter (2001), *A History of Babylonian Prices in the First Millennium BC. 1. Prices of Basic Commodities* (Heidelberger Studien zum Alten Orient 10; Heidelberg: Heidelverger Orientverlag).

Will, Edouard (1975a), "De l'aspect éthique des origines grecques de la mon naie," *Revue historique* 212: 209-31.

— (1975b), "Fonctions de la monnaie dans les cités grecques de l'époque classique," in M. Dentzer, P. Gauthier and T. Hackens (eds.), *Numismatique Antique: problèmes et méthods* (Études d'archéologie classique; Louvain: Éditions Peeters): 233-46.

Wray, L. Randall (1998), *Understanding Modern Money* (Cheltenham: Edward Elgar).

— (2001), Review of Kurke's "Coins, Bodies, Games, and Gold," *Journal of Economic Issues* (March).

— (2004) ed., *Credit and State Theories of Money: The Contributions of A. Mitchell Innes* (Cheltenham: Edward Elgar)

Wunsch, Cornelia (2002), "Debt, Interest, Pledge and Forfeiture in the Neo-Babylonian and Early Achaemenid Period: The Evidence from Private Archives," in Michael Hudson and Marc Van De Mieroop (eds.), *Debt and Economic Renewal in the Ancient Near East* (Bethesda, Md.: CDL Press): 221-55.

11.

General Discussion

This is an abridged stenographic version, edited by the participants, of the discussion that occurred at the conclusion of the colloquium on Friday, November 17, 2000. Incidental remarks are omitted, but some material is included from the discussions that followed individual papers where some controversy arose. M.H.

Hudson: The common point of contention running through most of these papers is whether accounting in the various periods under study served "minimally"—as a check against pilfering, dishonesty or shortfalls, and as a rough fiscal schedule of tax and rent payments—or "maximally" as an economic planning and management tool.

The "maximum" role of accounting is found early in the internal operations of the large institutions, when accounting procedures and formats, weights and measures, administered prices and money were first being put in place in the fourth and third millennia BC. These public institutions took the lead in developing accounting and management techniques.

But palaces later played mainly a fiscal function, taxing the economy and leasing land and enterprises to private managers. As this decentralization occurred, the degree of accounting detail and planning became more concerned simply with listing the scheduled deliveries and payments, and noting whether or not they were met. Private individuals did not organize their records on anywhere near as thoroughgoing a scale. The role of accounting thus narrowed as the economic center of gravity shifted from the palace to individual families.

Hallo: The great bulk of cuneiform documents consist of accounts. The reason we have them is because their creators were accountable. There cannot be accountability without an auditor. There would seem to be little reason to write up accounts if there were not an auditor.

Van De Mieroop: I think we all agree that there was accountability and responsibility. The role of account-keeping was institutional. Records were created because someone was reporting to a superior within the large institutions.

The question is, to what extent did the temple or palace go beyond this and use it for planning? What we need to explain is the existence of so much textual documentation within these institutions. What does it signify? I share Michael Jursa's minimalist approach.

Renger: The written record certainly does not provide a comprehensive picture of the whole economy. One problem is that these archives are segmented, as were the social systems themselves. Some areas are not affected by record-keeping at all. The size of this unaffected sphere increases in the Old Babylonian period, and indeed, from Ur III onward. Also growing are large segments of the economy unaffected by the large institutions.[1]

To trace the effect of accounting we need to understand the relationship between the bureaucratic structures and the rest of society. We must know how deep the bureaucracy was, and to correlate accounting documents with official ranks. There are scribal ranks, and ranks for entrepreneurs, royal officials and trade officials.

Michael Hudson's paper shows that there was much less need for money than would be the case today, as our modern specialization of labor has gone far beyond that of antiquity, requiring more payments than were necessary in earlier times.

Palaima: I agree that the central idea of accounting is accountability—institutional responsibility as well as personal responsibility. The Linear B records show a three-tiered hierarchy: craftsman, guild head, and either a palace or temple official. Regarding the distinction between accountability and planning, these records include estimates, projections and quotas. The officials calculate landholdings and what each unit should yield. Every written record has a potential consequence. The texts are prescriptive: This delivery is to be made in the future. It is a demand on outlying districts.

---

1 For a general outline see Johannes Renger, "Wirtschaftsgeschichte des alten Mesopotamien. Versuch einer Standortbestimmung," in A. Hausleiter, S. Kerner, B. Müller-Neuhoff, eds., *Material Culture and Mental Spheres—Rezeption archäologischer Denkrichtungen in der Vorderasiatischen Altertumskunde. Internationales Symposium für Hans J. Nissen, Berlin, 23.-24 Juni 2000*, (= AOAT 293; Münster 2002): 239-65.

Zaccagnini: We need to know how many people, and what kind or category of people, belong to the public institutions.

Van De Mieroop: Do we have any documentation for this?

Zaccagnini: The census data probably was used for military recruitment and corvée labor.

Wunsch: We find such lists in private archives. It is hard to identify them, because the key figures of the archive are not mentioned in them. A family may be involved in tax farming or may supply soldiers to fulfill military obligations, but it is hard to put these lists into context. Maybe there never were full official lists but the information only existed at the entrepreneurial level.

Jursa: The purpose of census lists was to oblige somebody to supply the people listed in these texts. It was always to charge someone to take responsibility. This supports the view of accounting as a means of control—what Moses Finley called the "police function."

Steinkeller: But you need to have some expectation as to what can be produced and what the state can take.

Wunsch: Archives on date orchards can be traced over many years, and show striking differences in estimates of the date crops. You can deal only with the income of a given year, and can tell the harvest only a few weeks before it is in. You cannot forecast such things as disease, bad weather or other disturbances. It is easier to forecast for a five- or ten-year period. It gets harder from year to year, because that is where the variation occurs around the normal trend.

Palaima: Still, the palace needs to have some kind of projection to know how it can feed its workers. If you know the labor force, you know the target that has to be delivered.

Englund: You have production norms, and then you have records. But we ourselves must reconstruct many of the totals that must have been inherent in the system. Someone must have added up all these records to create an overall total.

Gardiner: This was what the Domesday Book set out to do—to establish the land's yield. Obviously it varied from year to year. Taxes were based on the anticipated norm, not on the actual yields. The lords knew what their obligations would be. They themselves had to bear the brunt of the variation if the crop or revenue was low. The market value of the crop might be low if the crop were a bumper crop, by the way.

Hallo: Mathematical texts provide us with a norm, such as Gelb's exercise regarding the growth of a herd.[2]

Van De Mieroop: But this is just a mathematical game. There is little relevance to actual life.

Englund: Idealized curves always go upward. Real life has abrupt discontinuities. In the Drehem text that Bill cites—the key text to understanding dairy production in the Ur III period[3] —the growth and production of an artificial herd of cattle are charted over a ten-year period. The chart is based on strict production norms of the time, including those that regulate deliveries of butter oil and dried cheese to central household offices, as well as the set quota of calves, reckoned according to the number of adult cows. Gelb mistook this text to represent a true record of dairy accounting, based on his discovery that it presumed the use of the same "nice numbers"—that is, the same dairy equivalencies, such as five liters of butter oil per milk-bearing cow per year as a delivery quota—that are found in innumerable Ur III accounts. But that was a misunderstanding, now deep-seated in the field, concerning the difference between the artificial character of the debits or "projection section" of running accounts, and the credit sections that derive from receipts documenting the actual transportation, storage, and distribution of real goods and services.

The moral is that whenever the Ur III specialist sees in some account such easily factored numbers as, for instance, 75 liters of butter oil, he must consult his equivalency files—both for production norms and for exchange rates—before assuming that they represent actual deliveries.

Hallo: But what are projections, other than ideals?

Van De Mieroop: There has to be some link to reality.

Renger: What is all this record-keeping for? Jursa cites Finley regarding a "police function" with respect to higher authority. The king wants a

---

2 Ignace J. Gelb (1967), "Growth of a Herd of Cattle," *Journal of Cuneiform Studies* 21:64-69.

3 See R. Englund, "Regulating Dairy Productivity in the Ur III Period," *Orientalia* 64 (1995):377-429.

surplus to be produced. The palace must be paid, regardless. That's the basic "plan."

Jursa: Projecting yields and output by simplified mathematical models seems to have been done already in Ur III.

Van De Mieroop: On a purely definitional point, does Mesopotamia's "police" function mean an audit function?

Palaima: Pylos records are stored in central archives. All the records are political, in the sense that the palace wants to know this information.

We have three sets of female records. Women are listed (1) by profession and location; (2) how many children they have, boys and girls, according to two age groups (so right here the palace is estimating the future labor force); and (3) the rations that are due monthly. The basket scribe will write a note, "rations for women for so-and-so …"

Other records reflect the size and births of flocks. The Mycenaeans also projected these. We do not have their projections, but they must have existed. This seems to be implied in the documents. That evidently was the purpose of Gelb's exercise. What is significant is that all this is palatial, as part of a single processing system.

Steinkeller: Rations for the labor force were a key projection.

Van De Mieroop: But rations are an expenditure, not a forecast of output or income.

Steinkeller: You need to know both. You need to plan ahead. I plan ahead, but I don't have a plan that exists anywhere. I only have bills to pay, and I know about how much they will amount to. That's all I need to know, because I assume a continuity.

Van De Mieroop: Any record can serve as a planning device in principle. A checkbook can play this role. But does it do so in practice?

Palaima: The issue is planning versus authenticating. We have little ostensible planning material from the Linear B records. Their function was simply to authenticate transactions. We see this particularly in the sealing systems, which are entirely "authenticating" or oversight functions.

Van De Mieroop: Yes, most records are to cover one's tracks. Only a small proportion is for planning.

Steinkeller: But these may be highly important. One would expect many fewer records to be concerned with planning, because they take a broad overview, based on many, many individual transactions.

Van De Mieroop: Certainly there are fewer end-of-year accounts than on-the-spot accounts. It is the latter that would have been used for oversight at the top of the pyramid. But the function may be simply for workshops, for example, to say that this is how much raw material they got, and then to account for their change of inventories during the year by showing what they used the raw material for.

Palaima: There is no temple in the outlying districts, but there is a Mycenaean text saying that each district has temple bronze.

Hallo: Account texts preparing against the possibility of future audits by higher authority can be identified as "descriptive rituals" when they deal with expenditures incurred in a temple service.[4]

Jursa: What you might call "forward planning" in Neo-Babylonian times involved the use of simplified mathematical models, for example with regard to the average yield of fields in the case of renting out large tracts of land. In a very general way these models were based on practical experience. But such accounting was not or could not be based on exact empirical data.

Christopher Walker: The British Museum is audited only for about 1% of its transactions.

Palaima: Mycenaean planning was mainly in the military sphere. Its mentality was responsive. It is hard to find plans to build up a cloth workshop, but you can build up stocks to provision the military.

Fred Harrison: Was there really no planning? Was there no calculation of how or in what way the surplus was to be extracted? No calculation of the dependent population that had to be fed out of stocks from the harvest and inventories carried over?

Renger: Average crop yields were calculated in order to calculate expenditures and plan the disposition of revenues in kind or in money. We know that in some years harvests exceeded expectations. In other years

---

[4] See the article by Baruch A. Levine and W.W. Hallo on "Offerings to the Temple Gates at Ur," in HUCA 38 (1967).

they fell short.[5] This implies that there were expected yields. Otherwise, nobody would have calculated a shortfall and nobody would have said that some outlying region or administrative unit was short and owed a debt. So the Babylonians certainly were up to planning in terms of expectations.

Steinkeller: Lagash grain production expectations ran for ten years.

Hudson: Maurice Lambert used the word *planification*. Was he right or wrong?

Englund: Expectations underlay the planned economy. Field texts show projections based on yield-to-seed ratios.

Gardiner: All systems of taxation are based on estimated annual values. European taxes from the Domesday Book on were based on average output, not actual output.

Renger: "Taxes" did not exist, but the large institutions generated a surplus. There has to be something like auditing. Quotas were set. That was the kind of planning they had. Records of arrears from these quotas survive.[6] So such accounts acted as a control mechanism.

Piero Sraffa wrote a book on *Production of Commodities by Means of Commodities* (1960). We might use that approach as a kind of input/output study of Mesopotamia. What is remarkable is the high yield/seed ratio. This was not always achieved in practice each year, of course. There were disturbances.

---

[5] See RTC 407 and similar documents, for which see Johannes Renger, "Institutional, Communal, and Individual Ownership or Possession of Arable Land in Ancient Mesopotamia from the End of the Fourth to the End of the First Millennium B.C.," *Kent Law Review* 71 (1995): 285 with footnote 35; Renger, "On Economic Structures in Ancient Mesopotamia," *Orientalia* NS 63 (1994): 157-208, espec. 178f.; and Renger, *Überlegungen zur räumlichen Ausdehnung des Staates Ebla an Hand der agrarischen und viehwirtschaftlichen Gegebenheiten*, Istituto Universario Orientale, Napoli, Series Minor 27 (1986): 293-311.

[6] The entire institution of the "*Palastgeschäft*" in Old Babylonian and later times was based on such agreed-upon or set quotas. See Renger, "Das Palastgeschäft in der altbabylonischen Zeit," in A. C. V. M. Bongenaar, ed., *Interdependency of Institutions and Private Entrepreneurs* (= Proceedings of the 2nd MOS Symposium Leiden 1998) 2000: 153-83.

Palaima: In Mycenaean records each archive is site-specific, showing the extent to which there is a wide variability of possible ways to make accounts. Different sites and different times have different characteristics for their accounts and records. But on balance there is a transition from simplicity to increasing degrees of complexity. As Geoffrey Gardiner said, how do we extract from labor that which it may not want to give? The solution is to establish a system of coercion and rewards.

The Mycenaean system was a forcible overlay on a long pre-existing system. Their problem was: How do you conquer a land? You make people dedicated to the ideal of efficiency. Today we call this "civilization." The Mycenaean rulers were able to use brute force to enforce "efficiency," that is, forcing a population to serve the ruler and do what he says, deliver crops and handicrafts and raw materials to him. You could say that when one merely aims at efficiency, it is as if one has been conquered.

Hudson: So you are saying that civilization is a conquest that has become non-military in character. Populations today are acting as if they were conquered, without really having been subdued by force.

Gardiner: The means of getting a usufruct in Mesopotamia were different from those used in modern times, or even in classical antiquity. We might speak of different modes of exploiting labor. Today's governments levy taxes. Back then, the public institutions generated their own surplus. My understanding from your papers is that before they taxed the private sector of *its* surplus, they created their own surplus with their own flocks, workshops and dependent labor force. They then realized this surplus by trading their products at home and in foreign lands and other cities. To do this, they took the lead in creating basic market institutions that have survived ever since, although they were not price-making markets but used administered prices.

So the fiscal policy of Sumer and Babylonia was based on (1) shares of output on public assets (*e.g.*, by sharecroppers on temple and palace lands leased out to them, usually via intermediaries or "entrepreneurs"); (2) charging user fees (*e.g.*, stipulated fees levied on boatmen, ceremonial priests for officiating, *etc.*); (3) various other levies and contributions, as when craftsmen would sell their services or products, and often pay fees to the palace. In some cases these fees were for public monopolies; and (4) the sale of products via royal intermediaries (*e.g.* ale women), including merchants to whom goods were consigned from the workshops. There also was a fifth category: waging war and either looting or demanding a pay-off not to attack, as is reported to have occurred when Uruk was attacked by Kish in the reign of Gilgamesh. A related source of income would be regular tribute demanded from conquered cities and their populations, such as the grain tribute that Lagash levied on Umma c. 2400 BC. Finally, temples received voluntary contributions. In classical antiquity these would include designated offerings of gratitude to the patron gods of victorious cities from generals who had won battles and from merchants upon the successful conclusion of their voyages or caravans.

What is missing from these means of the palace and temples to obtain resources are taxes in the modern sense of the term, although I gather that there were excise taxes levied on particular products or services, including excise taxes or tariffs on long-distance trade.

How many of these fiscal activities involved account-keeping? How many were recorded? Were only regular flows of receipts recorded, or occasional ones such as military tribute too, and perhaps taxes on trade? Would they have been recorded in a single comprehensive annual royal account? That is what would be needed for real planning.

Steinkeller: Many kinds of transactions did not need accounting, or even written documentation, especially exchange. Scribes were found at the city gate for important transactions involving public accountability or contracts. But most trade among individuals would have not needed contracts or other documentation, unless they involved loans or unpaid balances. Contracts were required to provide evidentiary proof of debts and property transfers and loans.

In this respect it is hard to see how Babylonian society could have developed in the way it did without written accounts. Written records were needed only when the transactions involved the public institutions, and these records served as a check. Documents provided top management with basic information needed to plan and control the economy. Officials ran their departments much like enterprises, and planning could not have occurred without such data. Jack Goody said that all societies need some kind of forward planning and budgeting. That is the essence of rationality.

Lamia al-Gailani: What does one *not* read about in these archives? Was their scope broad enough to make realistic plans? Most research on early times leaves out production by families for their own use. I have my own garden and get food from it, but this doesn't get into statistics even today.

Gardiner: In Germany industry is more widespread than in Britain, but Germans too have subsistence farming. Industrial economies are not the same thing as market economies.

In 1920, 60 percent of the retail price index consisted of food. You cannot project food crops accurately. This is why agriculture always has to plan for a surplus. Otherwise, there is a risk of starvation. But market pricing complicates matters, to the extent that prices reflect shifts in supply and demand. It is easier to predict crops than prices in today's world. The demand for food is price-inelastic, so that prices decline in times of surplus. This creates a disaster under modern price-making markets. But that was not the case in antiquity. Agriculture was controlled mainly by accumulating and disbursing inventories of reserves.

Progress is not always for the better, and does not even become larger. In Britain five thousand years ago agriculture occurred on a gigantic scale. Fields and boundaries stretched for ten miles.

Hudson: Households were largely self-supporting down through feudal European times. Families grew their own crops, just as even today many families in Russia and Central Europe have their own gardens. Only a small portion of output passed through the marketplace, and even for products that did, immediate payment was not required. The fact that most market transactions were financed by debt rather than monetary payment created a need for written record-keeping, but not necessarily accounting in the way we have been discussing it.

Jursa: Normally one doesn't find anything about the purchase of real estate, gifts of fields and houses to the temple or similar transactions in accounting records. For such facts the written documentation would furnish information as *aide-memoires* and also would have evidential value, *e.g.*, as title deeds.

Hudson: You remarked that the Venetians were amazed to find the Turkish empire so unplanned, and that this seemed to be unheard of. Of course, the Turks invaded a highly organized society. There is a difference between a society that creates a structure for initiating its takeoff, and one that invades and lives off that society. Once an economic system is put in place, outsiders can take it over and run it on an ad hoc basis. Their plan is no more sophisticated than believing that all they have to do each year is to repeat the previous year, taking as much as they can until they break the back of the host economy. To take the surplus they do not even need to understand how the structure works or what its relationships are.

This discussion so far has focused on the contrast between oversight checks and real planning. How can any large economy work without planning? The sexagesimal weights and measures were a form of forward planning, at least to the extent that dependent workers received rations monthly, and decided how much to consume each day. The solution was found in standardization—and that seems to have been the first step toward planning, certainly its prerequisite.

According to Maurice Lambert's description of the Lagash bureaucracy, when the crops failed because of Lugalanda's invasion from Umma, palace food stocks were drawn down. When they didn't suffice to feed the labor force, rations were cut back so as to "pace" the supply. Was this planning, or simply a response to a new situation based on the shrinking stock of food inventories and the labor force that needed to be fed?

Steinkeller: Jack Goody said that all societies need to plan in order to survive from year to year in order to allocate resources over time. Any economic anthropologist would find this obvious. I cannot imagine that an institution as complex as Ebabbar did not use planning. If it did not do this itself, then it relied on others to do this, such as the Egibi and other private entrepreneurs that Cornelia has studied. Is Michael Jursa suggesting that there really was no planning?

Jursa: Our disagreement is more quantitative than qualitative. The issue is where to draw the line. The Ebabbar accountants had a good idea of how much of a food harvest they needed for the year. They certainly were able to compare the estimated demand with what they actually had in their storehouses, and to take the necessary measures if they expected a shortfall. I have no doubt about the existence of this kind of forward planning. But there are other things they were not able to do—things that simply did not occur to them.

As I pointed out in my paper, in agriculture the expected field rents were based on mathematical models rather than on data taken from the actual relevant accounts. Another example is the administration of temple estates located far to the south of Sippar. It would have been more efficient to deal locally than to bring the harvest of these estates halfway across the land to Sippar. But instead of acting efficiently in this way, the palace acted bureaucratically or simply traditionally. We cannot assume rational cost management, because the accountants of Ebabbar were not set up to do cost planning.[7]

Van De Mieroop: We cannot assume that the Ur III state aimed at efficiency either. The mere fact of detailed records does not mean that their statistics were used efficiently by planners.

Renger: Did they ever aim at cost efficiency? Is that rather an anachronistic modernist idea?

Wunsch: At some point the mass of information became too cumbersome. The inertia of collecting data took on a life of its own, to the point where it exceeded the ability to incorporate into rational plan-

---

[7] I cannot resist noting here, *ex post facto*, that Michael Jursa sets criteria for planning that hardly could be met by many sectors of the United States or Britain today. It remains normal for industries to use fixed proportions and standardized average crop yields rather than actual harvests in making projections. A recent news report tells of the bumper 2003 U.S. grain and soybean crop being left to rot because of inadequate railroad shipping capacity. Referring to "the unexpected surge in both the agriculture sector and the economy in general," the report notes that the condition of America's rail fleet has deteriorated steadily in recent years, causing freight rates to soar and consumer prices to rise even in the face of abundant harvests. "We looked ahead and saw what we thought would be a pretty flat economy," a Union Pacific spokesman is quoted as saying. A similar "unexpected" shortage developed six years earlier, in 1997. (See "Railroad Logjams Threaten Boom In the Farm Belt," *The Wall Street Journal*, Dec. 1, 2003).

The reason for such seemingly failed planning is that the railroads only buy as many cars as can be used every year. Their administrators see little reason to buy cars that would be used only once every five or six years when domestic harvests are abundant and those abroad fall short (as they did in China in 2003) spurring export demand. Such corporate planning does not take into account the economy's loss to farmers and consumers from not having surplus cars available.

One wonders what Neo-Babylonian rulers would make of the strange logic that has produced British and U.S. rail transport. The objective of corporate planning is not economy-wide efficiency. The more decentralized economies become, the more self-centered is the scope of their planning, in Neo-Babylonian times just as in today's world. M.H.

ning. At this point the link between record-keeping and actual planning deteriorated into mere habit. This must be one reason for the less intensive account-keeping after Ur III.

Gardiner: Planning and cost forecasting reflect the type of organization conducting these activities. They reflect its purpose and system of authority. Not everyone—certainly not the individuals who made many of the documents—had a clue about cost accounting, to say nothing of double entry book-keeping. There was only a nominal idea of costs. Most businessmen fly by the seat of their pants, so to speak. Conscious logic may not be as good as managerial instinct.

Palaima: At issue here is the notion of rational forecasting. We do not have year-to-year schemes in the Mycenaean system, but we do have tax collections for six products. The districts are taxed proportionally, and these proportions remain constant. Hence, the taxes are based on expected output. These expectations are the "plan."

It is impossible that the actual yields among these districts and products always remained constant. Therefore, they must have been in the character of quotas based on what was expected, what was owed to the palace. However, the yearly tax was kept too high to be paid on a regular basis. In such cases the palace could relinquish the sums due, recognizing that it could not cry over spilt milk, so to speak. It had got all that it could, under the circumstances.

Delivery shortfalls, debts and their social consequences

Zaccagnini: Both in the public and private sectors a debt note would be kept. A reason for book-keeping is that the organization needs a budget, to establish a norm for next year.

Palaima: If there is a shortfall, the Mycenaean record says, "So much they do not give." The king may grant an exemption, however. There is a phrase for this.

Englund: Are there penalties known to you about cultivators who could not meet their stipulated obligations or pay their debts?

Renger: Legal documents such as debt notes become more important than accounting documents in the Old Babylonian period.[8]

---

[8] Johannes Renger, "Wirtschaftsgeschichte des alten Mesopotamien. Versuch einer Standortbestimmung," in *op. cit.* (fn. 1), esp. 255f.

Jursa: The Ebabbar temple had to rely on rent-farmers to make their collections. The temple tried to squeeze out as much as it could from them. The backlog grew and grew, but nothing really seemed to happen. Bad things did happen to individual sharecroppers, but not to the rent farmers. The palace or temple had the right to claim arrears, but didn't. However, the rent farmers were able to squeeze people under them, and even to force labor out of them seemingly without end.

Steinkeller: Your talk mentioned wooden tablets. What was done on them? Could a general summary have been made on them, aggregated into a general balance, as occurred, for instance, in the Ur III *bala* system?

Jursa: Wooden writing boards were used to collect information regarding one type of transaction from multiple sources, *e.g.*, from individual receipts. The reason for using such boards is that one could write many individual entries over a longer period of time. (Clay tablets might dry up and are in any case far heavier and more difficult to handle.) But summary accounts, which normally would have used the data from the writing boards, were always on clay.

The point is that this documentation would not have been sufficient for a rational overall forecast. There is no indication that an overall summary was struck. We do know how they kept information. The fact that the archive is dead does not limit us here. We know what kinds of writing boards were used, and I cite them in my paper. We can see that the information was not meant to be complete. Its focus is on individual types of commodities and transactions, obviously with the intention of checking if everything that was due was delivered or paid as required. I can see no attempt to achieve an overall synthesis by combining information from different sources, for example from different writing boards.

Again, I believe that the main purpose of this system is to control, to check, and to prevent fraud. What we find in Neo-Babylonian Sippar is for the most part storage management. This involves of course some kind of forward planning, but only on a very basic level. The accounting system was clearly not meant, and I think not even able, to provide an overall view of the temple's economic dealings in a way that would have made possible "rational" management of the kind Dominic Rathbone finds in his texts from Roman Egypt.

Englund: So in the Neo-Babylonian period wood tablets were used to keep running accounts of what the rent-farmers owed?

Jursa: Yes. Any summary accounts must have started with these wooden boards. Then the totals were recorded on clay tablets. But only the main types of transactions were collected. Much detail exists only on the individual receipts. I cannot imagine that anyone went back to these receipts to compile overall totals.

This means that there may be only an accidental similarity between these receipt and delivery tablets, and actual double-entry bookkeeping—a similarity of matches, without a conscious pattern emerging. Where is the cross-checking and the running totals that you find in double-entry accounts?

Steinkeller: But there must have been *some* other totals.

Jursa: I think that is unlikely. What I am proposing is more than an argument from silence. The available evidence is compatible with the system of accounting as I would like to reconstruct it, and the system has a clear and logical purpose. Maybe we should not worry too much that it does not seem to do all we would expect it to.

Robson: To evaluate whether projections about the future were made, you need to look at the mathematical techniques being used. Tom Palaima's example of proportionality shows that they used a "norm" and simple proportions. There was no concept of statistical probability. The accounts were simple, based on periodic happenings. To have tried to predict non-periodic events such as crop failure or drought would have been alien to their way of thinking. So I conclude that they used accounts mainly for storage management.

Balanced accounts and the question of double-entry bookkeeping

Jursa: In the Ebabbar archive—a dead archive, to be sure—the primary documents reflect single transactions, drawn up at the time the transaction took place. Then, there were summations and balances, compiled from the receipts, often covering a period for more than one year.

Gardiner: So the term "balanced account" does not imply a running balance, such as appears in modern savings-bank passbooks.

Jursa: It certainly is not "balanced" in terms of double-entry bookkeeping. But this is the terminology that I find in the literature. You may tell me if it is appropriate or a modernism. Do you have a balanced account if you compare debit and credit to figure out the shortfall or "profit," write a kind of debt note or credit for it, and put down in writing that the period which you dealt with in the account is now entirely covered and all balances settled?

Property appears in Neo-Babylonian times. But there is no running link of the increase and drawdown of inventories with each receipt and delivery.

Hallo: These balanced accounts are internal within the province of Umma and other provinces of the Ur III state. Hence, one part of the palace or temple regime would not pay interest to another part. Only where the parties become more distant is interest paid. But you would still have balanced accounts to keep track of what is happening, what stocks are being built up or drawn down.

Robson: Somebody must have invented the accounting format as a means of organizing information. This means that we are dealing with information theory as well as management. The important thing is to think in tabular terms, rather than merely writing. Tables are well suited for summing up records. The evolution of tabular formats reflects a desire for cross-checking across the lines and up and down the columns.

This is not synonymous with what Hallo believes to be double-entry book-keeping, because the columns and lines are not checked.

Gardiner: Double-entry bookkeeping is meant to prevent fraud. The issue of receipts was just the start of this process. The question being posed is, how far did they get toward double-entry bookkeeping as it is understood today?

Double-entry bookkeeping has two sides to the transaction. These two sides, separately, are found in Babylonia. Bill Hallo has shown that the two elements that became double-entry bookkeeping were there in Babylonia, without its users seeming to understand its potential importance.

I don't see that the synthesis idea was there, because there are gaps: The receipts and debits do not match. This element of matching receipts and expenditures, income and outlays, assets and liabilities is the key to double-entry bookkeeping. We probably would need the tabular format to which Eleanor pointed to be able to do this in practice.

Hallo: At the root of double-entry bookkeeping would be a two-dimensional "graph-like" presentation of data—what Eleanor calls tabular. At least the thinking behind it seems to be tabular.

Robson: Not quite. The axis of organization is not the same thing as the axis of calculation down the tablet and across the tablet.

The training of scribes

Robson: We need to know the relationship between school mathematics and professional scribes and their practice. Most of these texts are exercises to train students. We have second-degree algebra, solid geometry and trigonometry, calculations of volume based on the height and diameter of grain piles.

Gardiner: There is an old Oxbridge toast: "Here's to higher mathematics: May it never be of use to anybody."

Hallo: Scribal training was a public function. A good place to start examining projection and budgeting would be cadastral surveys.

Even in the case of the water clock, you had to calculate the rate at which water dripped, and the clock's volume. Trial and error must have been used. It probably also was used to calculate "Pythagorean" triangles, such as the famous tablet at Yale (which is our most often viewed tablet).

Robson: I think we should distinguish between what we ourselves are able to do with these numbers, and what they could do back then. Were the early scribes really doing trigonometry? We cannot find arithmetic progressions actually used in the account tablets that survive.

Steinkeller: Yes we do.

Robson: No—only training documents.

Renger: For Larsa we have actual figures describing the growth of a herd.[9]

Van De Mieroop: There is a basic calculation: the number of sheep to produce X-number of lambs.

Hudson: Is there any way of knowing what proportion of output had to be devoted to the accounting process? In America, it takes most people at least an entire day to make their annual income-tax records; then, they must employ accountants on top of that. Did the accounting process become economically top-heavy? And was it limited to the public institutions?

---

9 See F.R. Kraus, *Staatliche Viehhaltung im altbabylonischen Lande Larsa* (Amsterdam 1966).

Van De Mieroop: Nobody knows. There is no basis for making such a calculation. We would like to know what the scribes did with their time. Did they do anything besides record-keeping? Which ones did the planning, if it occurred? At what level did they work: merely making receipts for particular transactions, or summarizing overall work? But we just don't know.

Gardiner: Auditing fees differ widely among countries even today. Under medieval rulers only part of the output had to be paid. Taxes were based on notional values, not actual values.

Ultimately, authorities were squeezing a surplus out of labor, forcing it to be turned over to the palace or other central agency. What they were doing was fundamental, but they did not quite seem to know or realize what they were doing, conceptually.

Englund: What is the link between the administrative accounts and the mathematical school texts in the Old Babylonian period?

Robson: One of the big complications is the fact that tables of squares and other tables are undated. So one cannot tell what comes first, but my feeling is that the school tables precede the administrative tables.

Gardiner: In today's world it is normal for education to lag behind practice.

Hallo: The Old Babylonian scribal schools copied real contracts. Lexical texts probably are abstracts of actual texts.

Robson: I would disagree with you.

Steinkeller: We need to distinguish between accountants and scribes. The terms should not be used interchangeably. The data were put on clay tablets only at the end of the process. Other media were used as the transactions were first being tabulated.

Hallo: Cuneiform terminology may give a hint of the early role of traders, auditors and the people who prepared the accounting records. The earliest word for "scribe" was umbisag, written with a sign derived from the sign for "counting" (šid).

The earliest word for trader was ibira or tibira, otherwise equated with "craftsman" or "metal-worker." It was a substrate word, but so was possibly the common word for trader, damgar, popularly explained as "husband or spouse of the purse." I discuss this in my *Origins* (Hallo 1996:68-77).

Palaima: In Mycenaean Greece, subordinates did the tabulating, not the administrators themselves.

Van De Mieroop: The scribe's role was to legitimize the transaction. That is why we are able to trace chains of responsibility.

Walker: Tablets often were filled in at the last minute.

Robson: The scribes practiced multiplication and division to help them get an overview of large numbers of transactions.

Wunsch: Ledgers and files followed certain models and their data were sorted according to certain principles, and then excerpted or totaled.

Gardiner: A major role must have been to prevent fraud.

Steinkeller: Planning was the main reason.

Jursa: I find no trace of planning to increase efficiency in the Neo-Babylonian period. I believe that at least in the Neo-Babylonian period accounting procedures were efficient enough to control the flow of commodities, to check on officials, and to prevent fraud. This must have been its main purpose. On the other hand, it seems that for structural reasons the accounting system's potential for forward planning was limited. This is why I take the "minimalist" position when it comes to accounting.

Hudson: The question is whether, "in the beginning," thousands of years before your own period, accounting was used for forecasting, planning and cost accounting in a relatively small-scale context that could be handled by its administrators. If this is the case, under later rulers the early reporting habits became ossified.

It seems to me that wherever one sees simplicity, one can infer a planning objective. Mere "police functions" do not require simplicity (look at the U.S. tax code). Planning and structuring requires it. The administrative calendar based on uniform 30-day months, for instance, seems to have been standardized for planning purposes. Otherwise, rations had to be given out that consisted of 29 days worth of food one lunar month, and 30 days the next. Standardized prices, weights and measures suggest to me that somebody at the top of the administrative pyramid wanted to get an overview. The arguments for early planning thus would include (1) the calendar composed of standardized months, (2) standardized, calendrically based weights and measures, and (3) the emergence of money.

The need to develop prices and money for centralized resource allocation

Arno Daastol: What I have learned from this colloquium is the degree to which money is an institution, not merely a physical commodity. There are many perspectives from which to view its evolution. Regarding the role of temples in establishing monetary relations, Rudolph Steiner was one of the few economists to say that money is the most spiritual phenomena of society. Anthropologists also have traced money back to sacralized social functions, while sociologists have discussed its significance beyond market exchange as such to issues involving status, prestige and so forth. As far as you can tell, why was silver designated over other commodities?

Renger: The kind of money that is used reflects the circumstances in which it is used. Anthropologists cite cowry shells which have no use value but serve only as an agreed-upon store of value and medium of exchange.

Englund: Copper preceded silver, and barley probably preceded copper. So there was not a single monetary commodity. But throughout all these changes there were price schedules of equivalencies. This was the key—a set of equivalencies.

Renger: Yes, there has been too much concentration on silver. Silver came in the Sumerian and Babylonian periods, then tin for a while. In the Kassite period, gold emerged. Then, after about 1200 BC, there was a return to silver. Egypt used gold. What is important is that throughout all the shift of the monetary medium from copper to silver to tin to gold and back to silver, you had a set of equivalencies.

Hallo: These ideal equivalencies were administered centrally rather than set by market supply and demand. Silver is easily shaped into spirals, which are found all over the Near East. Gold was too rare and valuable to use.

Hudson: Does this mean that its use in the Kassite period reflected a highly polarized society, where only the wealthy used the official monetary medium?

Gardiner: Money served as a catalyst. If we ask why silver or gold was selected, the answer may be that they had no other function. Today, the annual production of gold is 15 times its actual use. The rest is monetary, as a store of value.

Renger: We do not really know how silver came into Mesopotamia.

Hudson: Was it perhaps a religious contribution, and sanctified because the temples desired it, and it was they that advanced workshop output to merchants? Or was it "the money of the world," being demanded by societies surrounding Mesopotamia and hence useful in foreign trade?

Just to say that silver and gold were bartered for and had a value against other commodities doesn't explain what gave it this value or what motivated the demand. Was it as a gift, a prestigious donation to temples? Why silver rather than tin or copper? Was it because these were used industrially, leaving silver and gold to serve as socially designated signs of status?

Renger: If you talk about the role of money in Mesopotamia, you have four categories: a unit of account, a means of repaying debt, a store of value, and a medium of exchange in buying commodities.[10]

What functions do you need money for, and when do you need it? It's clear enough that you do need *something*, even when a neighbor helps you in a mutual-aid context. But reciprocity may proceed without regard for the particular value of goods and services involved.[11]

Mesopotamia used accounting between household units and the large institutions. But people themselves needed "money" only *after* it was invented. Even in Seleucid times silver coins were weighed rather than noted in the text by their face value, that is as stater.[12]

Englund: What is important is the development of equivalencies. This is the crux of money—a set of equivalencies, overseen by a central authority.

This is close to a banking function. The laws of Hammurapi (§51) established a convertibility between barley and silver at a fixed price ratio, ruling that debts were redeemable in barley as well as silver. This

---

[10] See Johannes Renger, "Subsistenzproduktion und redistributive Palastwirtschaft: Wo bleibt die Nische für das Geld?" in W. Schelkle und M. Nitsch, eds., *Rätsel Geld – Annäherungen aus ökonomischer, soziologischer und historischer Sicht* (Marburg 1995):271-324.

[11] See Renger, "Subsistenzproduktion und redistributive Palastwirtschaft: Wo bleibt die Nische für das Geld?" in W. Schelkle und M. Nitsch, eds., *Rätsel Geld–Annäherungen aus ökonomischer, soziologischer und historischer Sicht* (Marburg 1995):271-324.

[12] See *The Chicago Assyrian Dictionary*, vol. I/J (1960), 204 *s.v. istatirru.*

silver unit was set equal to a unit of labor time, which under the circumstances meant the rations allocated to labor, and also to the yield from a unit of land. Thus, land yields, labor time and commodities were part of a system whose unit of account was interchangeable.

Hudson: The way in which the Sumerians set up an equivalency between silver-money (the shekel), the crop yield of land rented out (and hence, a land area that would yield a given crop of barley as rations), and labor time (as measured in rations)—with a proportionality established between adult male labor, female and child labor—enabled accounts to be translated readily into monetary equivalency, labor-time equivalency, or for that matter any of the key commodities whose proportionality with the silver shekel and unit of barley was established in round numbers.

Money's purpose therefore was (a) to achieve a sense of proportionality among various commodities, labor time and the yields of standard land areas, and (b) to produce an overview by designating common denominators (barley and silver units) by which the overall scale of operations and economic surpluses could be reported. The monetary medium could change, as Bob Englund and Johannes Renger have pointed out, but price schedules based on administered prices kept the system workable. It is the overall set of proportions that represent the monetary system, not the commodity silver, copper or whatever.

In the beginning this set of proportions had to be administered, at least within the large institutions. The key was the overall system, not merely the phenomenon of money as a metallic commodity. There needed to be some unit or units of account against which to value other commodities, as well as labor time and land.

Convertibility within such schedules meant that the major commodities could be monetized in the sense of being used as means of debt settlement or other payments, or as a store of value to the extent that they had a monetary equivalency vis-à-vis silver. To establish a commodity's price equivalency was to monetize it. Thus, silver debts could be paid in dates.

I would like to note that this line of monetary development that our colloquium has traced is quite different from the individualistic "Austrian" theory, which assumes that the precious metals emerged as things to be bartered spontaneously in markets whose prices shifted continually in response to fluctuating supply and demand. Mesopotamia's redistributive system of administered prices minimized this kind of price anarchy. But free-market economists denigrate the positive effects of public planning, not acknowledging its initial catalytic role in structuring markets and pricing systems.

I also should add that when coinage was developed, it did not simplify matters and reduce costs. It actually introduced new complications as it made possible seignorage (issuing coins whose nominal face value exceeded that of their bullion content), clipping, depreciation and hence price inflation. So that idea that each monetary innovation has saved transaction costs does not hold up.

As for price flexibility, it was a leap "forward" in the sense of replacing the administered pricing that was part and parcel of early accounting systems. But it had been economically easier to settle transactions periodically by clearing debt balances at customary price ratios than to make a fresh one-the-spot "barter" payment for each transaction as is done today.

Conclusion

Hudson: I see two distinct strands of papers here. On the one hand is the "accountability" strand reflecting the evolving social and political context of accounting—the role played by the accountants and the officials who received or audited their accounts. On the other hand is the internal development of accounting techniques, starting with economic structuring and planning and developing into what Eleanor Robson calls information processing.

With regard to the economic aims and scope of accounting, it seems to me that there turns out to be a common denominator between the maximalists and minimalists. I gather that we all agree that accounting occurred mainly in the large institutions, starting in the Uruk period at the end of the fourth millennium. By Neo-Babylonian times the palace had absorbed the temples and its role had evolved from being a primary producer of crops and handicrafts to one of taxing the economy while temples received contributions. As this political role of the palaces shifted, the scope of their accounting narrowed from maximalist to minimalist, that is, from a detailed management of productive resources to a mere schedule of what they were to receive in taxes or as rents on their own lands or enterprises that were leased.

In a nutshell, the palace got out of the production business and into the taxing business. So when there appears to be an argument between Michael Jursa and Marc Van De Mieroop vis-à-vis Bob Englund and

Piotr Steinkeller over whether the key to understanding accounting records is their role of accountability or planning, the explanation turns largely on the fact that the situation changed from the highly centralized Uruk and Ur III periods to the less centralized Old-Babylonian and Neo-Babylonian periods as empires were formed and control became more military than economic in character in the first millennium BC.

What emerges from this discussion is a narrative of how the scope and aims of accounting became shallower and less intensive as economies became more "privatized," to use the modernist word of our first colloquium. We see a process of devolution. And contrary to what modern ideology would suggest, we find a priority of the public institutions rather than a private-sector organizational initiative and innovation of cost management techniques.

The "maximum" role of accounting is found early in the internal operations of the large institutions, when accounting procedures and formats, weights and measures, administered prices and money were first being put in place in the fourth and third millennia BC. These public institutions took the lead in developing accounting and management techniques.

But palaces later played mainly a fiscal function, taxing the economy and leasing land and enterprises to private managers. As this decentralization occurred, the degree of accounting detail and planning became more concerned simply with listing the scheduled deliveries and payments, and noting whether or not they were met. Private individuals did not organize their records on anywhere near as thoroughgoing a scale. The role of accounting thus narrowed as the economic center of gravity shifted from the palace to individual families.

To trace the effect of accounting we need to understand the relationship between the bureaucratic structures and the rest of society. We must know how deep the bureaucracy was, and correlate accounting documents with official ranks. There are scribal ranks, and ranks for entrepreneurs, royal officials and trade officials.

Michael Hudson's paper shows that there was much less need for money than would be the case today, as our modern specialization of labor has gone far beyond that of antiquity, requiring more payments than were necessary in earlier times.

BIBLIOGRAPHICAL ABBREVIATIONS

AfO	*Archiv für Orientforschung* (Graz/Wien).
AJA	*American Journal of Archaeology* (Princeton:Archaeological Institute of America).
AOAT	Alter Orient und Altes Testament (Kevelaer: Butzon&Bercker and Neukirchen-Vluyn:Neukirchener Verlag/Münster: Ugarit).
AOS	American Oriental Series (New Haven: American Oriental Society).
ATU	Archaische Texte aus Uruk (Berlin: Gebr. Mann).
AuOr	*Aula Orientalis* (Barcelona: AUSA).
BaM	*Baghdader Mitteilungen* (Berlin: Gebr. Mann).
BASOR	*Bulletin of the American School of Oriental Research* (Atlanta: American School of Oriental Research).
BBVO	Berliner Beiträge zum Vorderen Orient (Berlin: Reimer).
BiMes	Bibliotheca Mesopotamica (Malibu: Undena).
BiOr	*Bibliotheca Orientalis* (Leiden: Nederlands Instituut voor het Nabije Oosten).
BSA	Bulletin on Sumerian Agriculture (Cambridge).
HUCA	*Hebrew Union College Annual* (Cincinnati: Hebrew Union College).
JANES	*Journal of the Ancient Near Eastern Society* (New York: Jewish Theological Seminary).
JCS	*Journal of Cuneiform Studies* (Atlanta: American School of Oriental Research).
JESHO	*Journal of the Economic and Social History of the Orient* (Leiden: Brill).
JNES	*Journal of Near Eastern Studies* (Chicago: University of Chicago).
NABU	*Nouvelles assyriologique brèves et utilitaires* (Paris: Société pour l'Étude du Proche-Orient Ancien).
OBO	Orbis biblicus et orientalis (Freiburg/Schweiz: Freiburger Universitätsverlag and Göttingen: Vandenhoeck & Ruprecht).
OIP	Oriental Institute Publications (Chicago: University of Chicago Press).
OrAn	*Oriens Antiquus* (Rome: Centro per le Antichità e la Storia dell'Arte del Vicino Oriente).
PIHANS	Uitgaven van het Nederlands Historisch-Archaeologisch Instituut te Istanbul. Publications de l'Institut historique-archéologique néerlandais de Stamboul (Istanbul/Leiden: Nederlands Historisch-Archaeologisch Instituut).
RA	*Revue d'Assyriologie et d'Archéologie Orientale* (Paris: Presses Universitaires de France).
WZKM	*Wiener Zeitschrift für die Kunde des Morgenlandes* (Wien: Selbstverlag des Instituts für Orientalistik).
YNER	*Yale Near Eastern Researches* (New Haven–London: Yale University Press).

www.ingramcontent.com/pod-product-compliance
Lightning Source LLC
Chambersburg PA
CBHW041955260926
51850CB00017B/4
* 9 7 8 3 9 4 9 5 4 6 1 0 5 *